Library Wars

—Love & War—

14

STORY & ART BY *Kiiro Yumi*   ORIGINAL CONCEPT BY *Hiro Arikawa*

Library Wars
Love & War

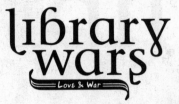

Contents

The Library Freedom Act

Libraries have the freedom to acquire their collections.

Libraries have the freedom to circulate
materials in their collections.

Libraries guarantee the privacy of their patrons.

Libraries oppose any type of censorship.

When libraries are imperiled,
librarians will join together
to secure their freedom.

library wars
Love & War

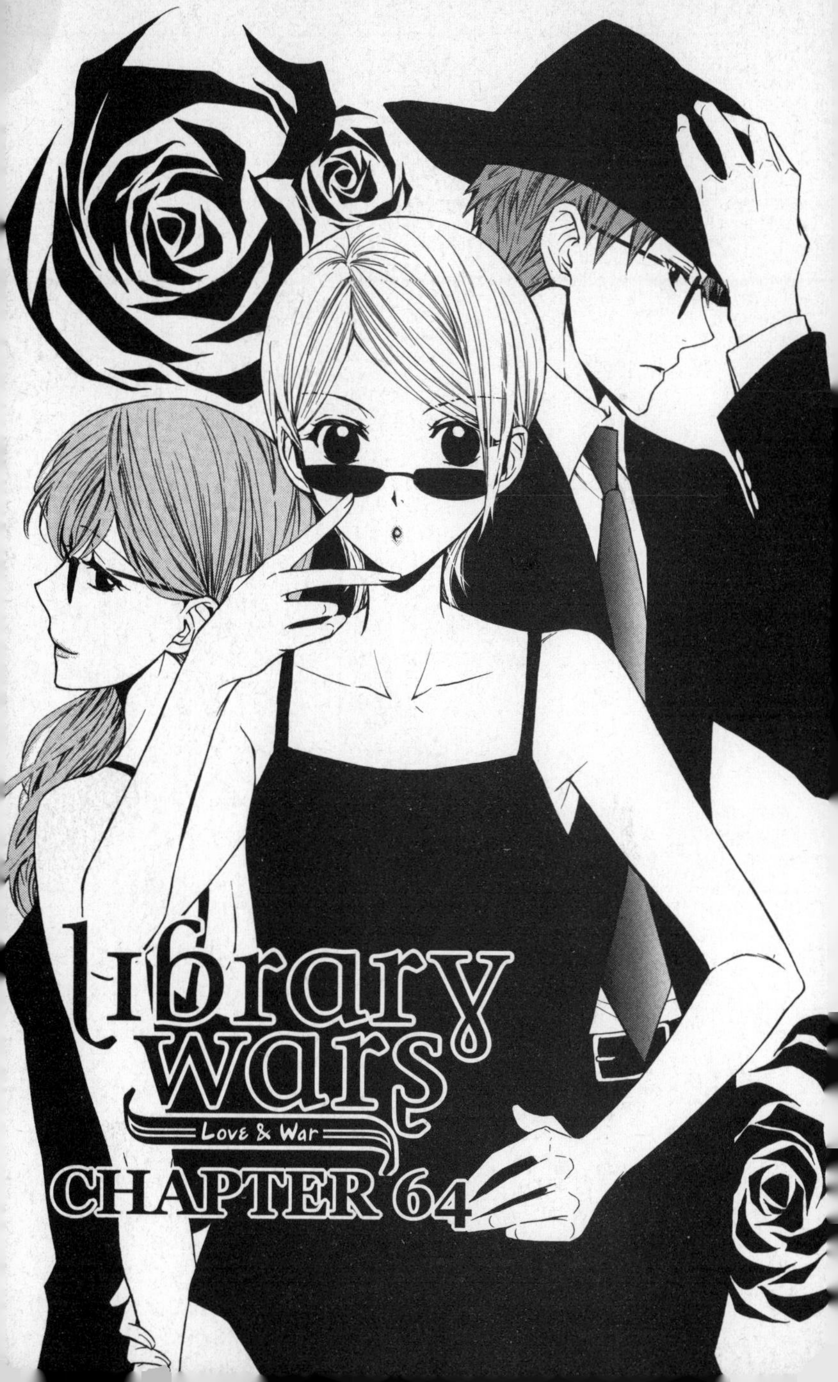
library wars
Love & War
CHAPTER 64

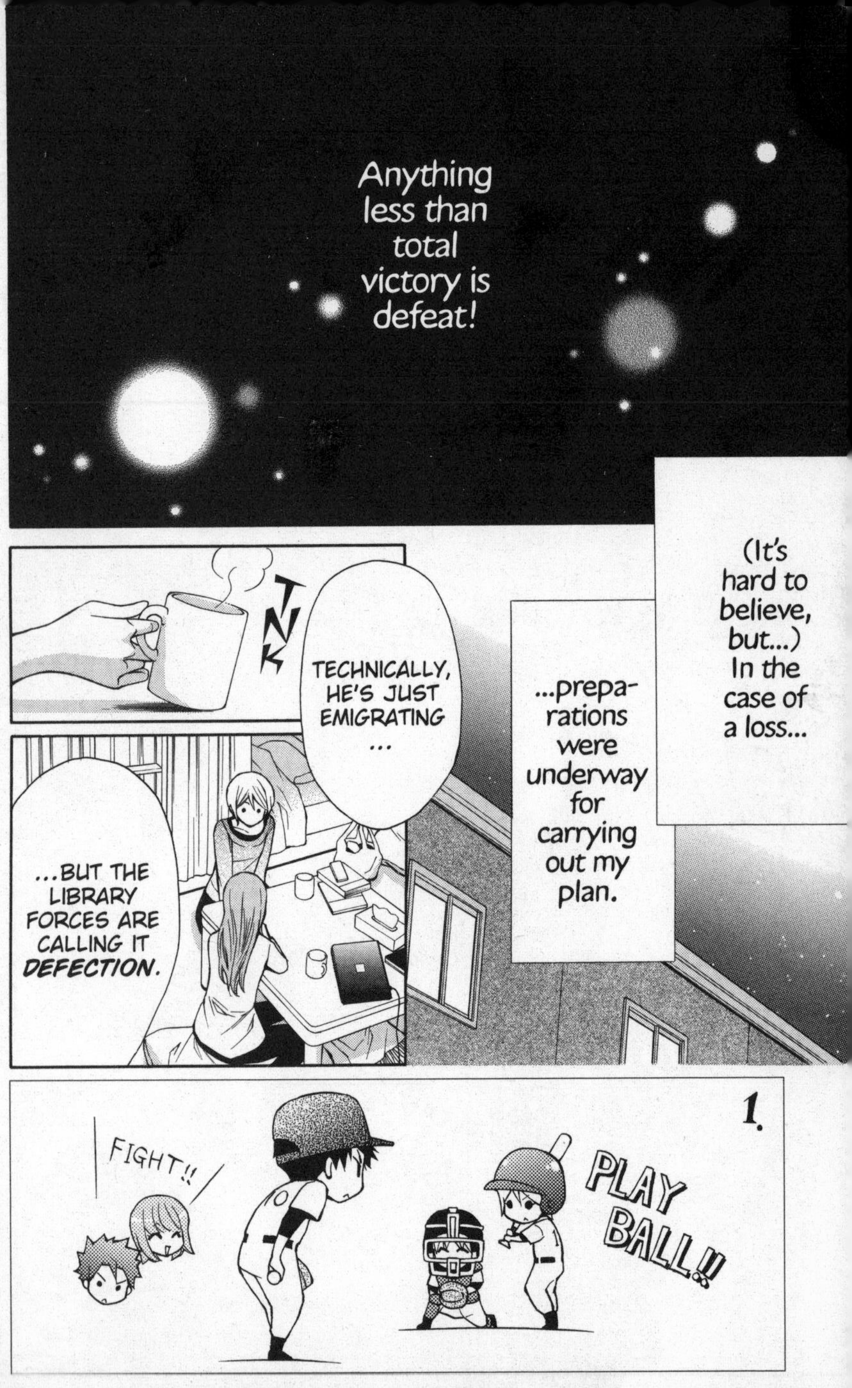
Anything less than total victory is defeat!
(It's hard to believe, but...) In the case of a loss...
...preparations were underway for carrying out my plan.
TECHNICALLY, HE'S JUST EMIGRATING...
TNK
...BUT THE LIBRARY FORCES ARE CALLING IT *DEFECTION*.
1.
PLAY BALL!!
FIGHT!!

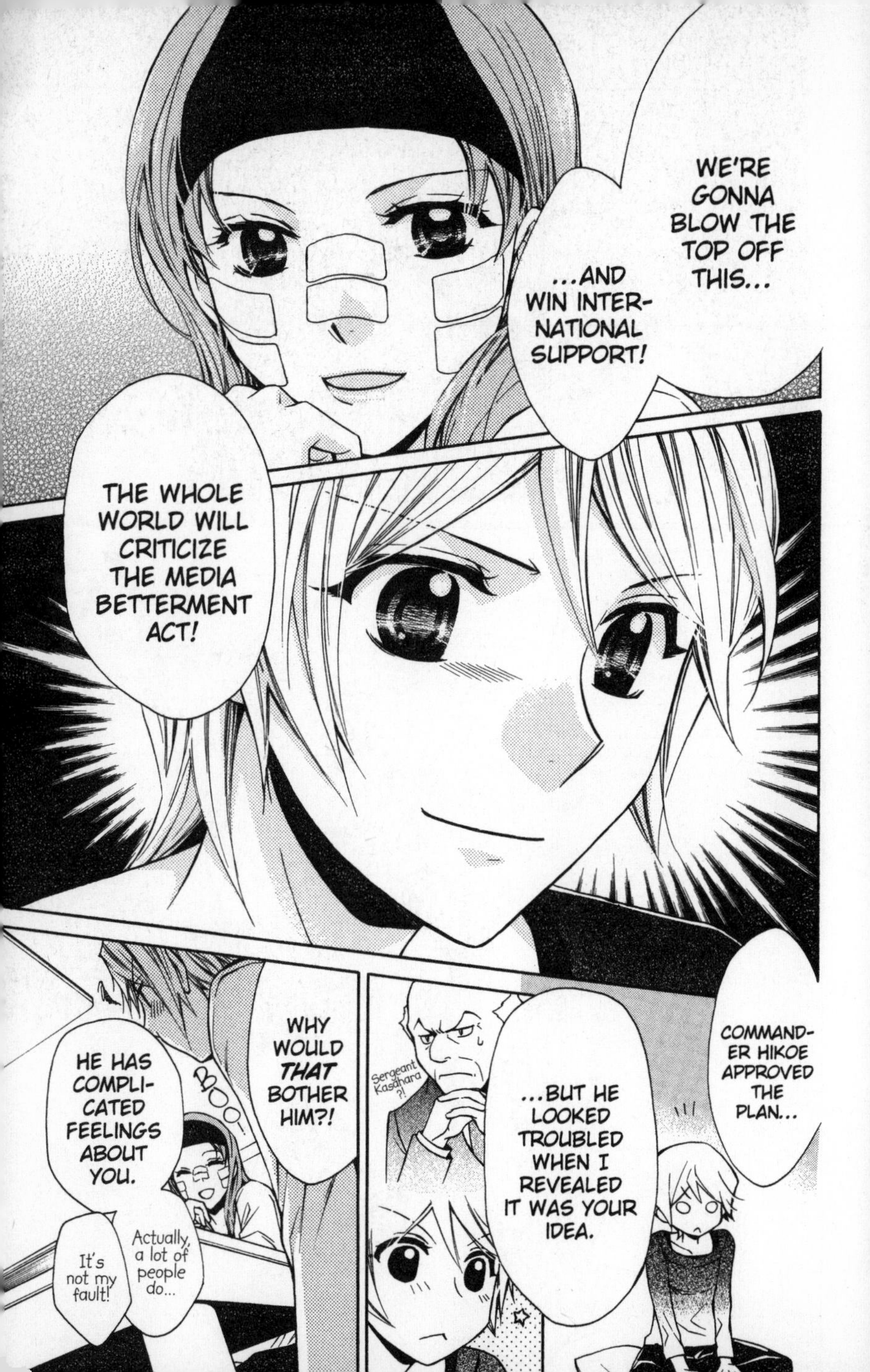
WE'RE GONNA BLOW THE TOP OFF THIS...
...AND WIN INTER-NATIONAL SUPPORT!
THE WHOLE WORLD WILL CRITICIZE THE MEDIA BETTERMENT ACT!
COMMAND-ER HIKOE APPROVED THE PLAN...
...BUT HE LOOKED TROUBLED WHEN I REVEALED IT WAS YOUR IDEA.
Sergeant Kasahara?!
WHY WOULD *THAT* BOTHER HIM?!
HE HAS COMPLI-CATED FEELINGS ABOUT YOU.
BOO
Actually, a lot of people do...
It's not my fault!

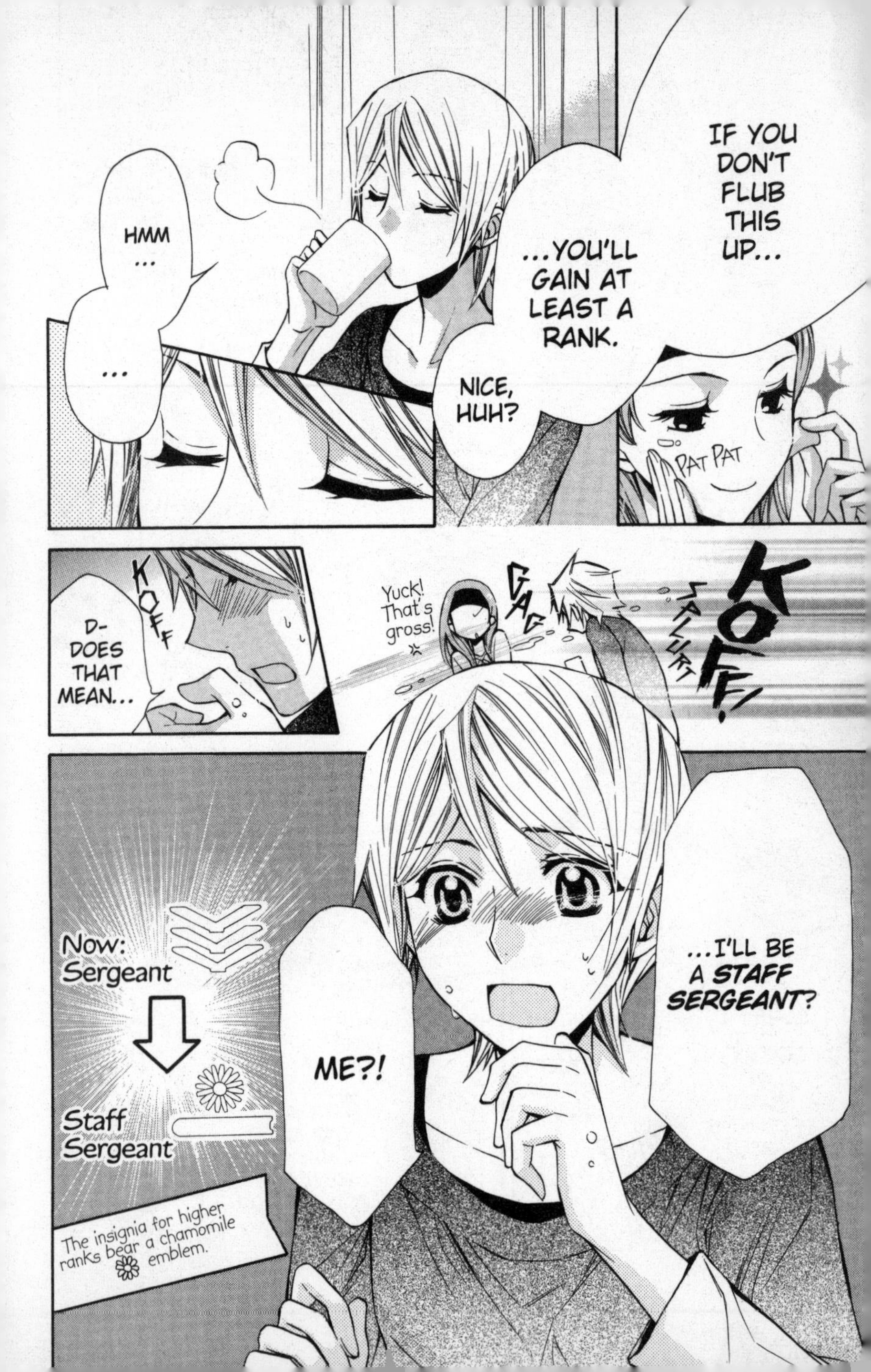
IF YOU DON'T FLUB THIS UP...
...YOU'LL GAIN AT LEAST A RANK.
NICE, HUH?
PAT PAT
HMM...
...
KOFF!
SPLURT
GAG
Yuck! That's gross!
KOFF
D-DOES THAT MEAN...
...I'LL BE A STAFF SERGEANT?
ME?!
Now: Sergeant
Staff Sergeant
The insignia for higher ranks bear a chamomile emblem.

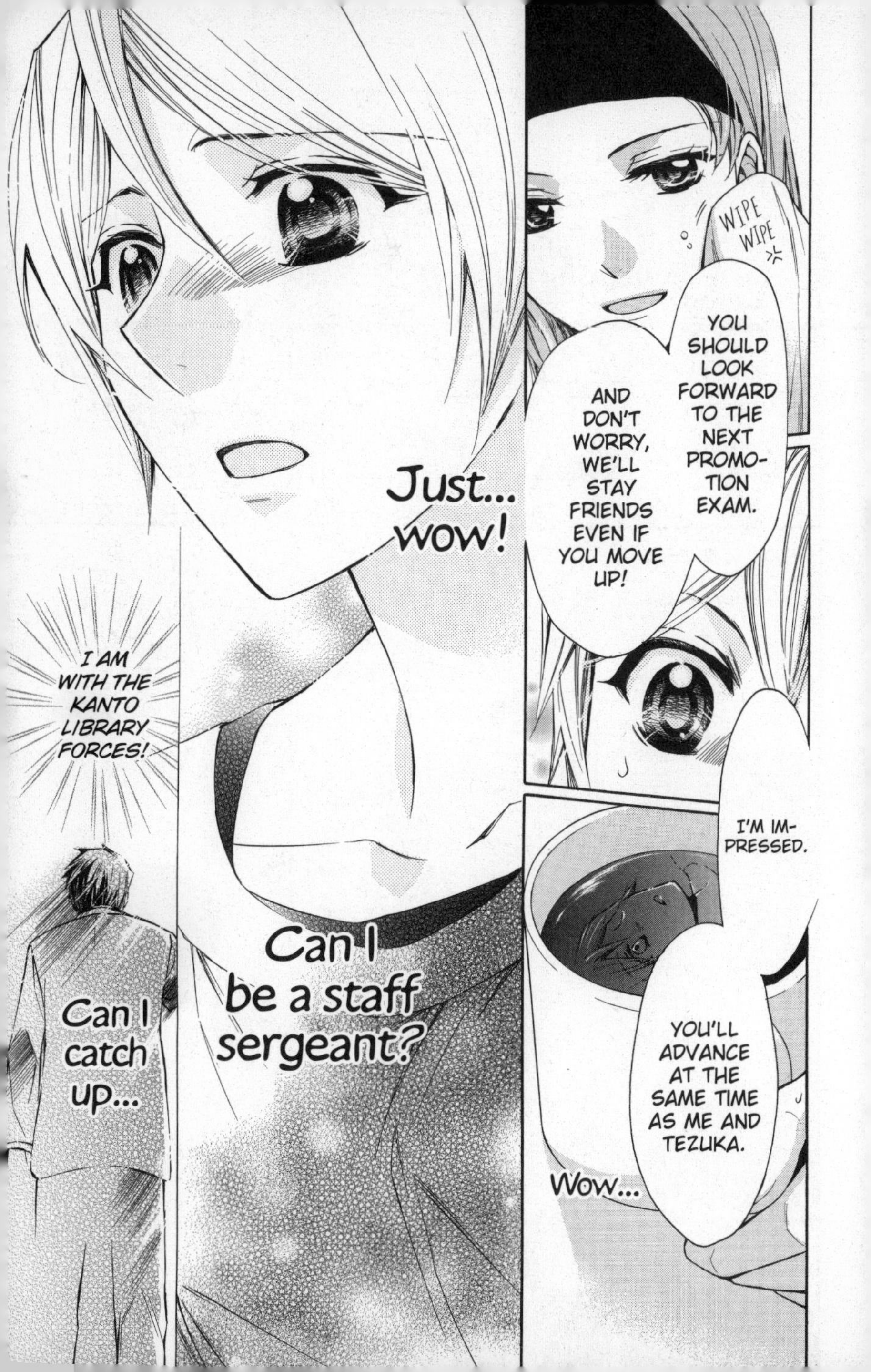
WIPE WIPE
YOU SHOULD LOOK FORWARD TO THE NEXT PROMOTION EXAM.
AND DON'T WORRY, WE'LL STAY FRIENDS EVEN IF YOU MOVE UP!
I'M IMPRESSED.
YOU'LL ADVANCE AT THE SAME TIME AS ME AND TEZUKA.
Wow...
Just... wow!
Can I be a staff sergeant?
I AM WITH THE KANTO LIBRARY FORCES!
Can I catch up...

...to Instructor Dojo eight years ago?

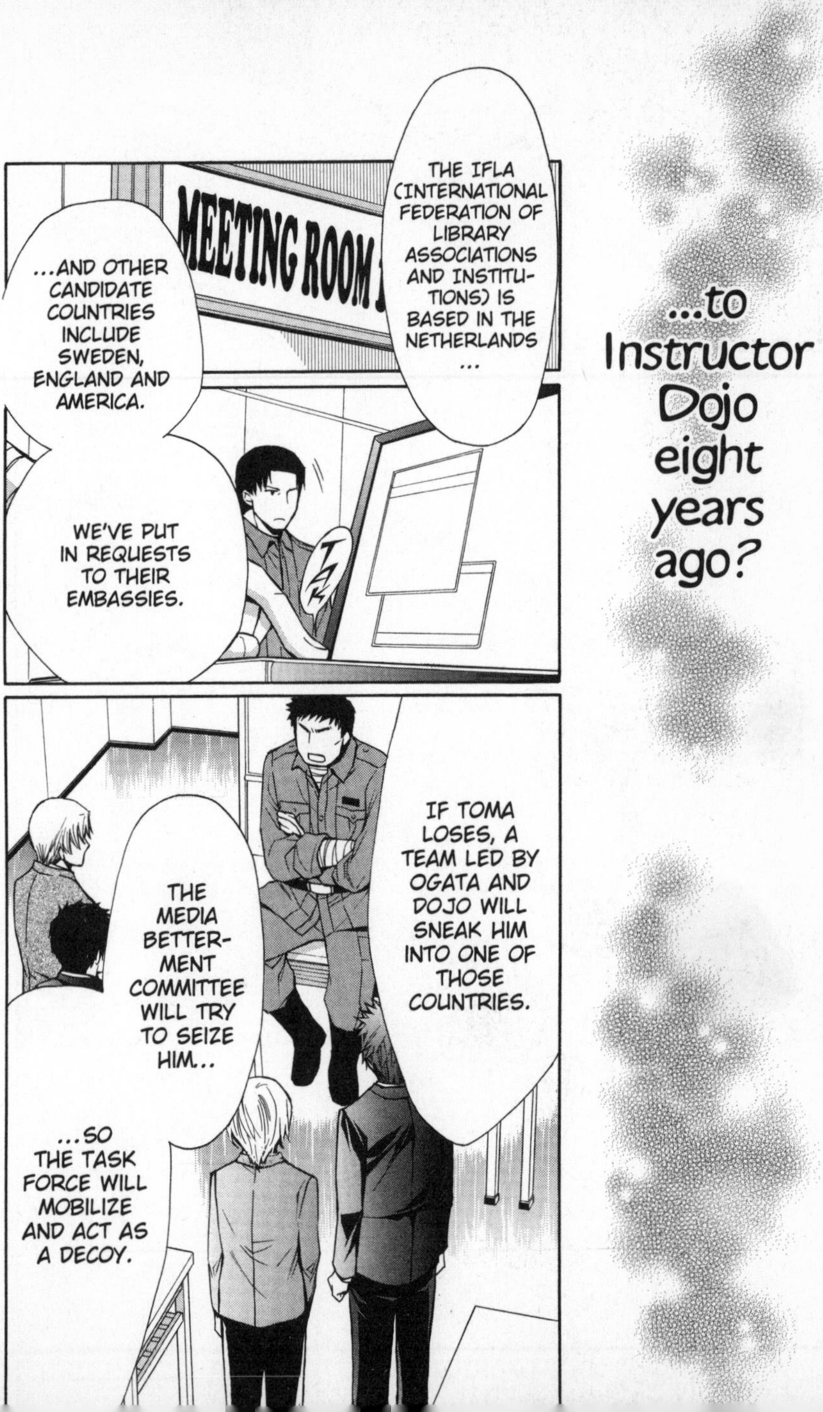
THE IFLA (INTERNATIONAL FEDERATION OF LIBRARY ASSOCIATIONS AND INSTITUTIONS) IS BASED IN THE NETHERLANDS ...
MEETING ROOM
...AND OTHER CANDIDATE COUNTRIES INCLUDE SWEDEN, ENGLAND AND AMERICA.
TAK
WE'VE PUT IN REQUESTS TO THEIR EMBASSIES.
IF TOMA LOSES, A TEAM LED BY OGATA AND DOJO WILL SNEAK HIM INTO ONE OF THOSE COUNTRIES.
THE MEDIA BETTERMENT COMMITTEE WILL TRY TO SEIZE HIM...
...SO THE TASK FORCE WILL MOBILIZE AND ACT AS A DECOY.

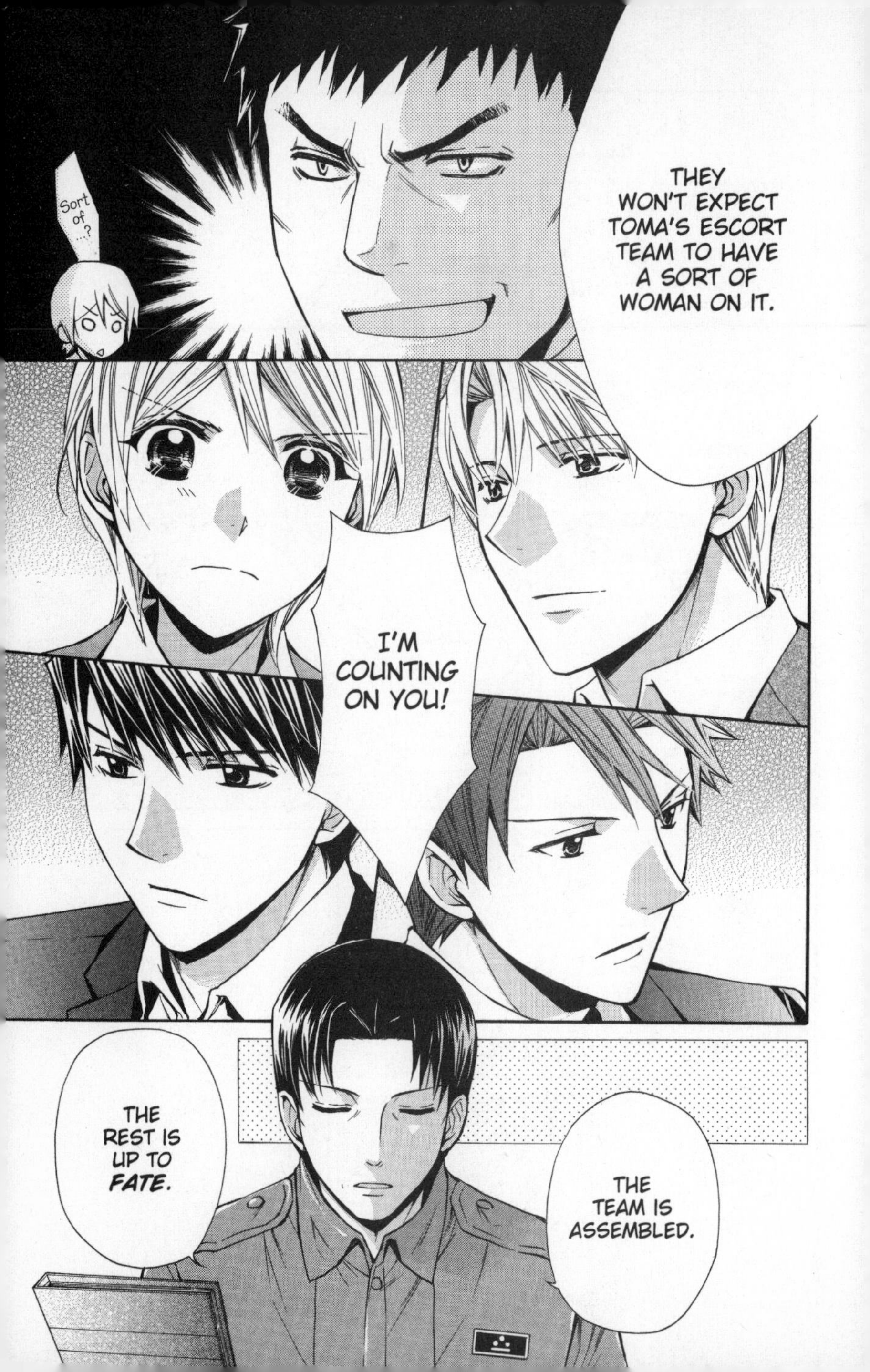
THEY WON'T EXPECT TOMA'S ESCORT TEAM TO HAVE A SORT OF WOMAN ON IT.
Sort of ...?
I'M COUNTING ON YOU!
THE TEAM IS ASSEMBLED.
THE REST IS UP TO *FATE*.

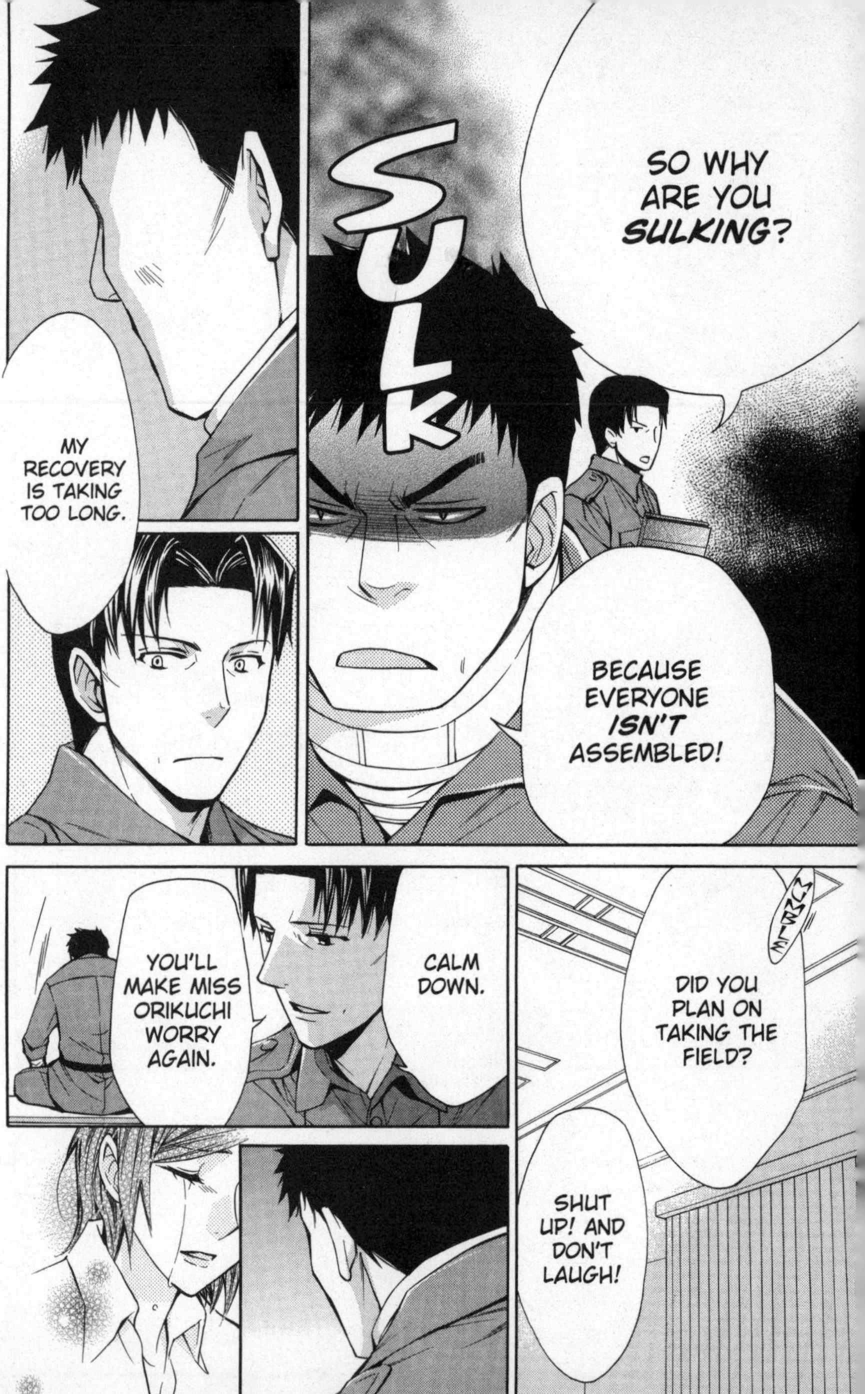
SO WHY ARE YOU *SULKING*?
SULK
BECAUSE EVERYONE *ISN'T* ASSEMBLED!
MY RECOVERY IS TAKING TOO LONG.
MUMBLE
DID YOU PLAN ON TAKING THE FIELD?
SHUT UP! AND DON'T LAUGH!
CALM DOWN.
YOU'LL MAKE MISS ORIKUCHI WORRY AGAIN.

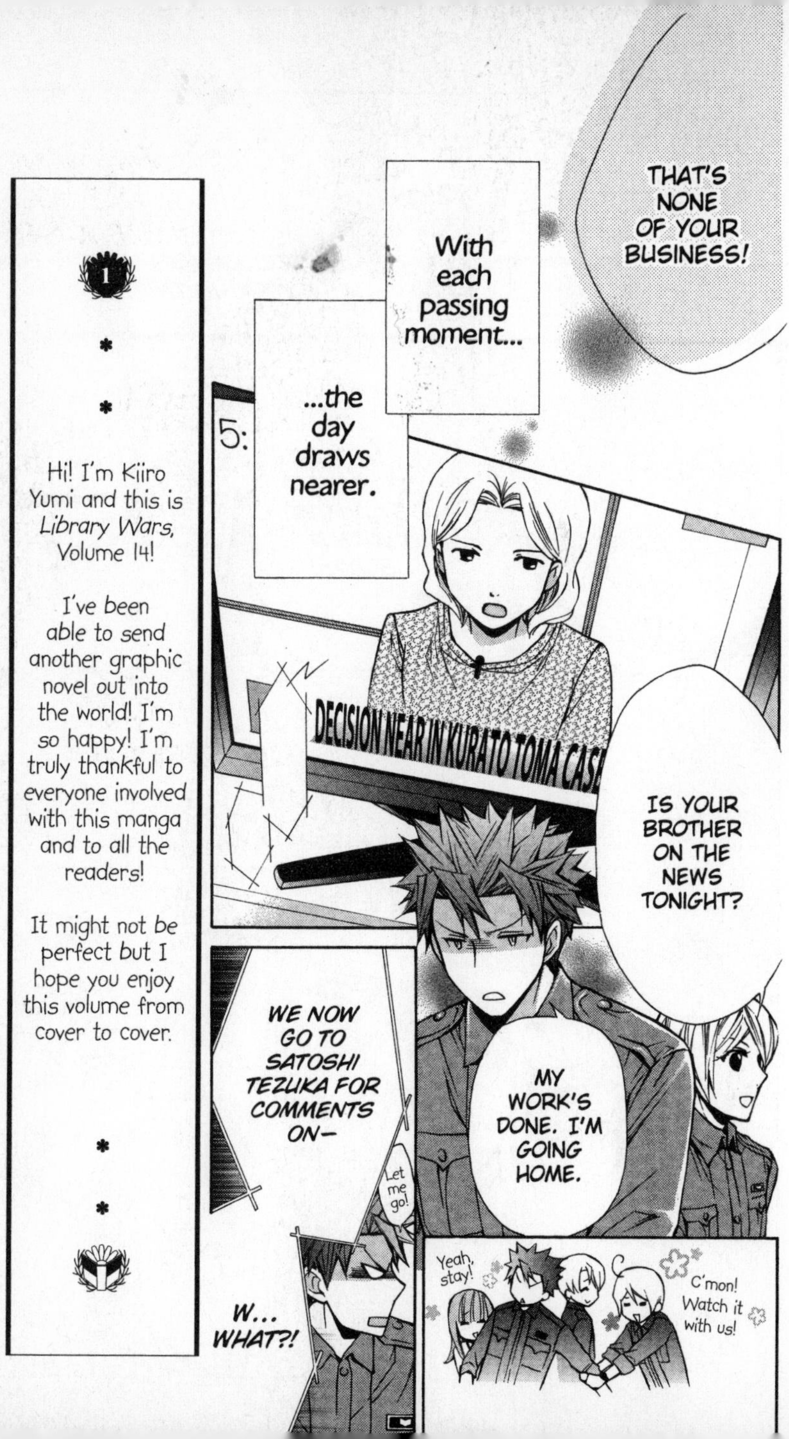
THAT'S NONE OF YOUR BUSINESS!
With each passing moment...
...the day draws nearer.
5:
DECISION NEAR IN KURATO TOMA CAS
IS YOUR BROTHER ON THE NEWS TONIGHT?
MY WORK'S DONE. I'M GOING HOME.
C'mon! Watch it with us!
Yeah, stay!
WE NOW GO TO SATOSHI TEZUKA FOR COMMENTS ON—
Let me go!
W... WHAT?!

1

*

*

Hi! I'm Kiiro Yumi and this is *Library Wars*, Volume 14!

I've been able to send another graphic novel out into the world! I'm so happy! I'm truly thankful to everyone involved with this manga and to all the readers!

It might not be perfect but I hope you enjoy this volume from cover to cover.

*

*

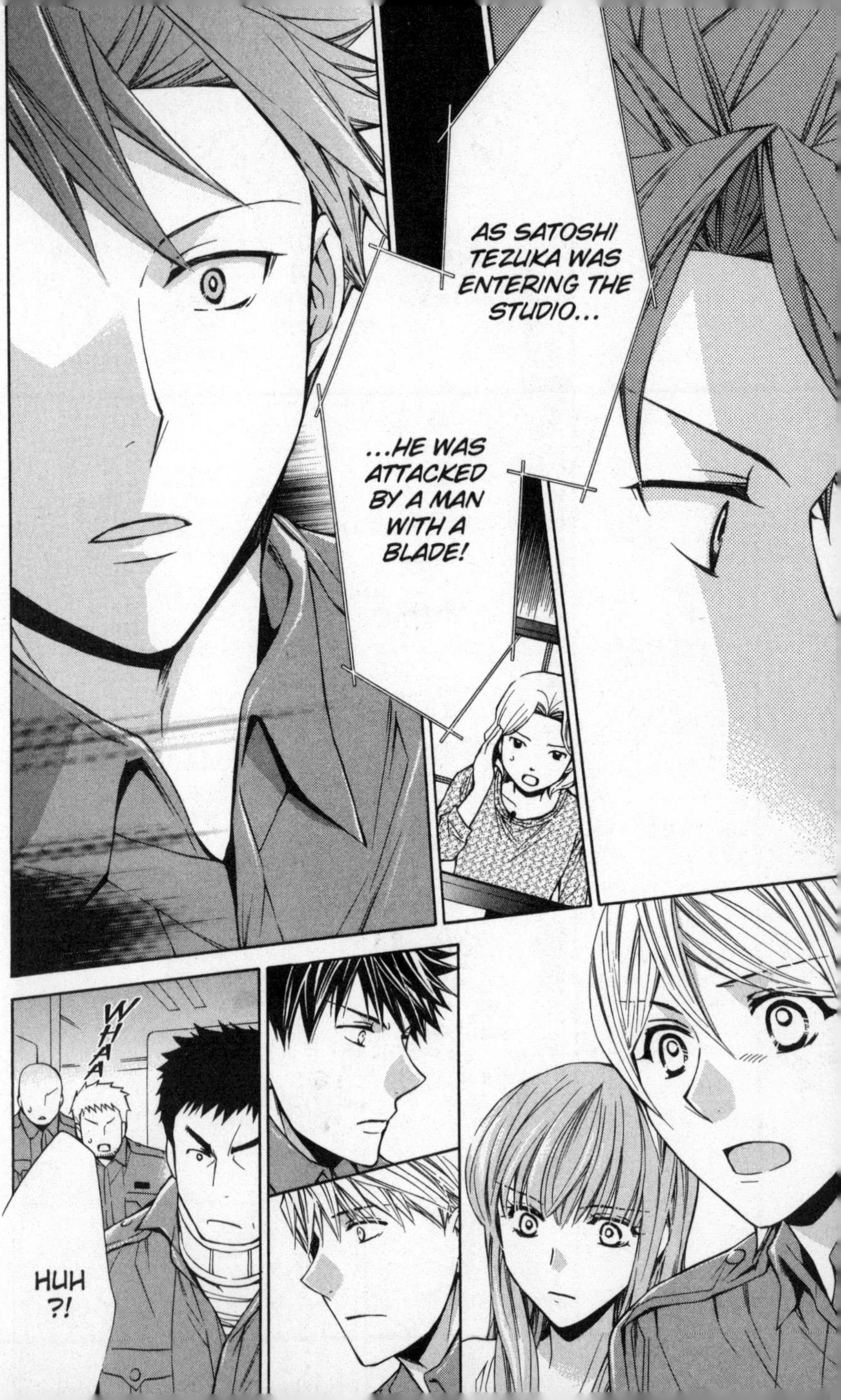
AS SATOSHI TEZUKA WAS ENTERING THE STUDIO...
...HE WAS ATTACKED BY A MAN WITH A BLADE!
WHAA
HUH ?!

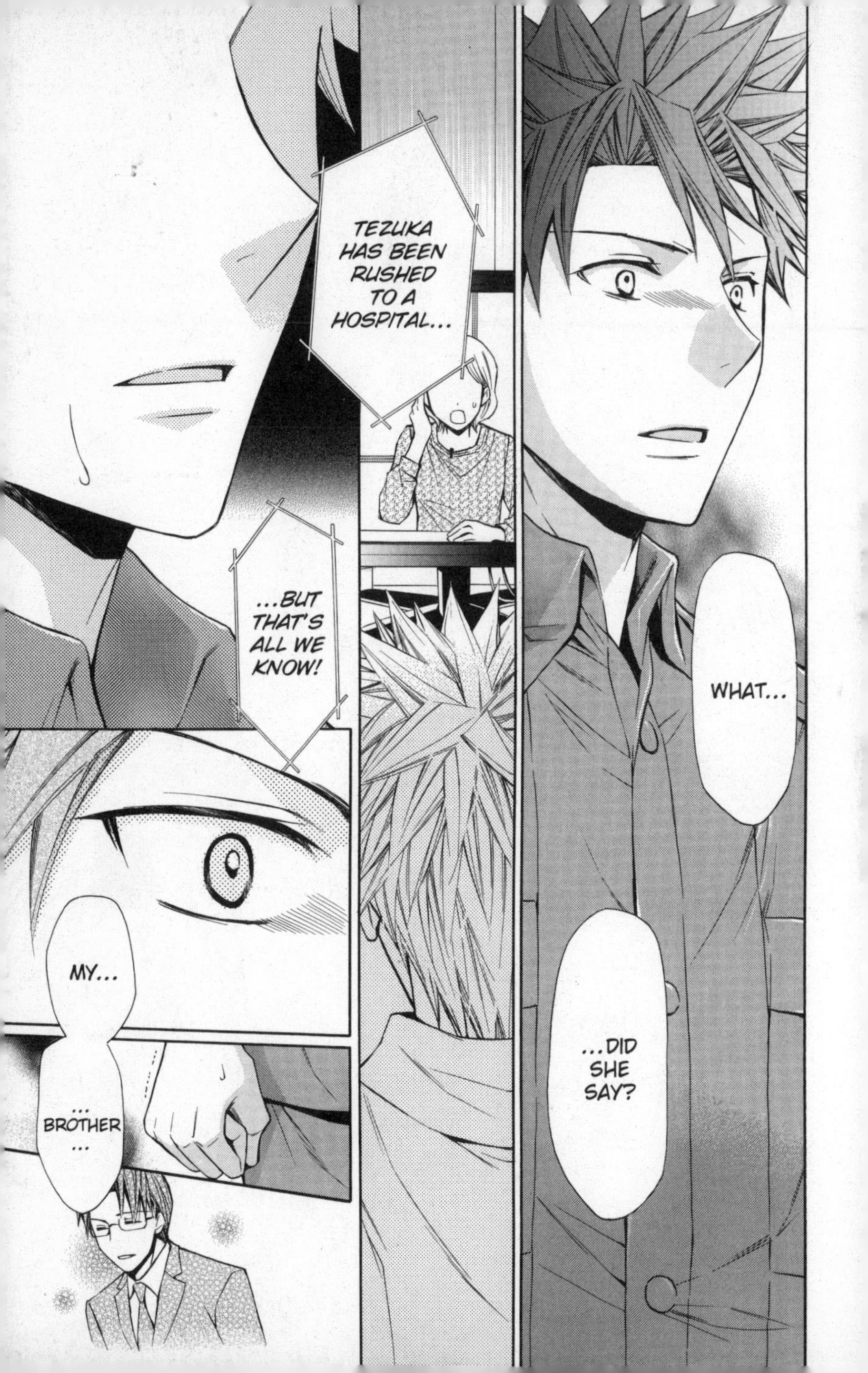
WHAT...
...DID SHE SAY?
TEZUKA HAS BEEN RUSHED TO A HOSPITAL...
...BUT THAT'S ALL WE KNOW!
MY...
...BROTHER...

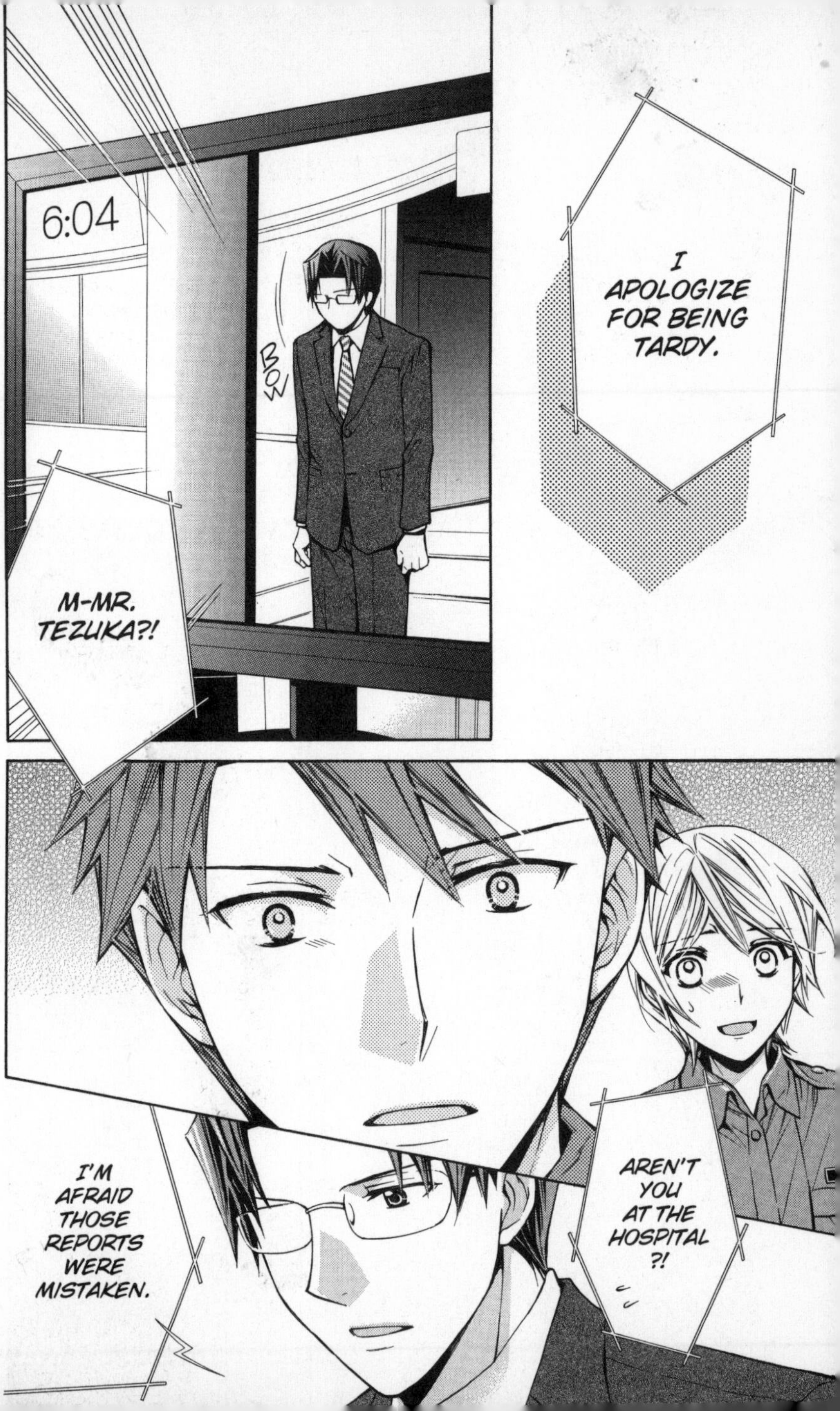
I APOLOGIZE FOR BEING TARDY.
6:04
BOW
M-MR. TEZUKA?!
AREN'T YOU AT THE HOSPITAL ?!
I'M AFRAID THOSE REPORTS WERE MISTAKEN.

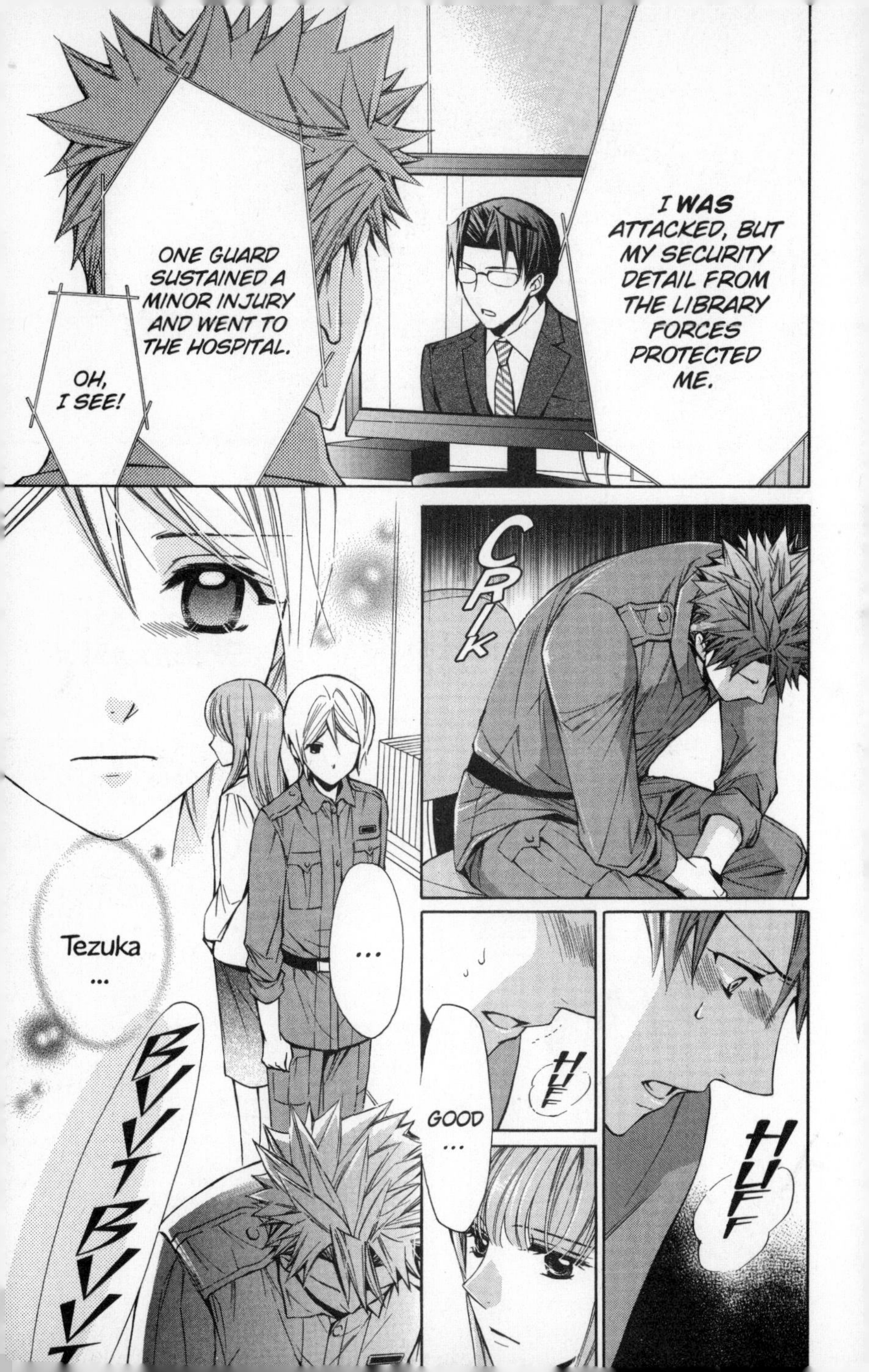
I WAS ATTACKED, BUT MY SECURITY DETAIL FROM THE LIBRARY FORCES PROTECTED ME.
ONE GUARD SUSTAINED A MINOR INJURY AND WENT TO THE HOSPITAL.
OH, I SEE!
CRIK
HUFF
HUFF
GOOD ...
...
Tezuka ...
BUTTBUT

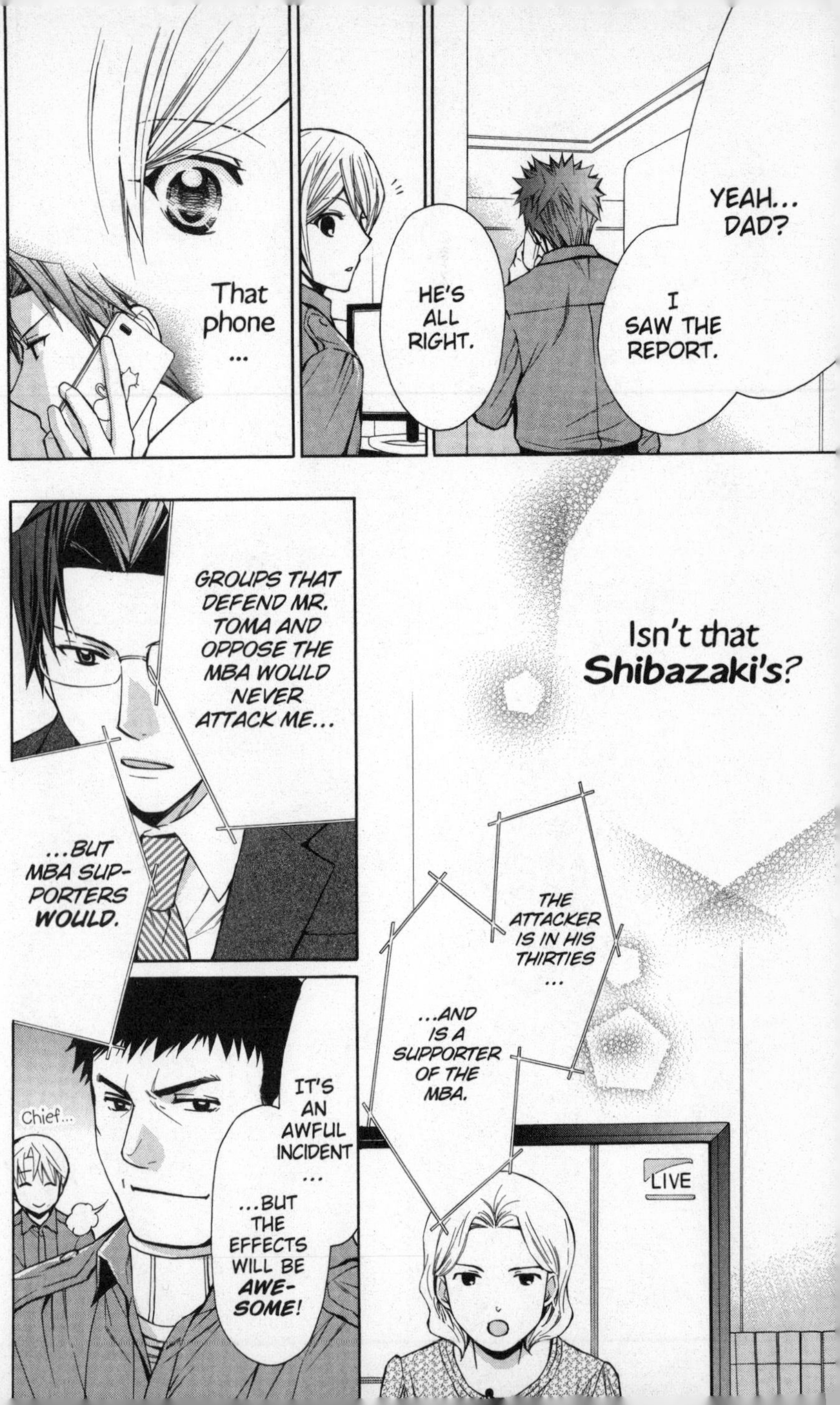
YEAH... DAD?
I SAW THE REPORT.
HE'S ALL RIGHT.
That phone ...
Isn't that **Shibazaki's**?
THE ATTACKER IS IN HIS THIRTIES ...
...AND IS A SUPPORTER OF THE MBA.
LIVE
GROUPS THAT DEFEND MR. TOMA AND OPPOSE THE MBA WOULD NEVER ATTACK ME...
...BUT MBA SUPPORTERS **WOULD.**
IT'S AN AWFUL INCIDENT ...
...BUT THE EFFECTS WILL BE **AWESOME!**
Chief...

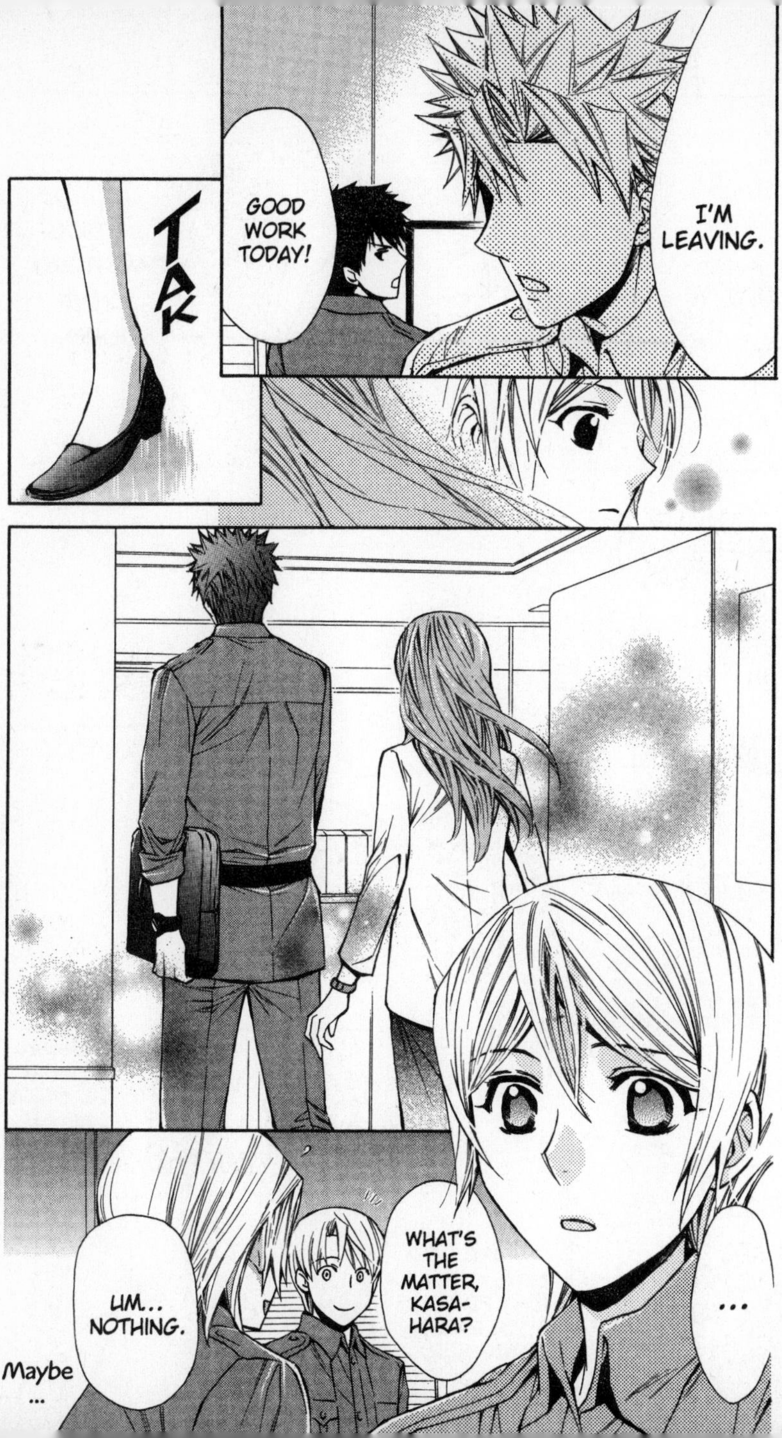
I'M LEAVING.
GOOD WORK TODAY!
TAK
...
WHAT'S THE MATTER, KASA-HARA?
UM... NOTHING.
Maybe ...

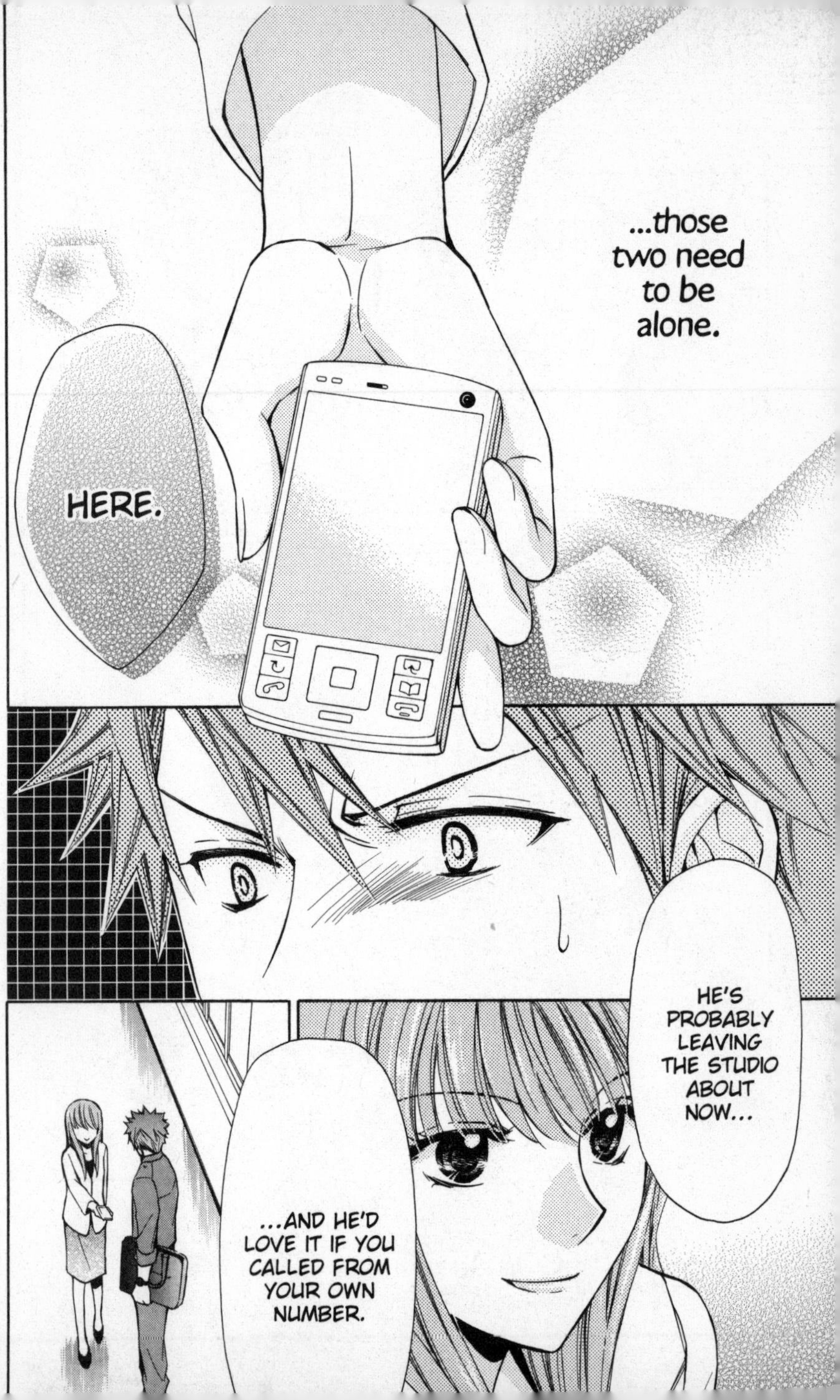
...those two need to be alone.
HERE.
HE'S PROBABLY LEAVING THE STUDIO ABOUT NOW...
...AND HE'D LOVE IT IF YOU CALLED FROM YOUR OWN NUMBER.

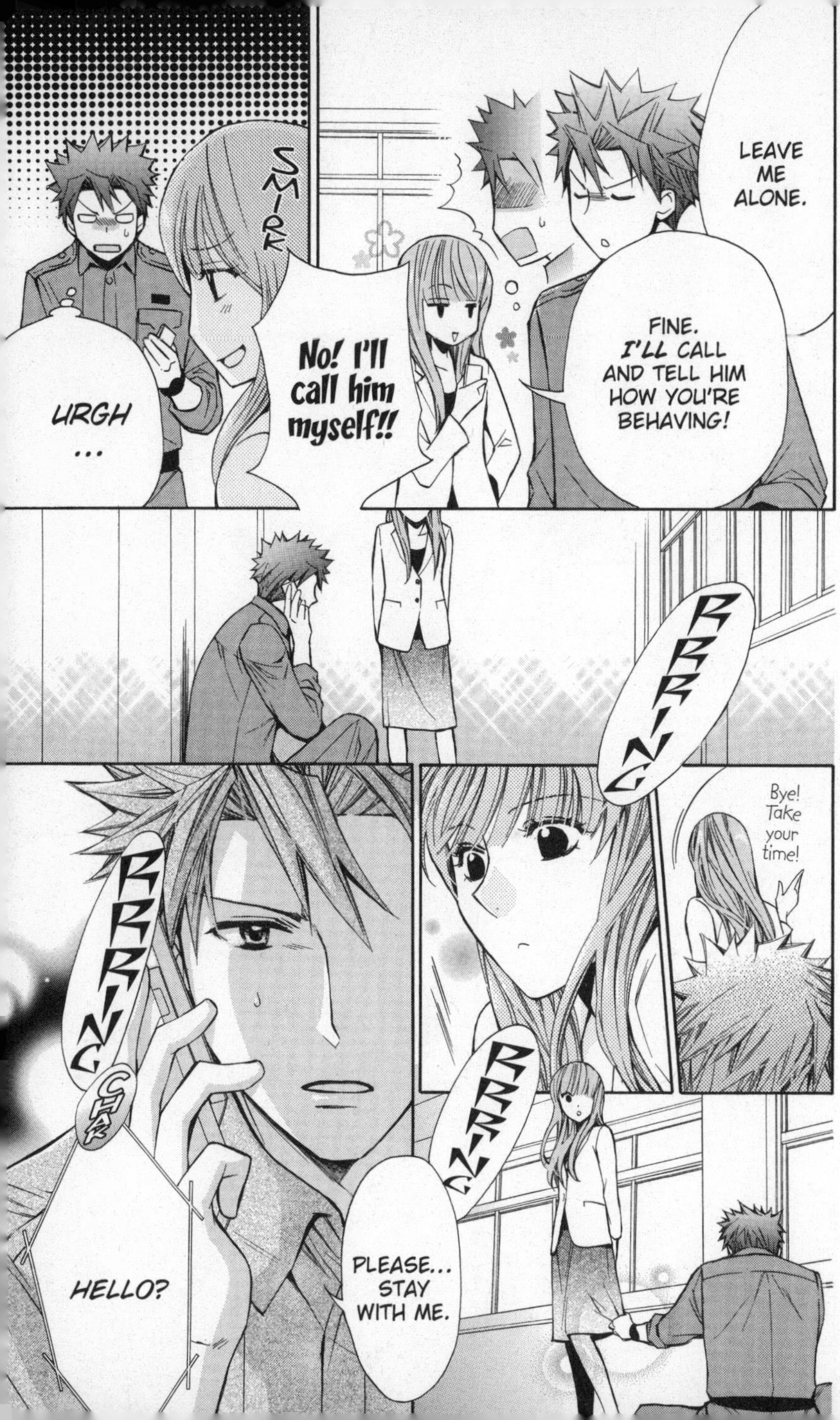
LEAVE ME ALONE.
FINE. I'LL CALL AND TELL HIM HOW YOU'RE BEHAVING!
No! I'll call him myself!!
SMIRK
URGH...
RRRING
Bye! Take your time!
RRRING
RRRING
CHAK
HELLO?
PLEASE... STAY WITH ME.

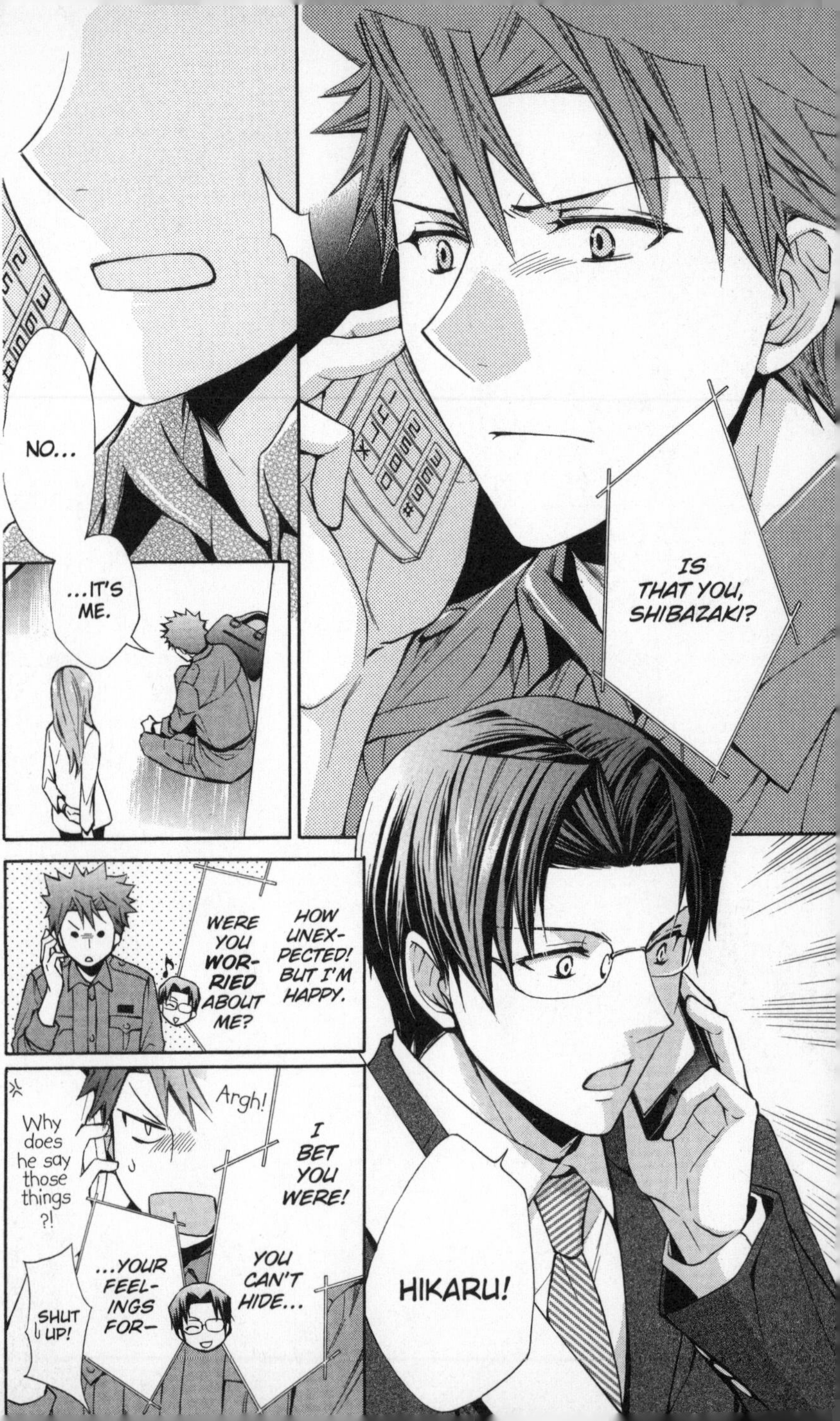
IS THAT YOU, SHIBAZAKI?
NO...
...IT'S ME.
HIKARU!
HOW UNEXPECTED! BUT I'M HAPPY.
WERE YOU WORRIED ABOUT ME?
Argh!
I BET YOU WERE!
Why does he say those things?!
YOU CAN'T HIDE...
...YOUR FEELINGS FOR—
SHUT UP!

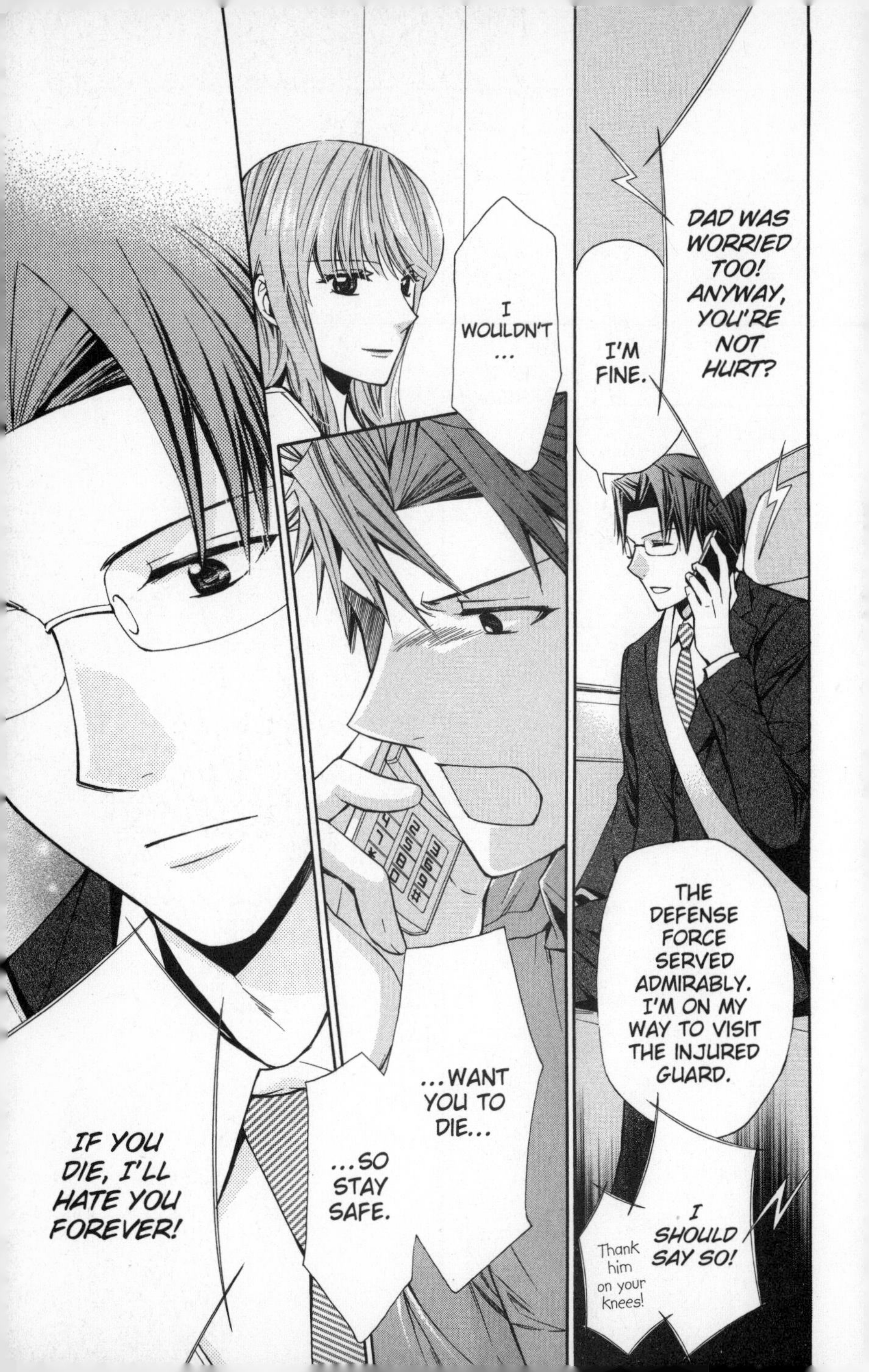
DAD WAS WORRIED TOO! ANYWAY, YOU'RE NOT HURT?
I'M FINE.
THE DEFENSE FORCE SERVED ADMIRABLY. I'M ON MY WAY TO VISIT THE INJURED GUARD.
I SHOULD SAY SO!
Thank him on your knees!
I WOULDN'T ...
...WANT YOU TO DIE...
...SO STAY SAFE.
IF YOU DIE, I'LL HATE YOU FOREVER!

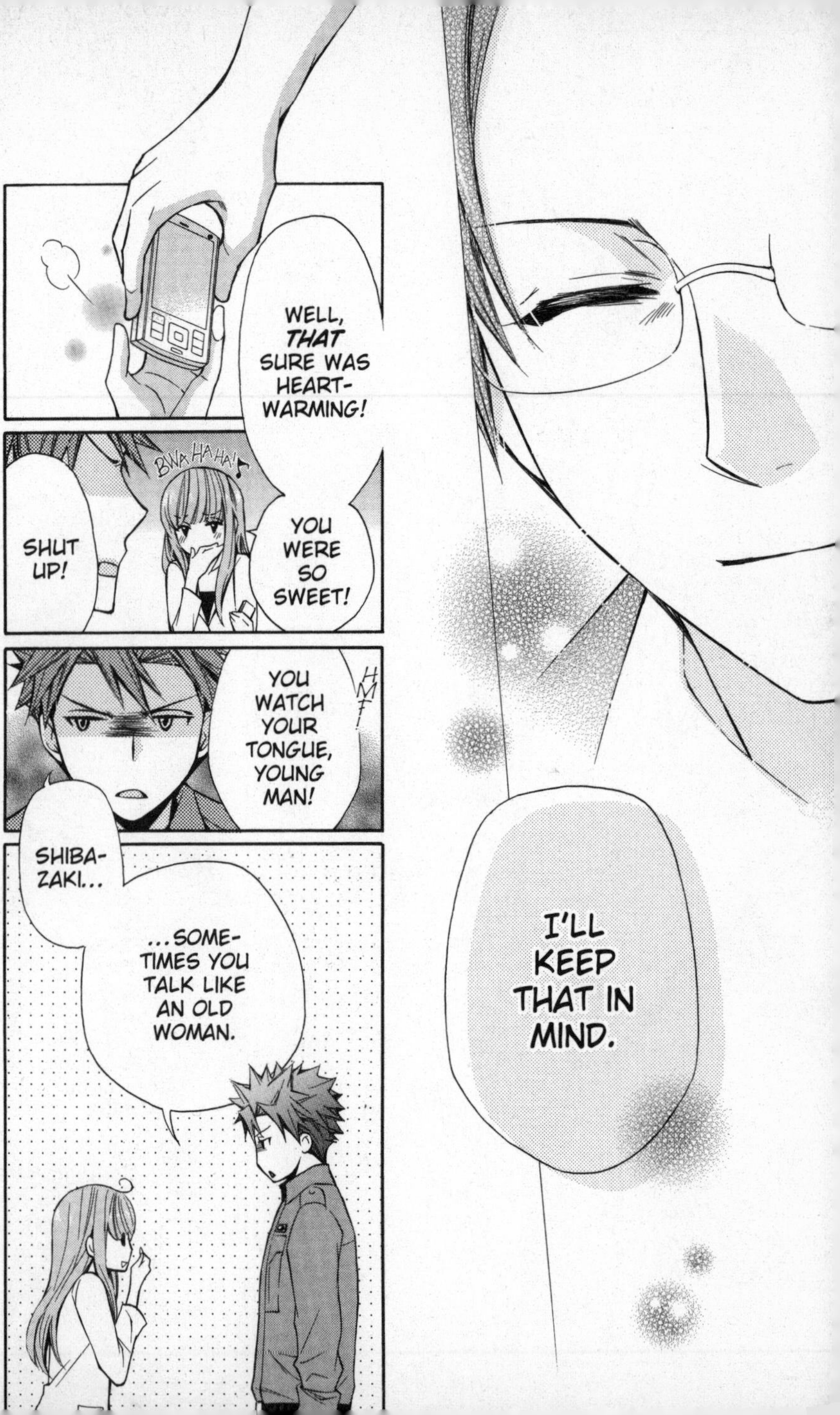
I'LL KEEP THAT IN MIND.
WELL, *THAT* SURE WAS HEART-WARMING!
BWAHAHA!
YOU WERE SO SWEET!
SHUT UP!
HMF!
YOU WATCH YOUR TONGUE, YOUNG MAN!
SHIBA-ZAKI...
...SOME-TIMES YOU TALK LIKE AN OLD WOMAN.

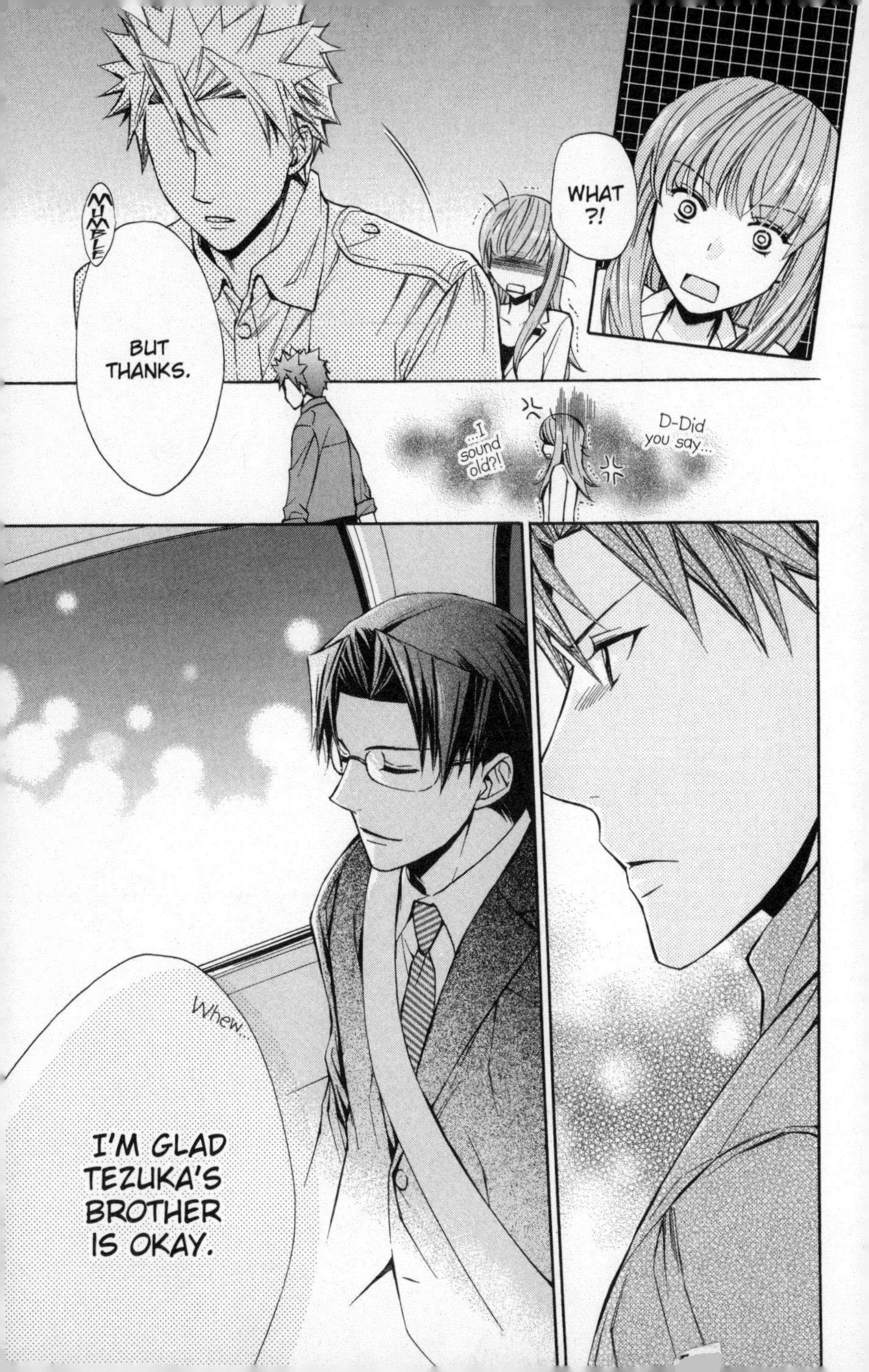
WHAT ?!
MUMBLE
BUT THANKS.
D-Did you say...
...I sound old?!
Whew...
I'M GLAD TEZUKA'S BROTHER IS OKAY.

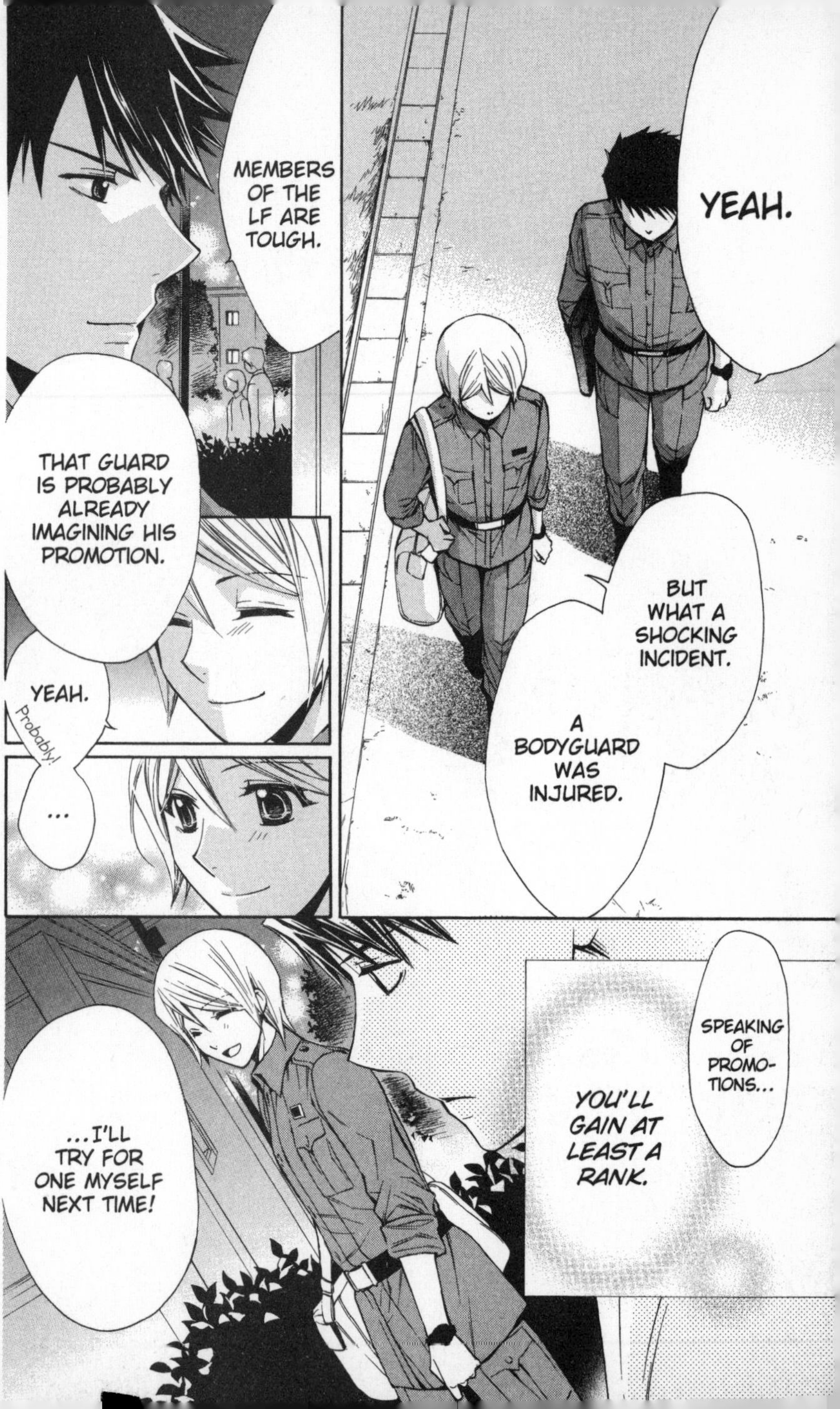
YEAH.
BUT WHAT A SHOCKING INCIDENT.
A BODYGUARD WAS INJURED.
MEMBERS OF THE LF ARE TOUGH.
THAT GUARD IS PROBABLY ALREADY IMAGINING HIS PROMOTION.
YEAH.
Probably!
...
SPEAKING OF PROMOTIONS...
YOU'LL GAIN AT LEAST A RANK.
...I'LL TRY FOR ONE MYSELF NEXT TIME!

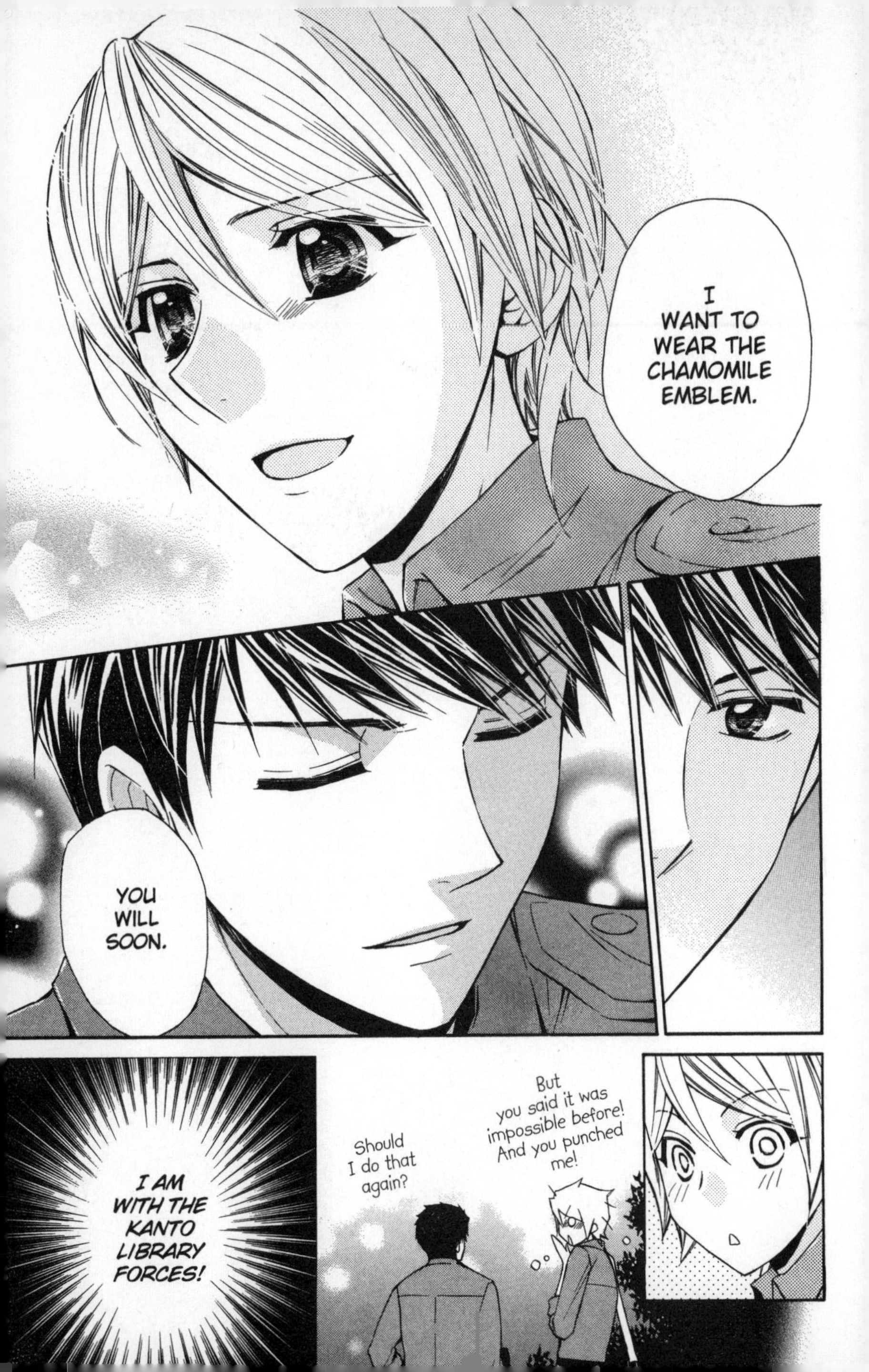
I WANT TO WEAR THE CHAMOMILE EMBLEM.
YOU WILL SOON.
But you said it was impossible before! And you punched me!
Should I do that again?
I AM WITH THE KANTO LIBRARY FORCES!

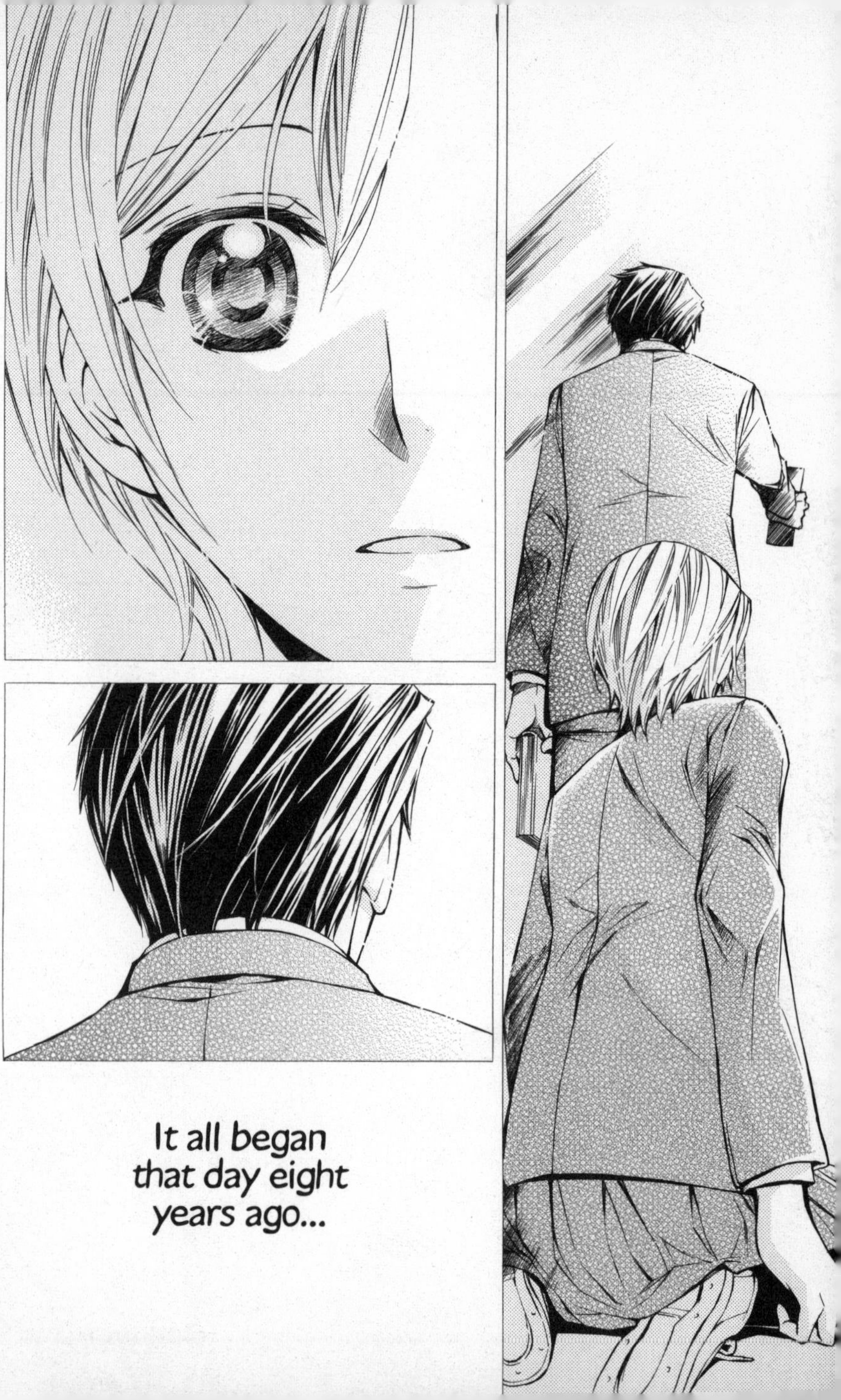
It all began that day eight years ago...

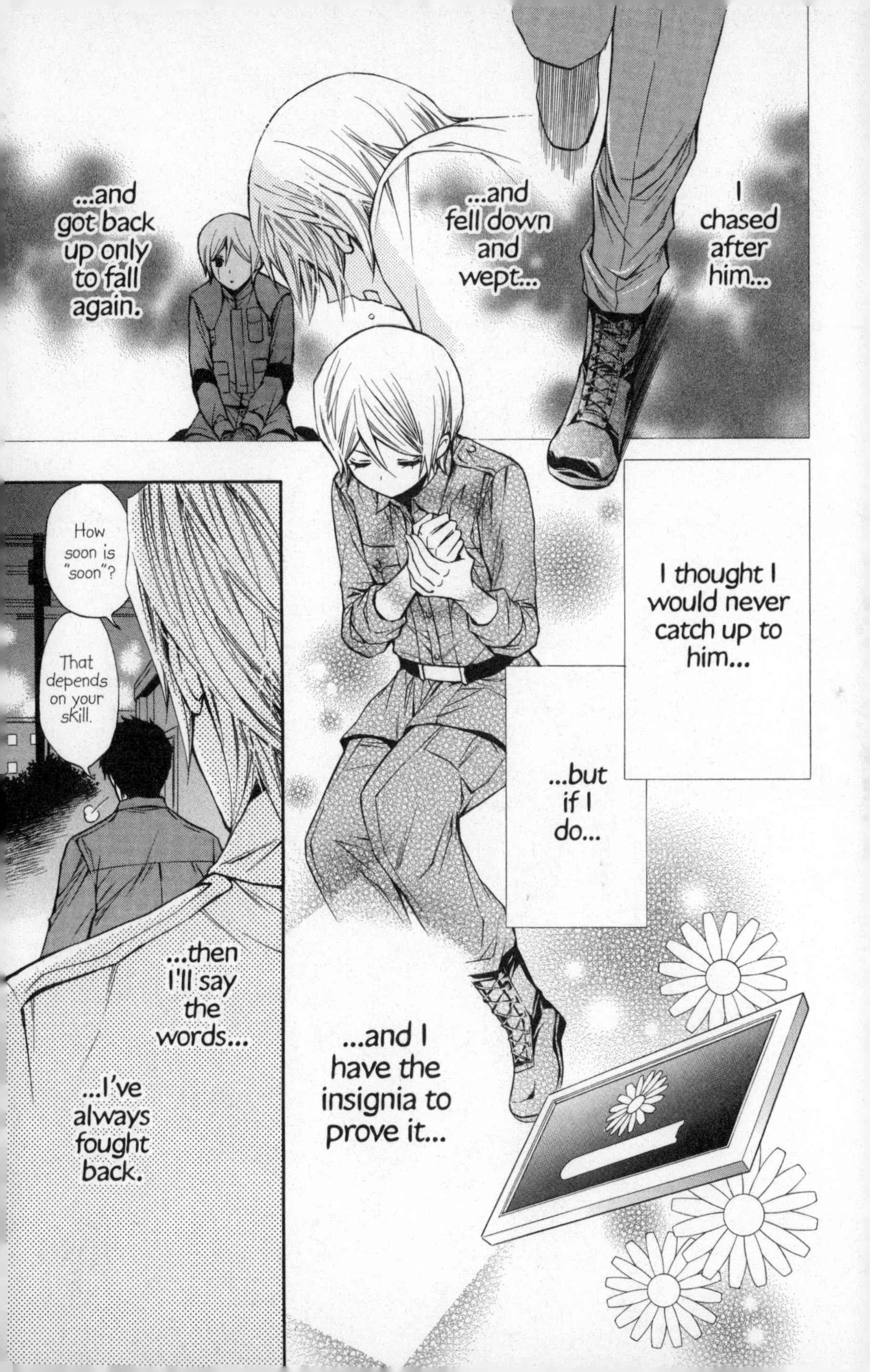
I chased after him...
...and fell down and wept...
...and got back up only to fall again.
I thought I would never catch up to him...
...but if I do...
...and I have the insignia to prove it...
How soon is "soon"?
That depends on your skill.
...then I'll say the words...
...I've always fought back.

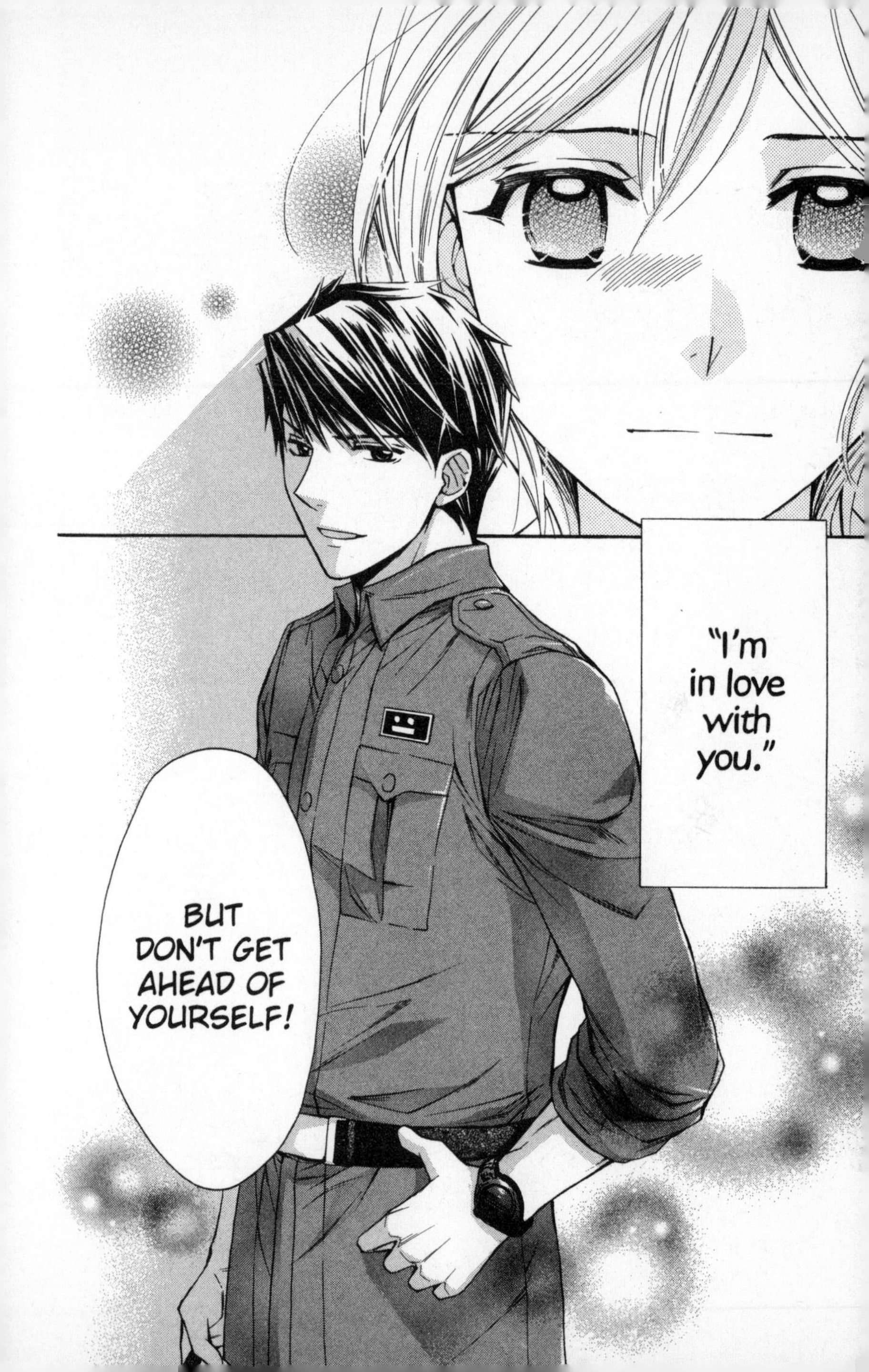
"I'm in love with you."
BUT DON'T GET AHEAD OF YOURSELF!

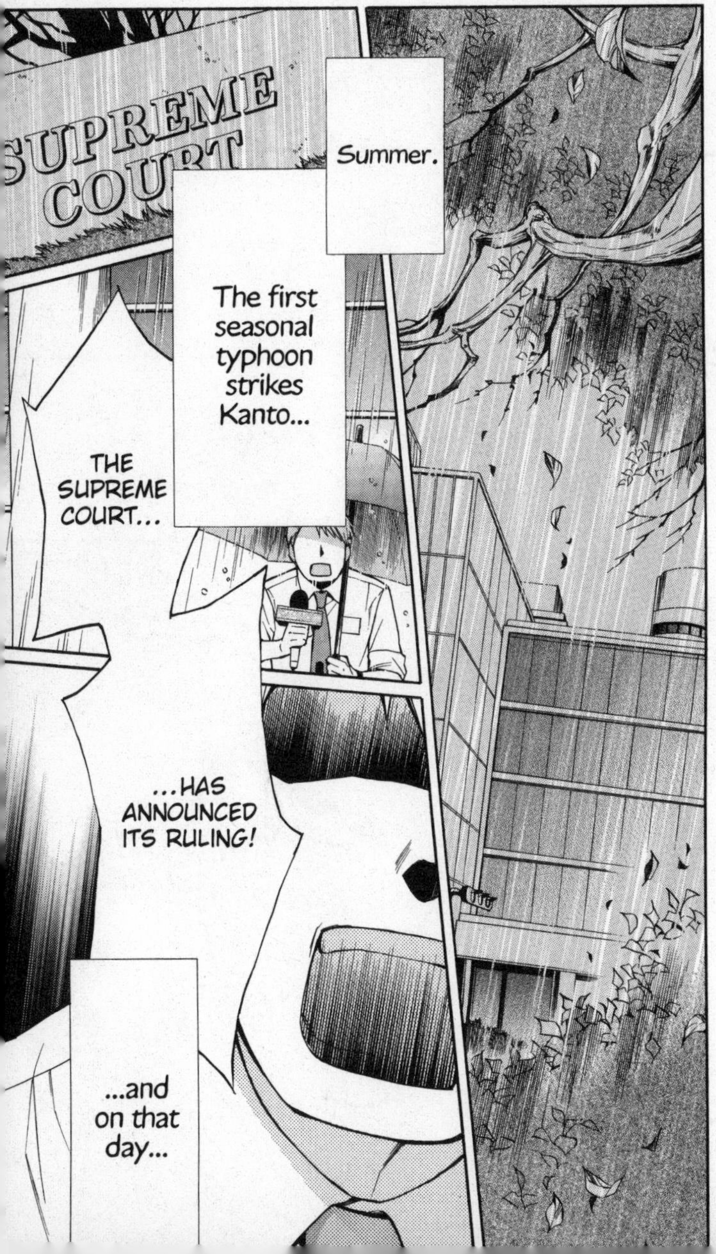
Summer.
The first seasonal typhoon strikes Kanto...
THE SUPREME COURT...
...HAS ANNOUNCED ITS RULING!
...and on that day...

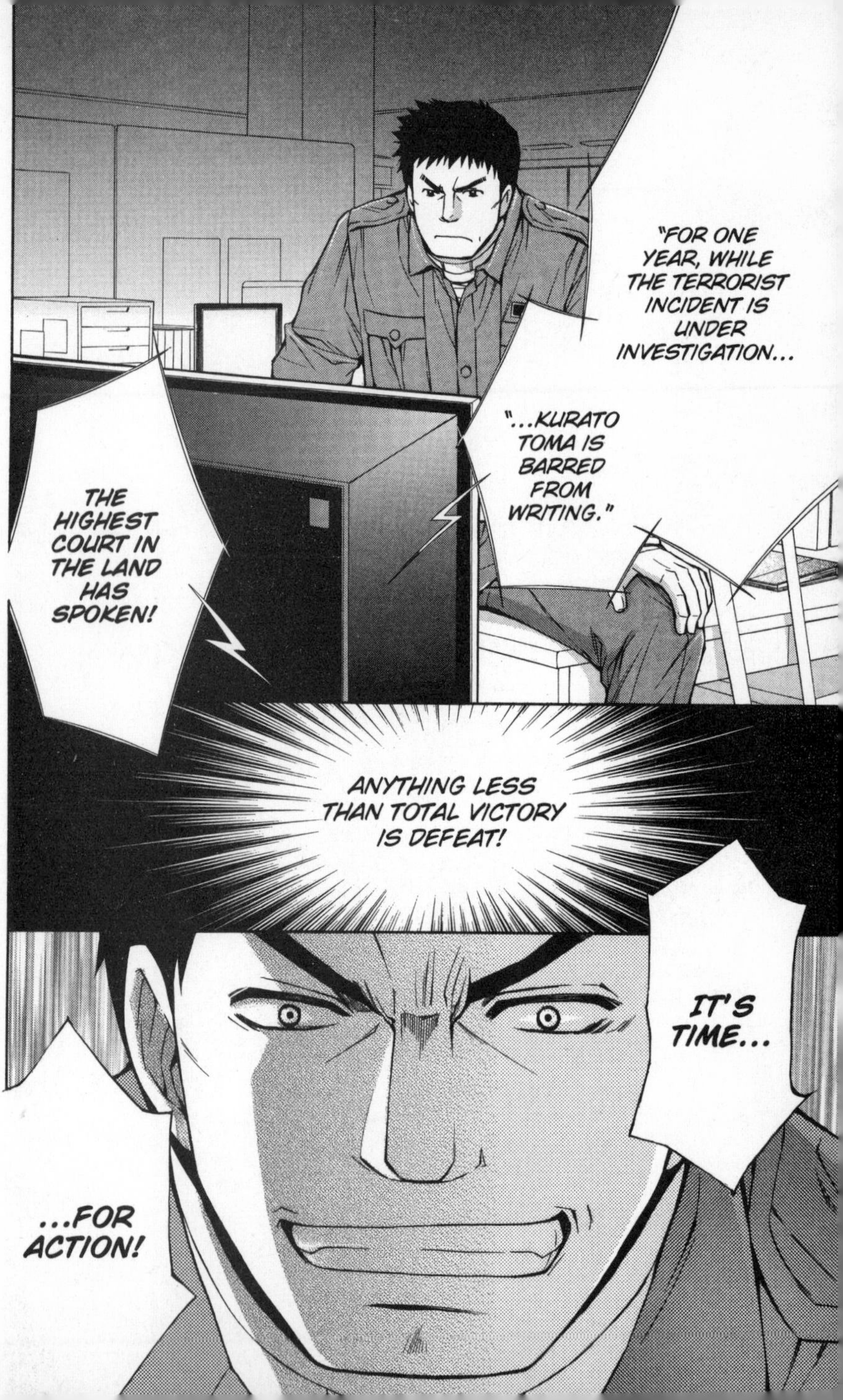
"FOR ONE YEAR, WHILE THE TERRORIST INCIDENT IS UNDER INVESTIGATION...
"...KURATO TOMA IS BARRED FROM WRITING."
THE HIGHEST COURT IN THE LAND HAS SPOKEN!
ANYTHING LESS THAN TOTAL VICTORY IS DEFEAT!
IT'S TIME...
...FOR ACTION!

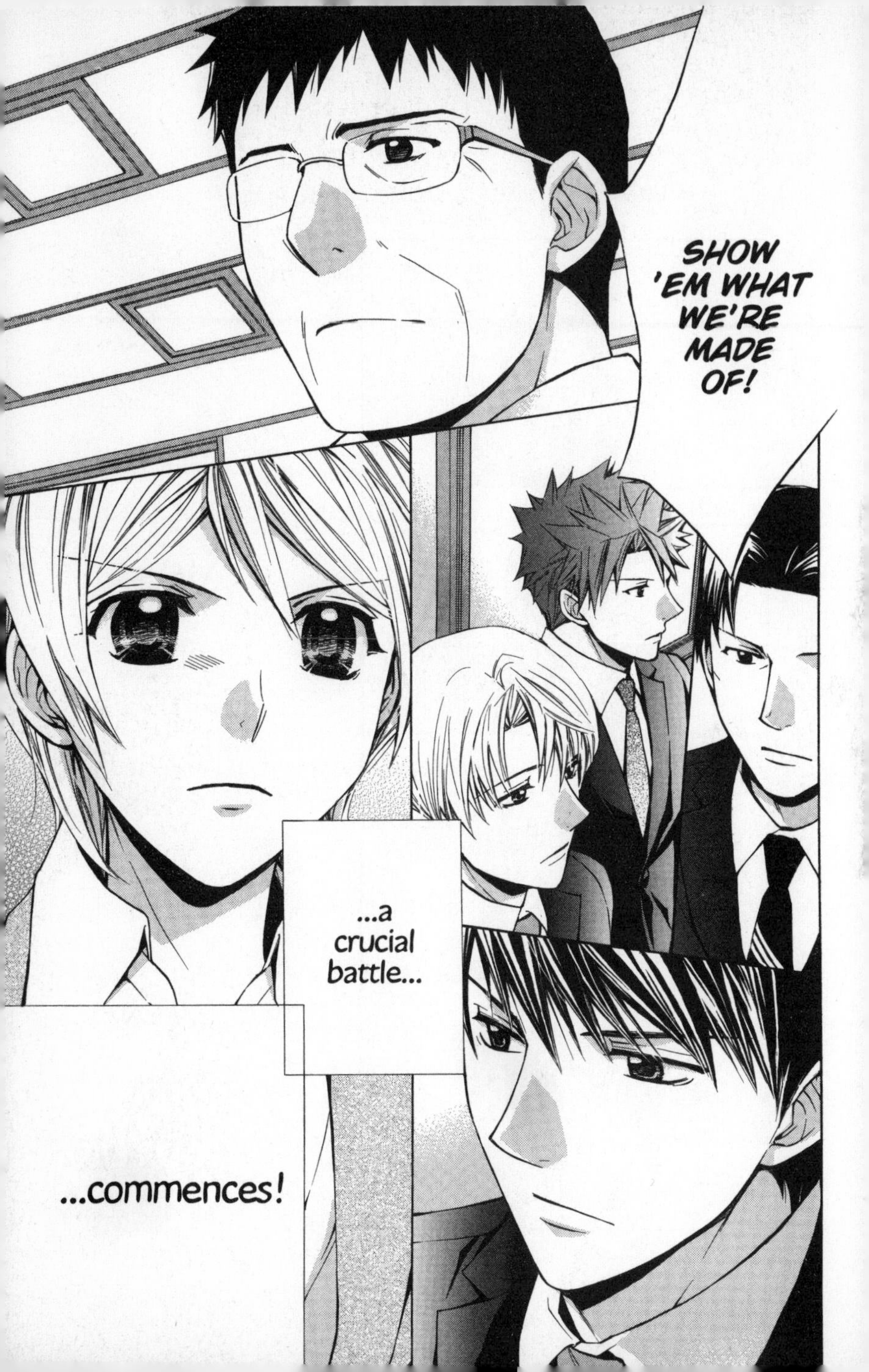
SHOW 'EM WHAT WE'RE MADE OF!
...a crucial battle...
...commences!

Satoshi Is Thankful for Modern Conveniences (A Call Recording App)

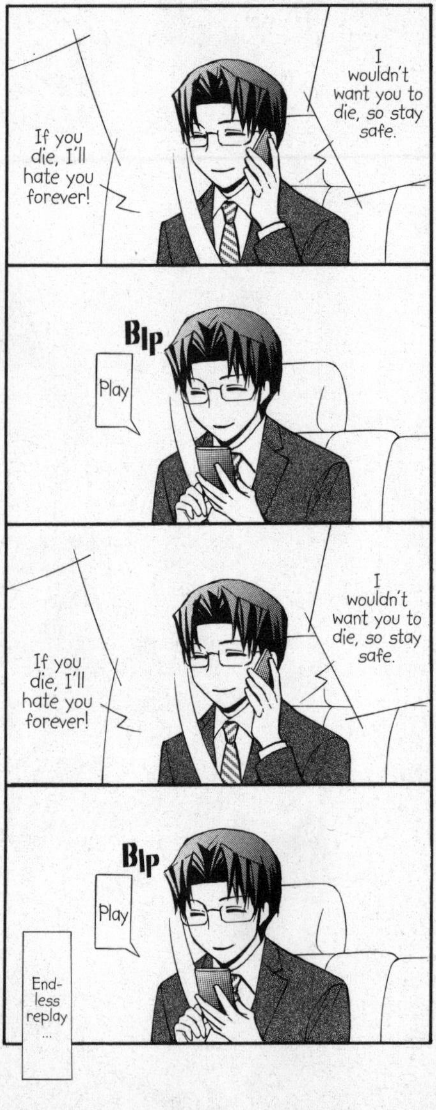
I wouldn't want you to die, so stay safe.
If you die, I'll hate you forever!
BIP
Play
I wouldn't want you to die, so stay safe.
If you die, I'll hate you forever!
BIP
Play
End-less replay ...

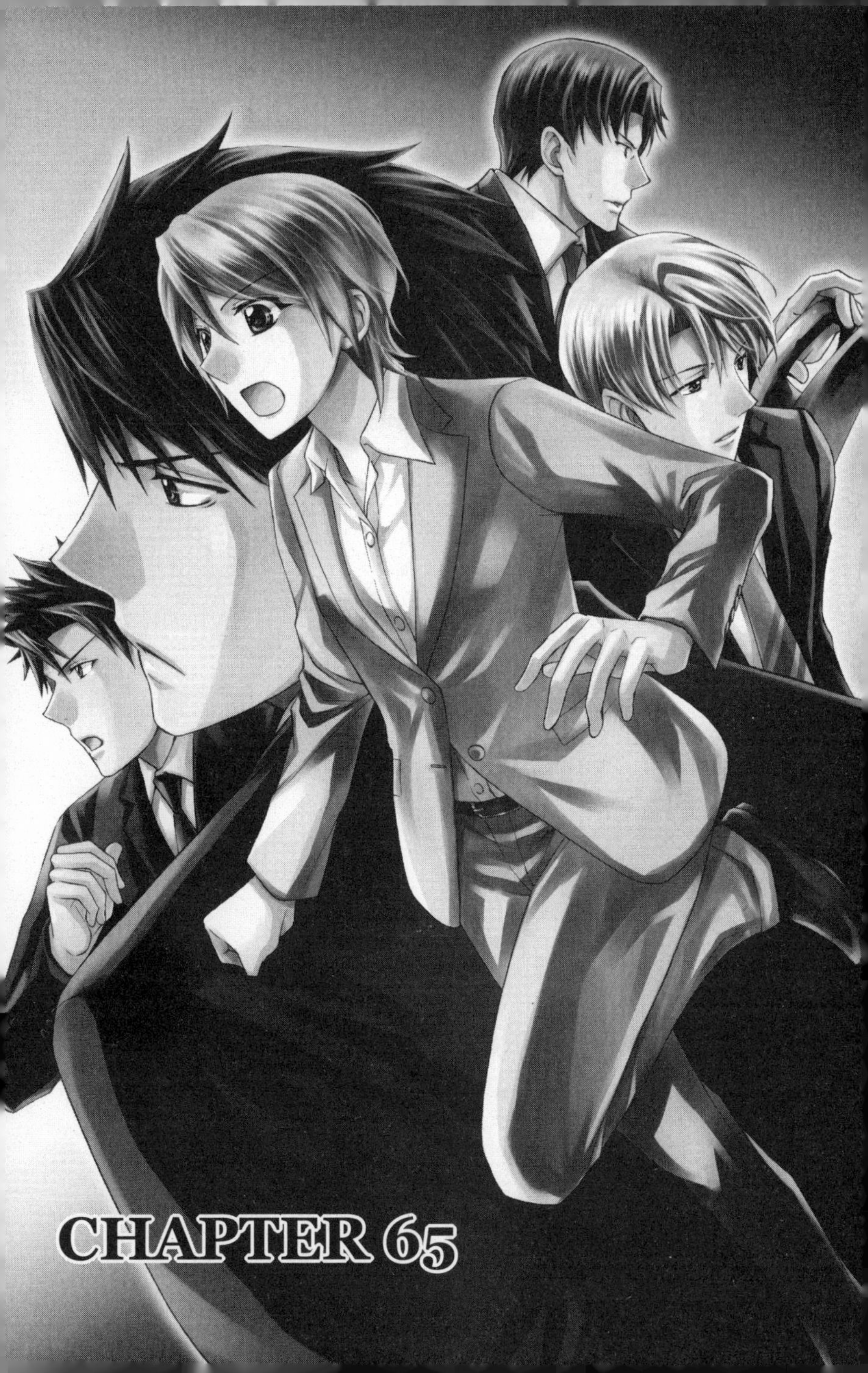
CHAPTER 65

Grew Up in the Country

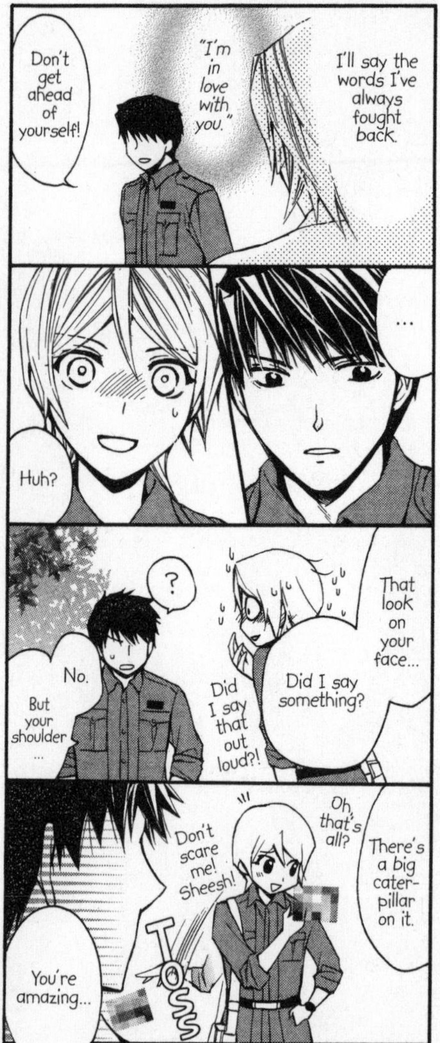

I'll say the words I've always fought back.
"I'm in love with you."
Don't get ahead of yourself!
...
Huh?
That look on your face...
Did I say something?
Did I say that out loud?!
?
No.
But your shoulder ...
There's a big cater-pillar on it.
Oh, that's all?
Don't scare me! Sheesh!
TOSS
You're amazing...

It was so big even I would have jumped!

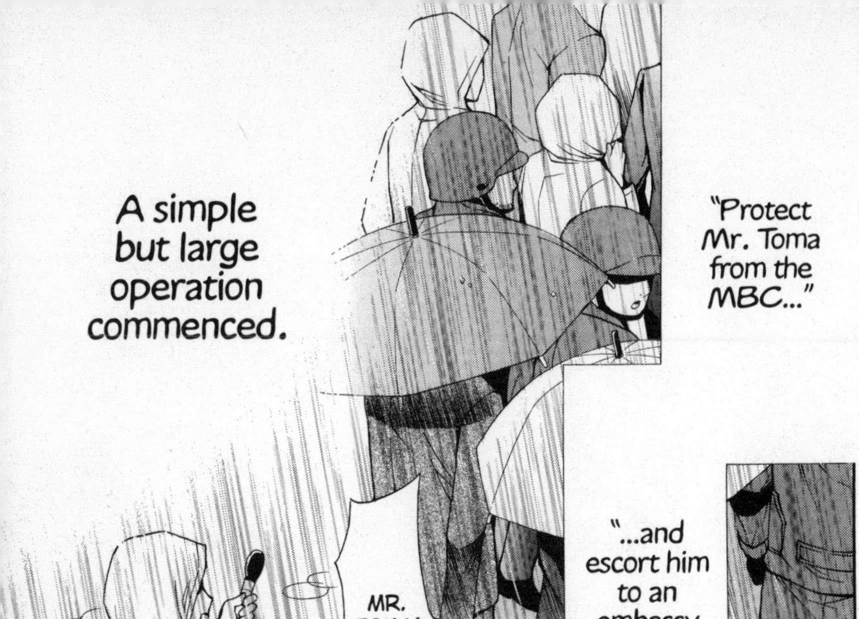
"Protect Mr. Toma from the MBC..."
A simple but large operation commenced.
"...and escort him to an embassy for defection."
MR. TOMA!
WHAT IS YOUR REACTION TO THE RULING?

2.

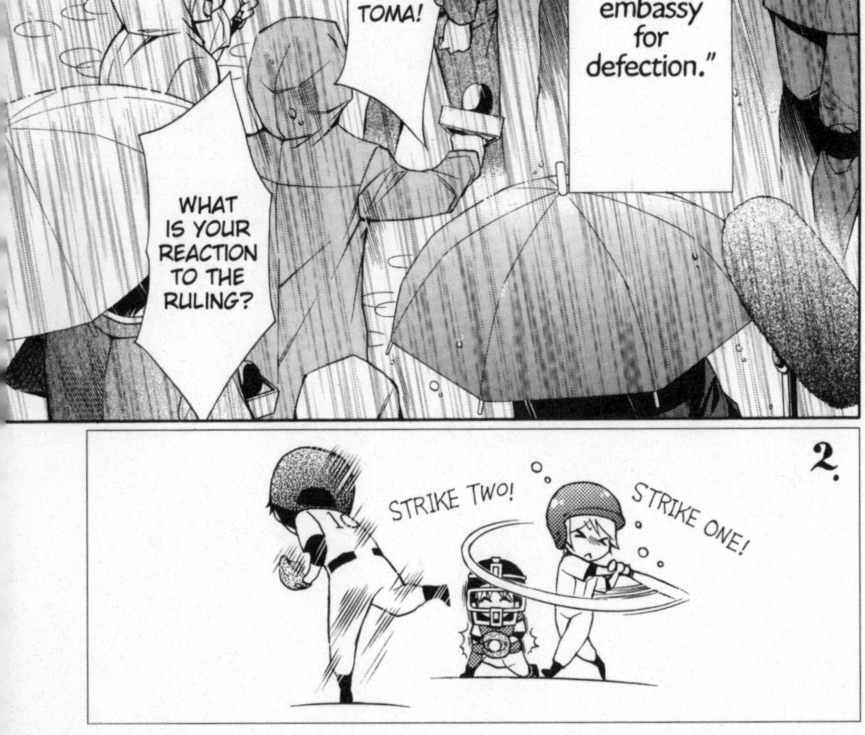
STRIKE ONE!
STRIKE TWO!

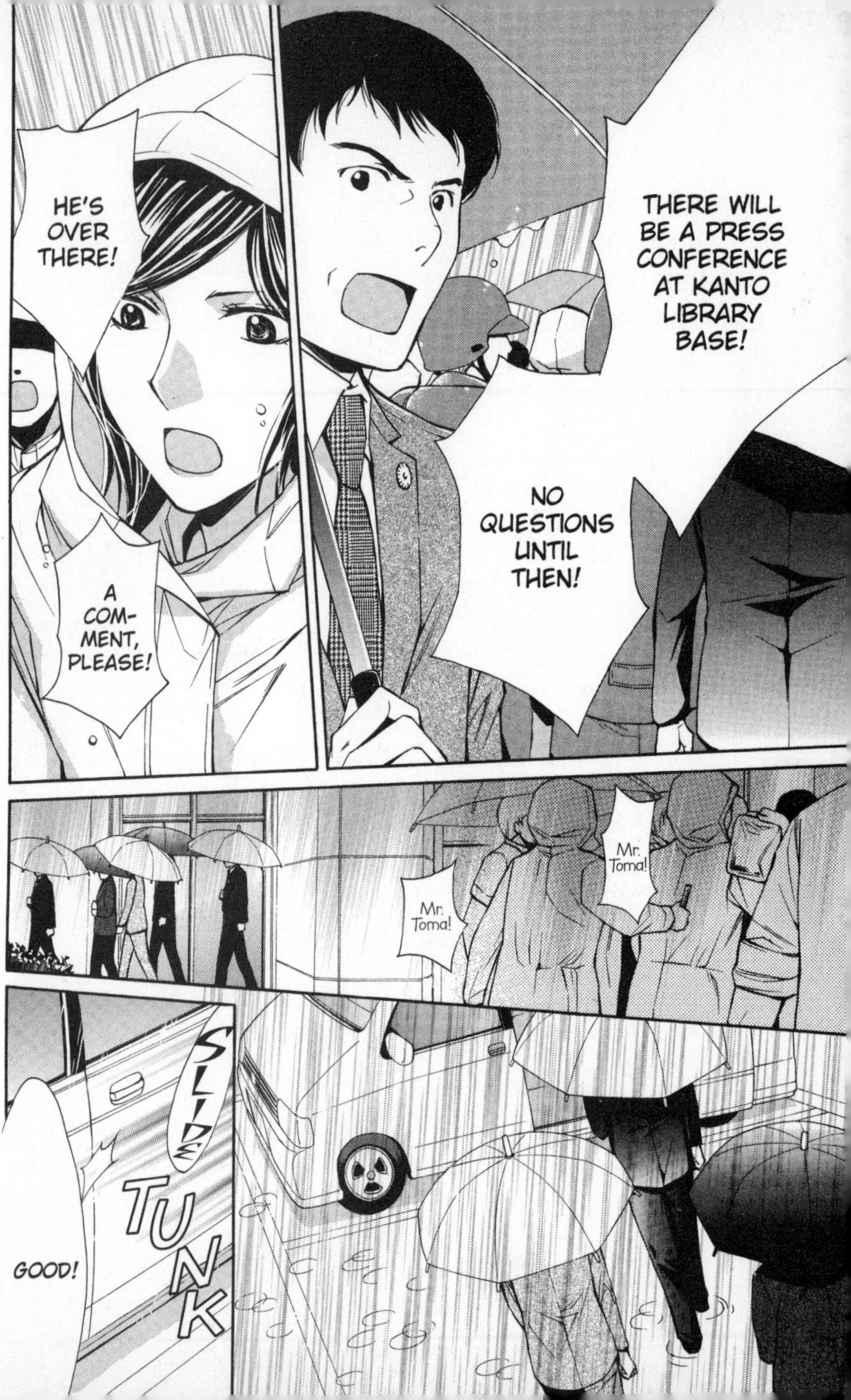
THERE WILL BE A PRESS CONFERENCE AT KANTO LIBRARY BASE!
NO QUESTIONS UNTIL THEN!
HE'S OVER THERE!
A COM-MENT, PLEASE!
Mr. Toma!
Mr. Toma!
SLIDE
TUNK
GOOD!

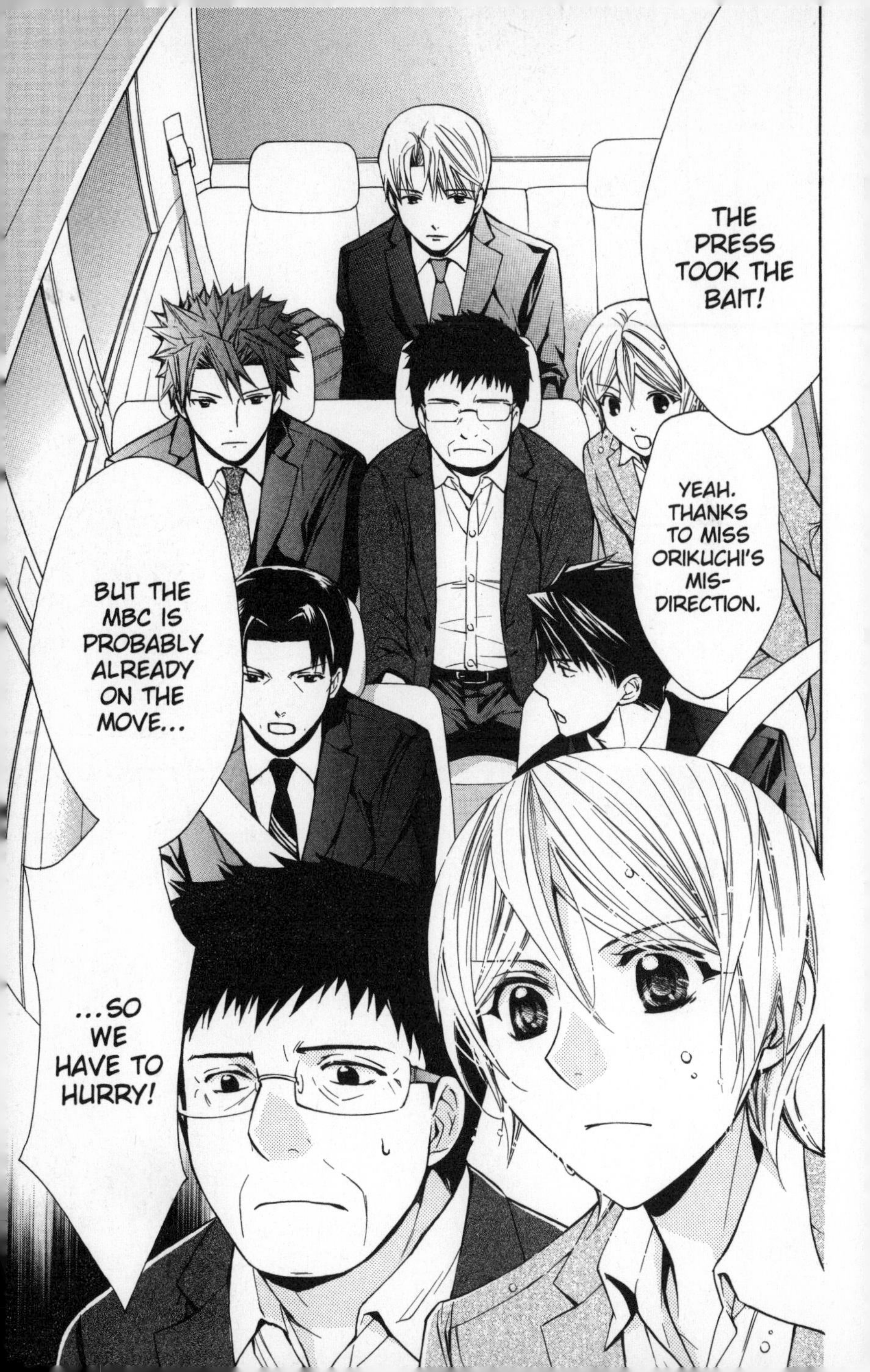
THE PRESS TOOK THE BAIT!
YEAH. THANKS TO MISS ORIKUCHI'S MIS-DIRECTION.
BUT THE MBC IS PROBABLY ALREADY ON THE MOVE...
...SO WE HAVE TO HURRY!

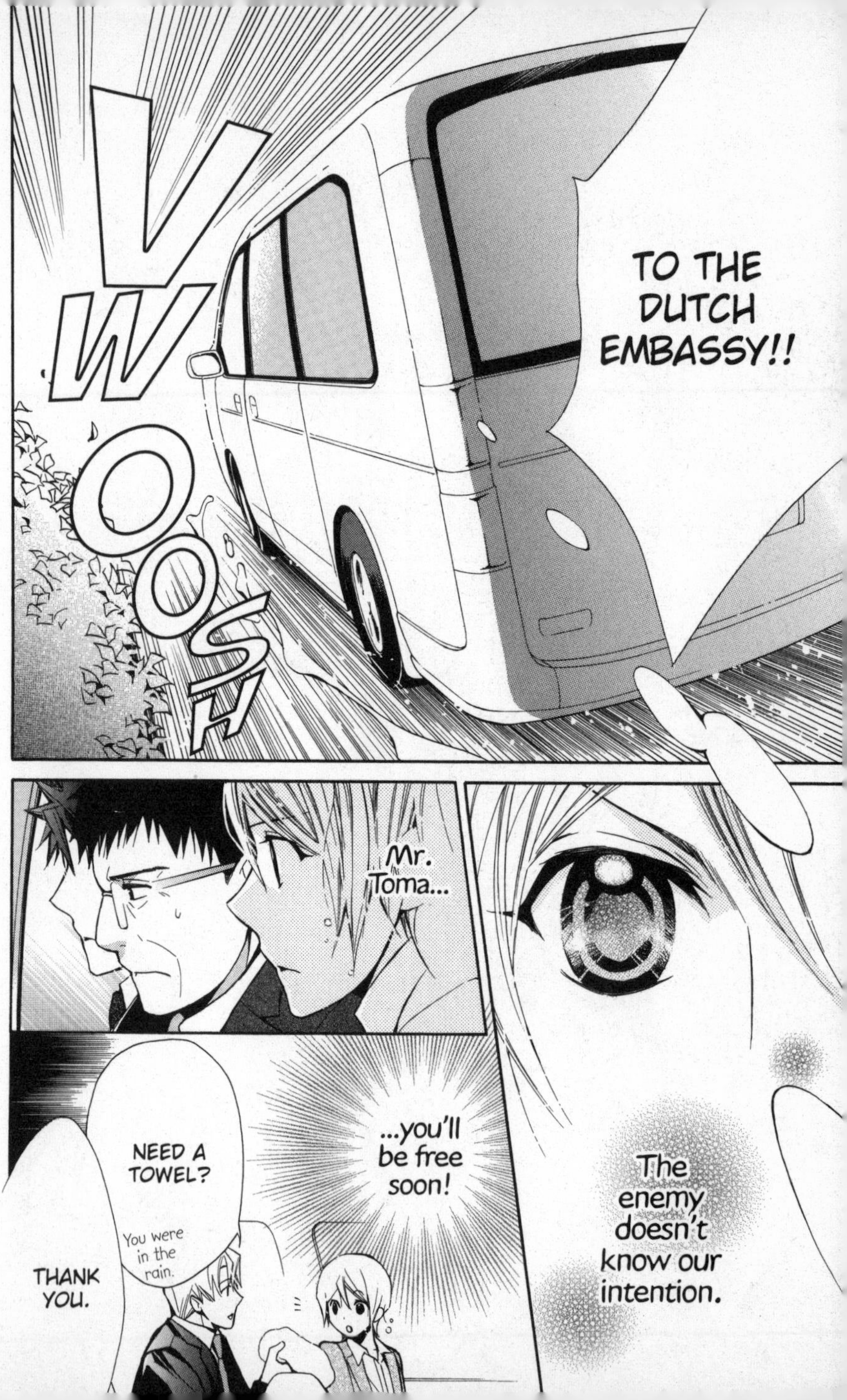
TO THE DUTCH EMBASSY!!
VWOOOSH
The enemy doesn't know our intention.
Mr. Toma...
...you'll be free soon!
NEED A TOWEL?
You were in the rain.
THANK YOU.

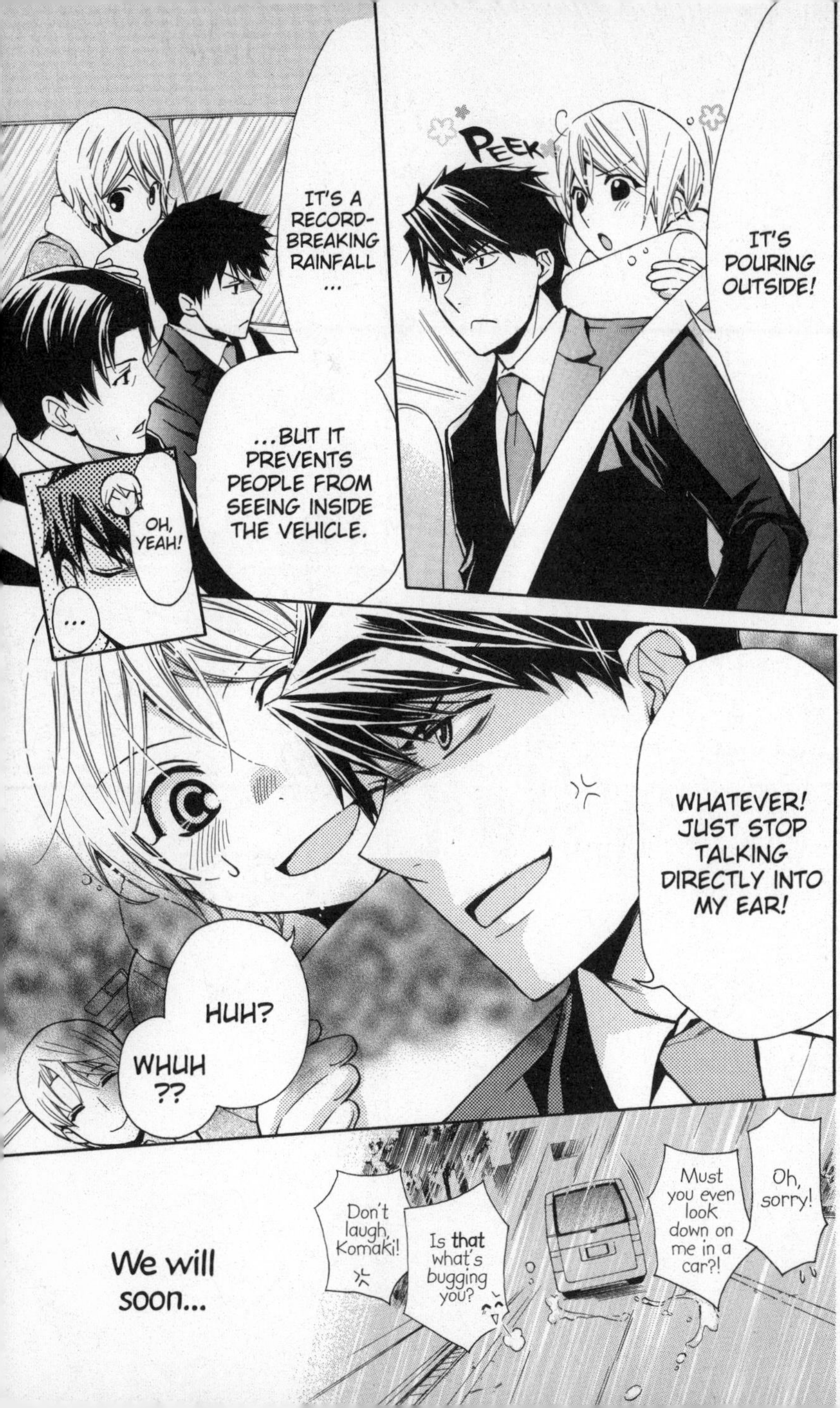
PEEK
IT'S POURING OUTSIDE!
IT'S A RECORD-BREAKING RAINFALL ...
...BUT IT PREVENTS PEOPLE FROM SEEING INSIDE THE VEHICLE.
OH, YEAH!
...
WHATEVER! JUST STOP TALKING DIRECTLY INTO MY EAR!
HUH?
WHUH ??
Oh, sorry!
Must you even look down on me in a car?!
Is that what's bugging you?
Don't laugh, Komaki!
We will soon...

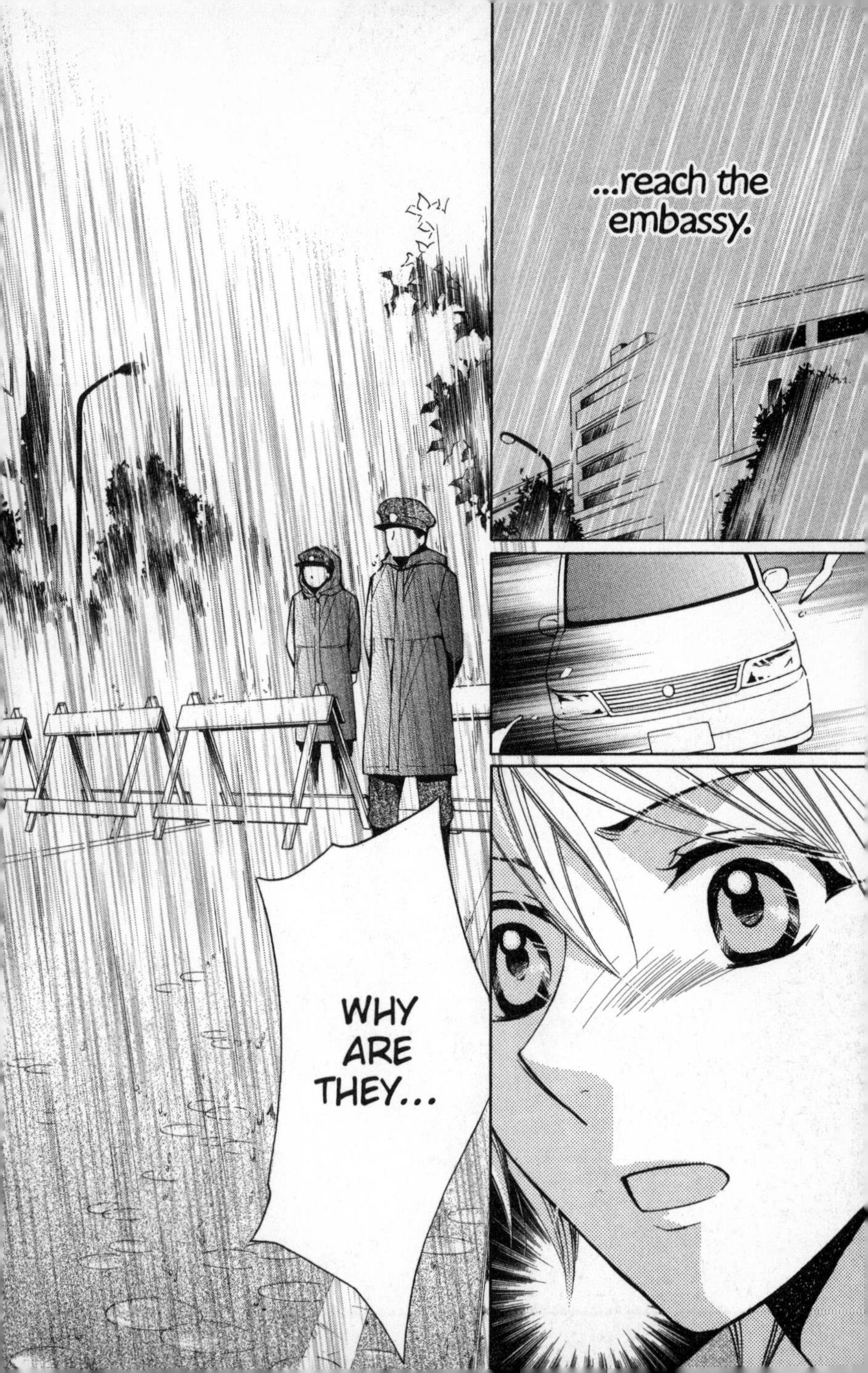
...reach the embassy.
WHY ARE THEY...

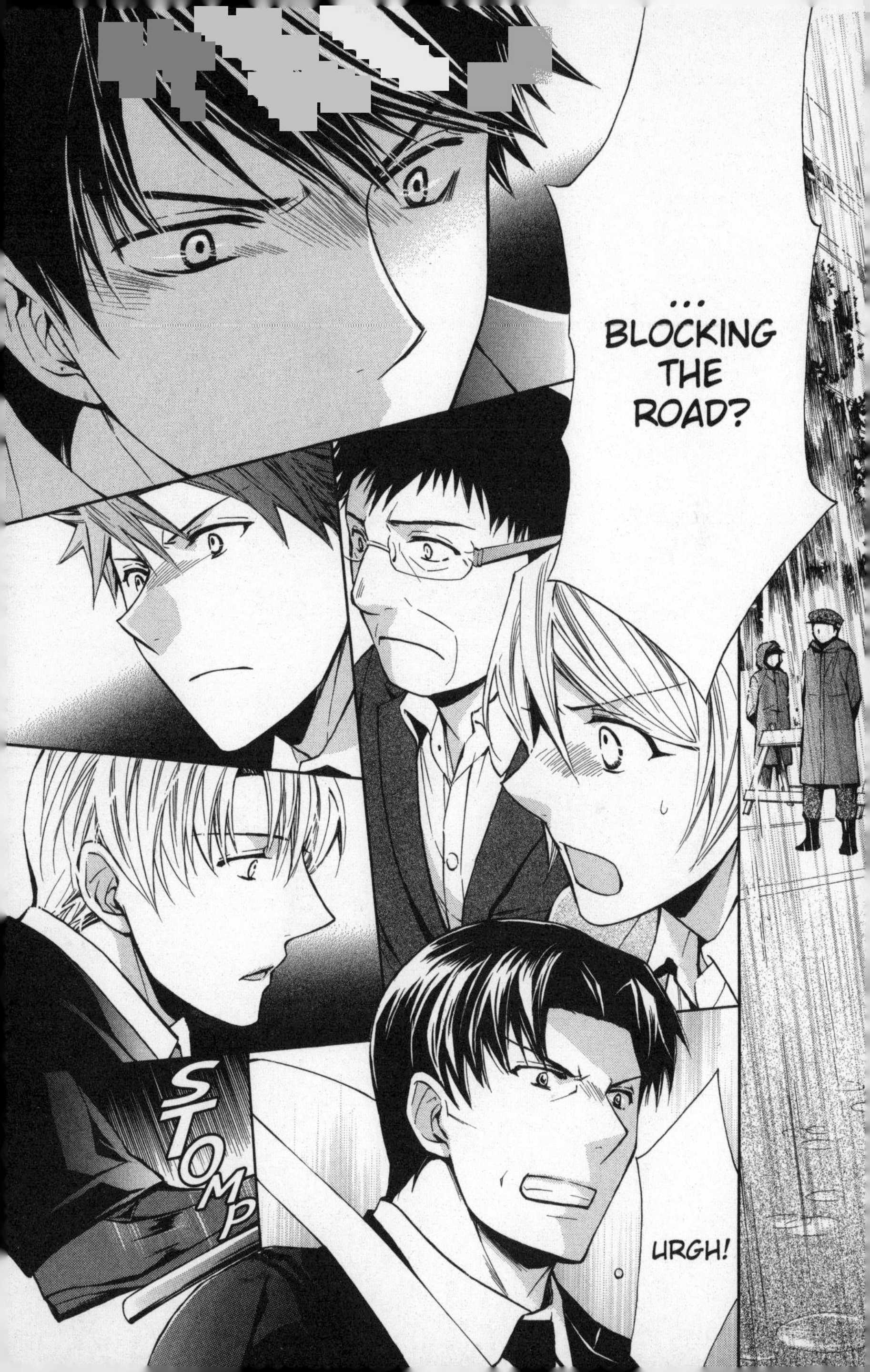
... BLOCKING THE ROAD?
URGH!
STOMP

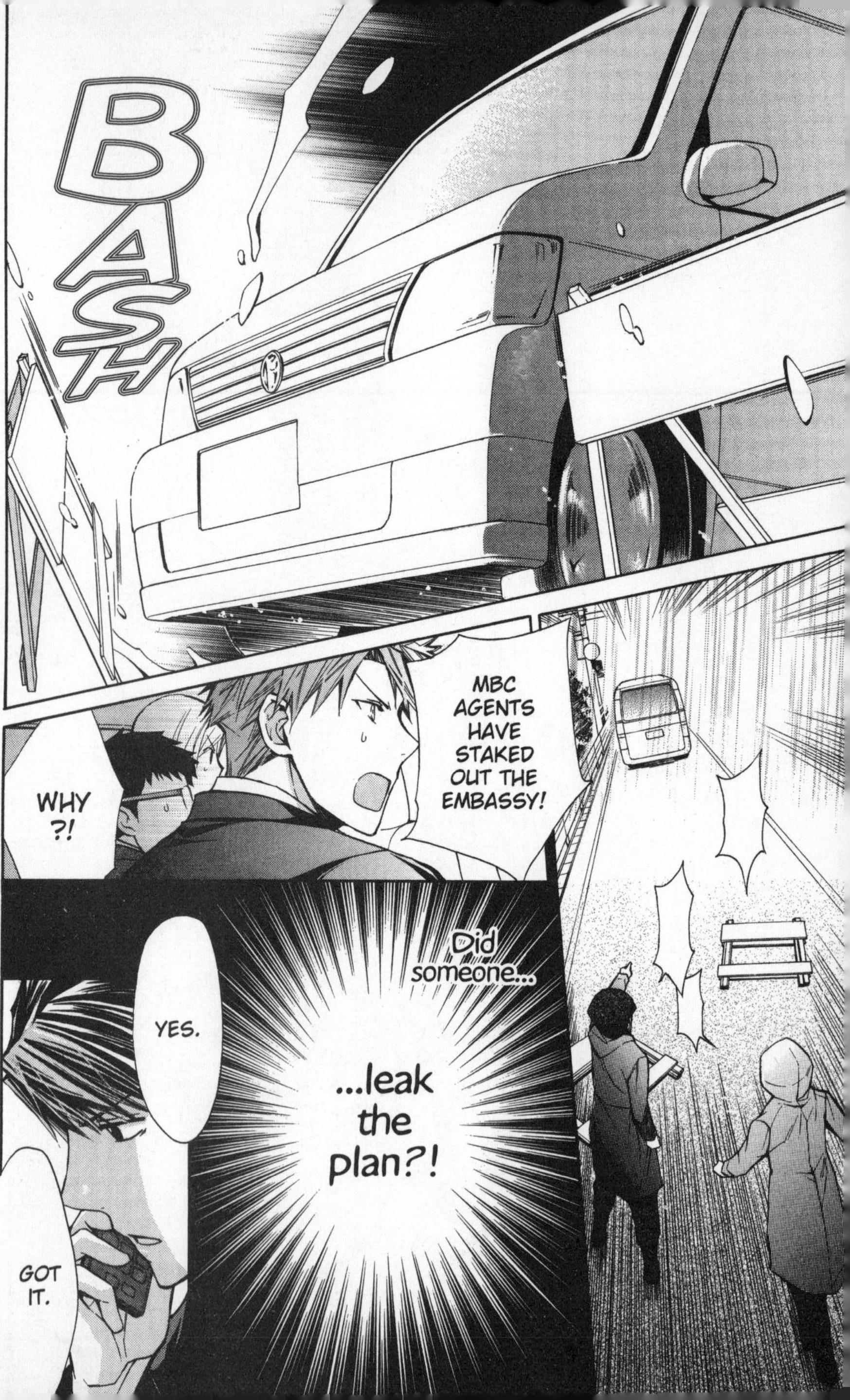
BASH
MBC AGENTS HAVE STAKED OUT THE EMBASSY!
WHY?!
Did someone...
...leak the plan?!
YES.
GOT IT.

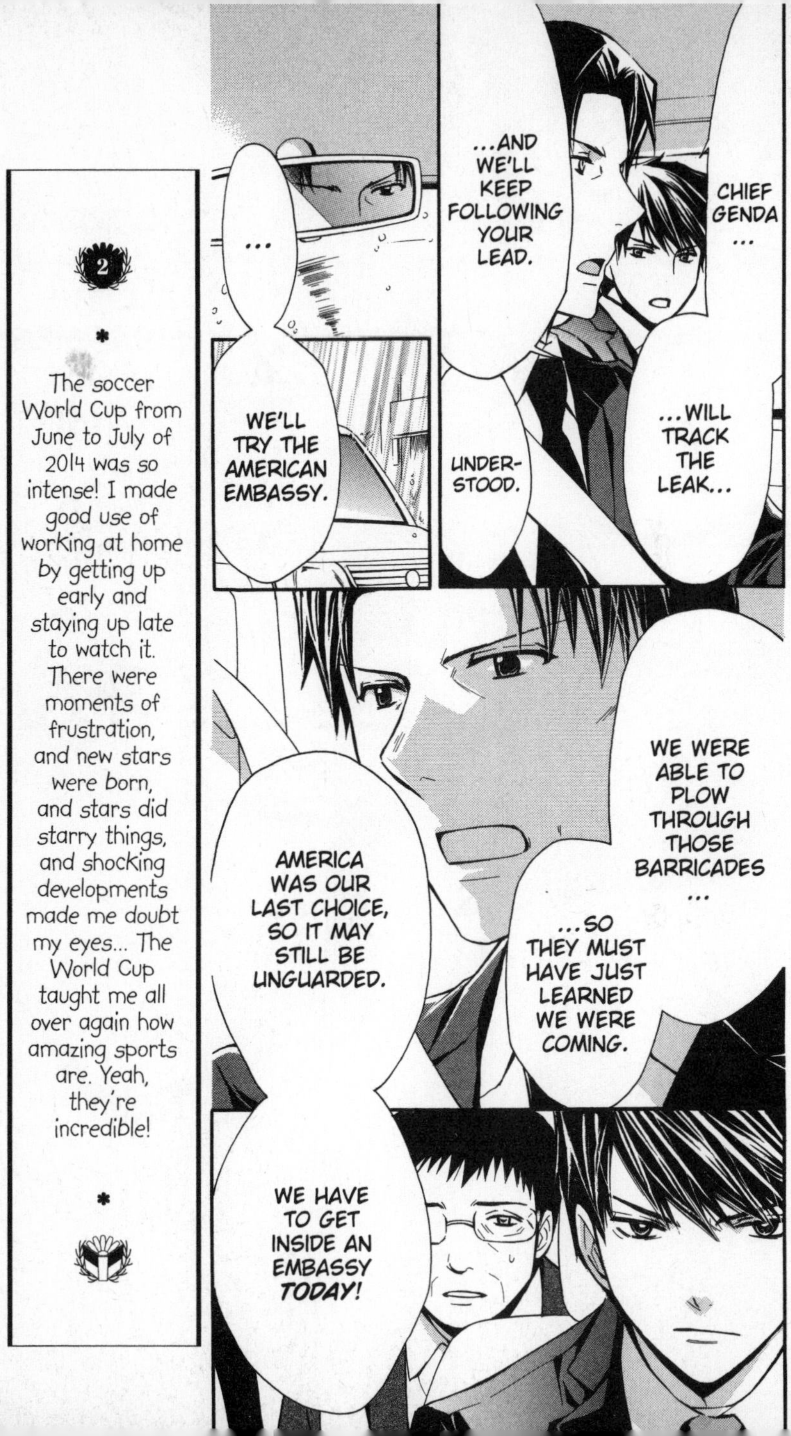
CHIEF GENDA...
...WILL TRACK THE LEAK...
...AND WE'LL KEEP FOLLOWING YOUR LEAD.
UNDERSTOOD.
...
WE'LL TRY THE AMERICAN EMBASSY.
WE WERE ABLE TO PLOW THROUGH THOSE BARRICADES...
...SO THEY MUST HAVE JUST LEARNED WE WERE COMING.
AMERICA WAS OUR LAST CHOICE, SO IT MAY STILL BE UNGUARDED.
WE HAVE TO GET INSIDE AN EMBASSY *TODAY!*

2

*

The soccer World Cup from June to July of 2014 was so intense! I made good use of working at home by getting up early and staying up late to watch it. There were moments of frustration, and new stars were born, and stars did starry things, and shocking developments made me doubt my eyes... The World Cup taught me all over again how amazing sports are. Yeah, they're incredible!

*

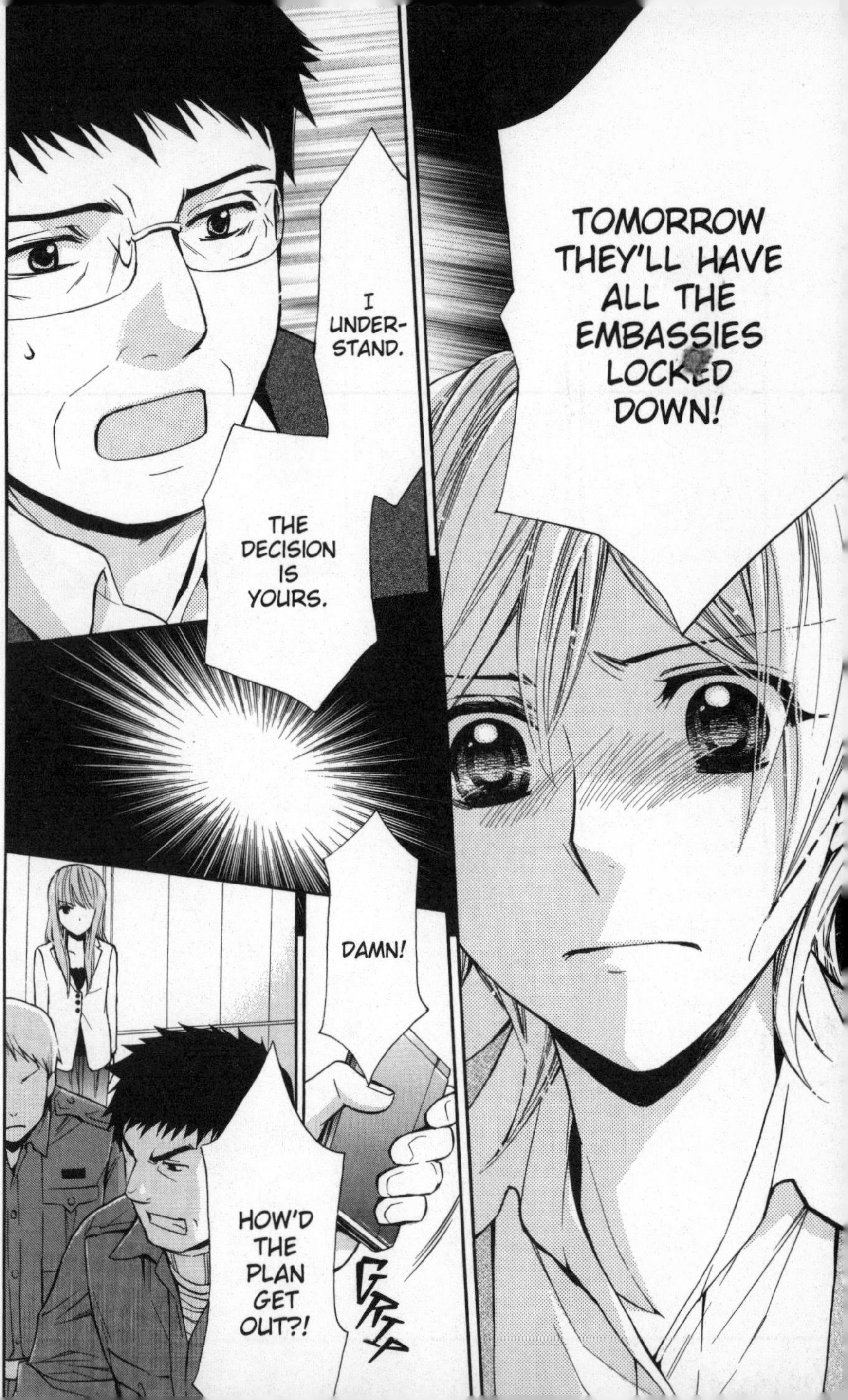
TOMORROW THEY'LL HAVE ALL THE EMBASSIES LOCKED DOWN!
I UNDER-STAND.
THE DECISION IS YOURS.
DAMN!
HOW'D THE PLAN GET OUT?!
GRIP

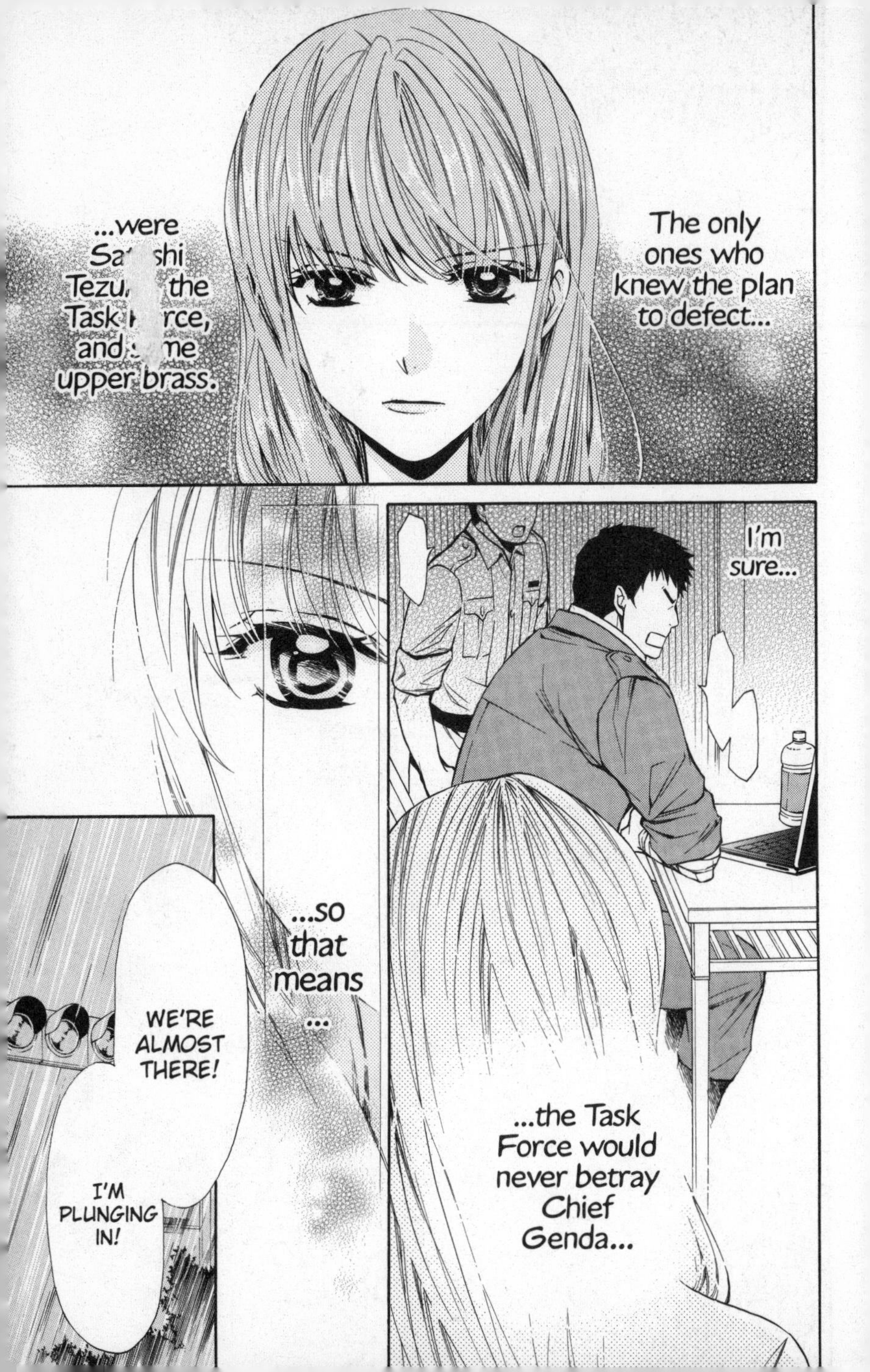
The only ones who knew the plan to defect...
...were Satoshi Tezuka, the Task Force, and some upper brass.
I'm sure...
...so that means...
...the Task Force would never betray Chief Genda...
WE'RE ALMOST THERE!
I'M PLUNGING IN!

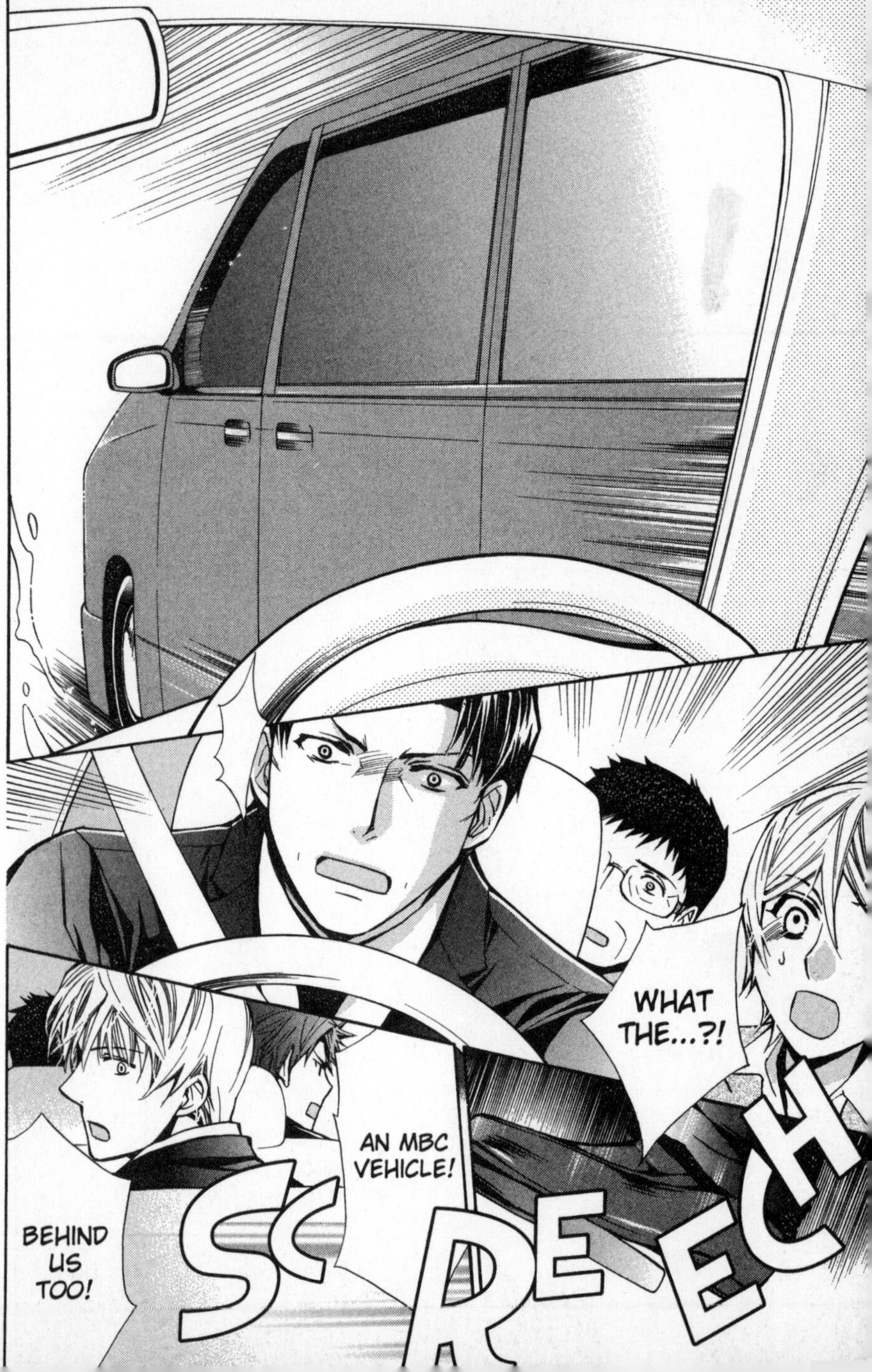
WHAT THE...?!
AN MBC VEHICLE!
BEHIND US TOO!
SCREECH

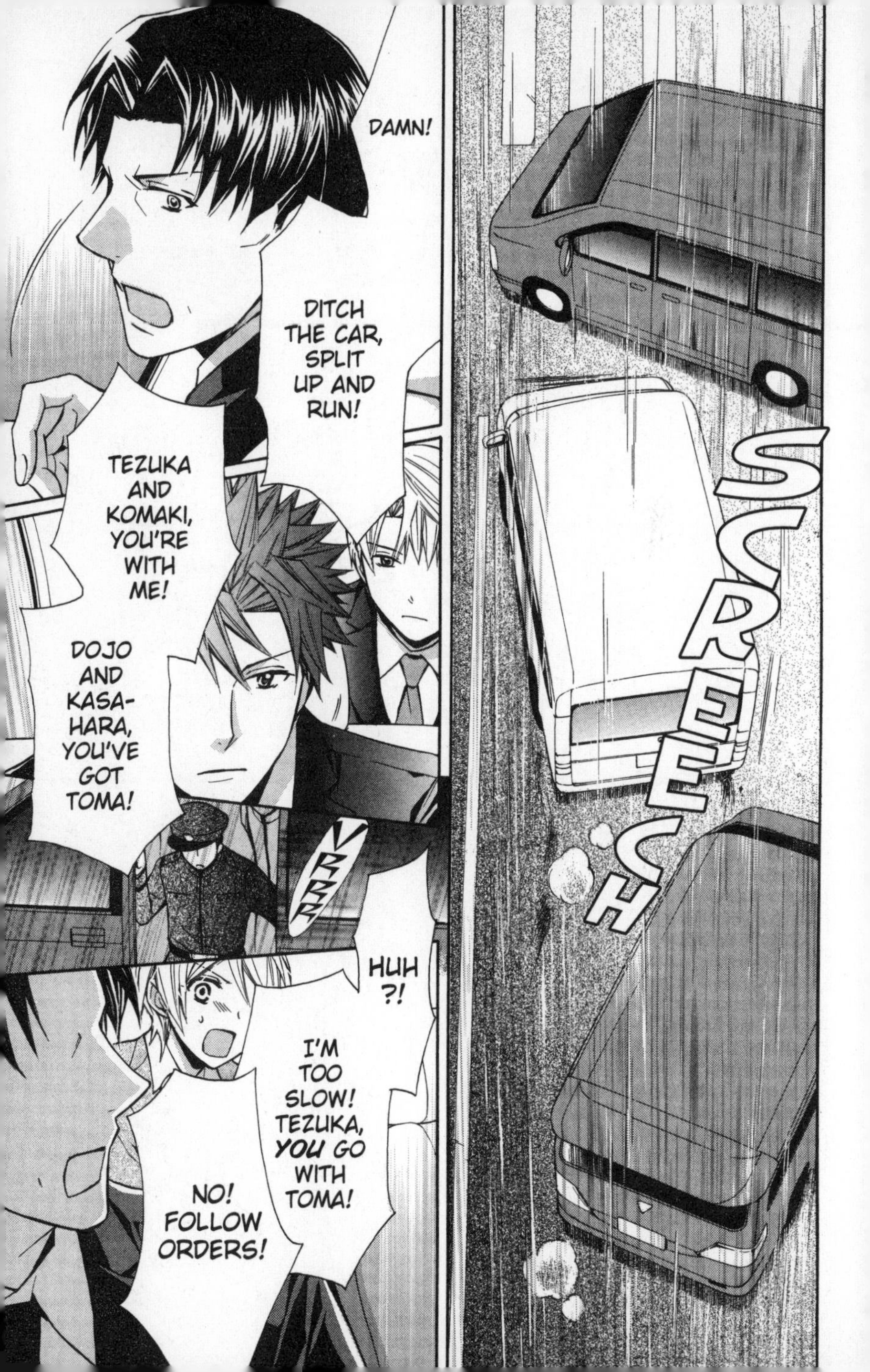

SCREEECH
DAMN!
DITCH THE CAR, SPLIT UP AND RUN!
TEZUKA AND KOMAKI, YOU'RE WITH ME!
DOJO AND KASAHARA, YOU'VE GOT TOMA!
VRRR
HUH?!
I'M TOO SLOW! TEZUKA, *YOU* GO WITH TOMA!
NO! FOLLOW ORDERS!

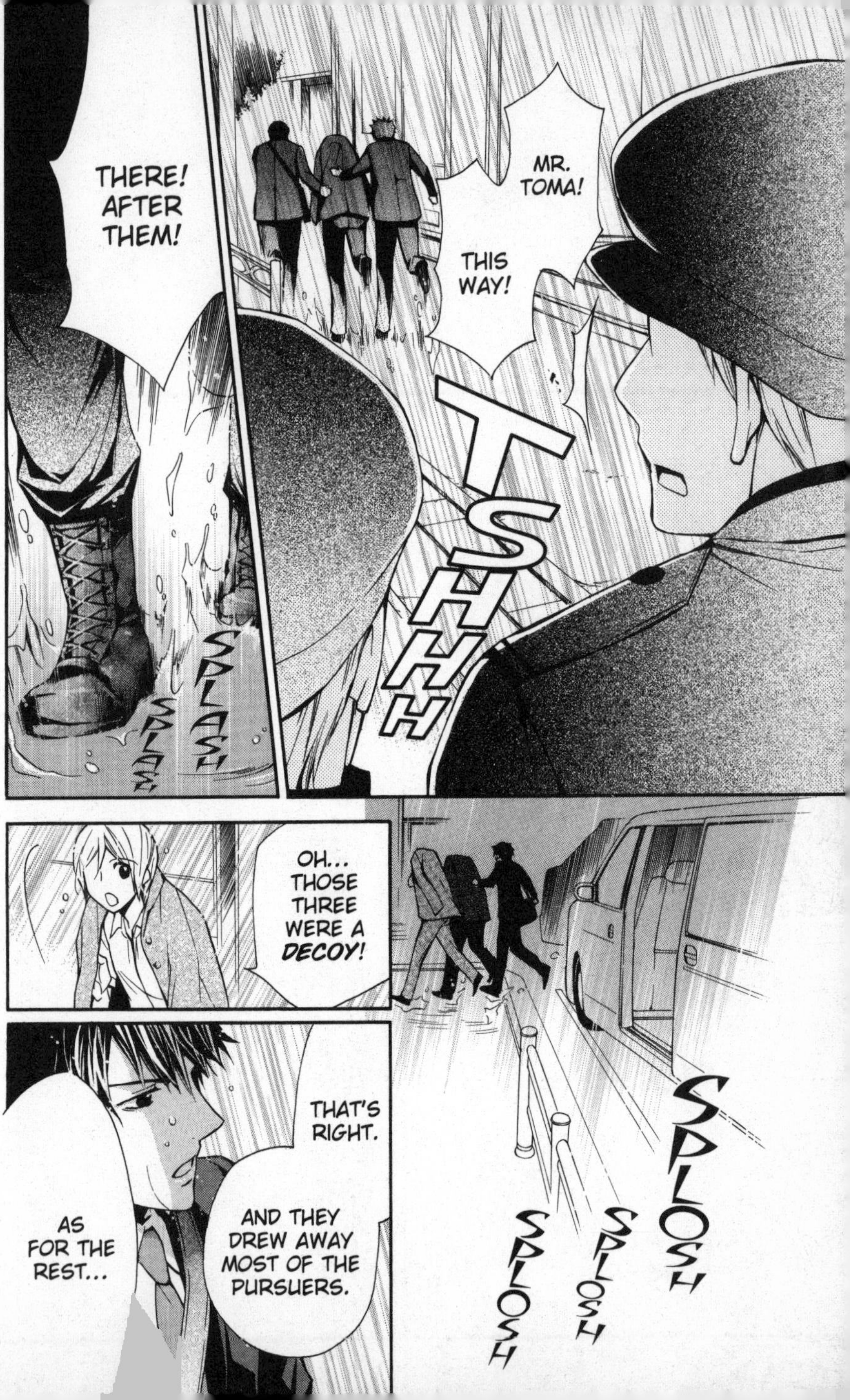
MR. TOMA!
THIS WAY!
TSHHHH
THERE! AFTER THEM!
SPLASH
SPLASH
SPLOSH
SPLOSH
SPLOSH
OH... THOSE THREE WERE A *DECOY*!
THAT'S RIGHT.
AND THEY DREW AWAY MOST OF THE PURSUERS.
AS FOR THE REST...

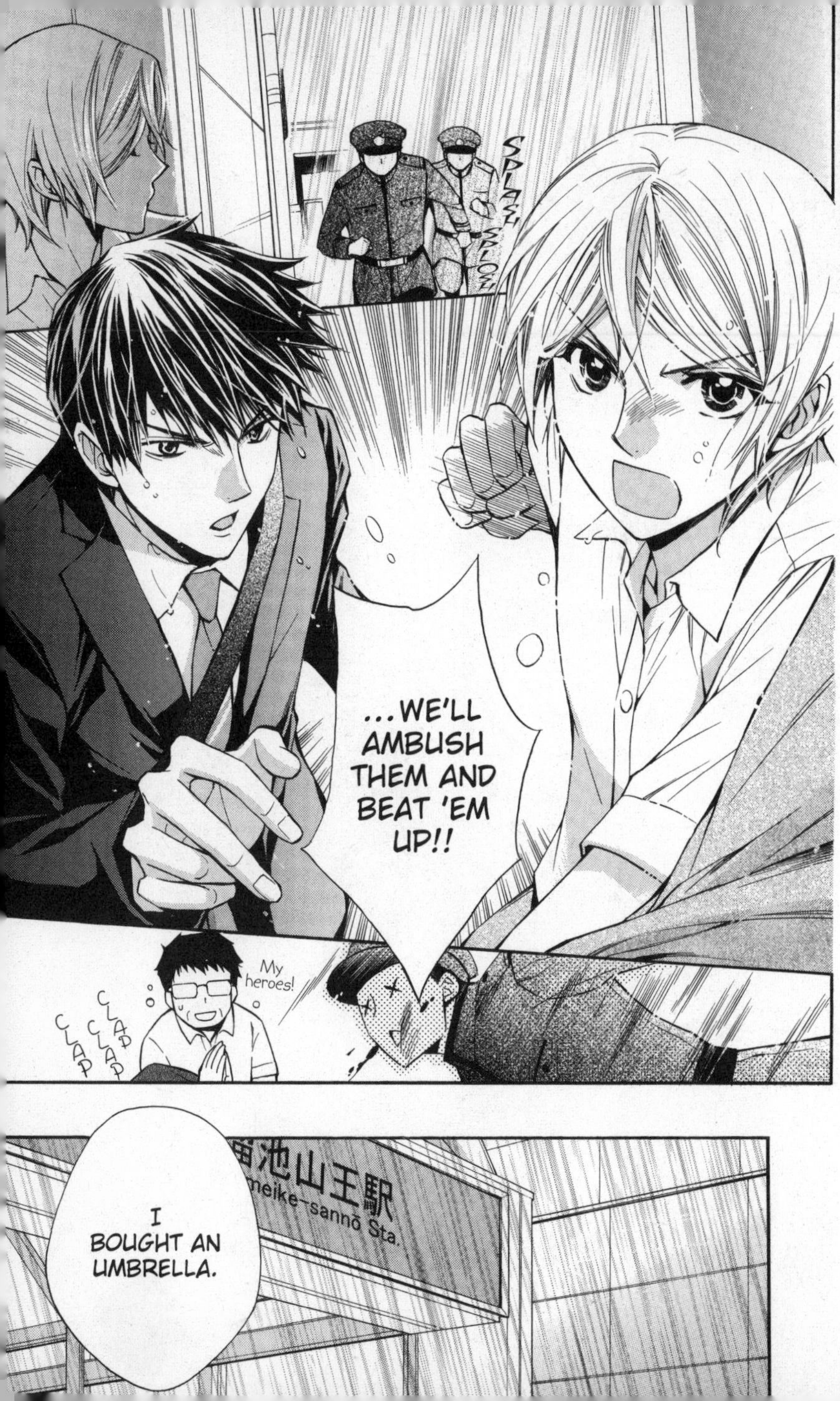
SPLASH
SPLOSH
...WE'LL AMBUSH THEM AND BEAT 'EM UP!!
My heroes!
CLAP CLAP
CLAP CLAP
池山王駅
meike-sannō Sta.
I BOUGHT AN UMBRELLA.

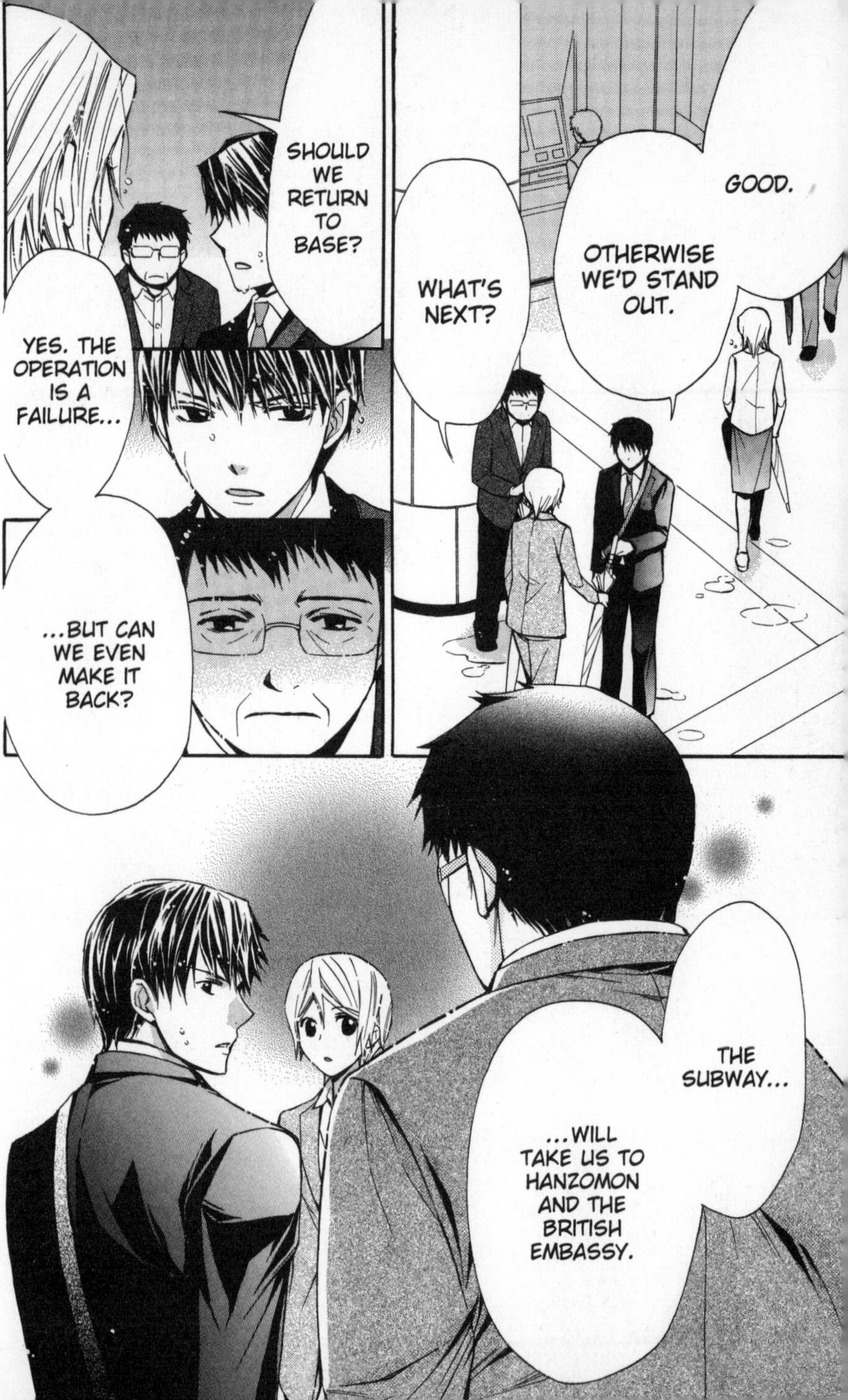
GOOD.
OTHERWISE WE'D STAND OUT.
WHAT'S NEXT?
SHOULD WE RETURN TO BASE?
YES. THE OPERATION IS A FAILURE...
...BUT CAN WE EVEN MAKE IT BACK?
THE SUBWAY...
...WILL TAKE US TO HANZOMON AND THE BRITISH EMBASSY.

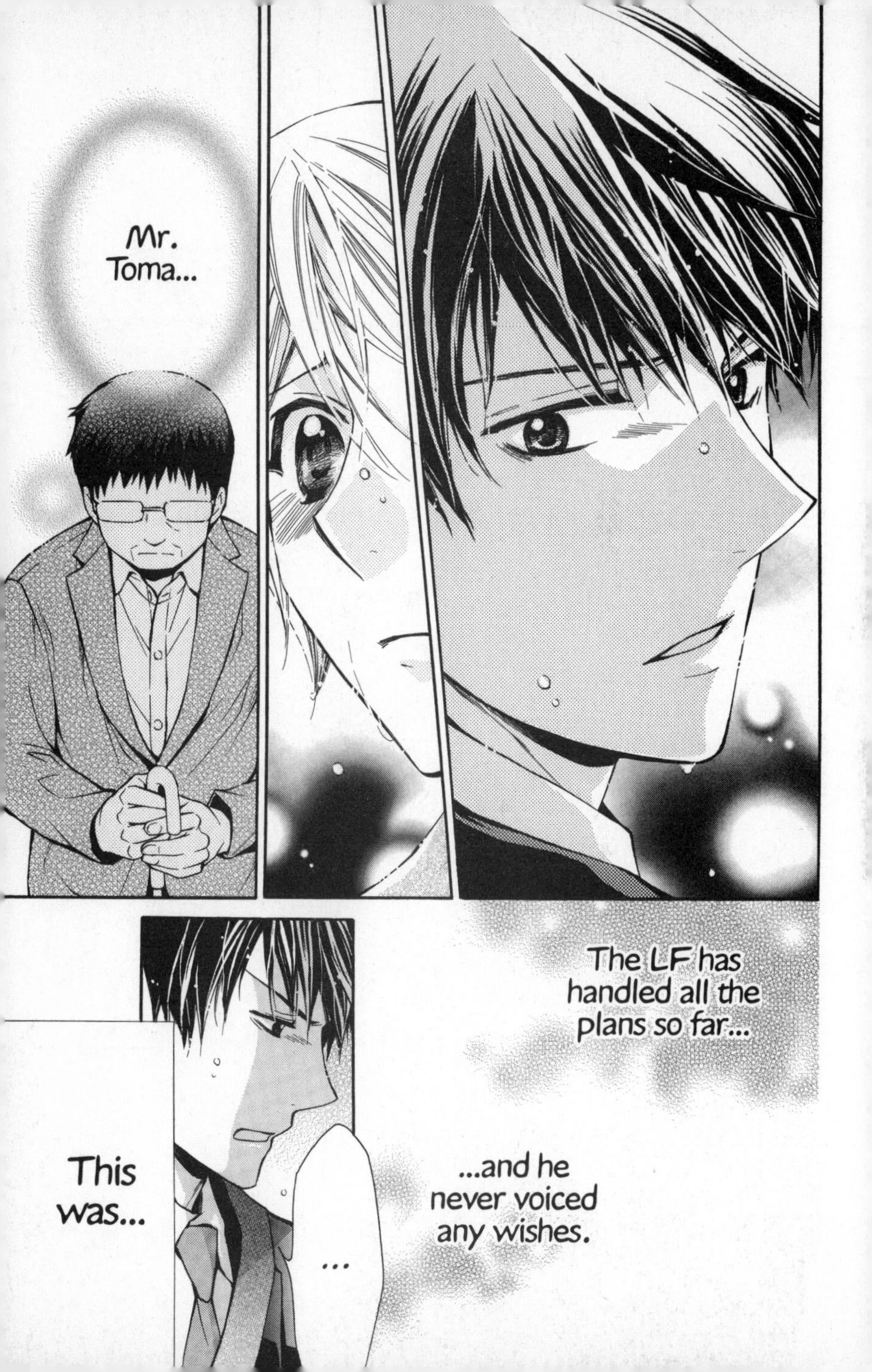
Mr. Toma...
The LF has handled all the plans so far...
...and he never voiced any wishes.
This was...
...

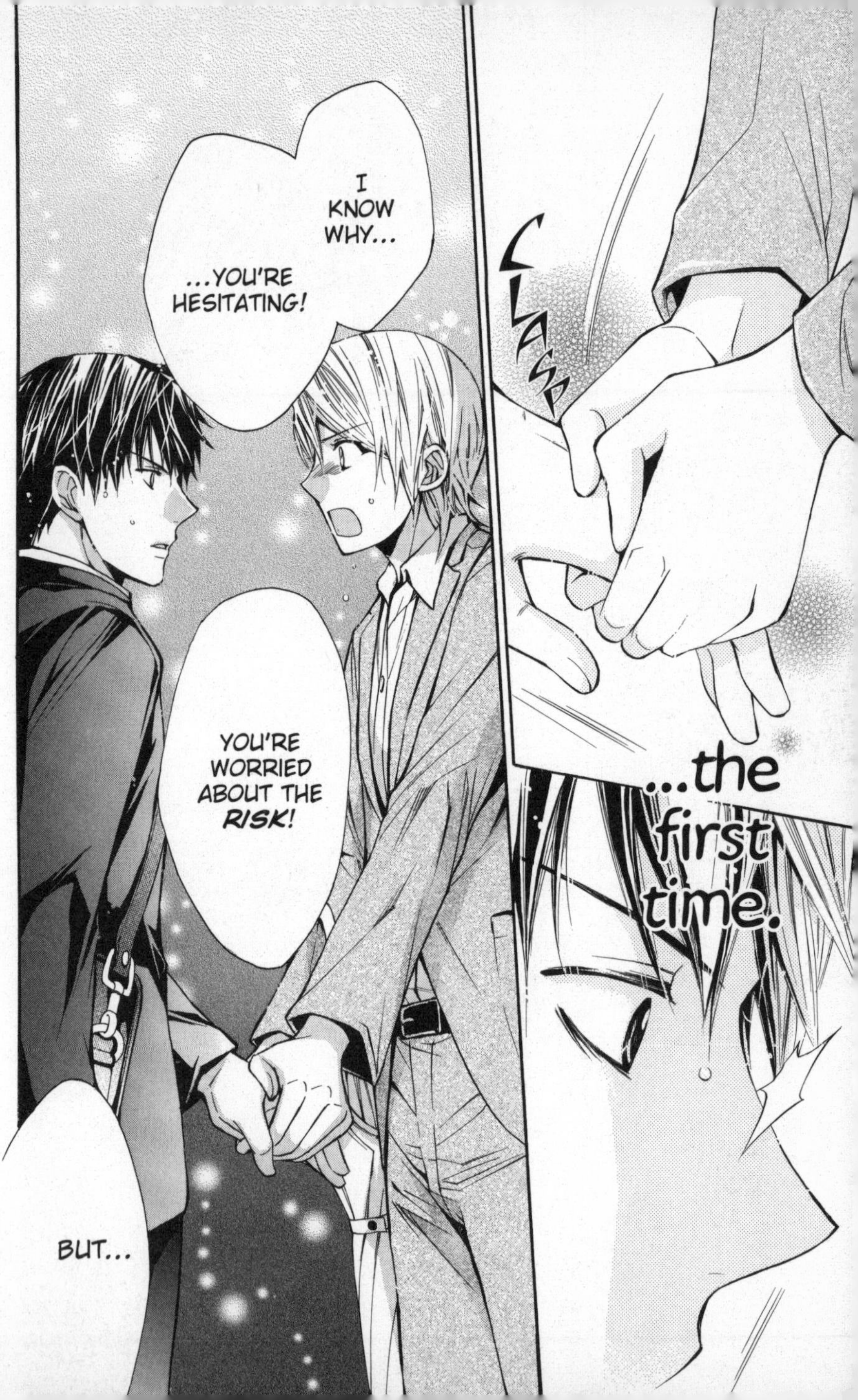
CLASP
...the first time.
I KNOW WHY...
...YOU'RE HESITATING!
YOU'RE WORRIED ABOUT THE RISK!
BUT...

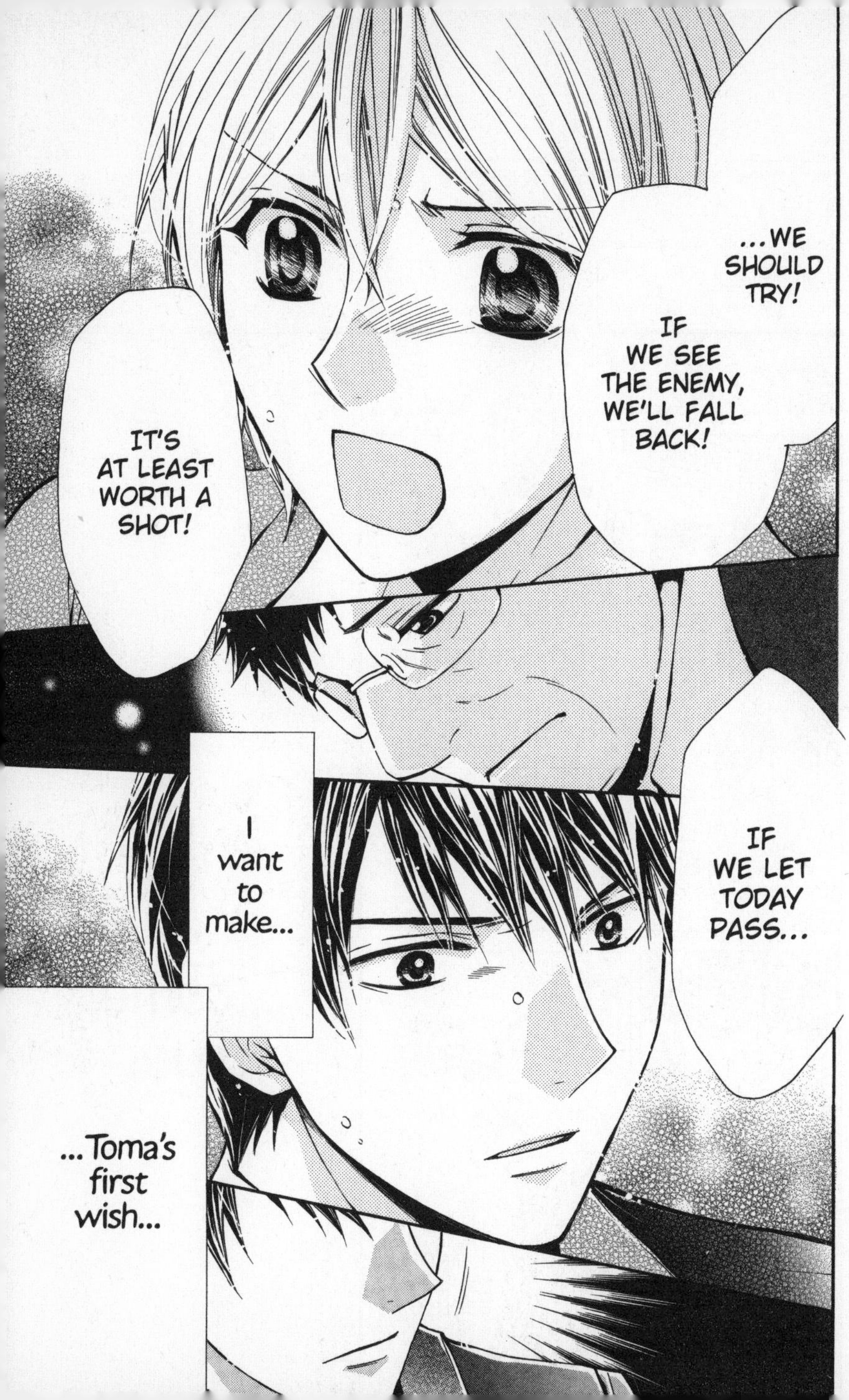
...WE SHOULD TRY!
IF WE SEE THE ENEMY, WE'LL FALL BACK!
IT'S AT LEAST WORTH A SHOT!
IF WE LET TODAY PASS...
I want to make...
...Toma's first wish...

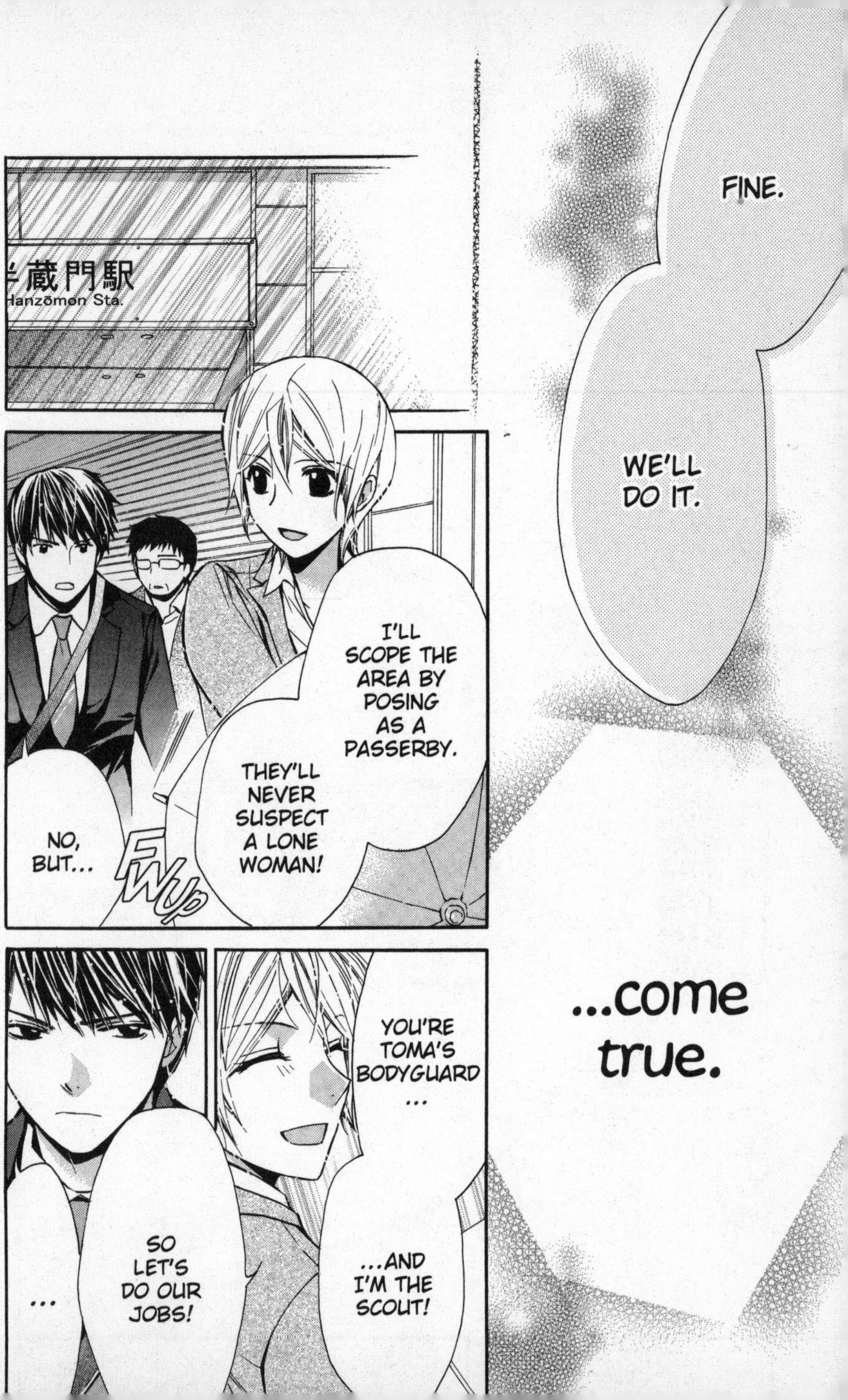
FINE.
WE'LL DO IT.
...come true.
蔵門駅
Hanzōmon Sta.
I'LL SCOPE THE AREA BY POSING AS A PASSERBY.
THEY'LL NEVER SUSPECT A LONE WOMAN!
FWUP
NO, BUT...
YOU'RE TOMA'S BODYGUARD...
...AND I'M THE SCOUT!
SO LET'S DO OUR JOBS!
...

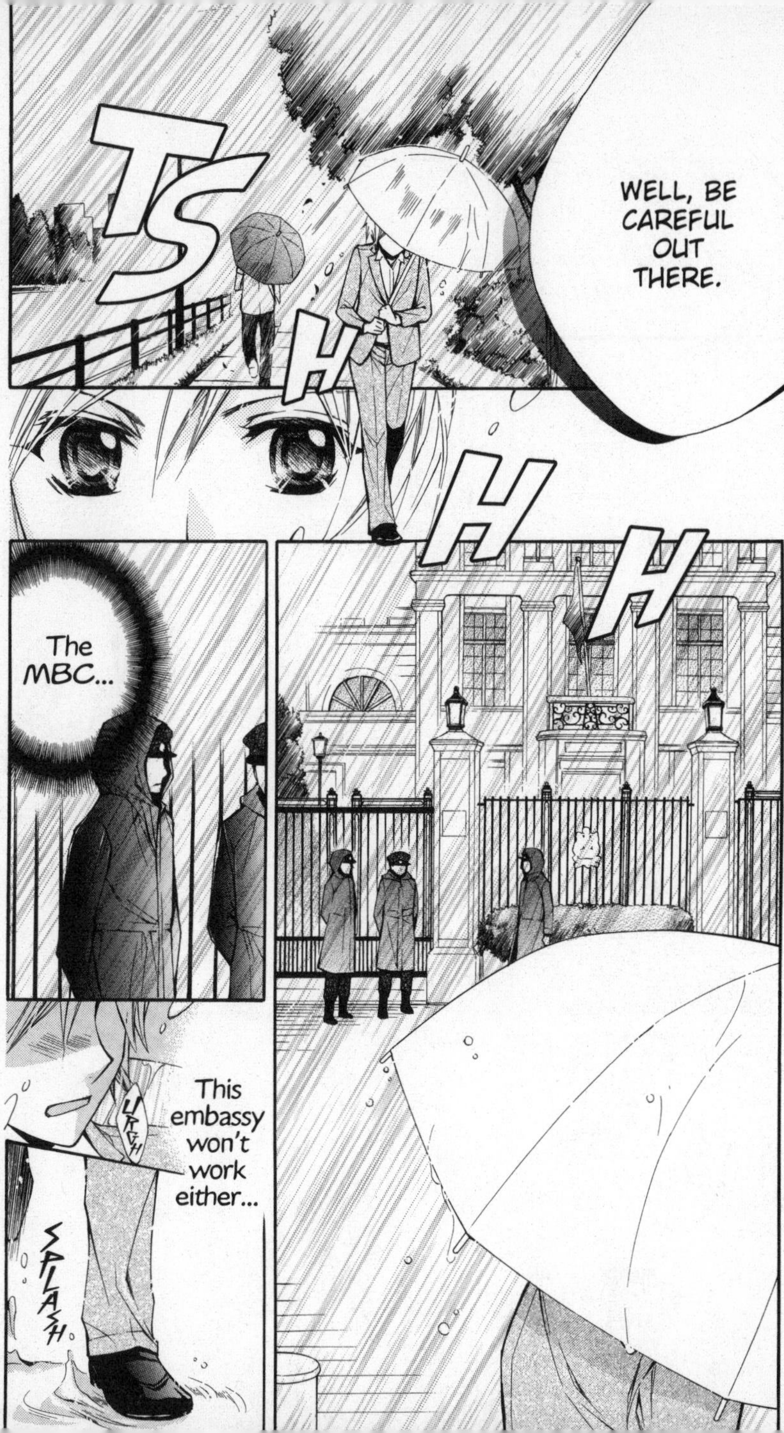
WELL, BE CAREFUL OUT THERE.
TSHHHH
The MBC...
URGH
This embassy won't work either...
SPLASH

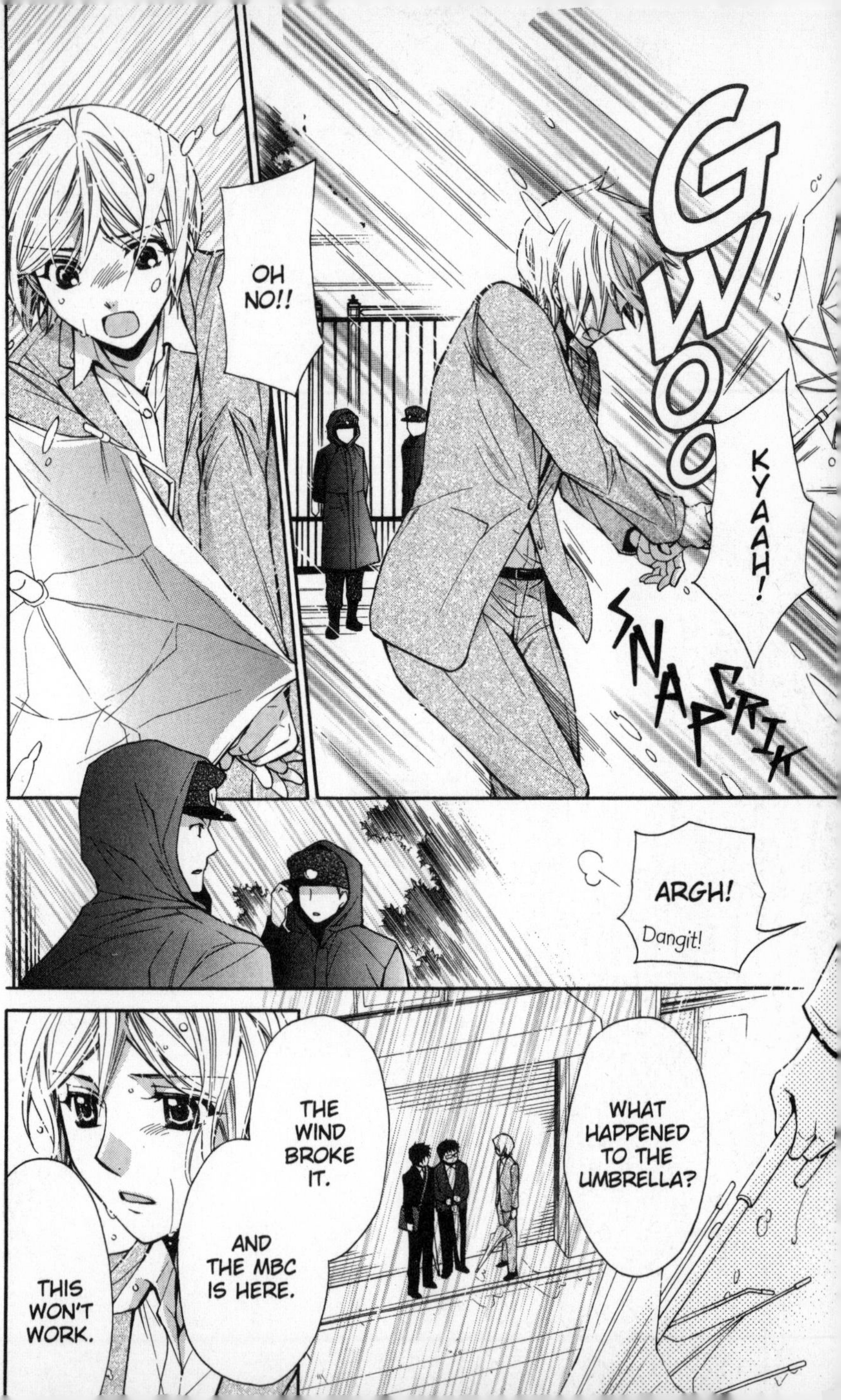
GWOOO
KYAAH!
SNAP CRIK
OH NO!!
ARGH!
Dangit!
WHAT HAPPENED TO THE UMBRELLA?
THE WIND BROKE IT.
AND THE MBC IS HERE.
THIS WON'T WORK.

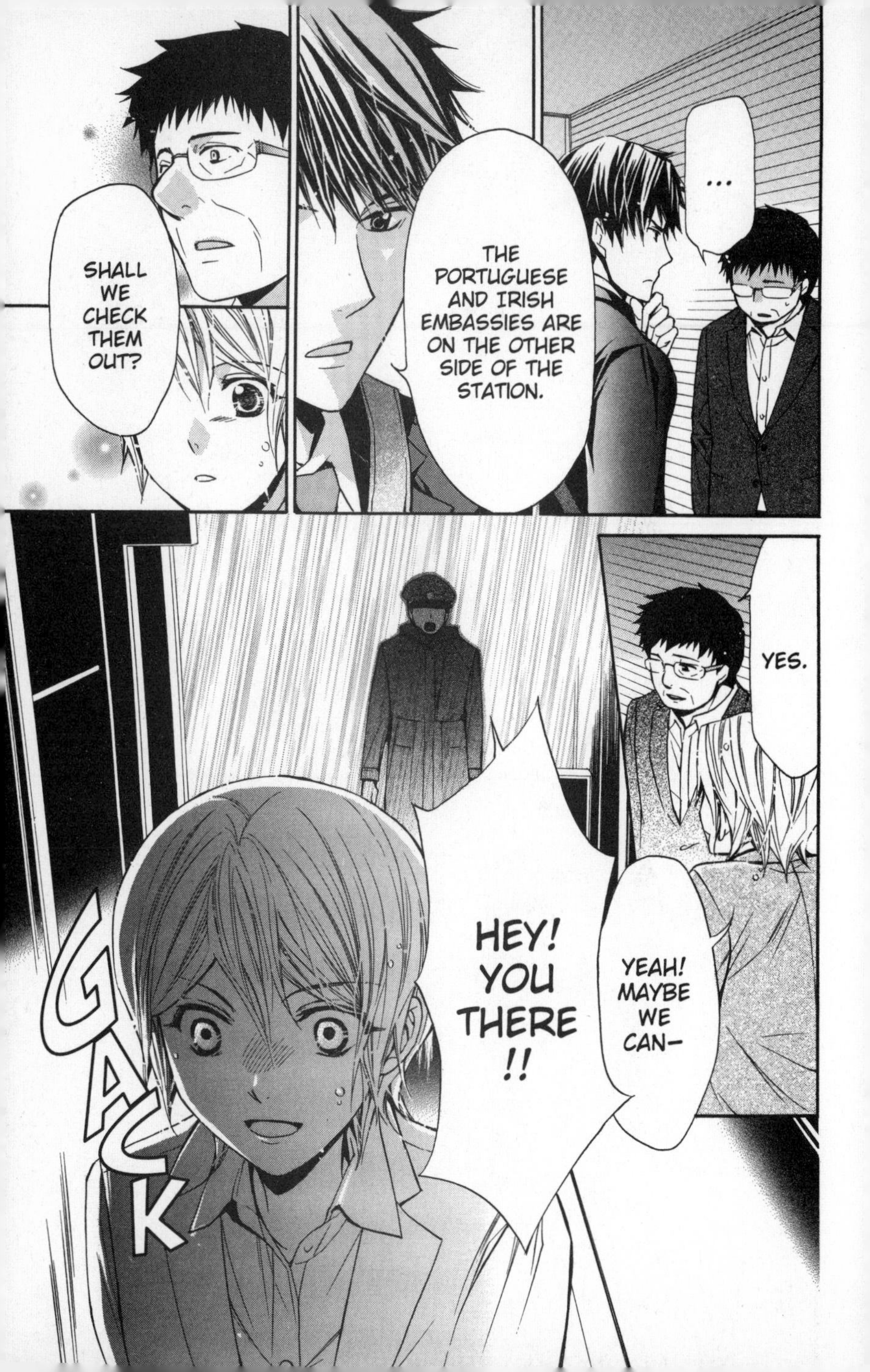
...
THE PORTUGUESE AND IRISH EMBASSIES ARE ON THE OTHER SIDE OF THE STATION.
SHALL WE CHECK THEM OUT?
YES.
YEAH! MAYBE WE CAN—
HEY! YOU THERE!!
GACK

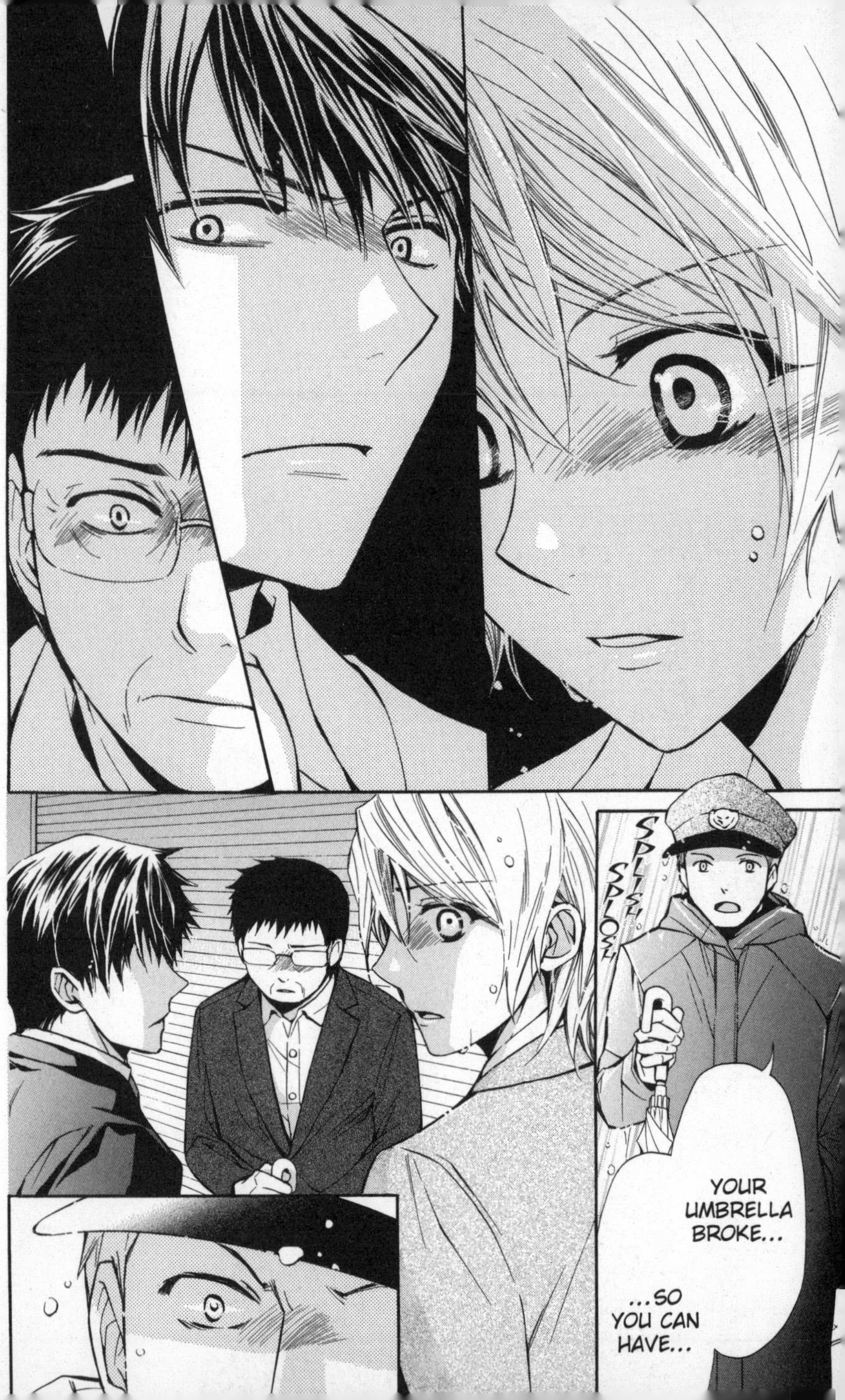
SPLISH SPLOSH
YOUR UMBRELLA BROKE...
...SO YOU CAN HAVE...

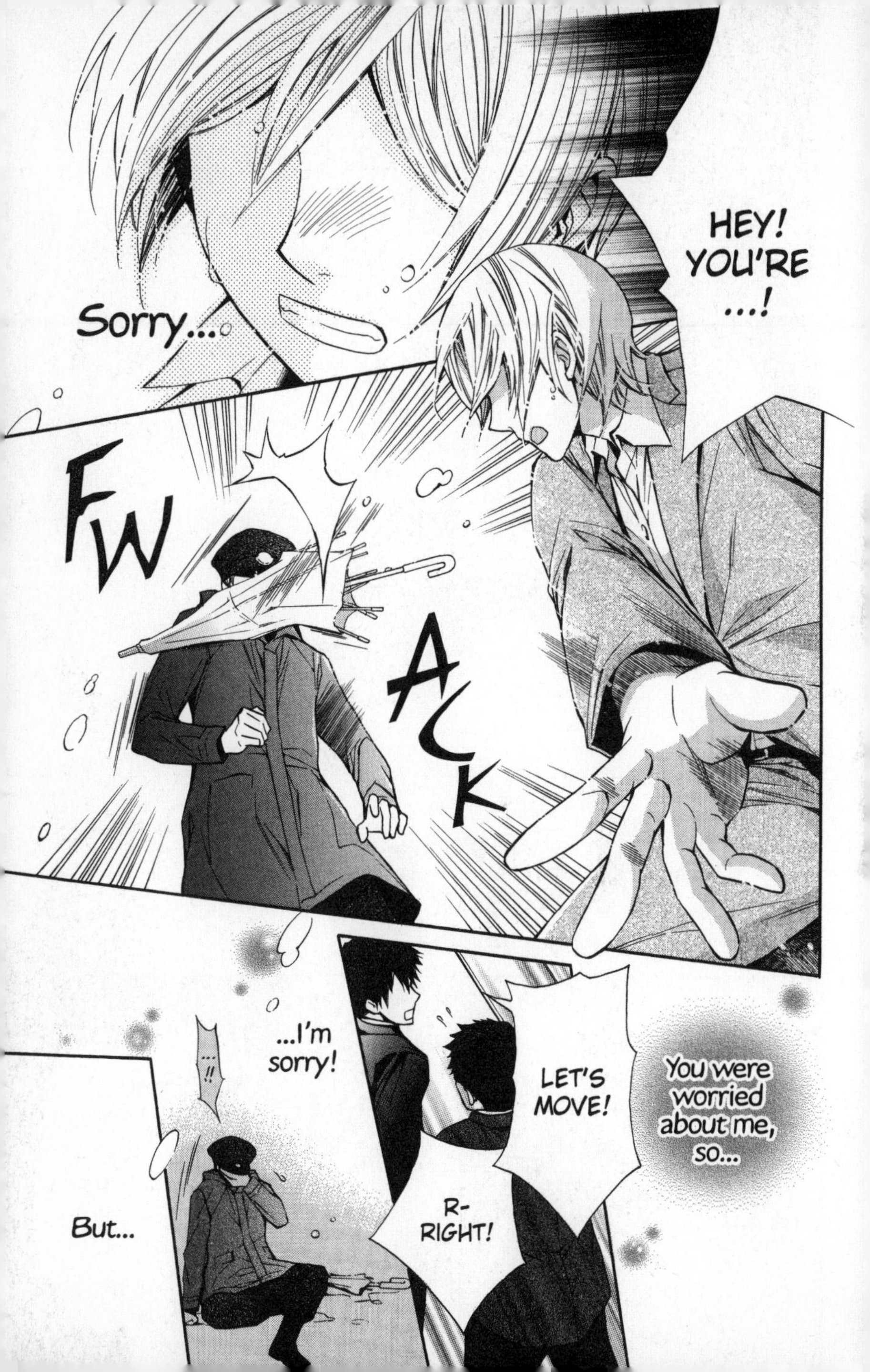
HEY! YOU'RE ...!
Sorry...
FWACK
You were worried about me, so...
LET'S MOVE!
R-RIGHT!
...I'm sorry!
...!!
But...

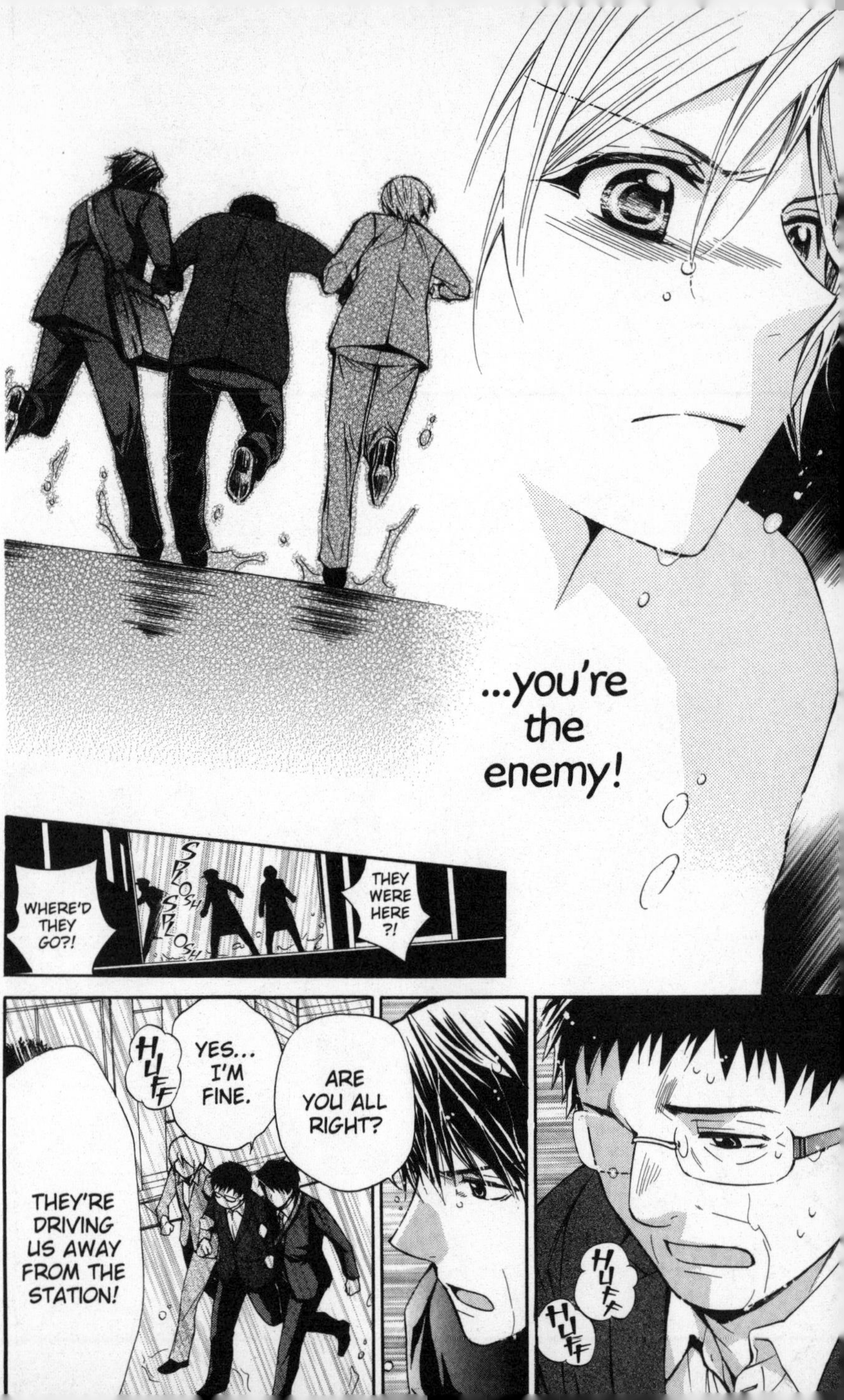
...you're the enemy!
THEY WERE HERE?!
SPLOSH
SPLOSH
WHERE'D THEY GO?!
HUFF
HUFF
ARE YOU ALL RIGHT?
YES... I'M FINE.
HUFF
THEY'RE DRIVING US AWAY FROM THE STATION!

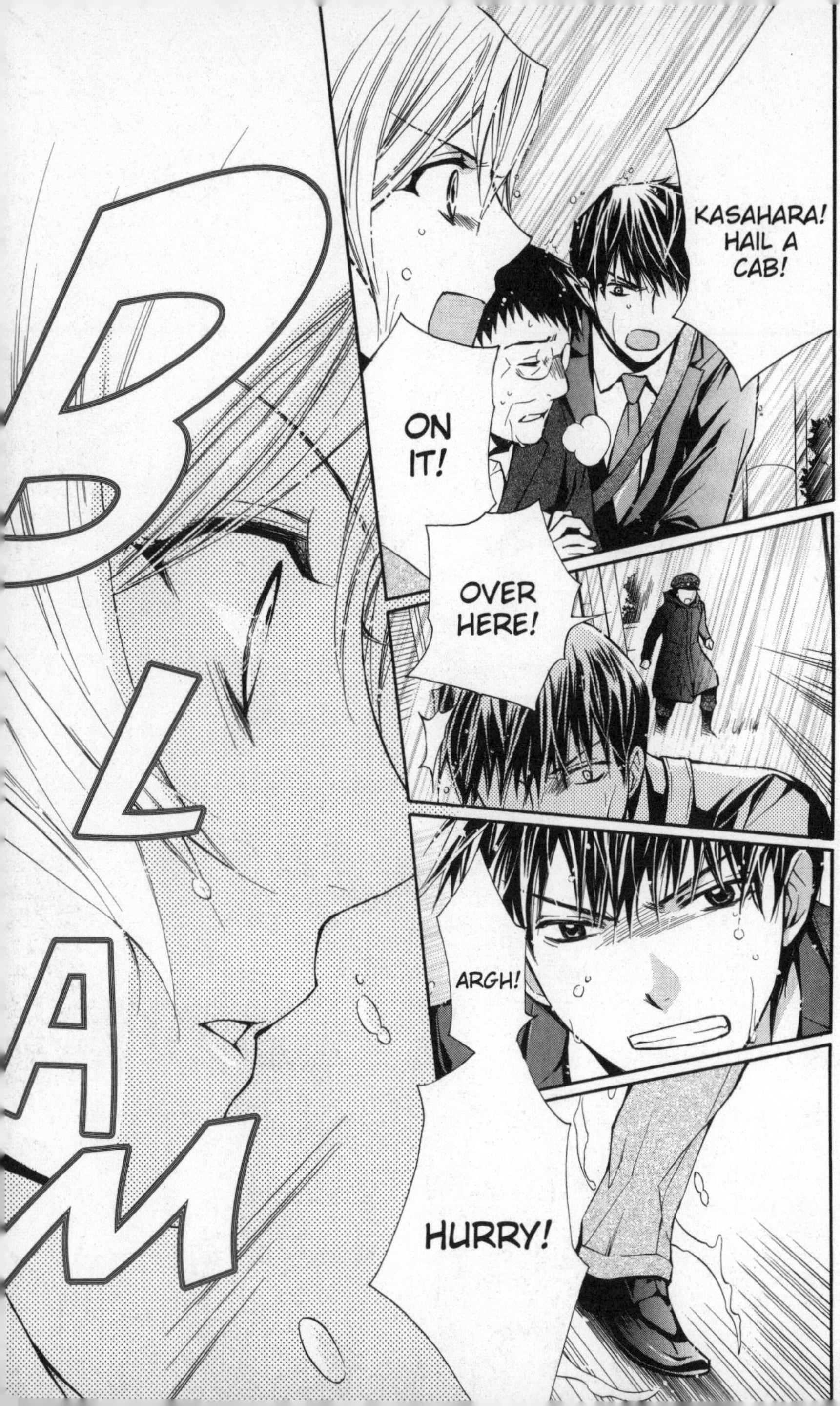
KASAHARA! HAIL A CAB!
ON IT!
OVER HERE!
ARGH!
HURRY!
BLAM

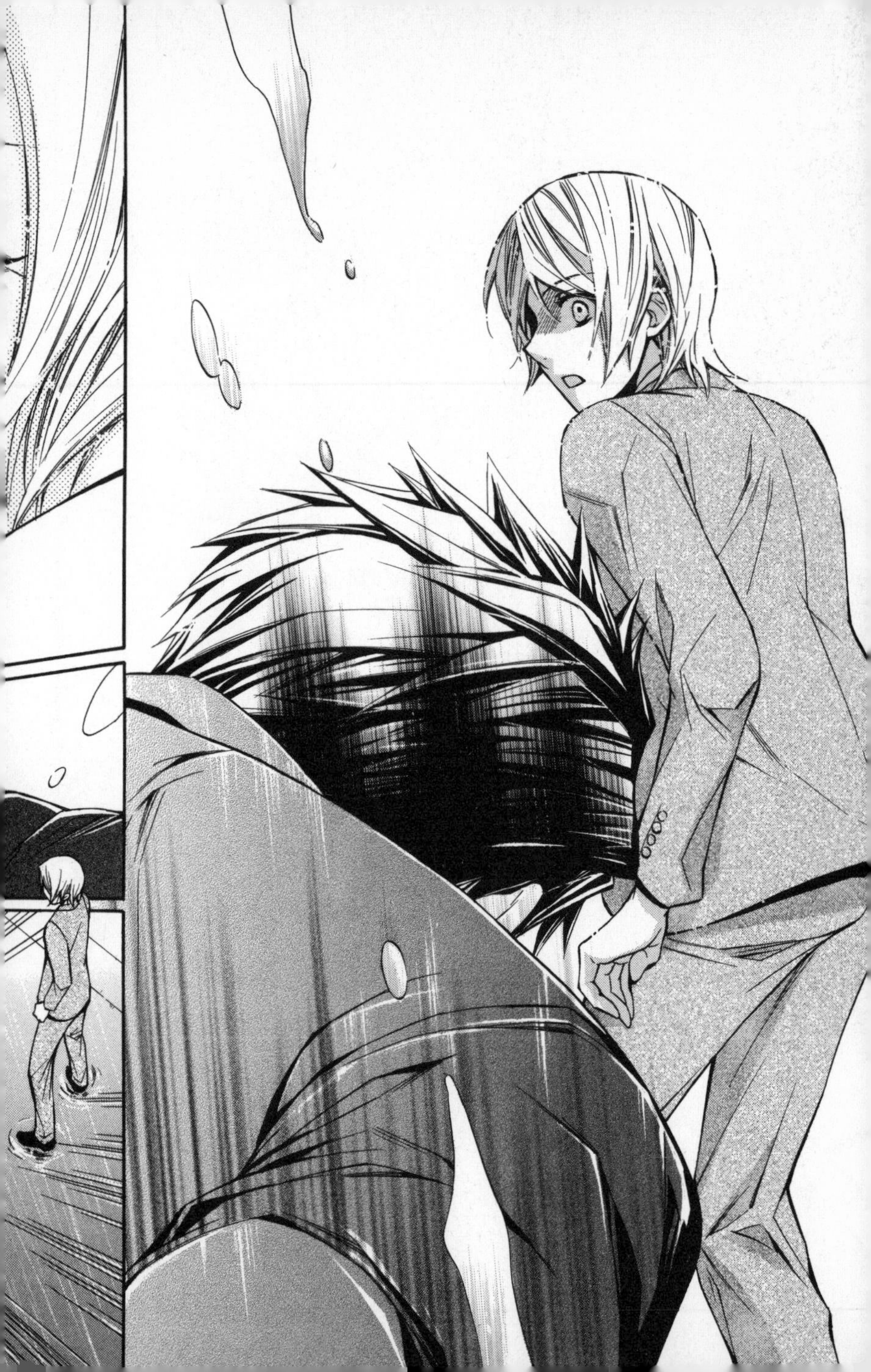

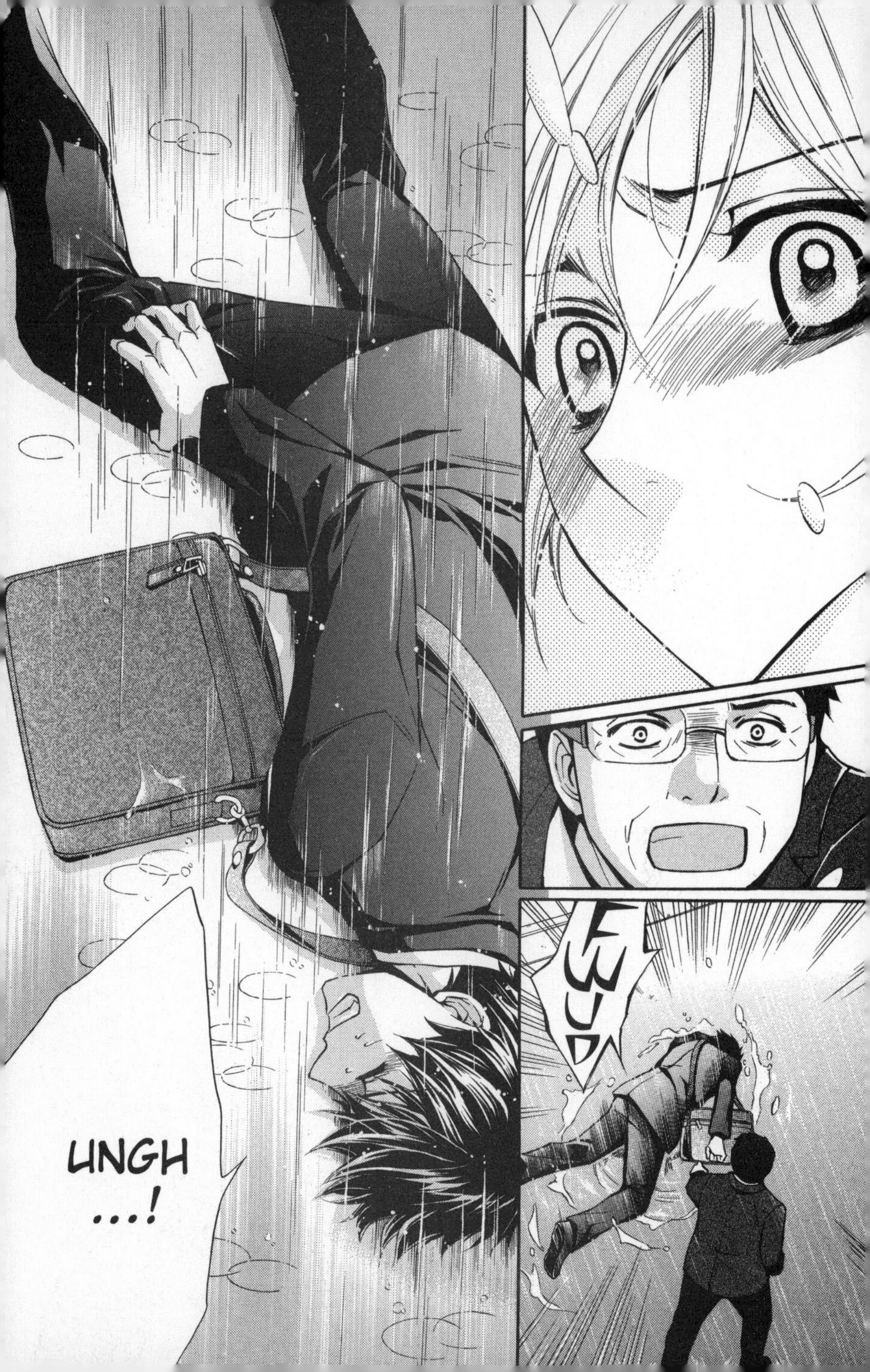
THUD
UNGH
...!

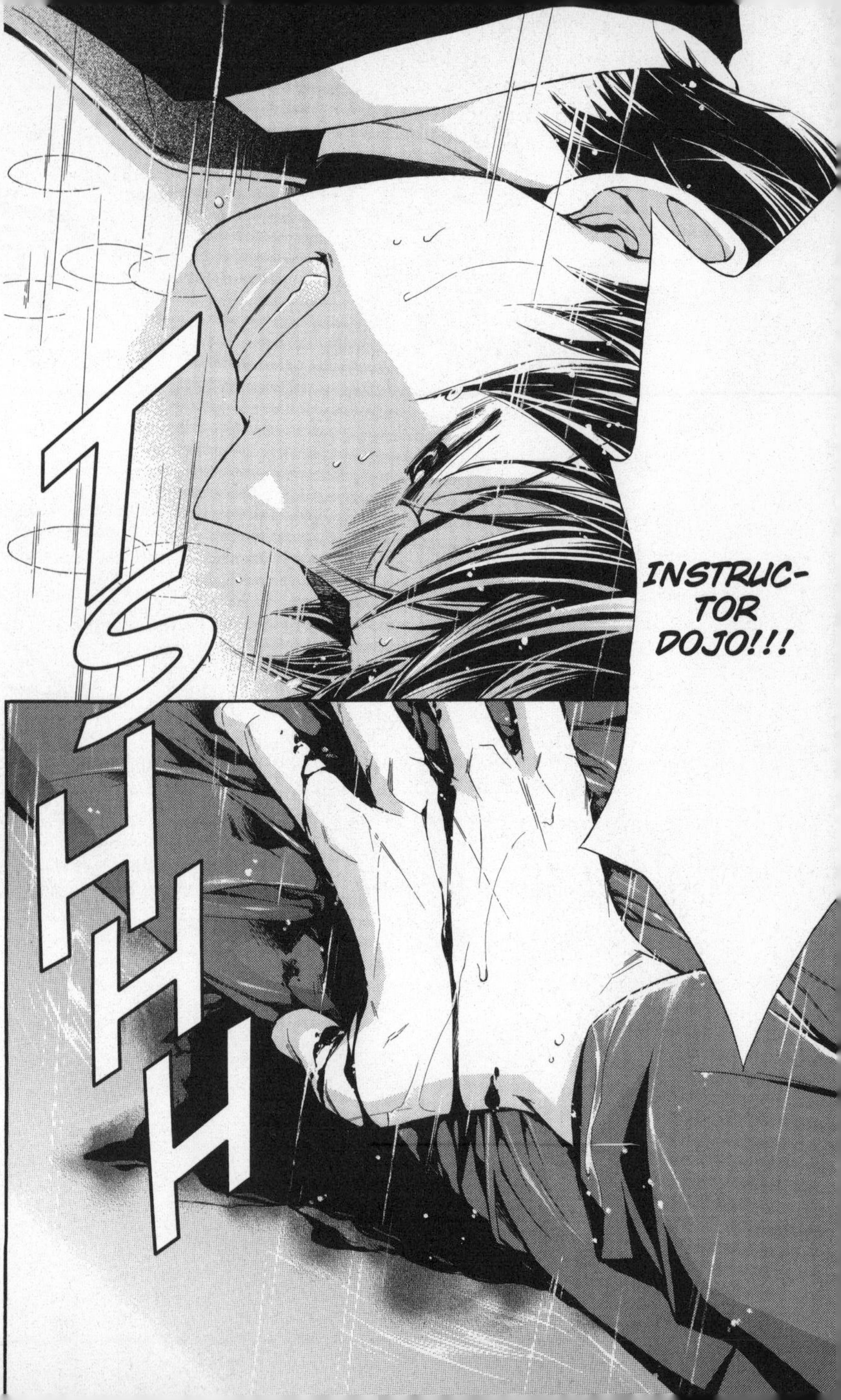
INSTRUC-
TOR
DOJO!!!
TSSHHHH

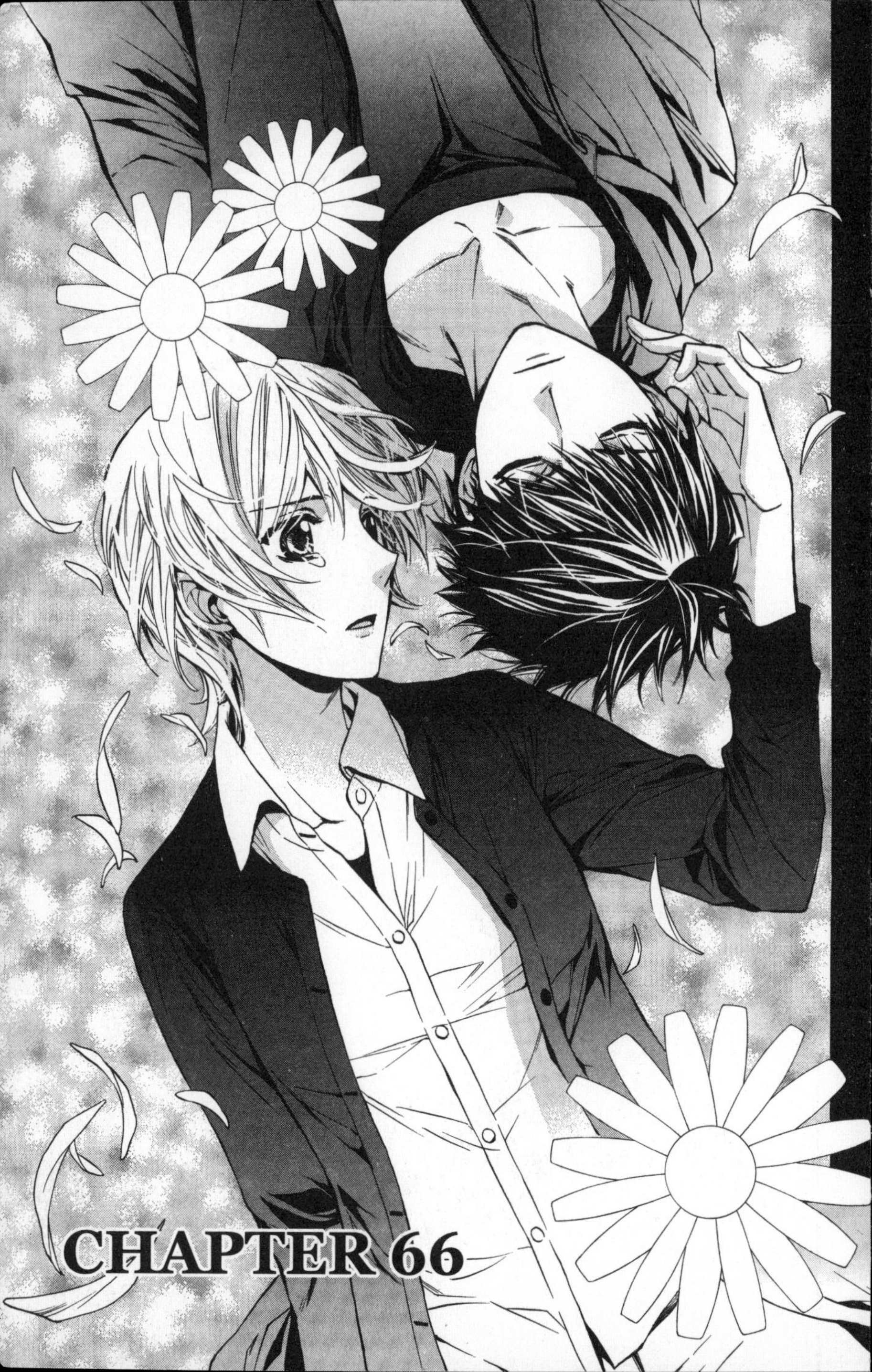

CHAPTER 66

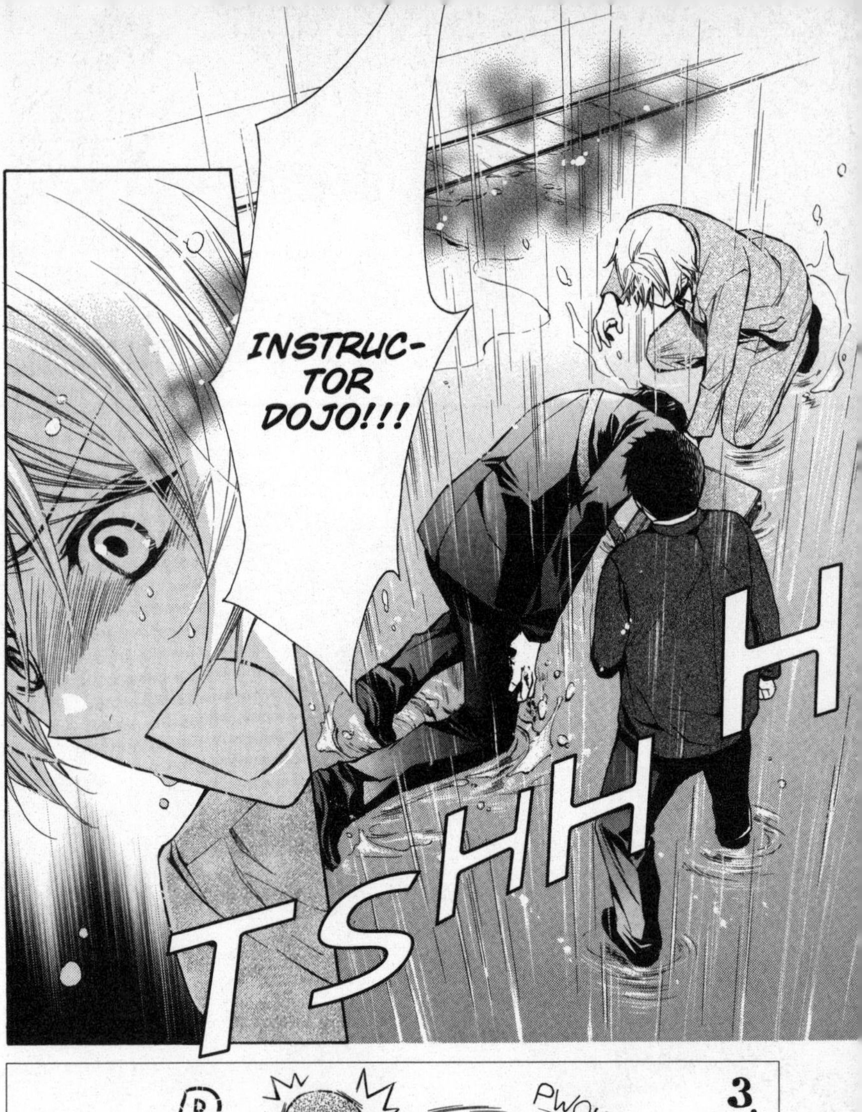
INSTRUC-
TOR
DOJO!!!
TSHHH

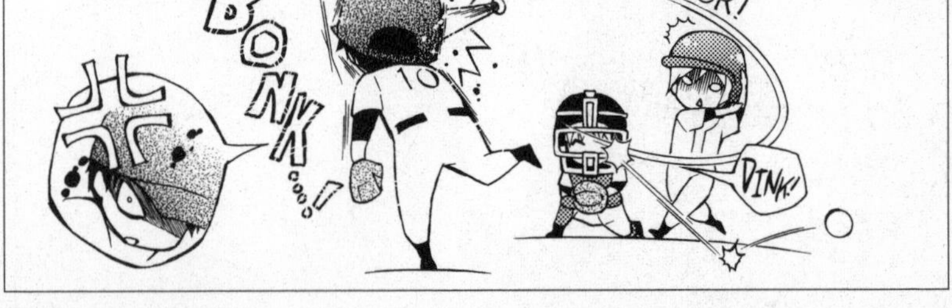
3.
PWOK!
DINK!
BONK!

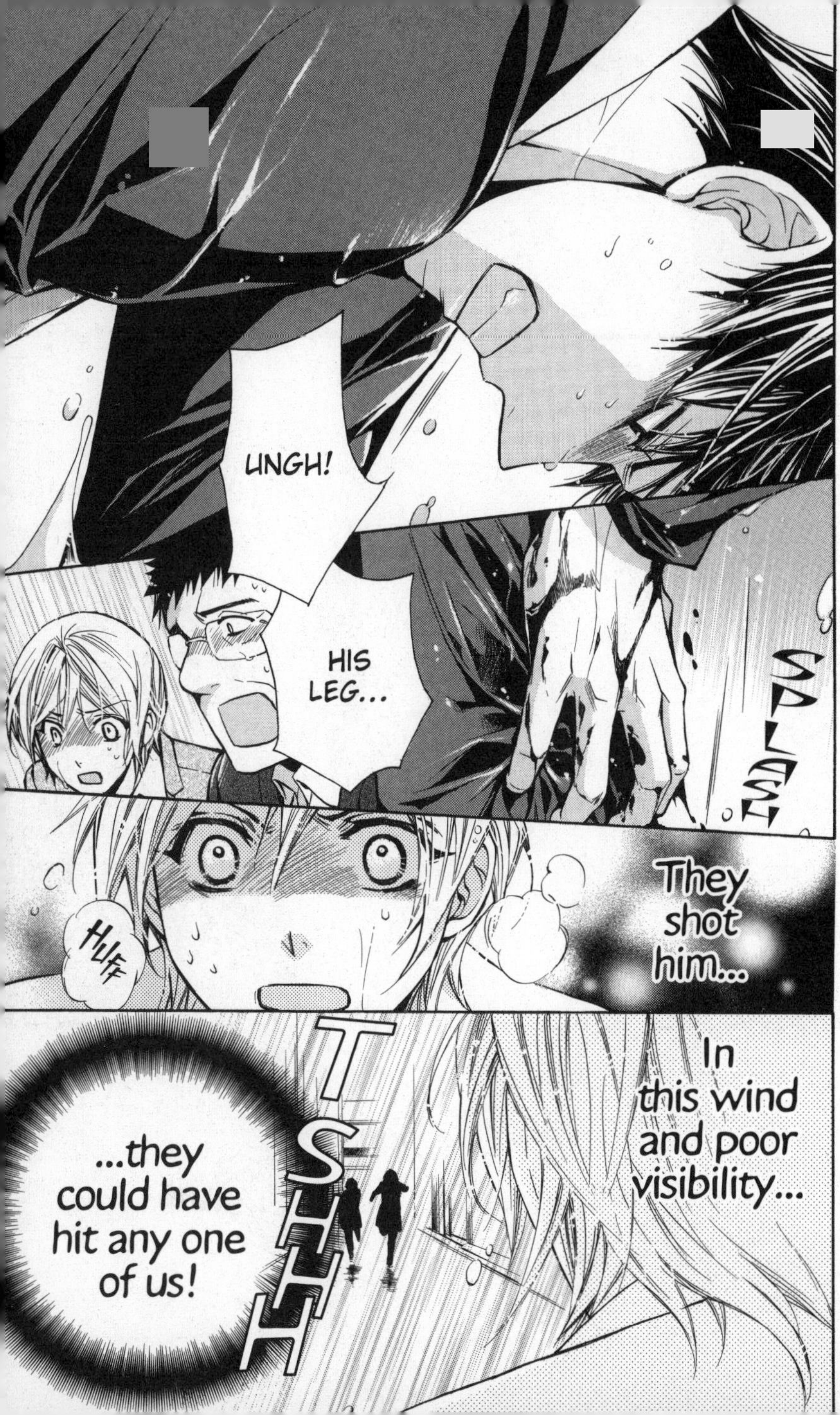
UNGH!
SPLASH
HIS LEG...
They shot him...
HUFF
In this wind and poor visibility...
TSHHH
...they could have hit any one of us!

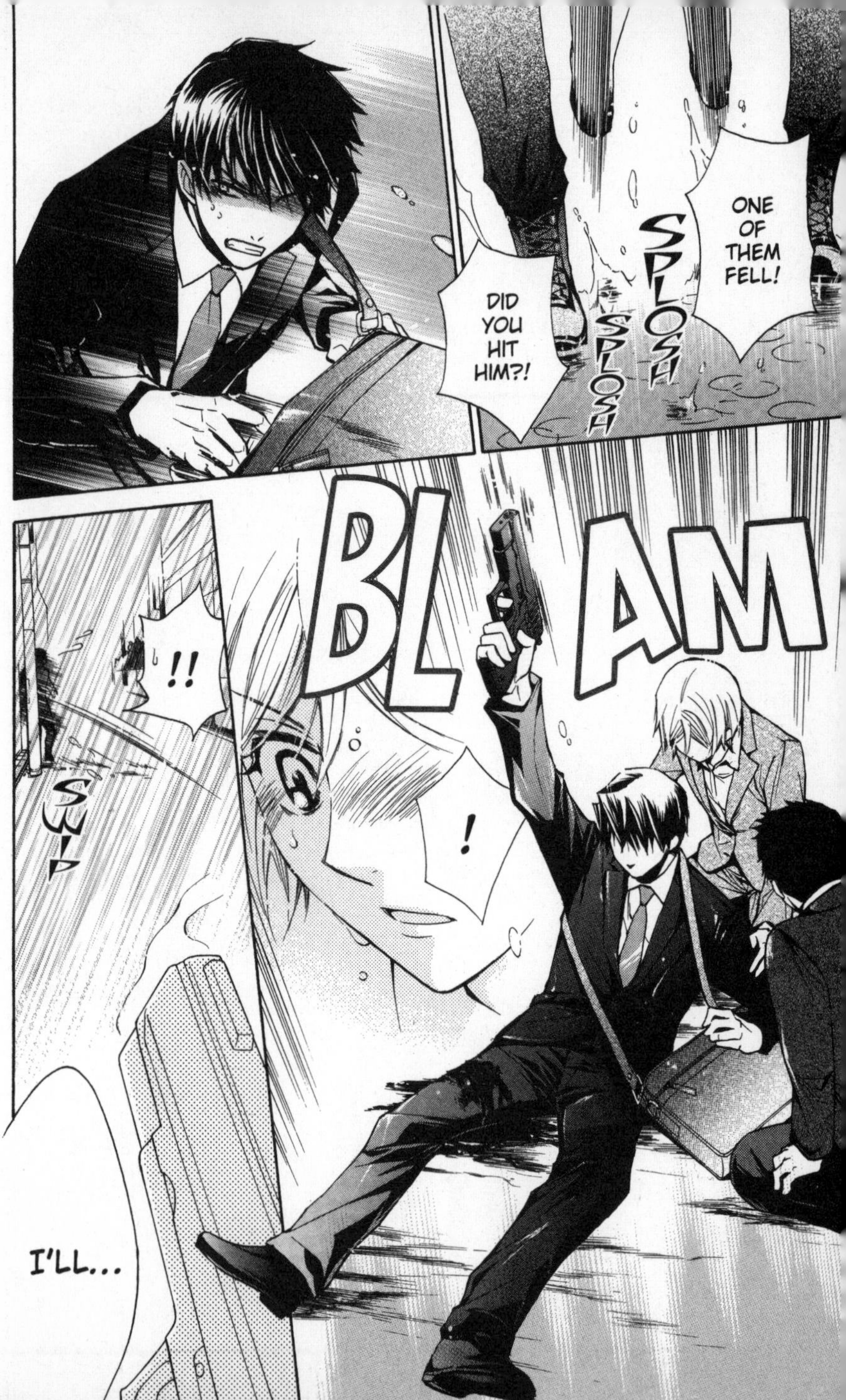
ONE OF THEM FELL!
SPLOSH
SPLOSH
DID YOU HIT HIM?!
BLAM
!
!!
SWIP
I'LL...

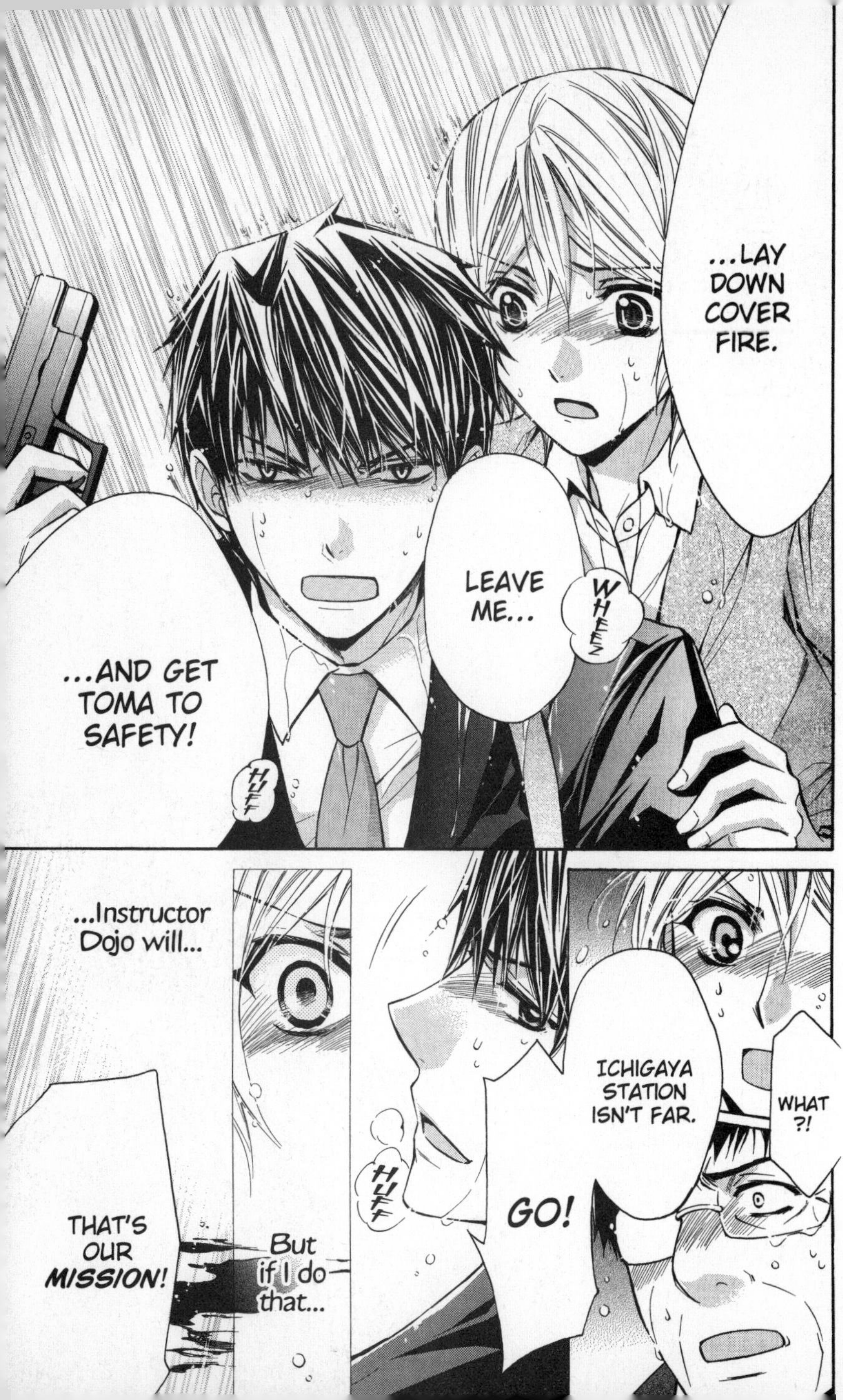
...LAY DOWN COVER FIRE.
WHEEZ
LEAVE ME...
...AND GET TOMA TO SAFETY!
HUFF
WHAT?!
ICHIGAYA STATION ISN'T FAR.
GO!
HUFF
But if I do that...
...Instructor Dojo will...
THAT'S OUR MISSION!

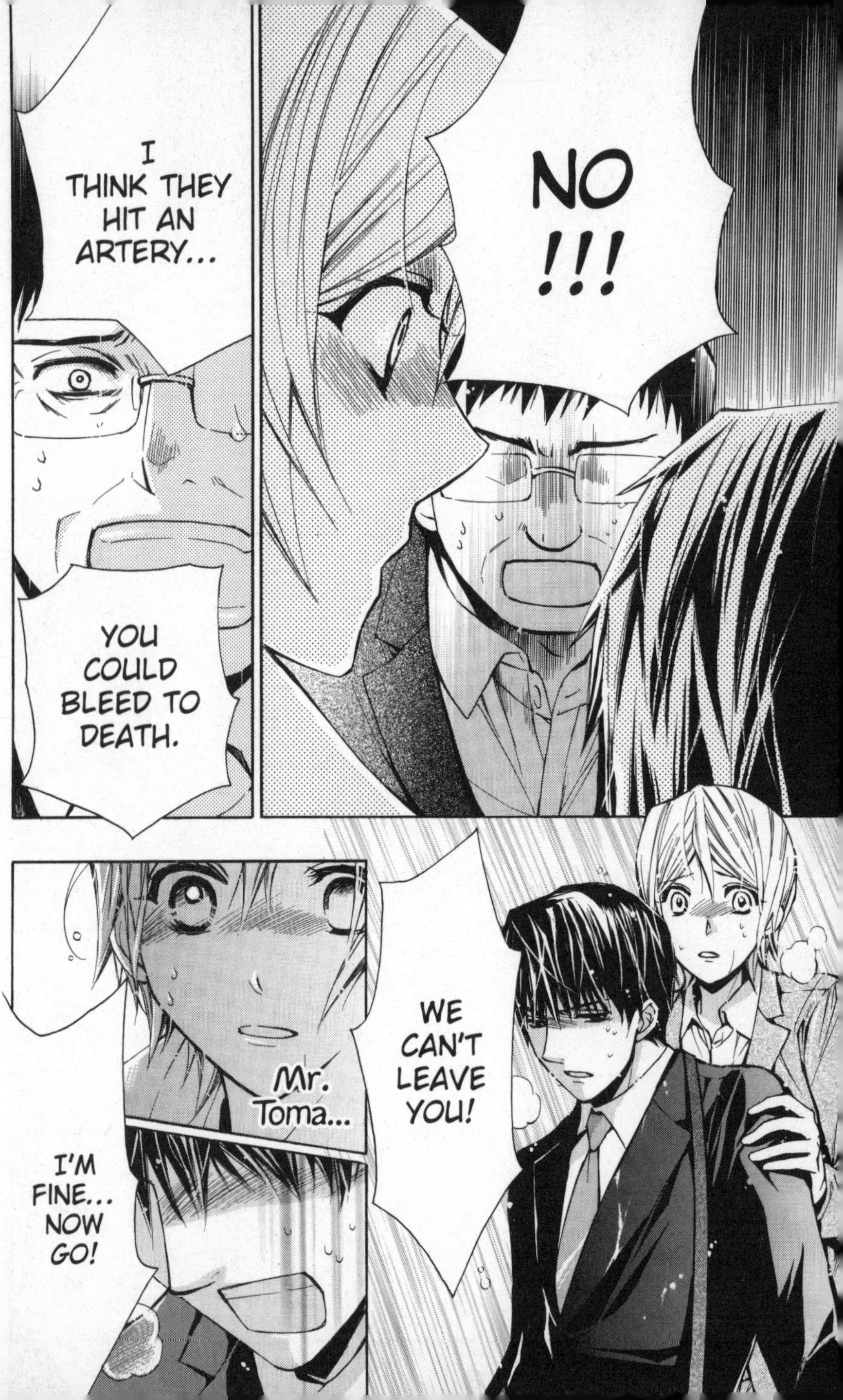
NO !!!
I THINK THEY HIT AN ARTERY...
YOU COULD BLEED TO DEATH.
WE CAN'T LEAVE YOU!
Mr. Toma...
I'M FINE... NOW GO!

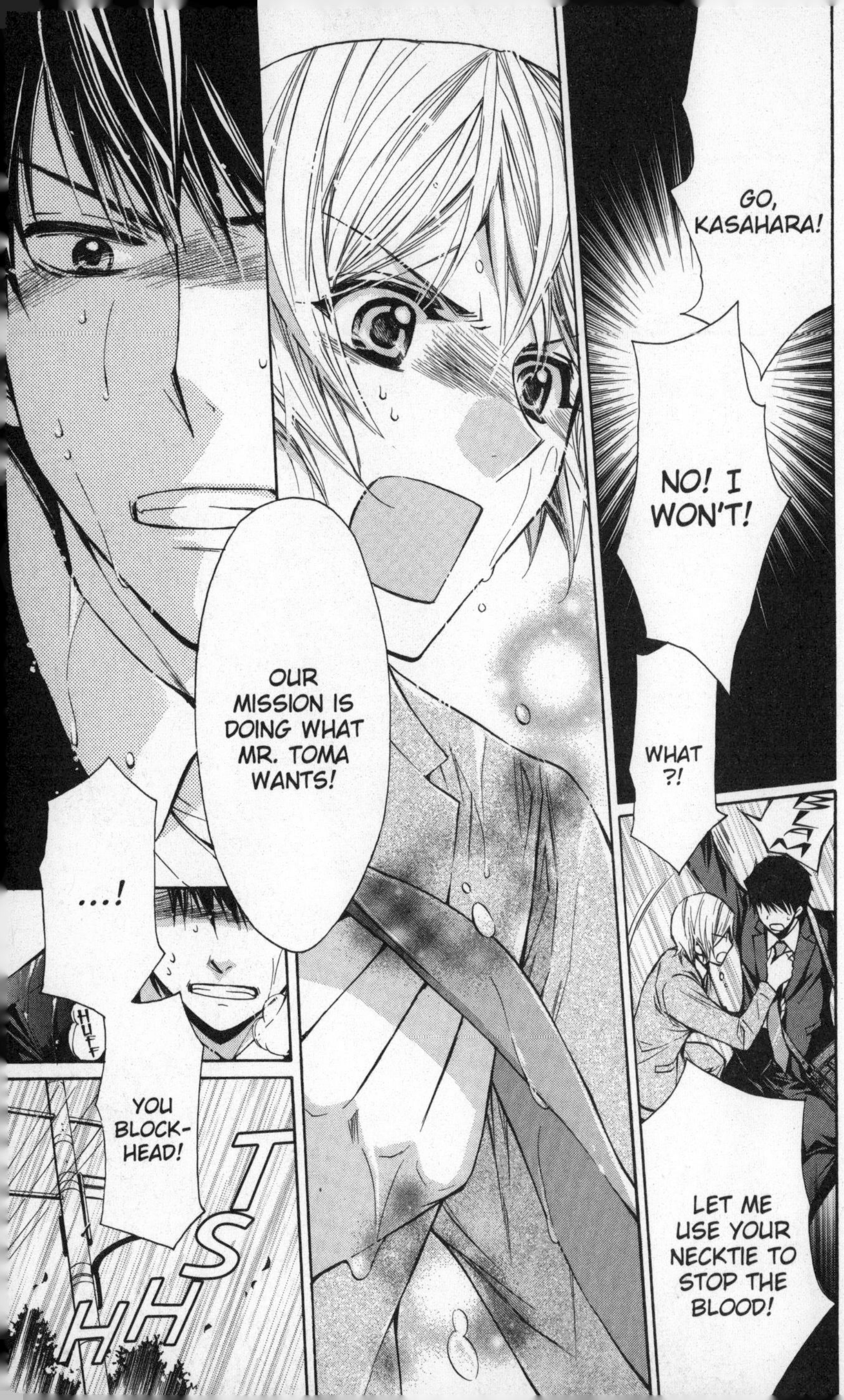
GO, KASAHARA!
NO! I WON'T!
WHAT ?!
BLAM
LET ME USE YOUR NECKTIE TO STOP THE BLOOD!
OUR MISSION IS DOING WHAT MR. TOMA WANTS!
...!
HUFF
YOU BLOCK-HEAD!
TSHH

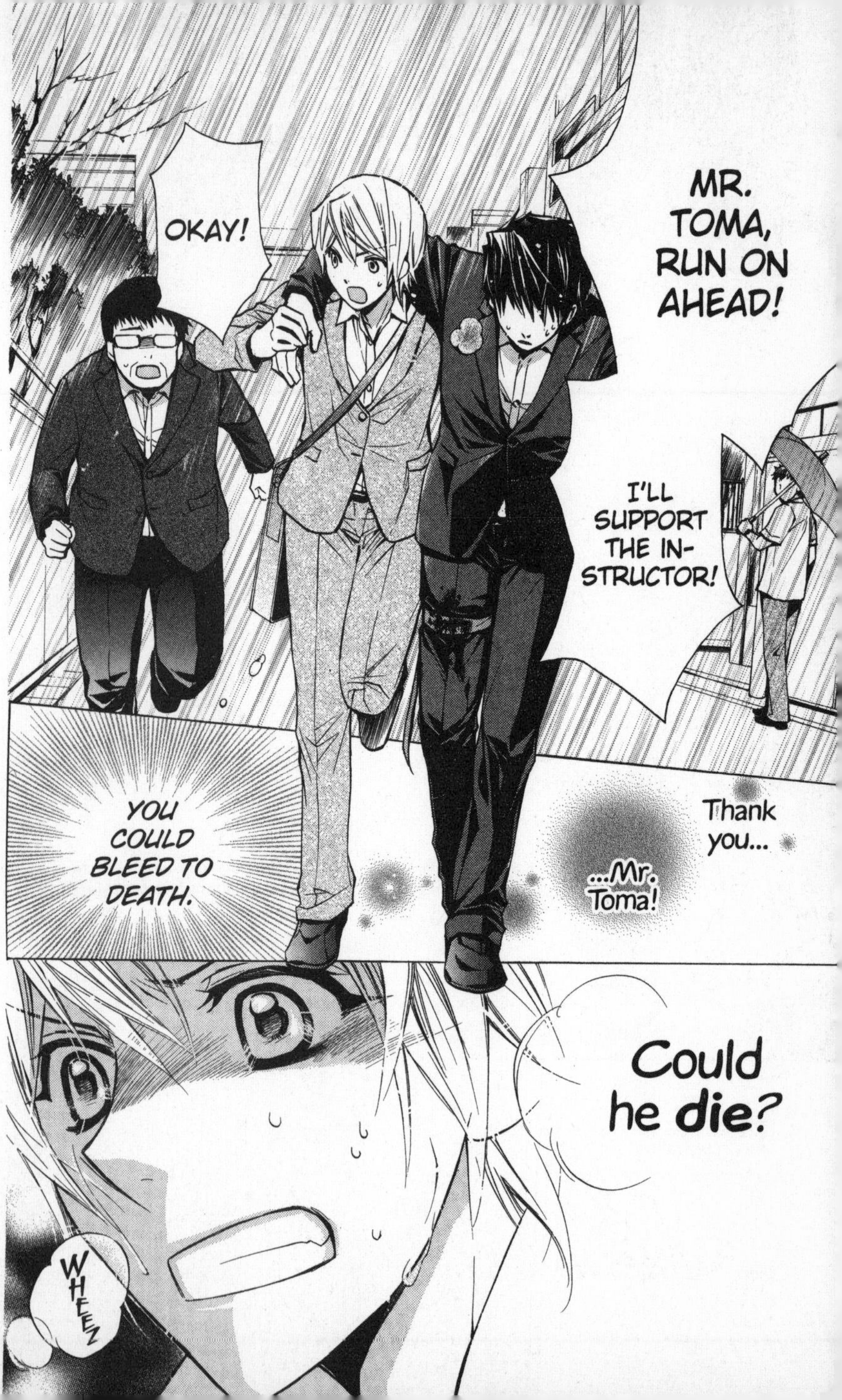
MR. TOMA, RUN ON AHEAD!
I'LL SUPPORT THE IN-STRUCTOR!
OKAY!
Thank you...
...Mr. Toma!
YOU COULD BLEED TO DEATH.
Could he die?
WHEEZ

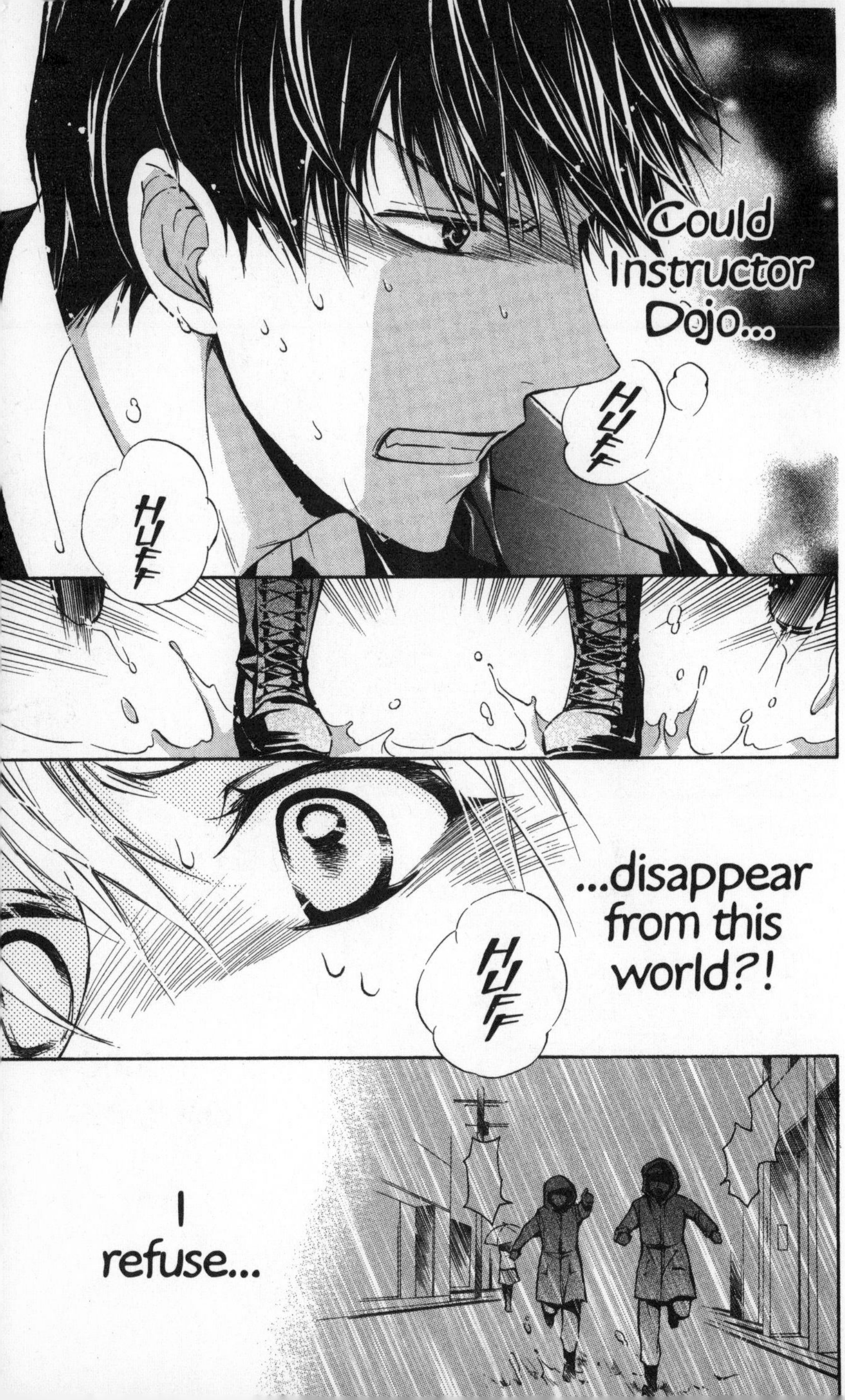
Could Instructor Dojo...
HUFF
HUFF
...disappear from this world?!
HUFF
I refuse...

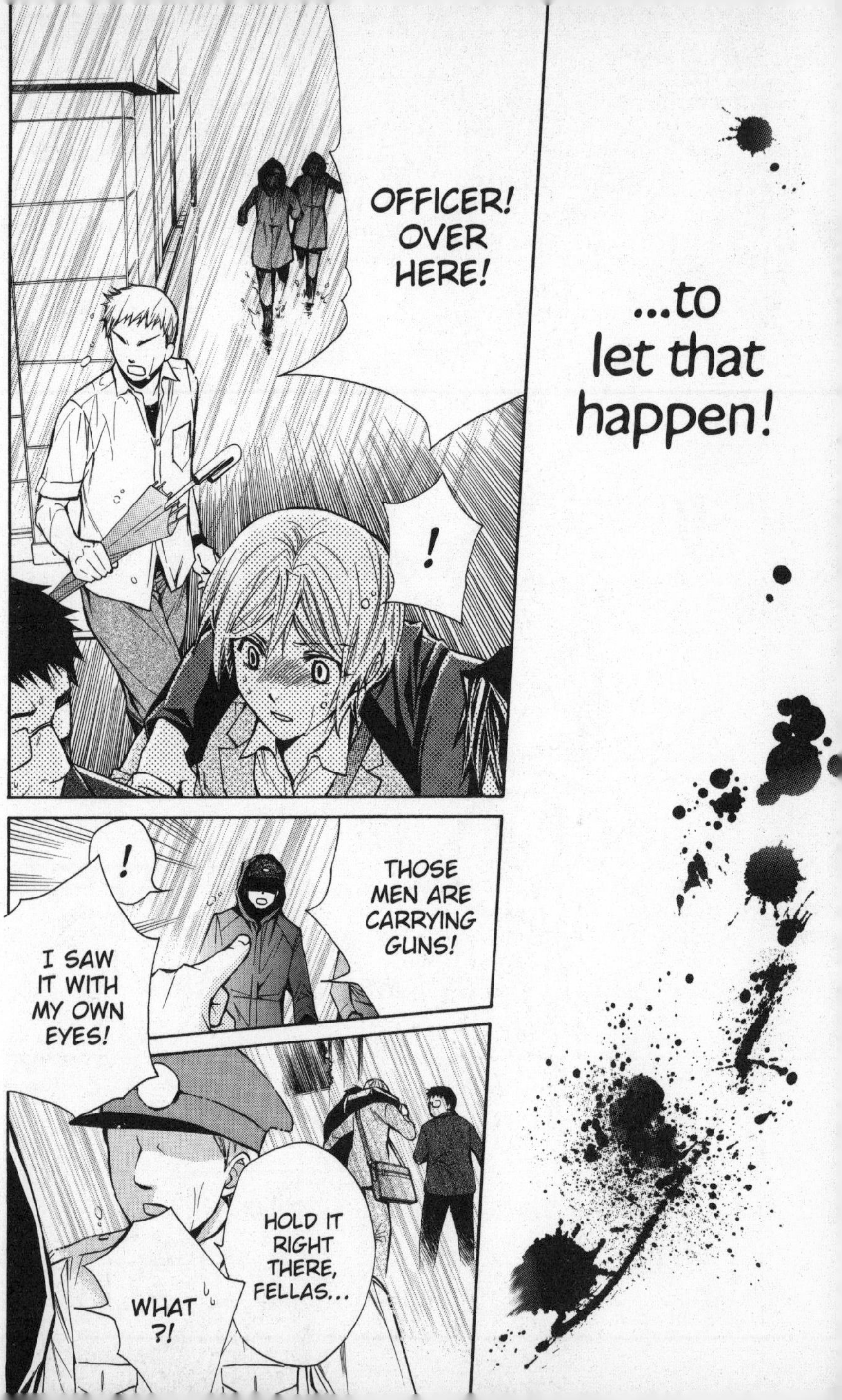
...to let that happen!
OFFICER! OVER HERE!
!
THOSE MEN ARE CARRYING GUNS!
!
I SAW IT WITH MY OWN EYES!
HOLD IT RIGHT THERE, FELLAS...
WHAT ?!

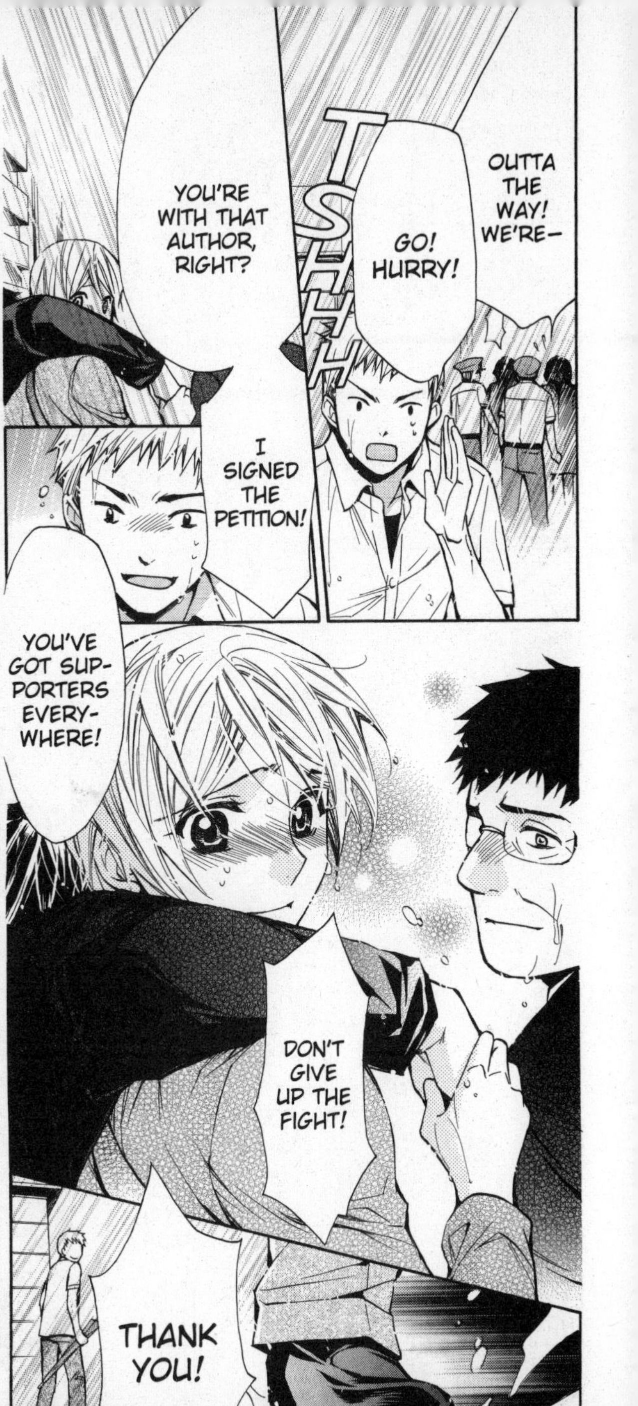
OUTTA THE WAY! WE'RE—
GO! HURRY!
TSHHH
YOU'RE WITH THAT AUTHOR, RIGHT?
I SIGNED THE PETITION!
YOU'VE GOT SUP-PORTERS EVERY-WHERE!
DON'T GIVE UP THE FIGHT!
THANK YOU!

3

*

I'm sorry if I haven't replied to fan mail, but I read it all. Thanks so much! Some readers are under the impression that I'm a man, but I'm a woman! (lol) I think my pen name and this kind of caricature

→ 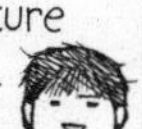

are to blame but, unfortunately, that caricature is an extremely faithful representation of me... I did a good job on it. Yep.

*

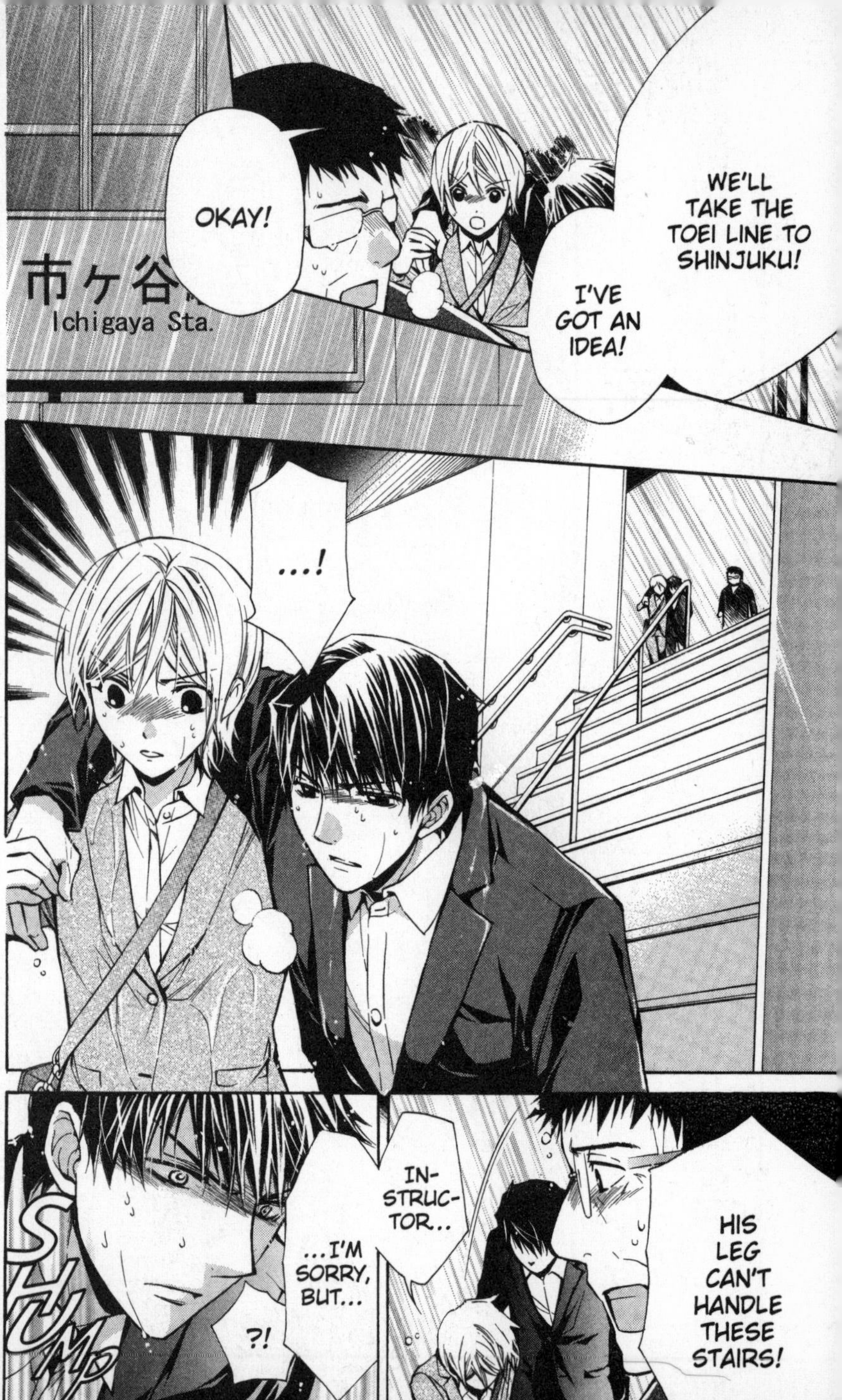
WE'LL TAKE THE TOEI LINE TO SHINJUKU!
I'VE GOT AN IDEA!
市ヶ谷
Ichigaya Sta.
OKAY!
...!
HIS LEG CAN'T HANDLE THESE STAIRS!
INSTRUCTOR...
...I'M SORRY, BUT...
?!
SHUMP

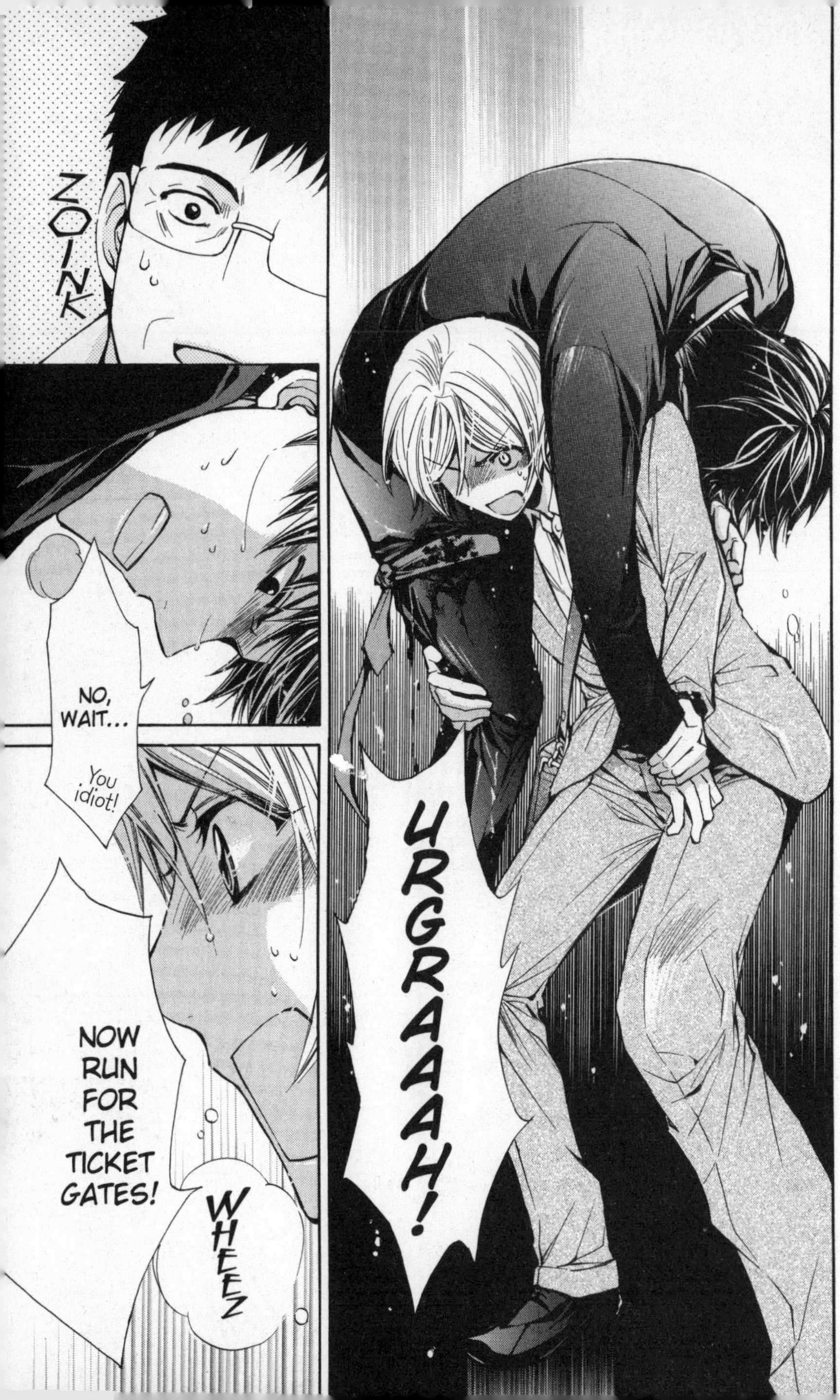
URGRAAAH!
ZOINK
NO, WAIT...
You idiot!
NOW RUN FOR THE TICKET GATES!
WHEEZ

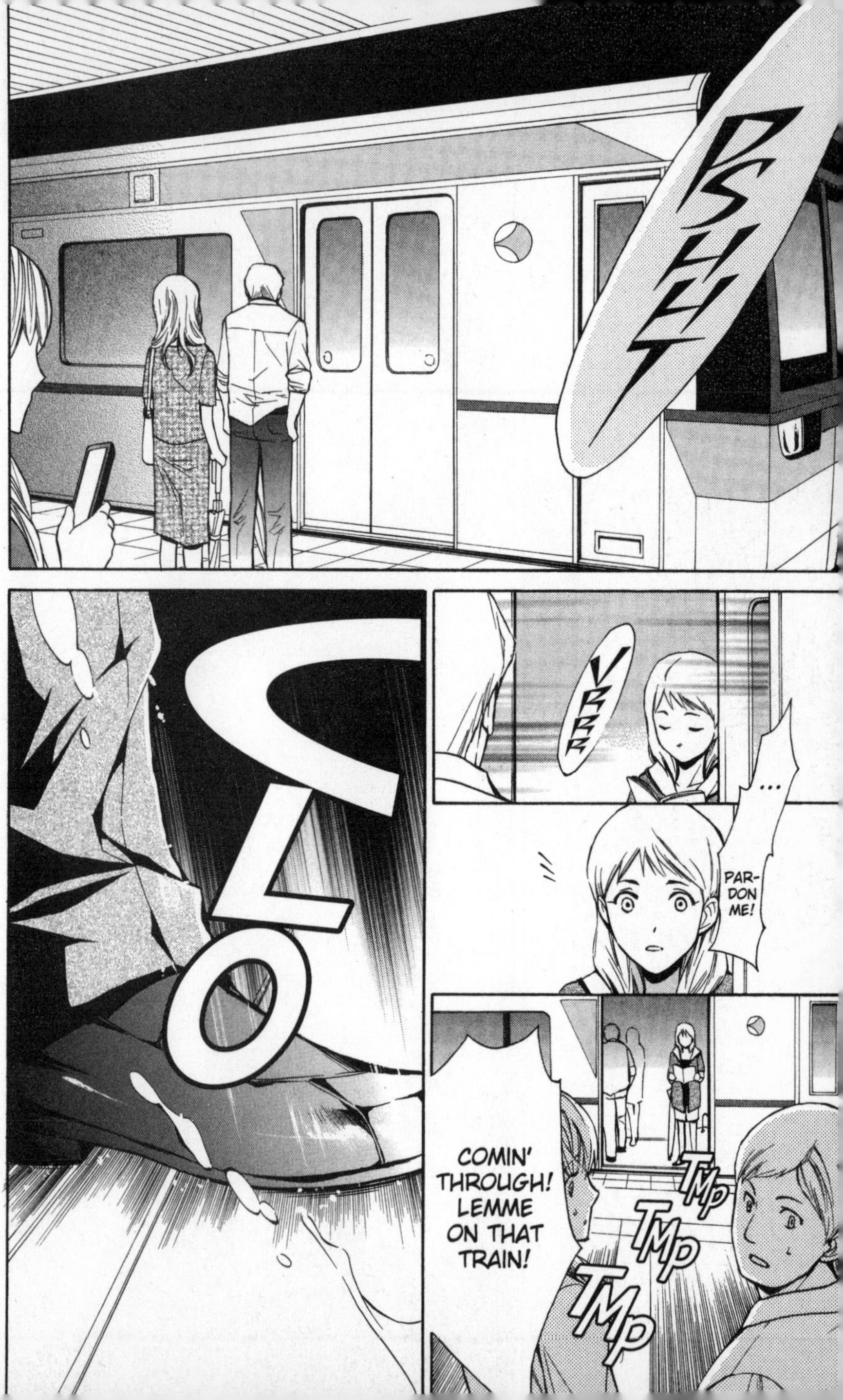
PSHHT
VRRR
...
PAR-DON ME!
COMIN' THROUGH! LEMME ON THAT TRAIN!
TMP TMP TMP
CLO

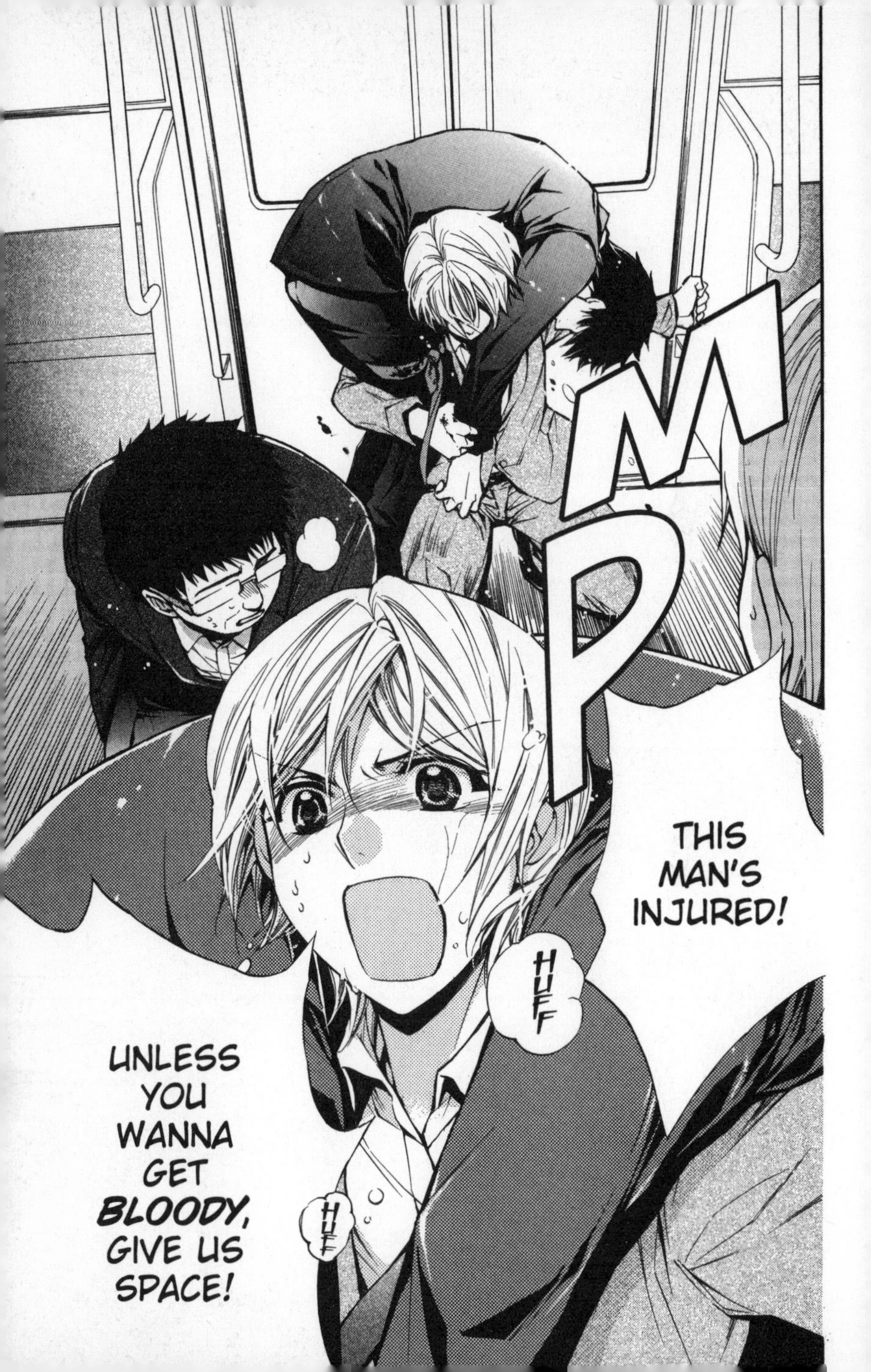
MP
THIS MAN'S INJURED!
HUFF
UNLESS YOU WANNA GET *BLOODY,* GIVE US SPACE!
HUFF

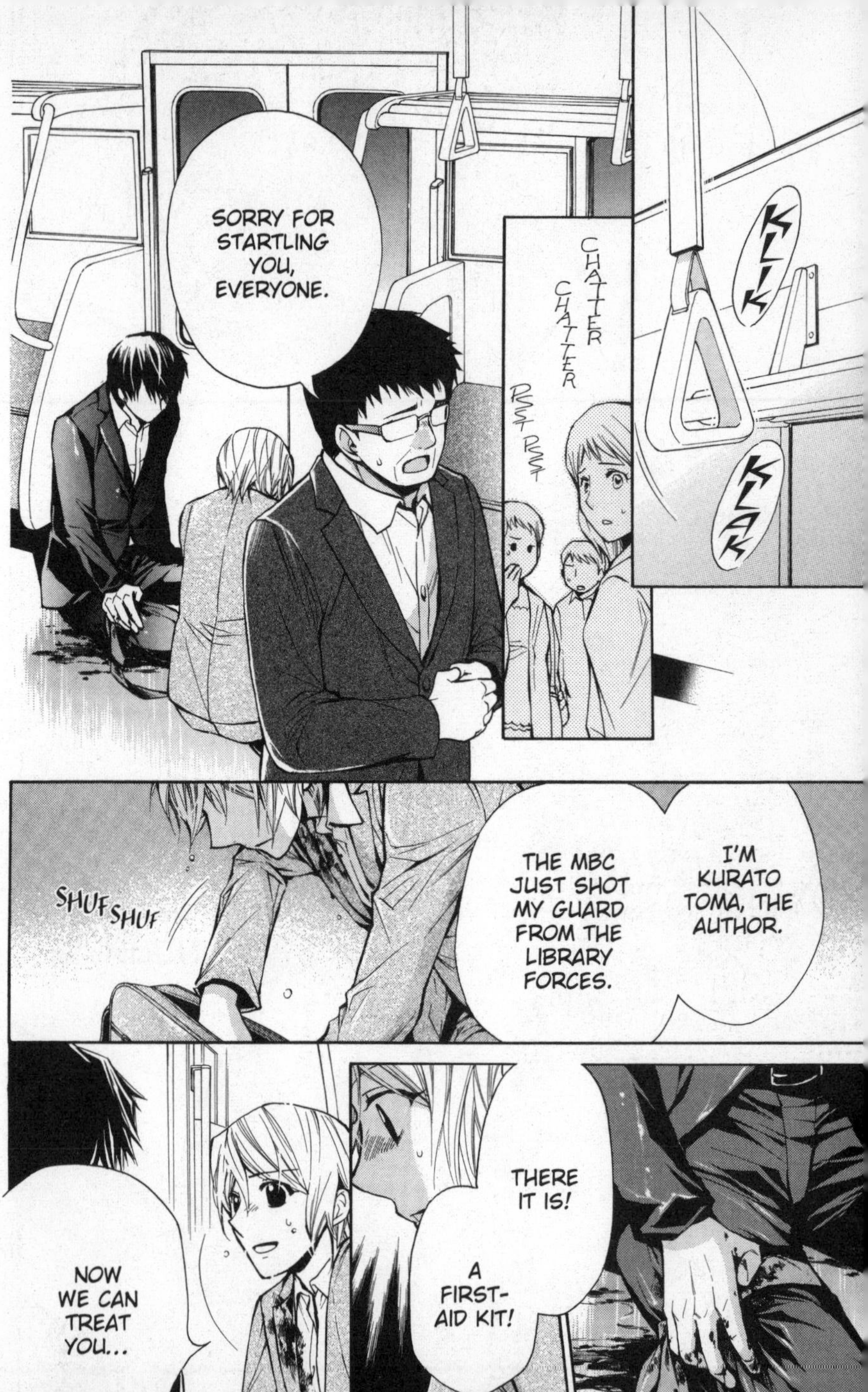
KLIK
KLAK
CHATTER CHATTER
PSST PSST
SORRY FOR STARTLING YOU, EVERYONE.
I'M KURATO TOMA, THE AUTHOR.
THE MBC JUST SHOT MY GUARD FROM THE LIBRARY FORCES.
SHUF SHUF
THERE IT IS!
A FIRST-AID KIT!
NOW WE CAN TREAT YOU...

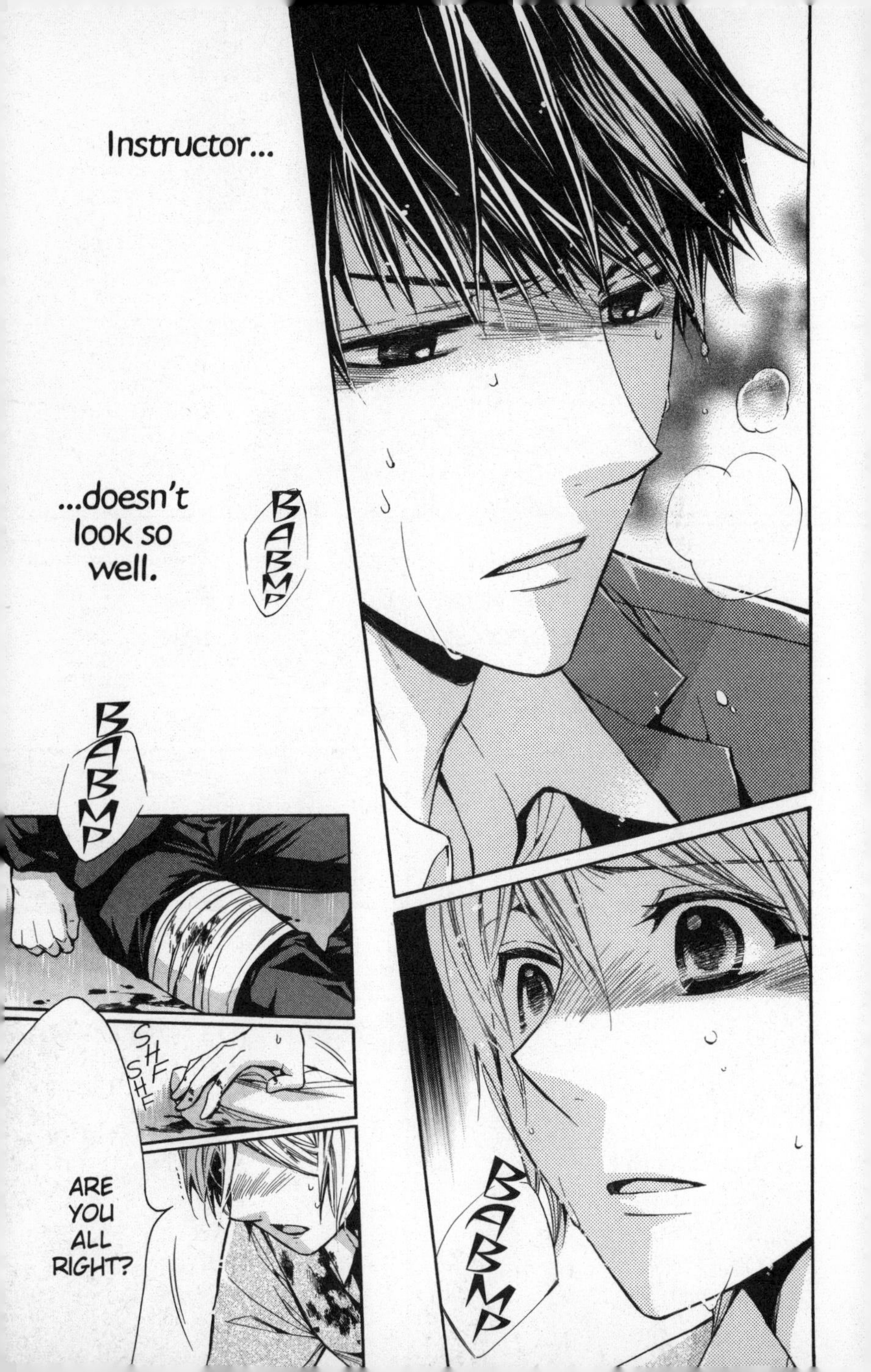
Instructor...
...doesn't look so well.
BABMP
BABMP
BABMP
SHF SHF
ARE YOU ALL RIGHT?

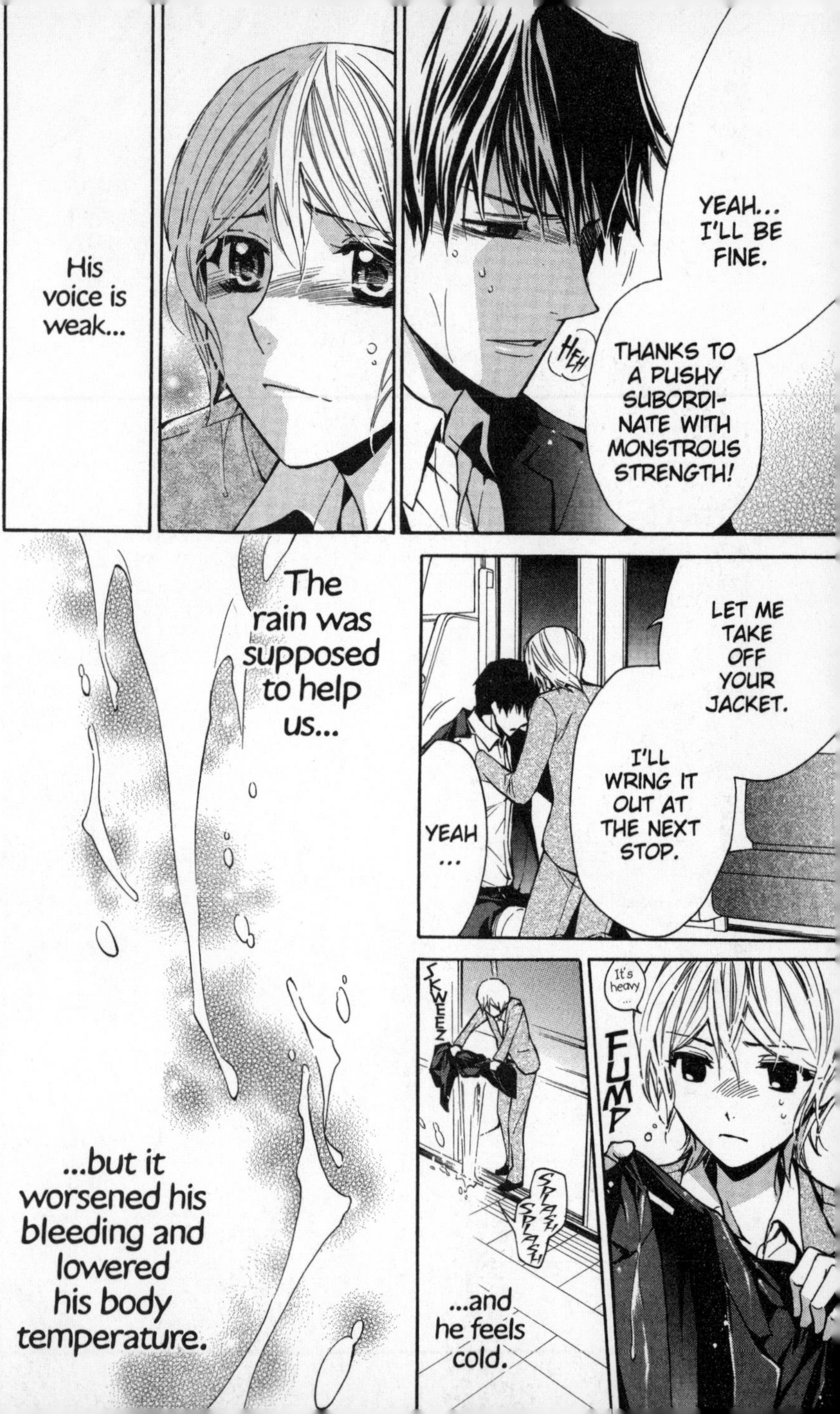
YEAH... I'LL BE FINE.
HEH
THANKS TO A PUSHY SUBORDINATE WITH MONSTROUS STRENGTH!
His voice is weak...
LET ME TAKE OFF YOUR JACKET.
I'LL WRING IT OUT AT THE NEXT STOP.
YEAH...
It's heavy...
FUMP
SKWEEZ
SPLASH SPLASH
...and he feels cold.
The rain was supposed to help us...
...but it worsened his bleeding and lowered his body temperature.

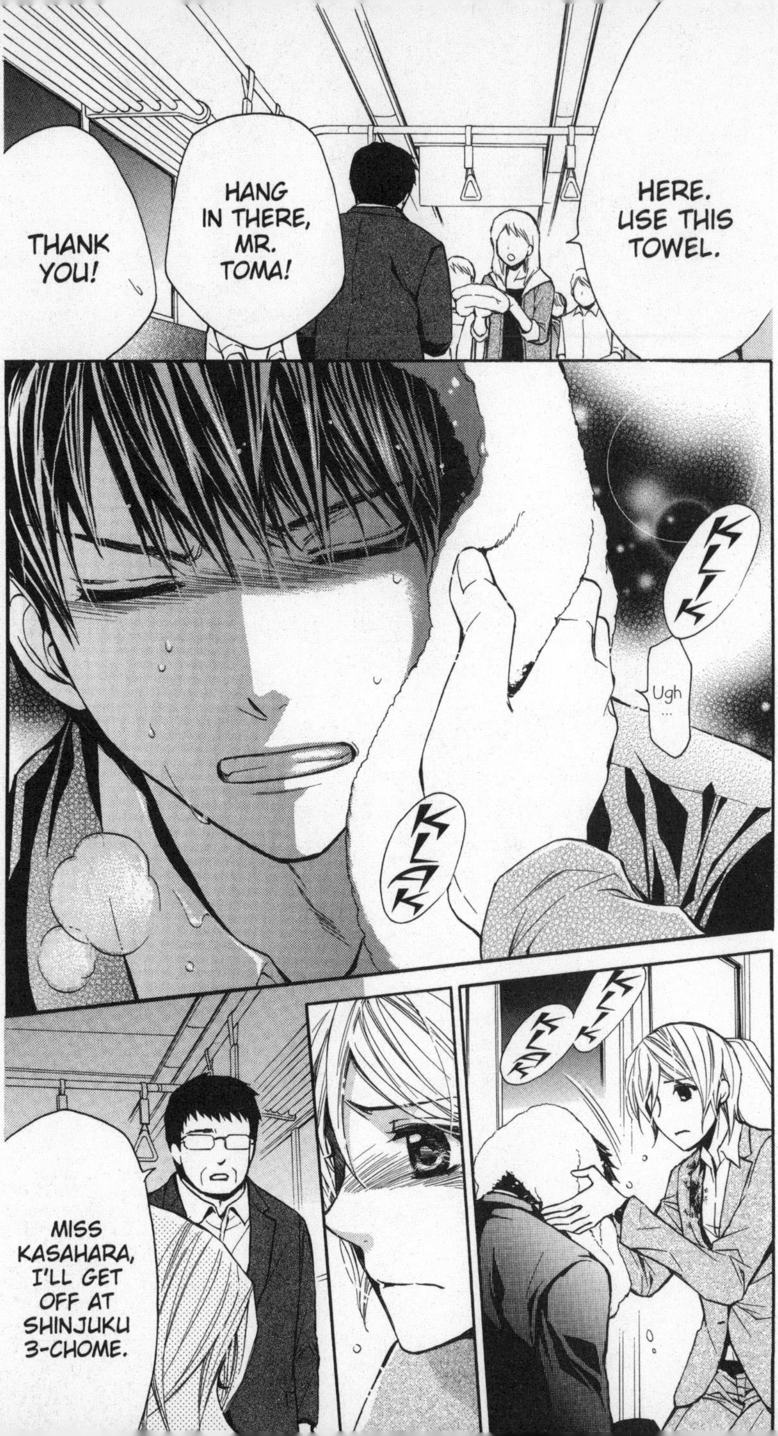
HERE. USE THIS TOWEL.
HANG IN THERE, MR. TOMA!
THANK YOU!
KLIK
Ugh...
KLAK
KLIK
KLAK
MISS KASAHARA, I'LL GET OFF AT SHINJUKU 3-CHOME.

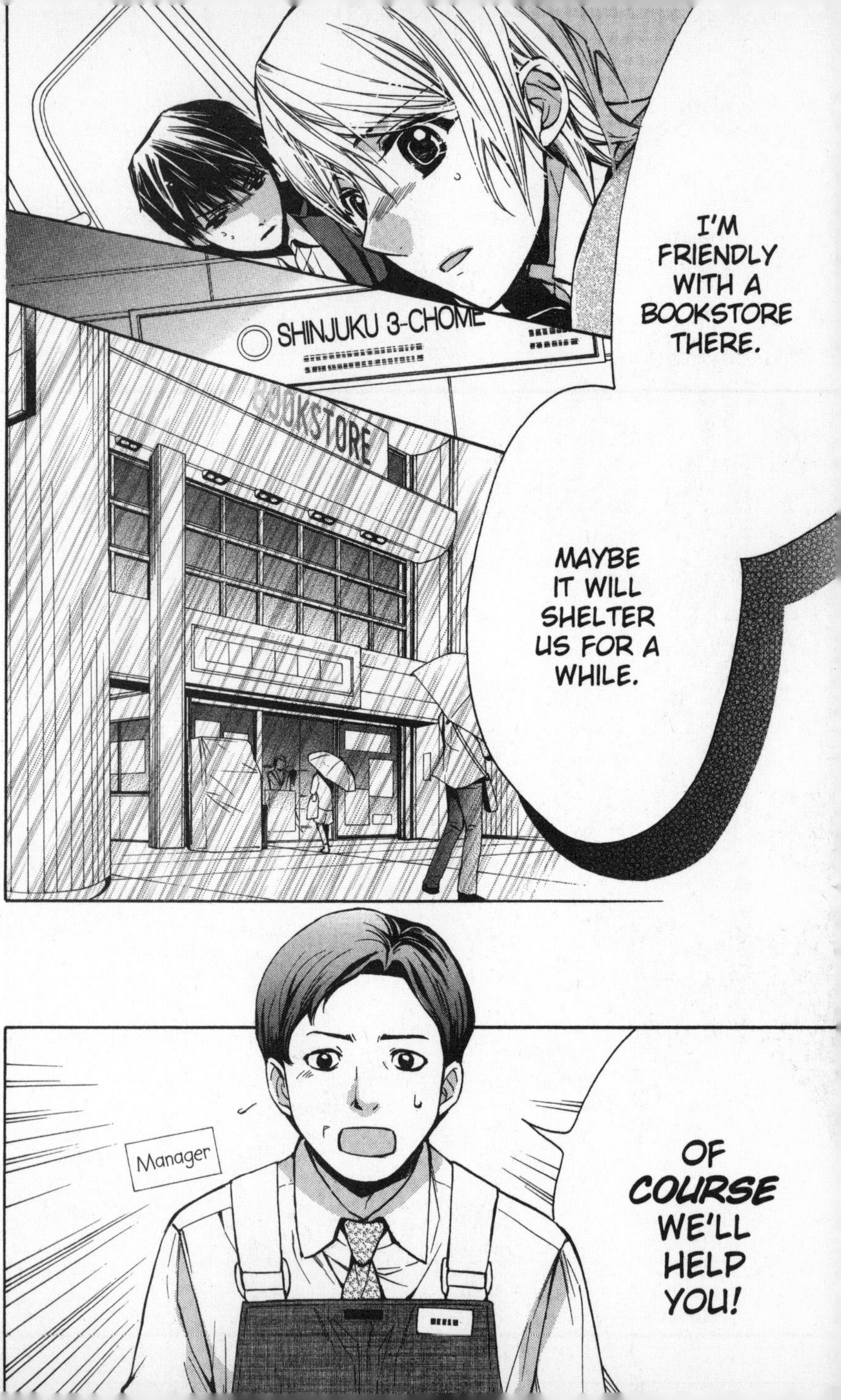
I'M FRIENDLY WITH A BOOKSTORE THERE.
SHINJUKU 3-CHOME
BOOKSTORE
MAYBE IT WILL SHELTER US FOR A WHILE.
OF COURSE WE'LL HELP YOU!
Manager

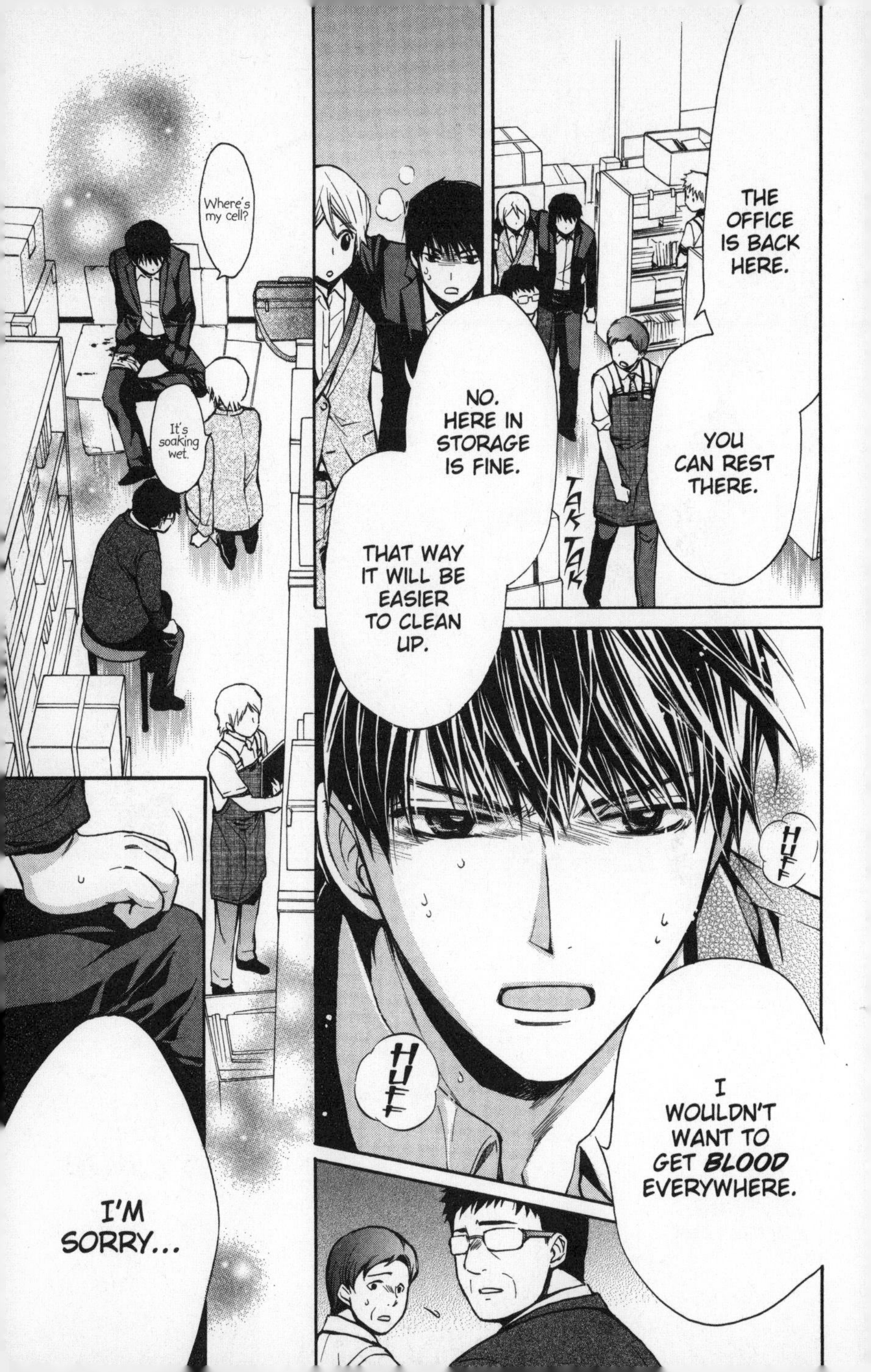
THE OFFICE IS BACK HERE.
YOU CAN REST THERE.
TAK TAK
NO. HERE IN STORAGE IS FINE.
THAT WAY IT WILL BE EASIER TO CLEAN UP.
HUFF
I WOULDN'T WANT TO GET *BLOOD* EVERYWHERE.
HUFF
Where's my cell?
It's soaking wet.
I'M SORRY...

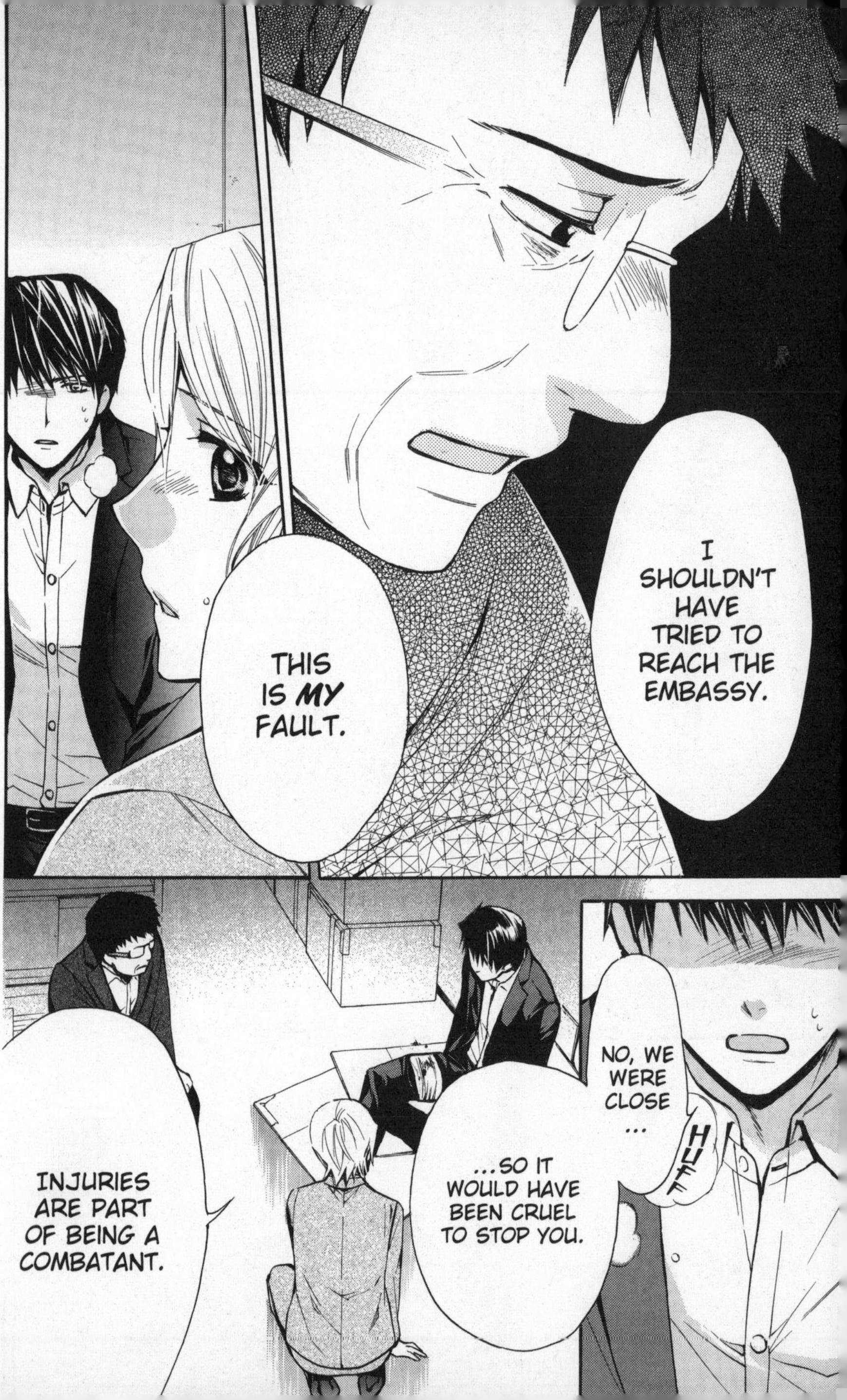
I SHOULDN'T HAVE TRIED TO REACH THE EMBASSY.
THIS IS MY FAULT.
NO, WE WERE CLOSE ...
HUFF
...SO IT WOULD HAVE BEEN CRUEL TO STOP YOU.
INJURIES ARE PART OF BEING A COMBATANT.

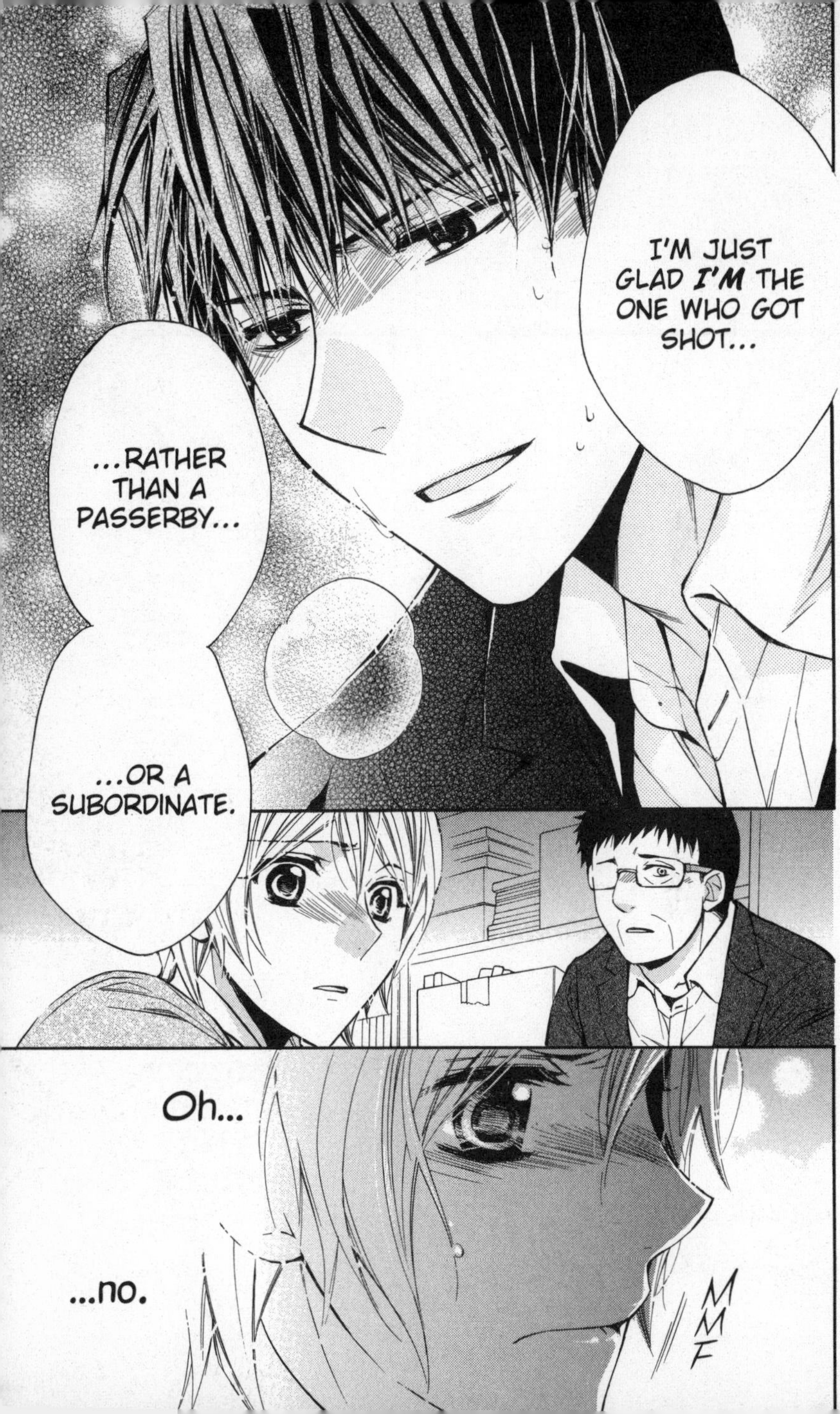
I'M JUST GLAD *I'M* THE ONE WHO GOT SHOT...
...RATHER THAN A PASSERBY...
...OR A SUBORDINATE.
Oh...
...no.
MMF

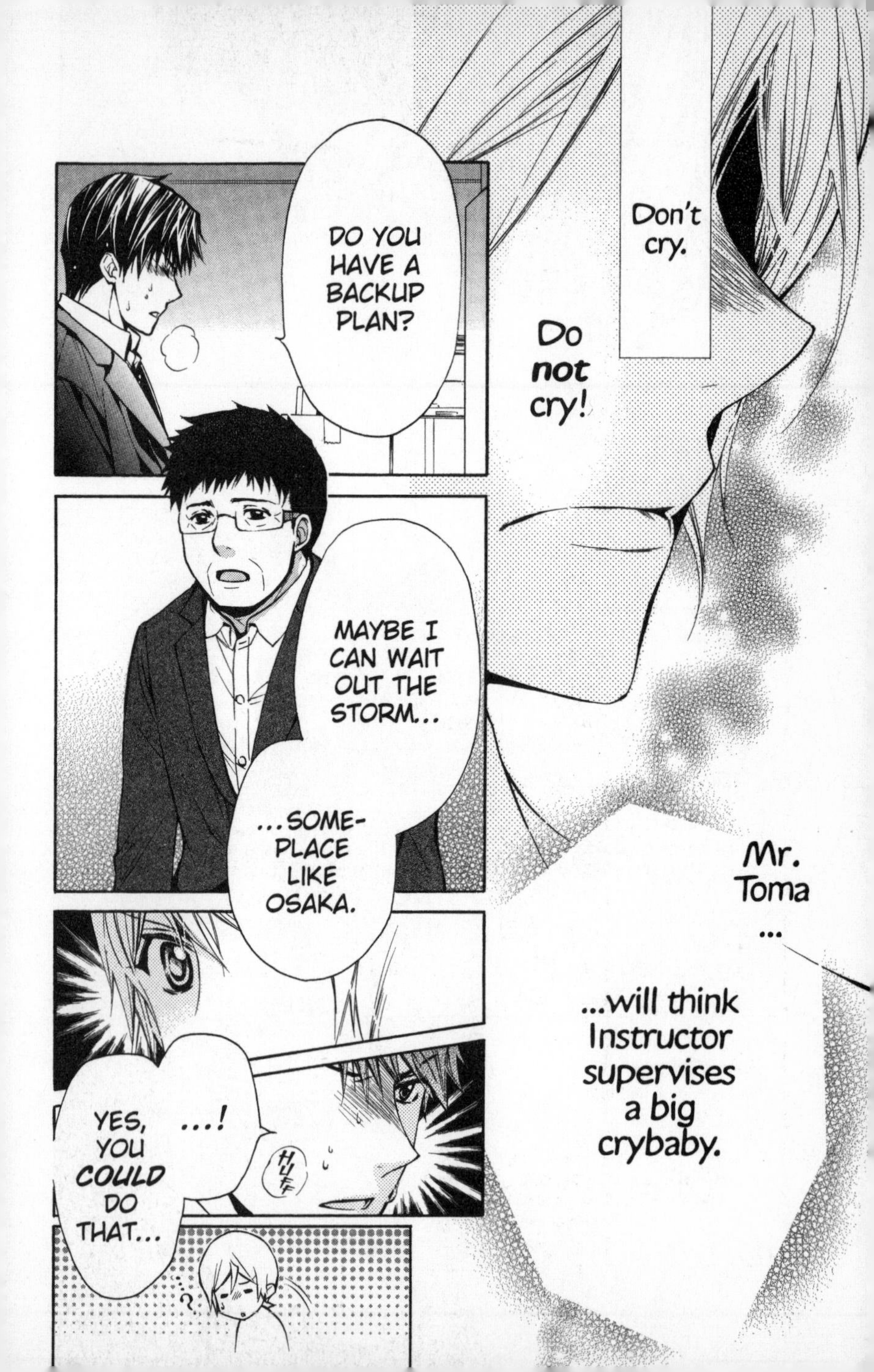
Don't cry.
Do *not* cry!
Mr. Toma ...
...will think Instructor supervises a big crybaby.
DO YOU HAVE A BACKUP PLAN?
MAYBE I CAN WAIT OUT THE STORM...
...SOME-PLACE LIKE OSAKA.
...!
YES, YOU *COULD* DO THAT...
HUFF
?

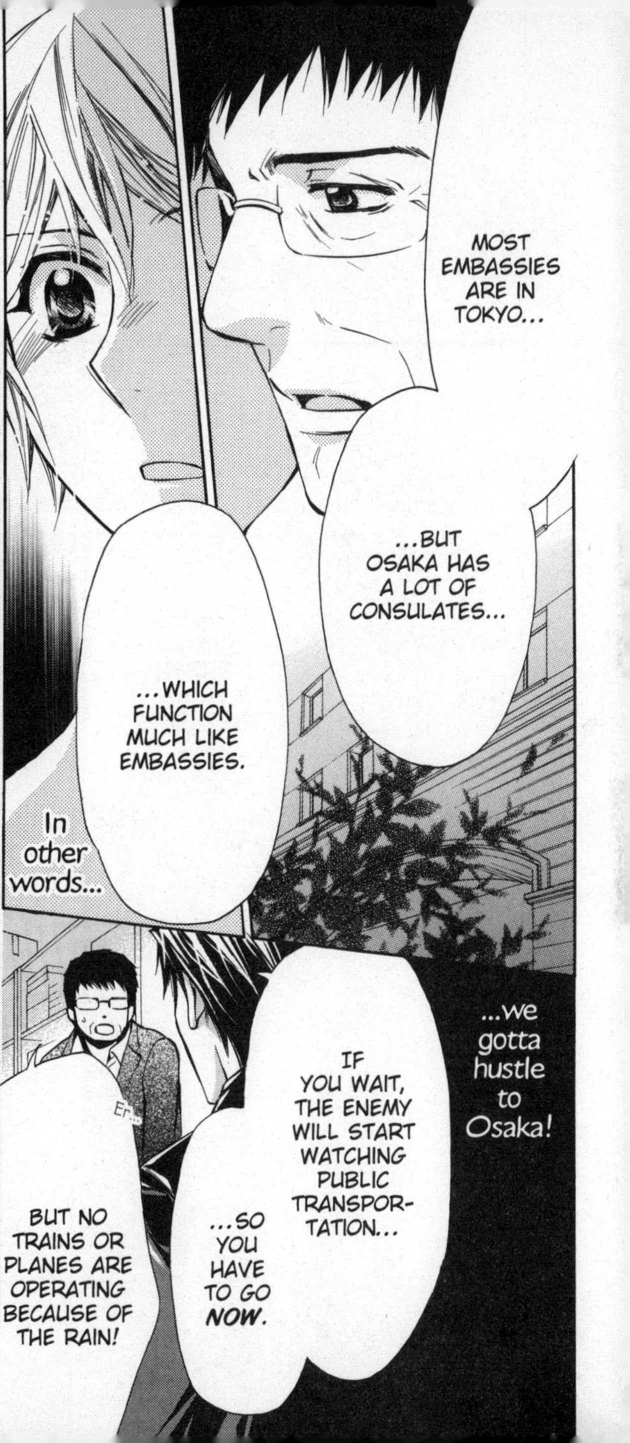
MOST EMBASSIES ARE IN TOKYO...
...BUT OSAKA HAS A LOT OF CONSULATES...
...WHICH FUNCTION MUCH LIKE EMBASSIES.
In other words...
...we gotta hustle to Osaka!
IF YOU WAIT, THE ENEMY WILL START WATCHING PUBLIC TRANSPOR-TATION...
...SO YOU HAVE TO GO **NOW.**
Er...
BUT NO TRAINS OR PLANES ARE OPERATING BECAUSE OF THE RAIN!

4

Since beginning to work at home, I've watched every episode of a morning TV show. (I watch a lot of daytime ones too. Really sordid ones!) I always enjoy it, but recently it's been somewhat sad. I'll fill you in a little...

Two times...in a row...a childhood friend's whole-hearted love for the heroine has gone unfulfilled...and that's rough!!!

Of course, the main guy who wins her love is cool too! *SIGH* But it's so sad... I always fall for the loser in a love triangle!

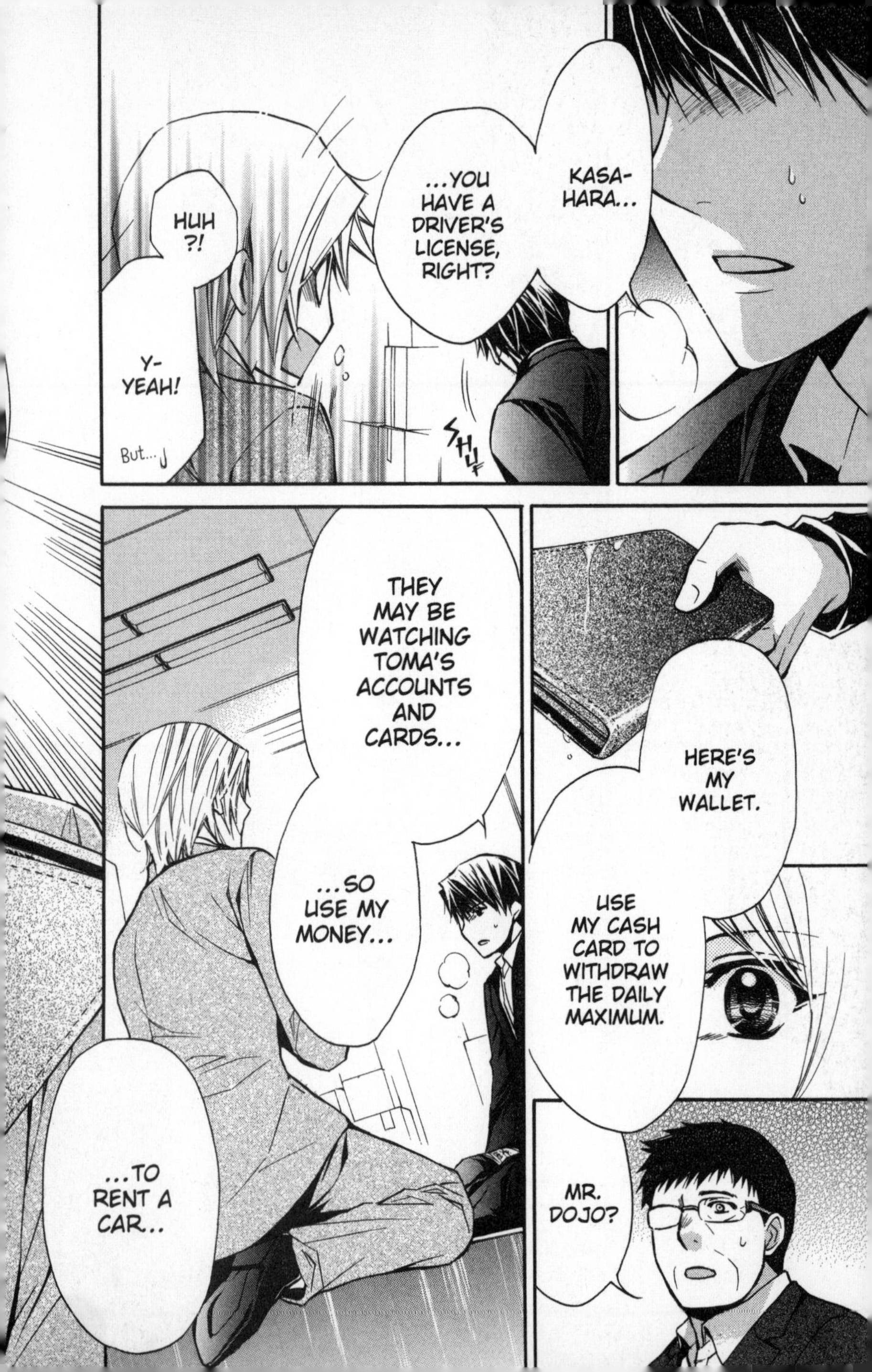
KASA-
HARA...
...YOU HAVE A DRIVER'S LICENSE, RIGHT?
SHUF
HUH ?!
Y-YEAH!
But...
HERE'S MY WALLET.
USE MY CASH CARD TO WITHDRAW THE DAILY MAXIMUM.
MR. DOJO?
THEY MAY BE WATCHING TOMA'S ACCOUNTS AND CARDS...
...SO USE MY MONEY...
...TO RENT A CAR..

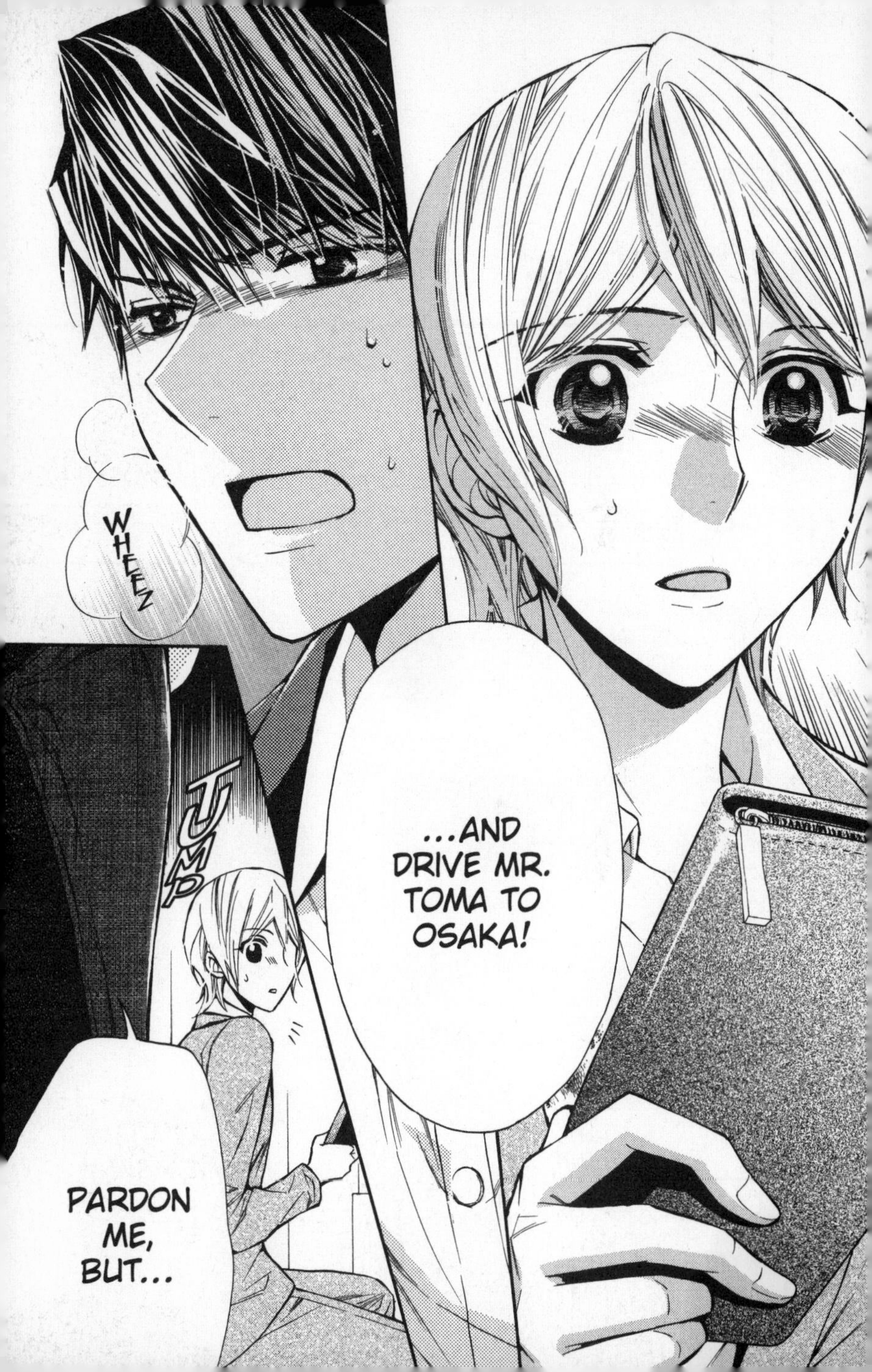
...AND DRIVE MR. TOMA TO OSAKA!
WHEEZ
TUMP
PARDON ME, BUT...

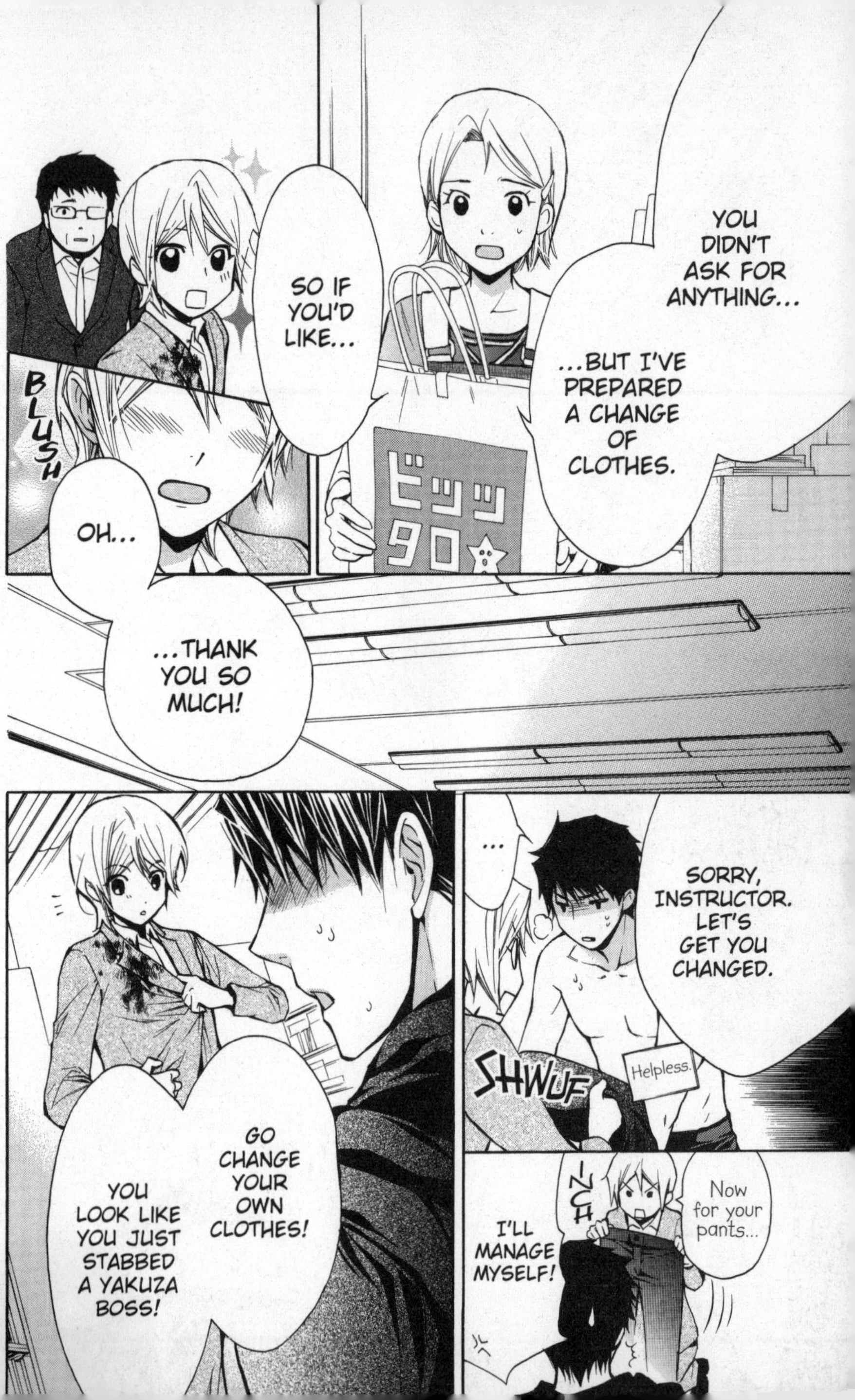
YOU DIDN'T ASK FOR ANYTHING...
...BUT I'VE PREPARED A CHANGE OF CLOTHES.
ビッツ
90
SO IF YOU'D LIKE...
BLUSH
OH...
...THANK YOU SO MUCH!
...
SORRY, INSTRUCTOR. LET'S GET YOU CHANGED.
SHWUF
Helpless.
Now for your pants...
INCH
I'LL MANAGE MYSELF!
GO CHANGE YOUR OWN CLOTHES!
YOU LOOK LIKE YOU JUST STABBED A YAKUZA BOSS!

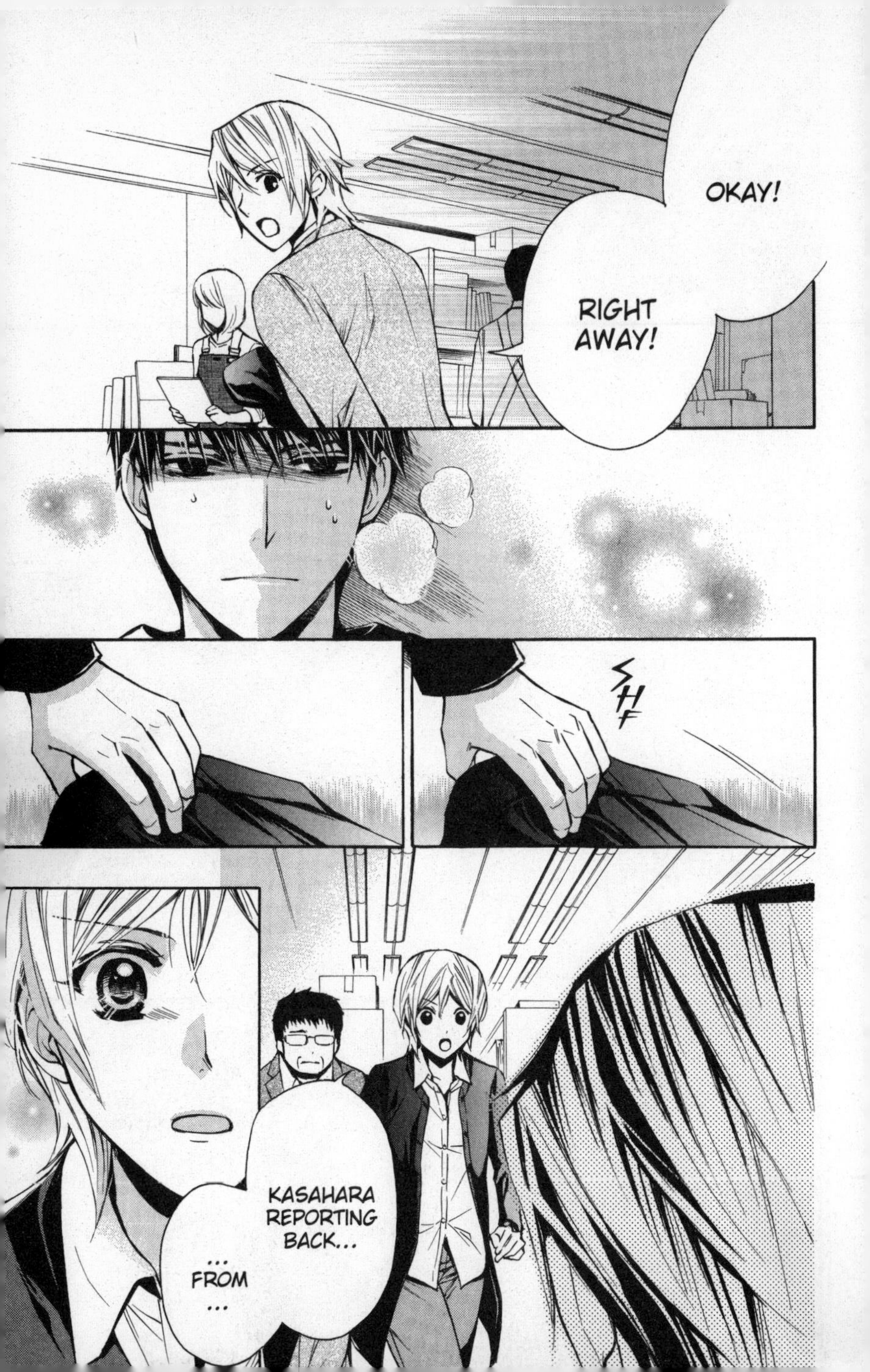
OKAY!
RIGHT AWAY!
SHF
KASAHARA REPORTING BACK...
...FROM
...

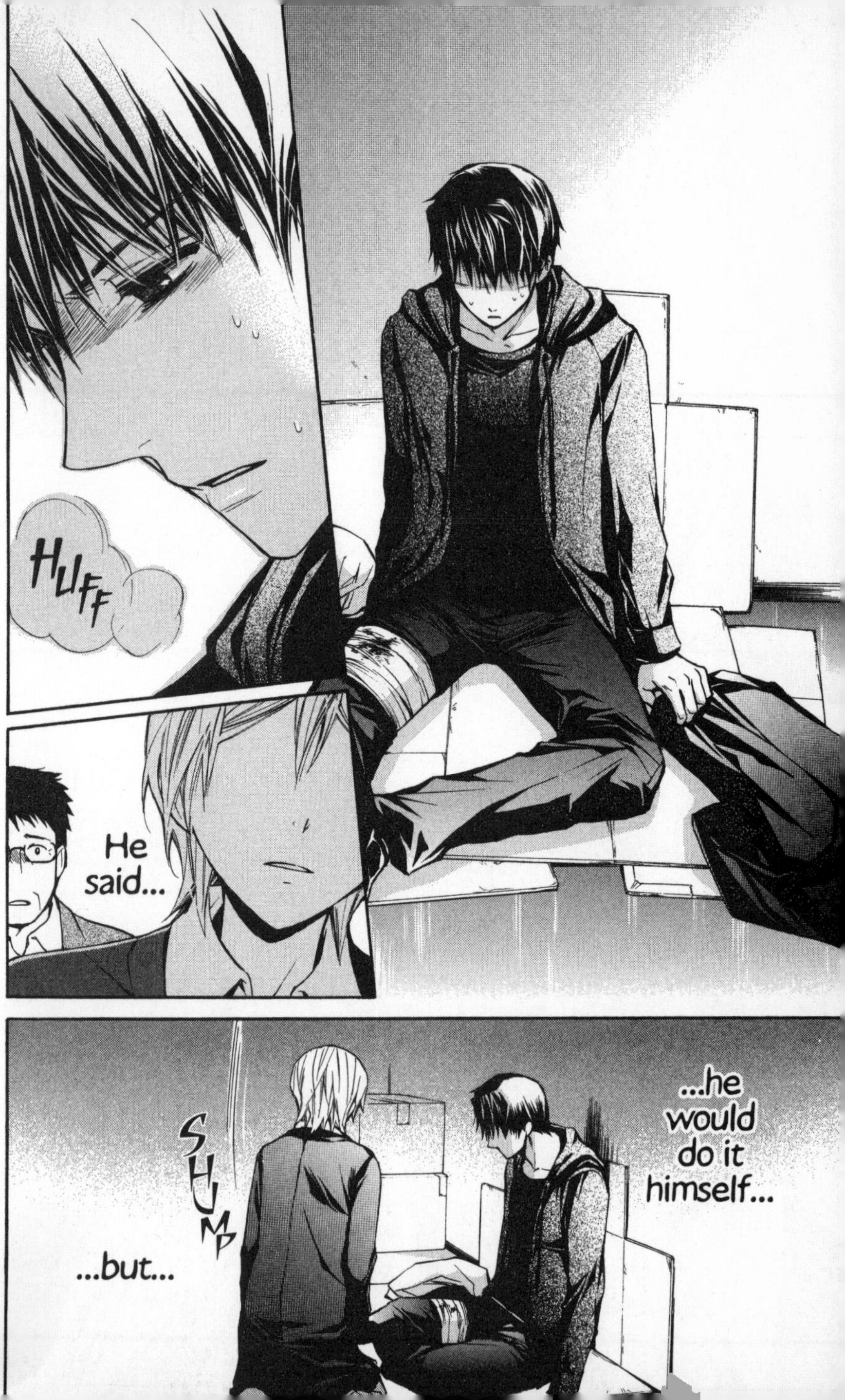
HUFF
He said...
...he would do it himself...
SHUMP
...but...

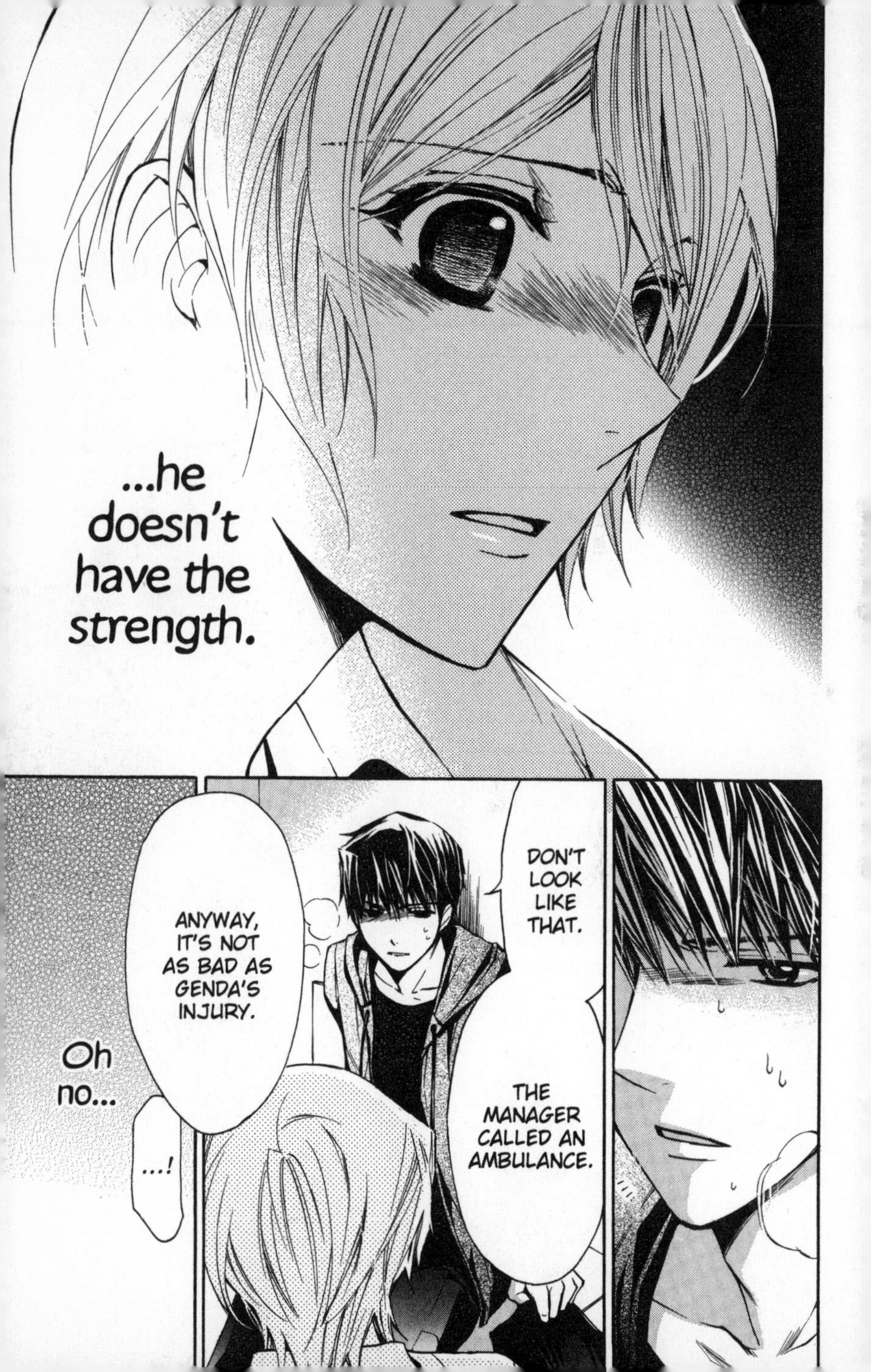
...he doesn't have the strength.
DON'T LOOK LIKE THAT.
THE MANAGER CALLED AN AMBULANCE.
ANYWAY, IT'S NOT AS BAD AS GENDA'S INJURY.
...!
Oh no...

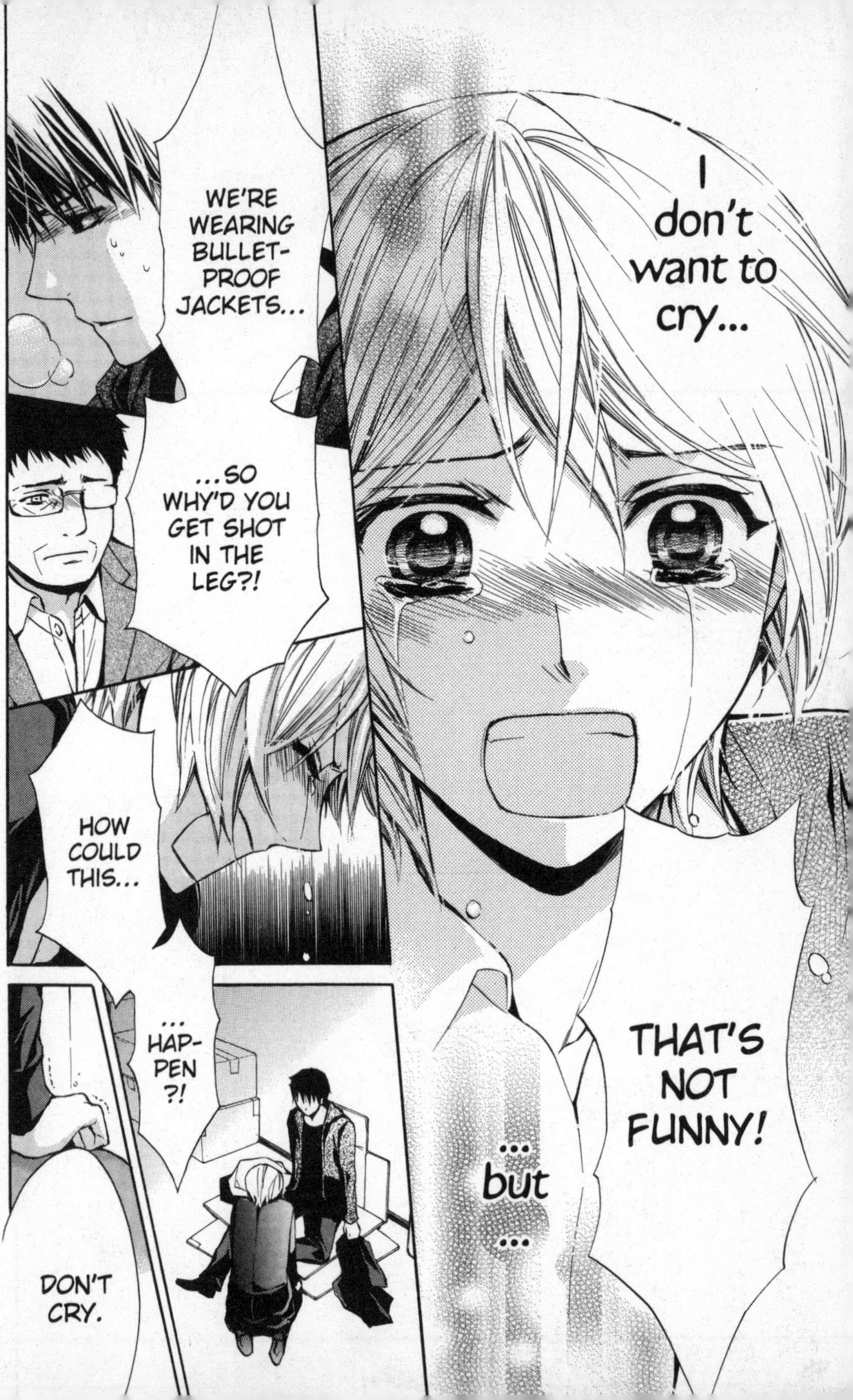

I don't want to cry...
THAT'S NOT FUNNY!
...but...
WE'RE WEARING BULLET-PROOF JACKETS...
...SO WHY'D YOU GET SHOT IN THE LEG?!
HOW COULD THIS...
...HAP-PEN?!
DON'T CRY.

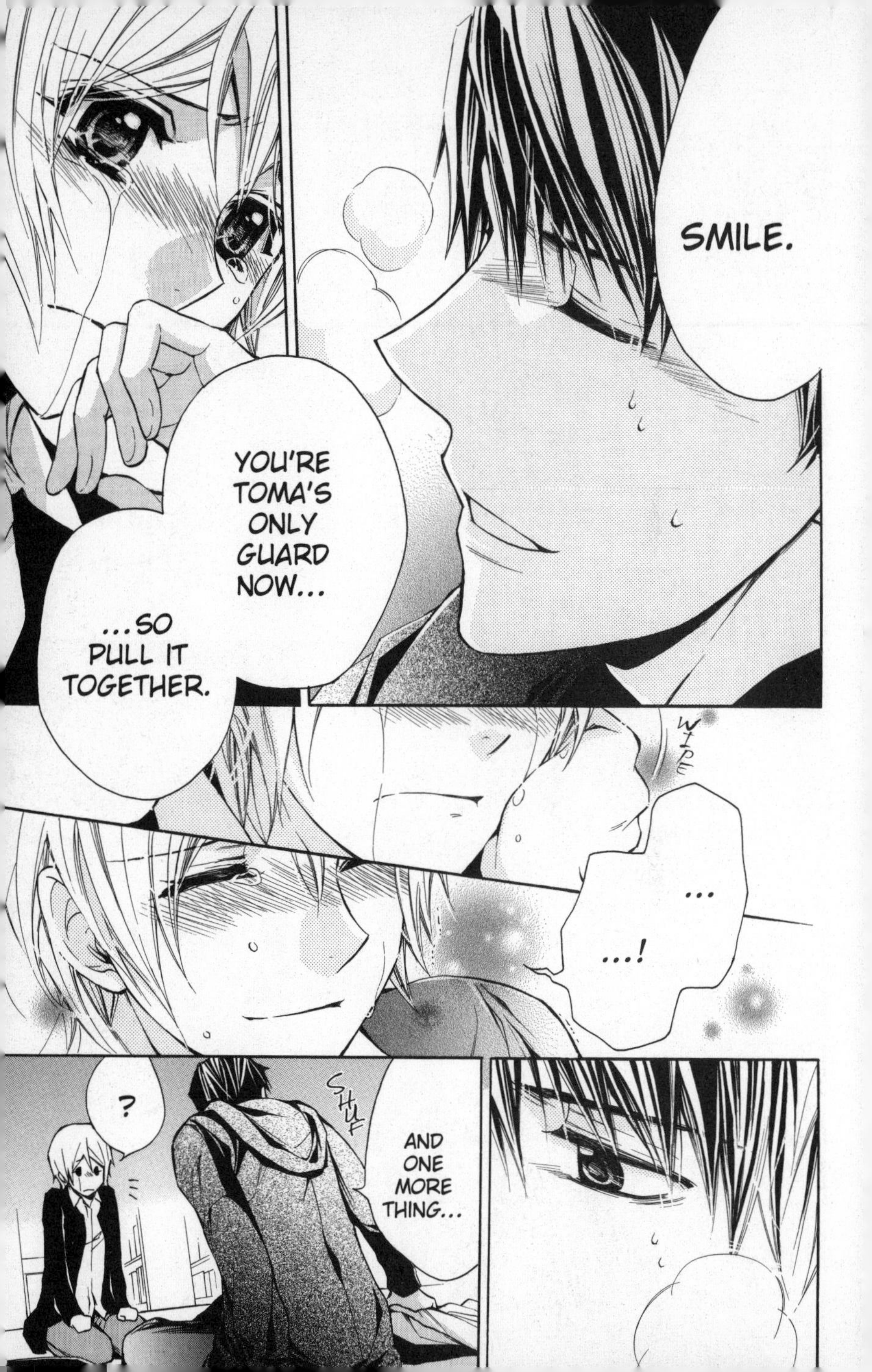
SMILE.
YOU'RE TOMA'S ONLY GUARD NOW...
...SO PULL IT TOGETHER.
WIPE
...
...!
SHUF
AND ONE MORE THING...
?

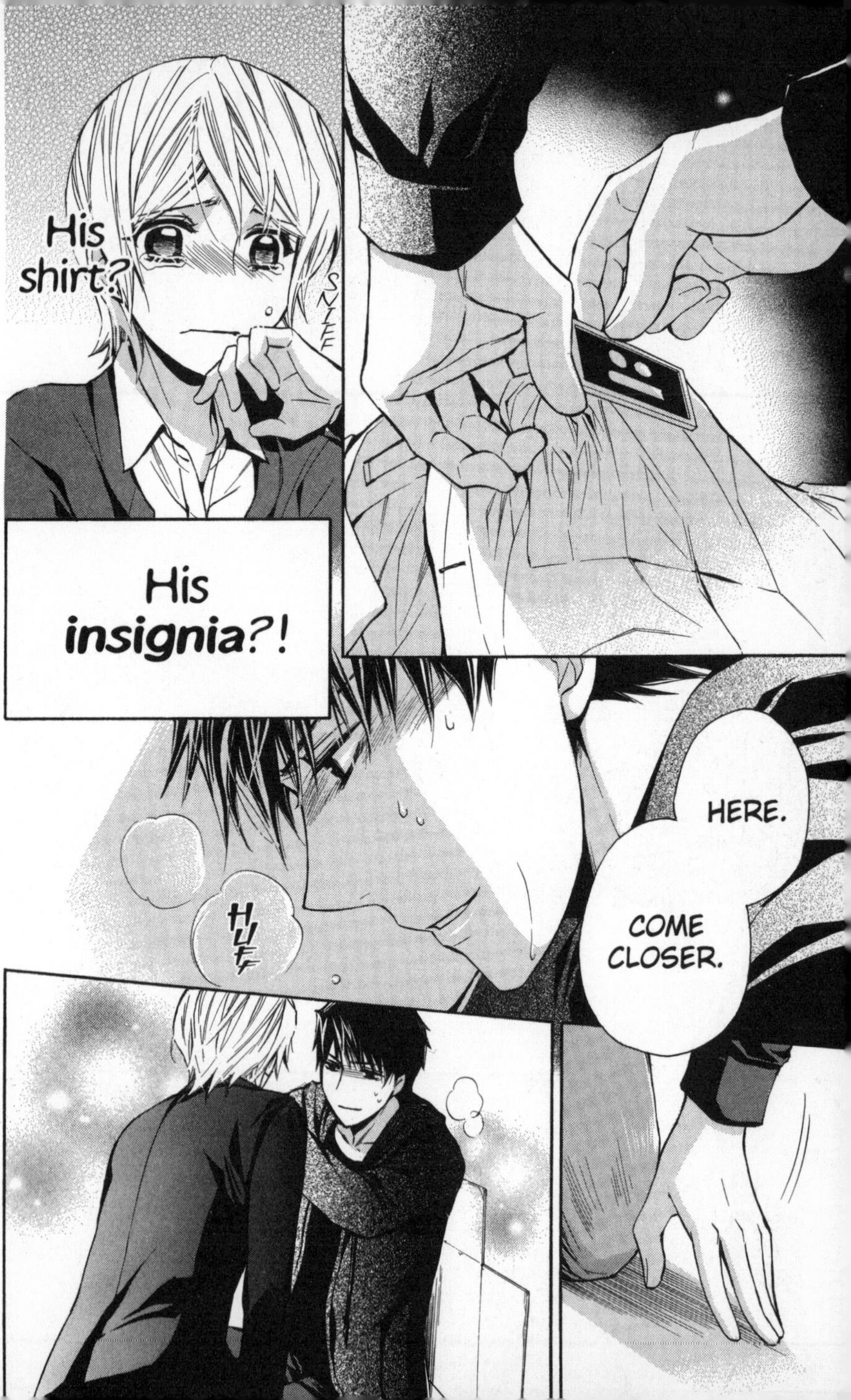
His shirt?
SNIFF
His insignia?!
HERE.
COME CLOSER.
HUFF

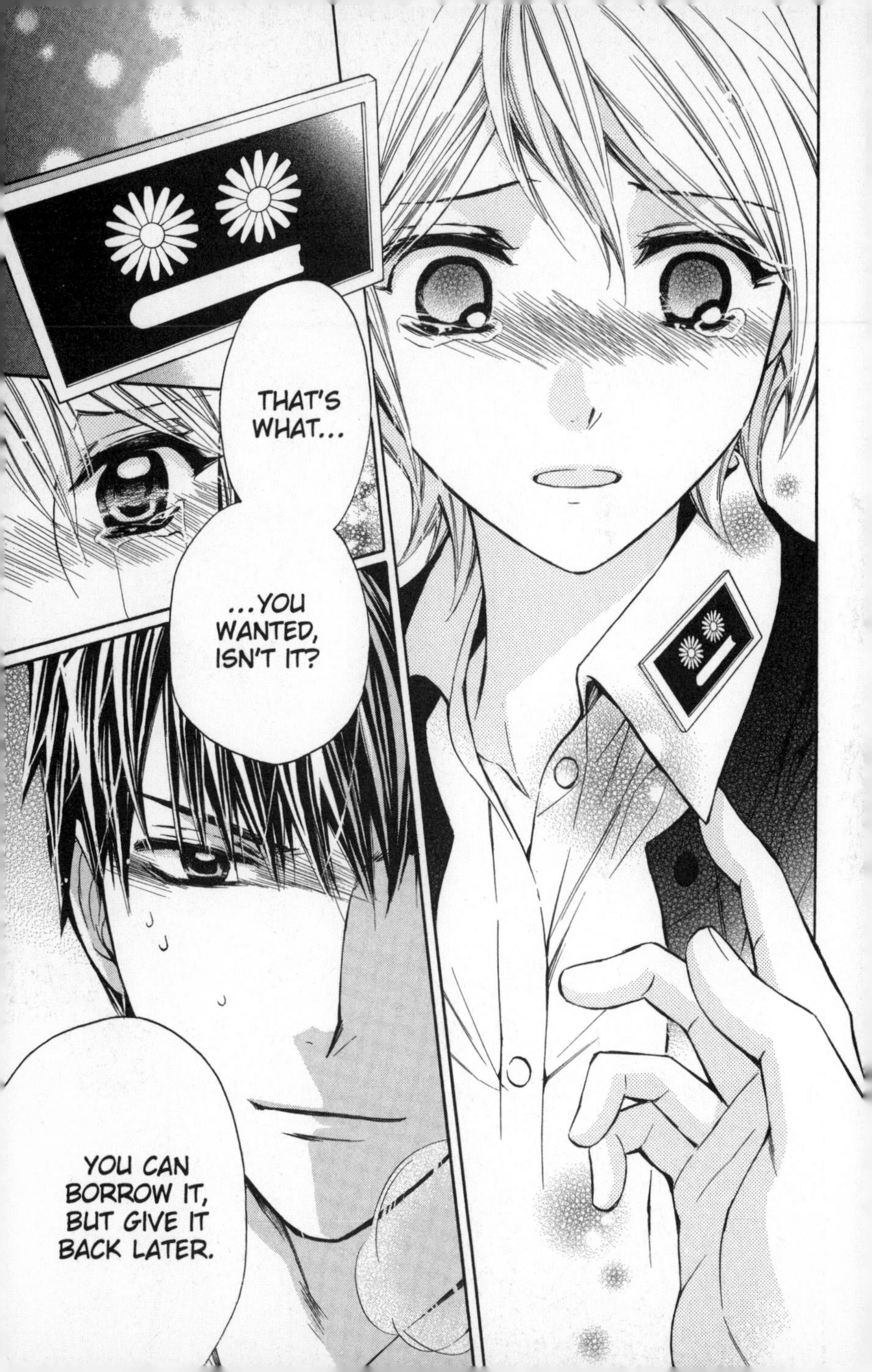
THAT'S WHAT...
...YOU WANTED, ISN'T IT?
YOU CAN BORROW IT, BUT GIVE IT BACK LATER.

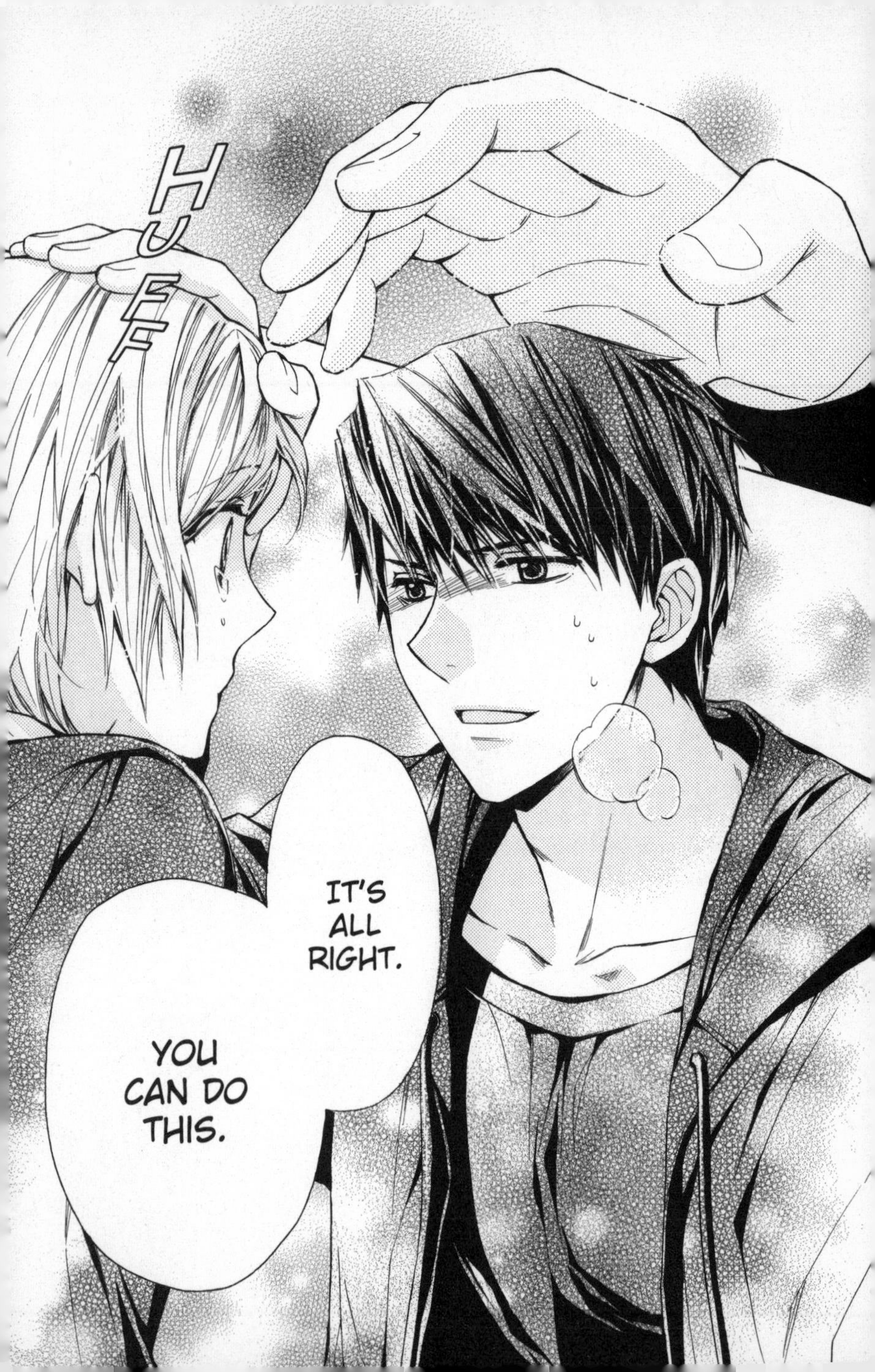
HUFF
IT'S ALL RIGHT.
YOU CAN DO THIS.

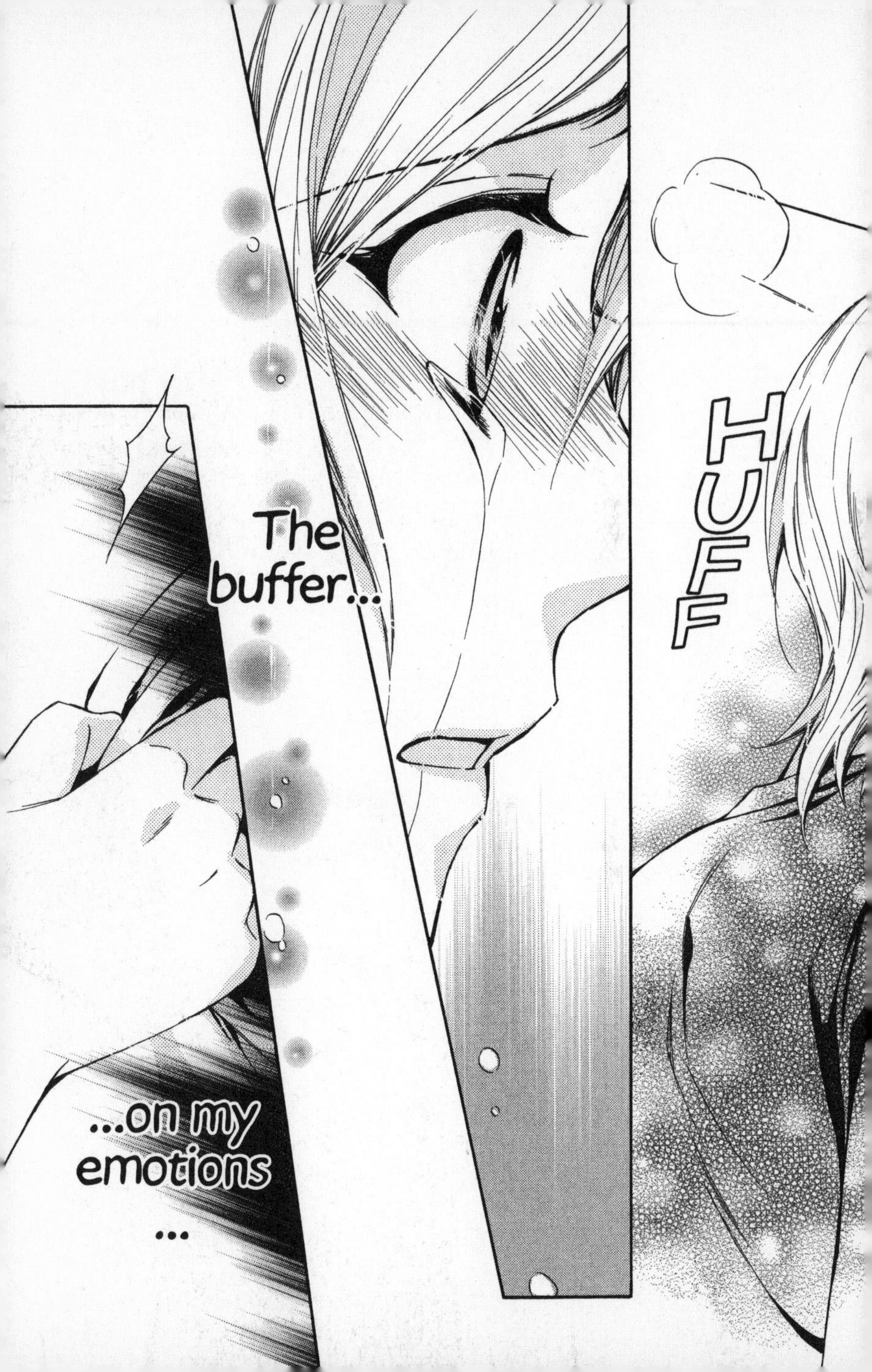
HUFF
The buffer...
...on my emotions...

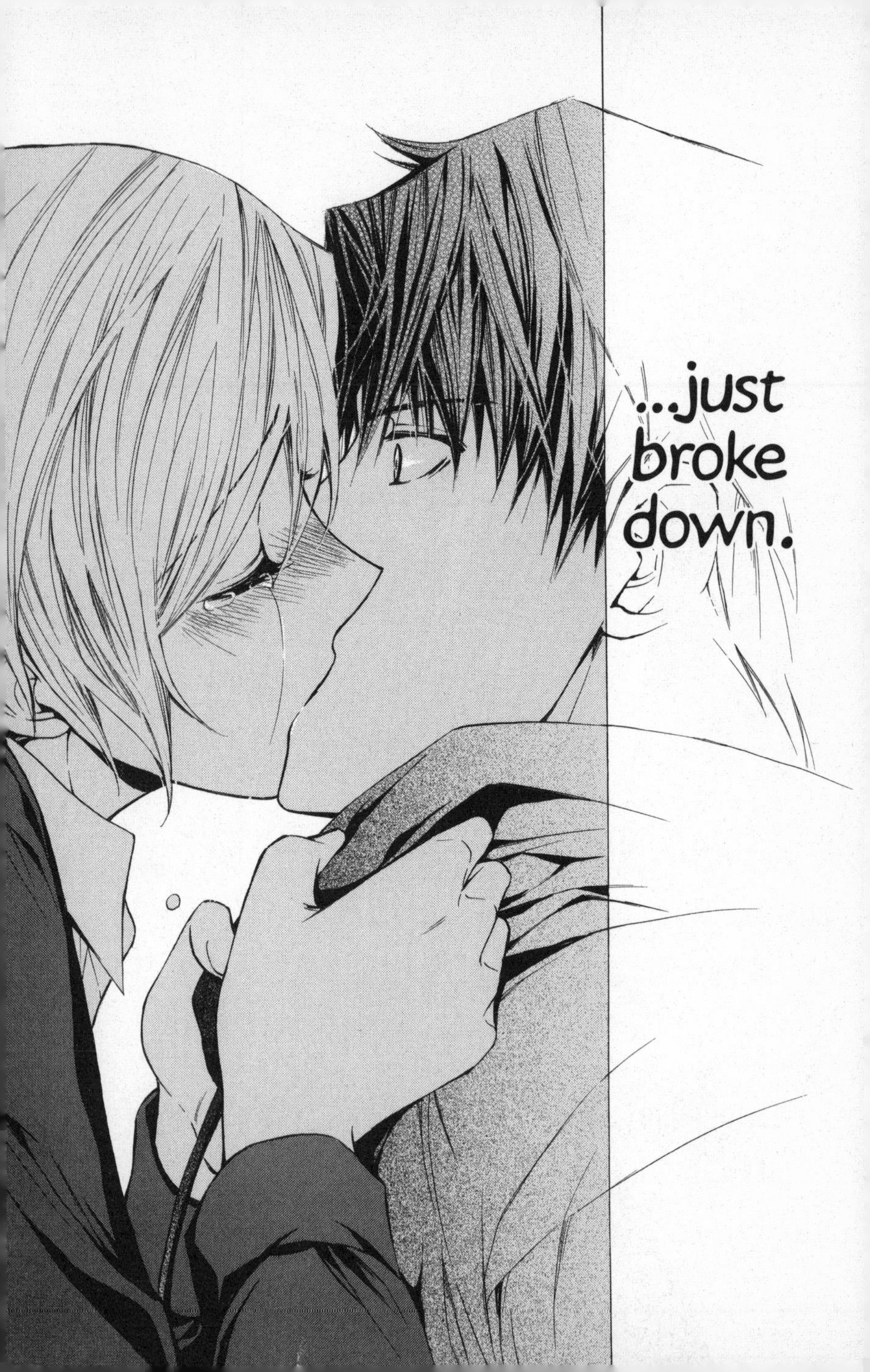
...just broke down.

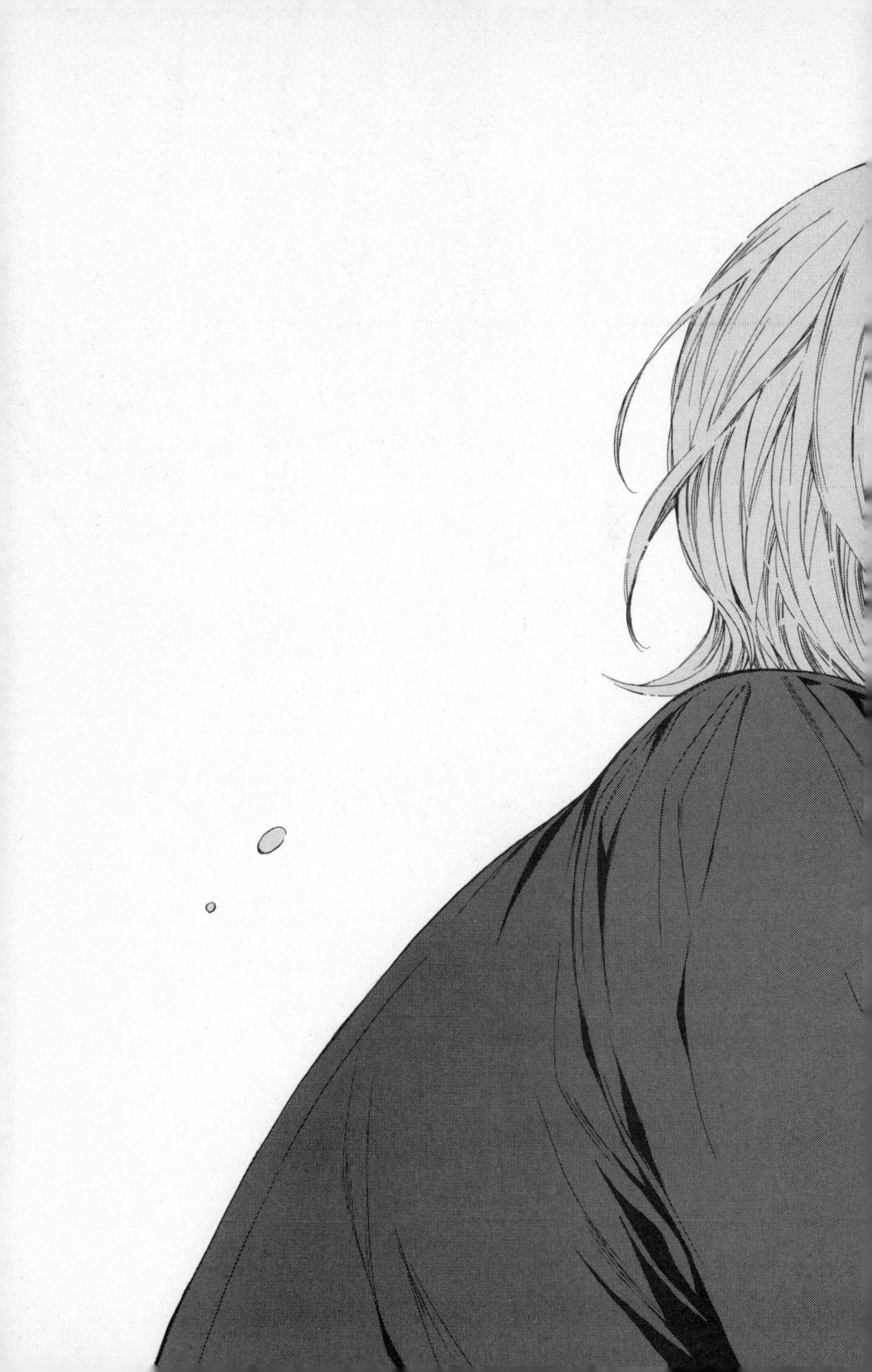

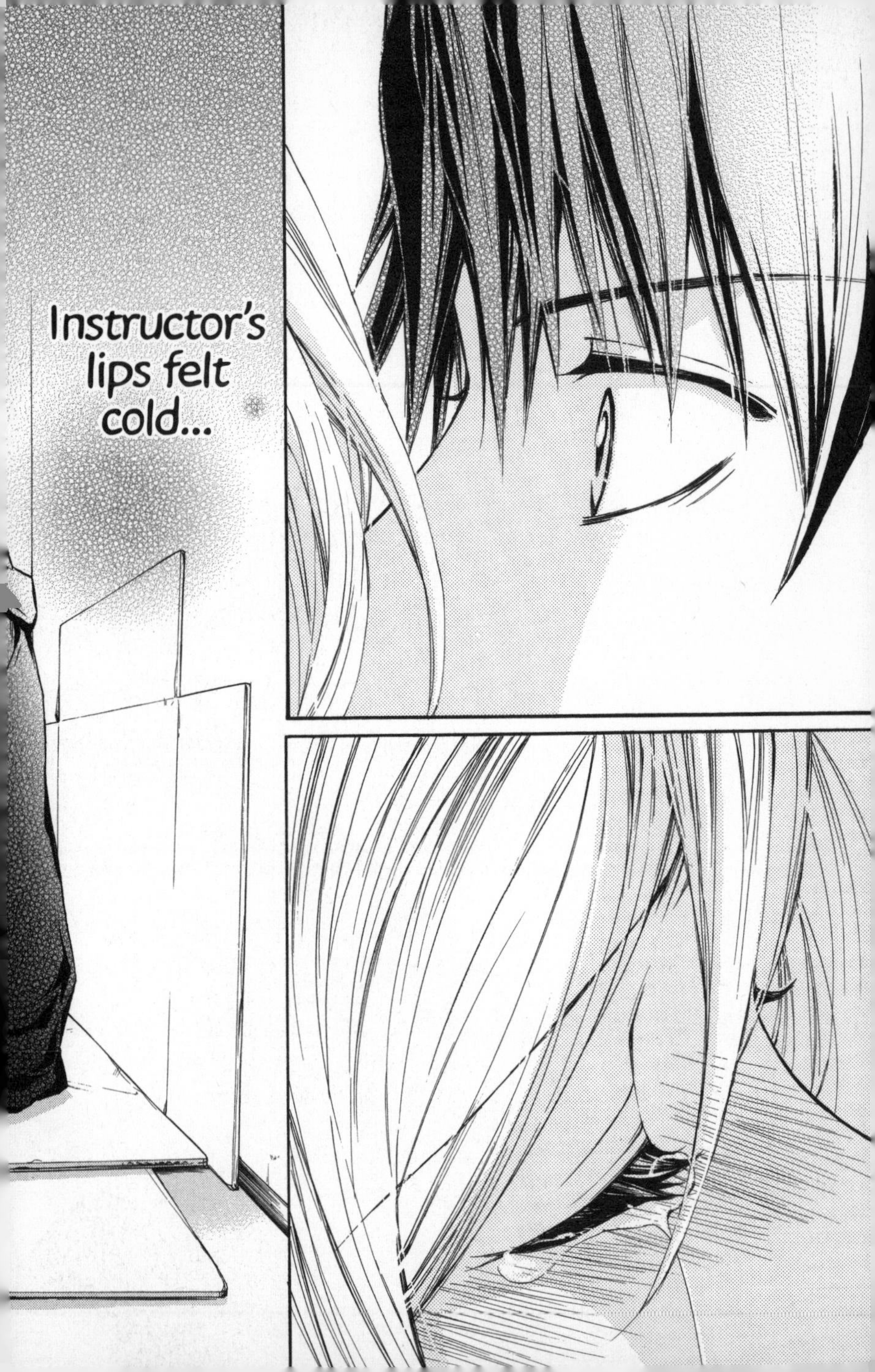
Instructor's lips felt cold...

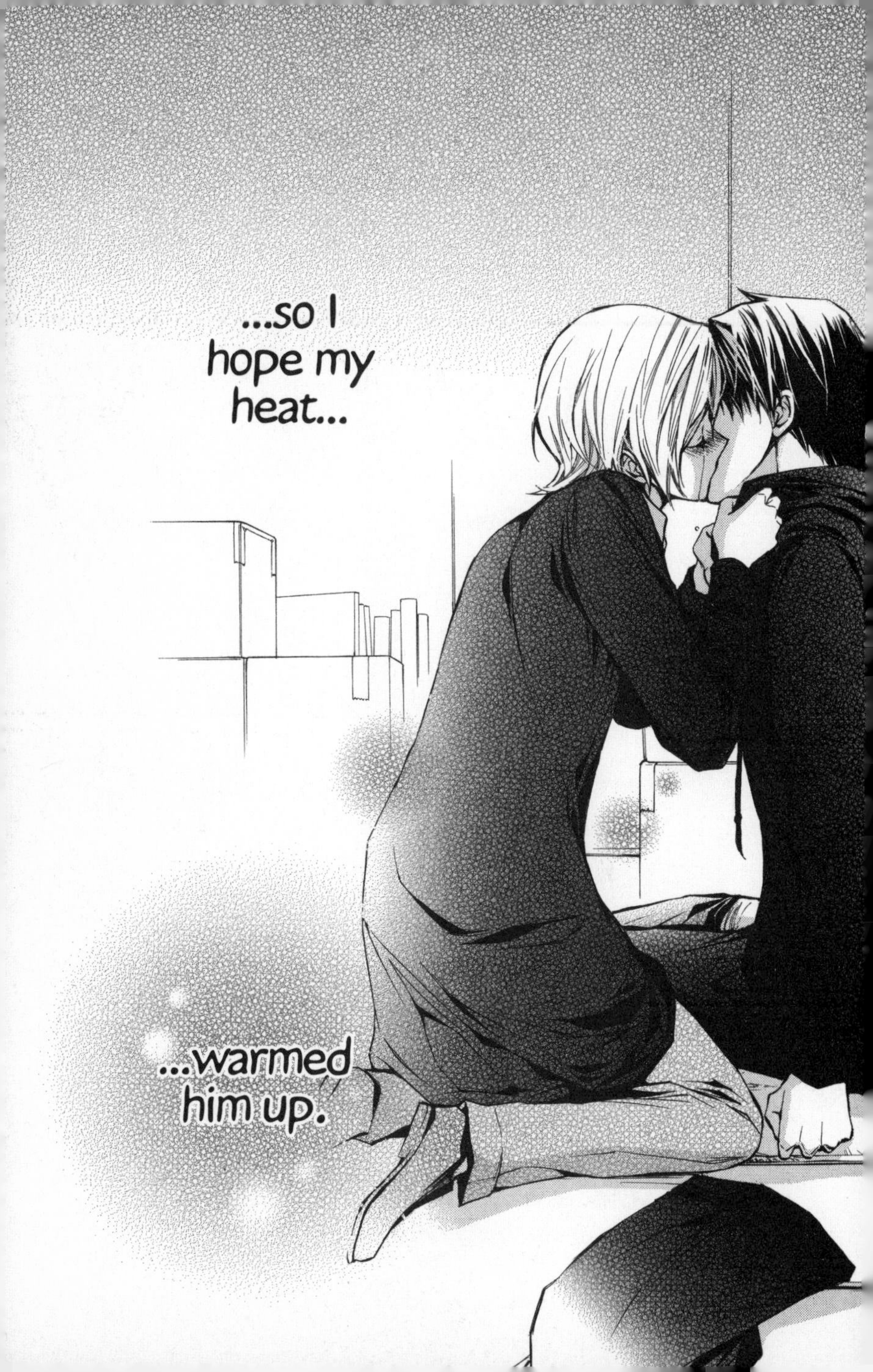
...so I hope my heat...
...warmed him up.

Secret Admirer part 13

I was carrying out my mission even as a sense of foreboding assailed me.

Looking back, I think I pretended not to notice...

...what had caused it.

Is this foreshadowing my death?!

✻ Searching for Mr. Toma.

Don't look for Moburo in Chapters 66 or 67!
He isn't there!

CHAPTER 67

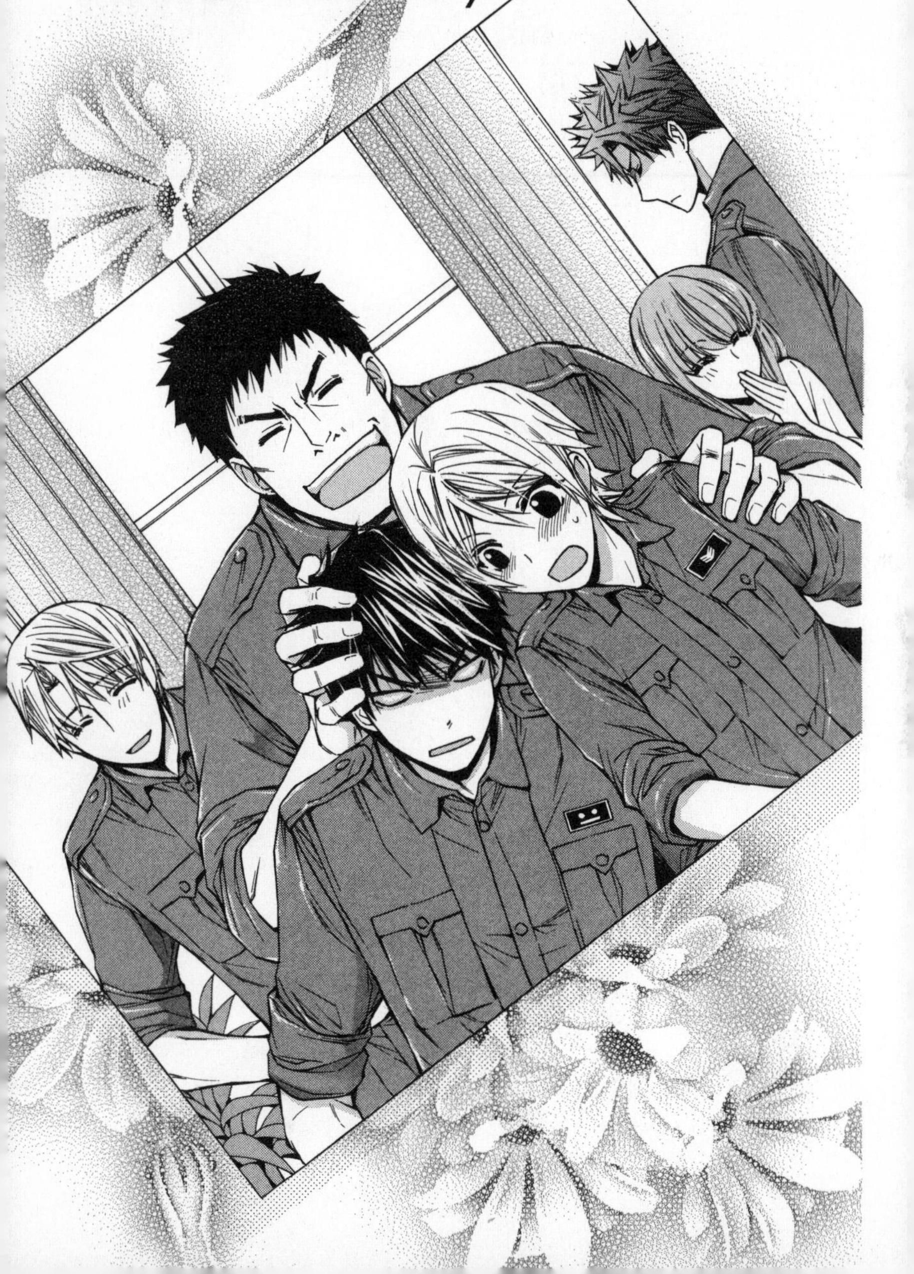

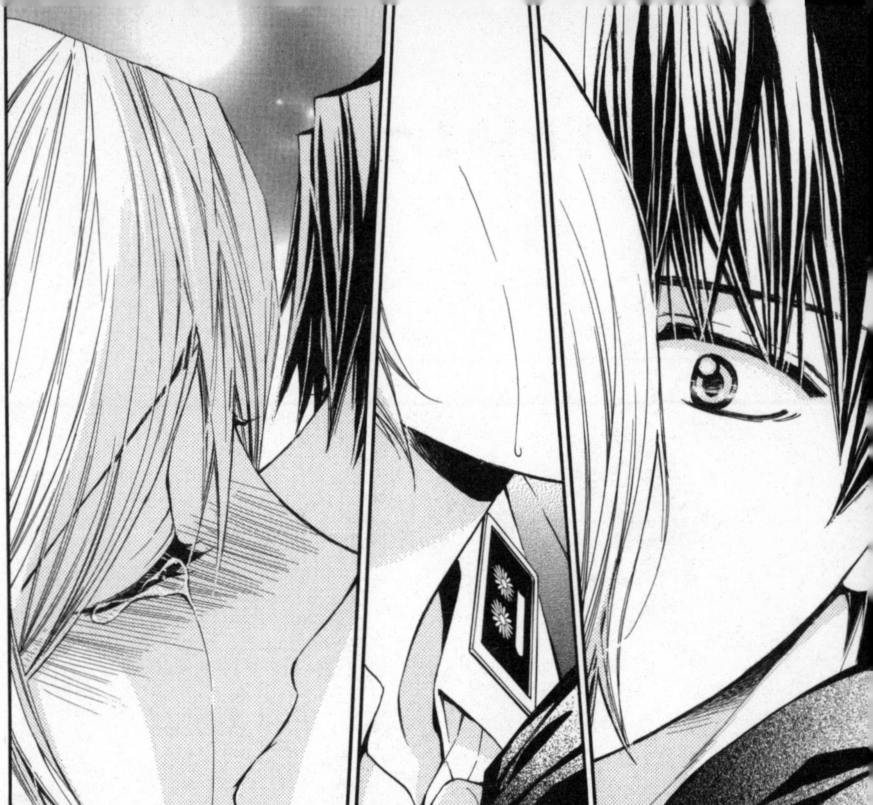

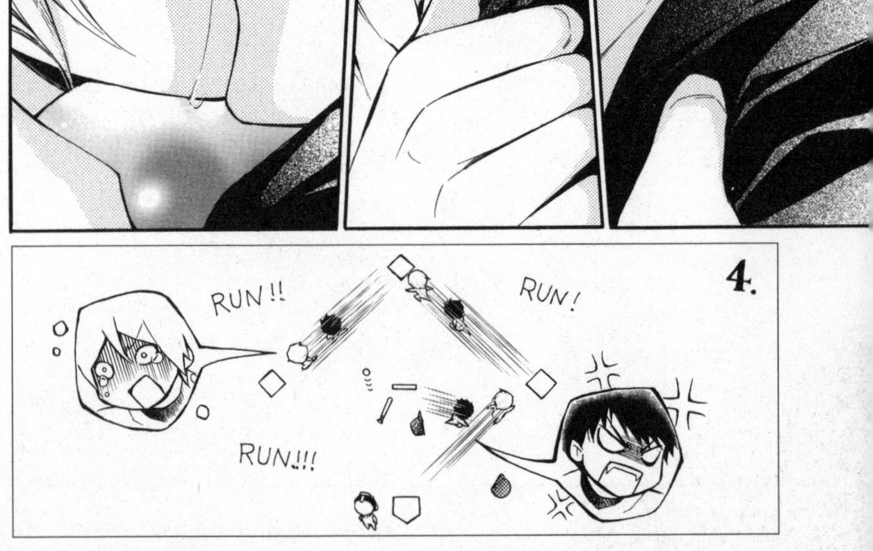
4.
RUN!
RUN!!
RUN!!!

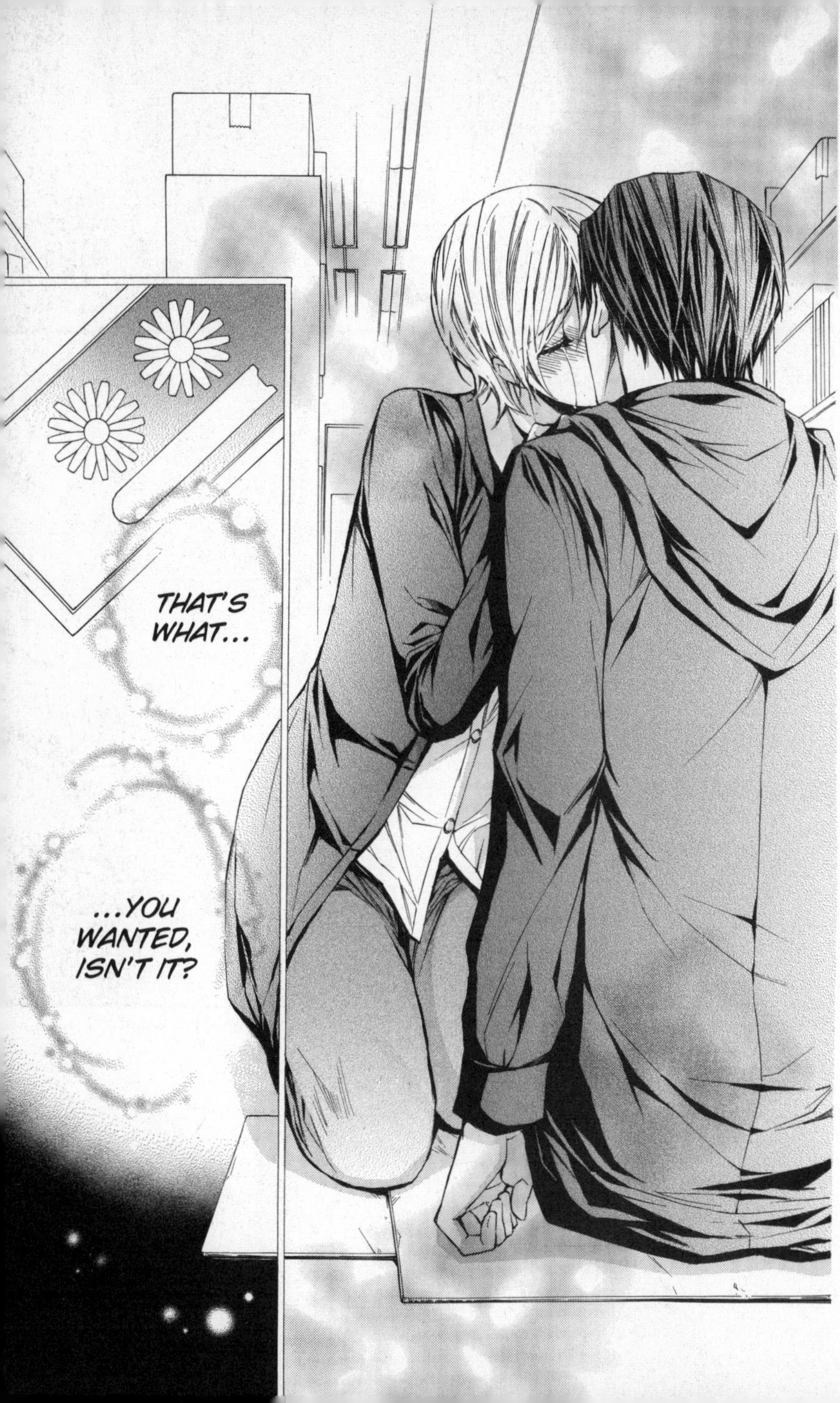
THAT'S WHAT...
...YOU WANTED, ISN'T IT?

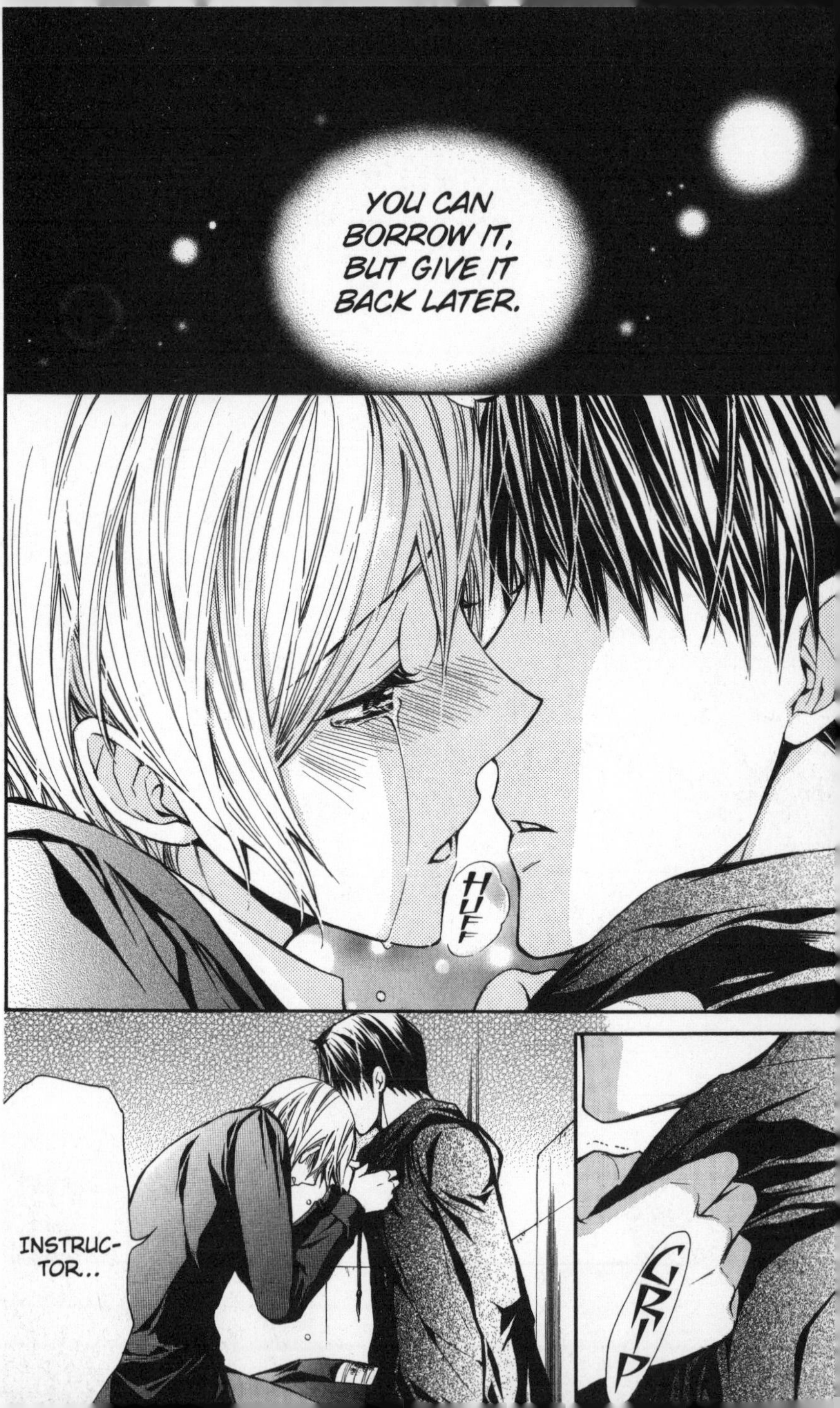
YOU CAN BORROW IT, BUT GIVE IT BACK LATER.
HUFF
GRIP
INSTRUCTOR...

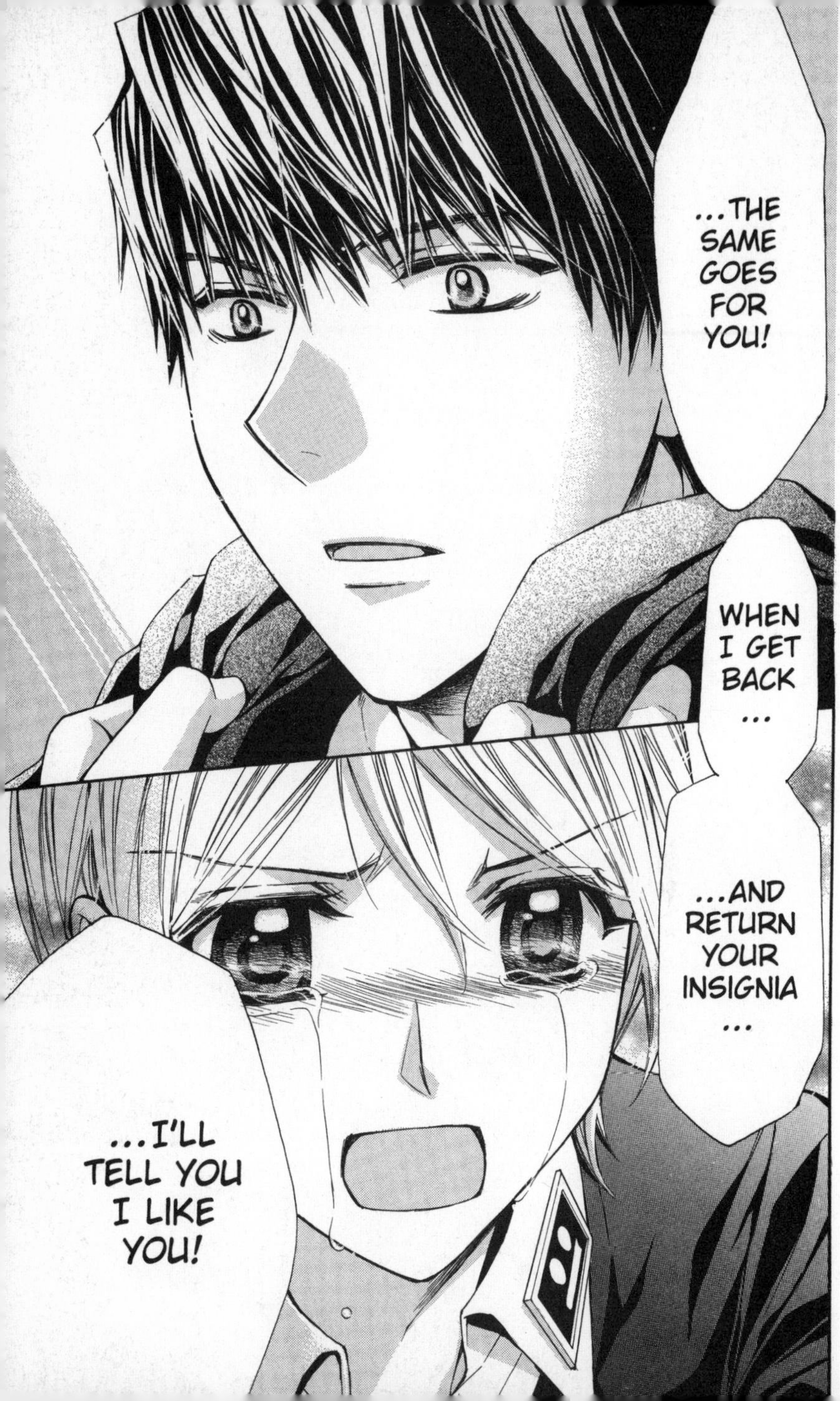
...THE SAME GOES FOR YOU!
WHEN I GET BACK ...
...AND RETURN YOUR INSIGNIA ...
...I'LL TELL YOU I LIKE YOU!

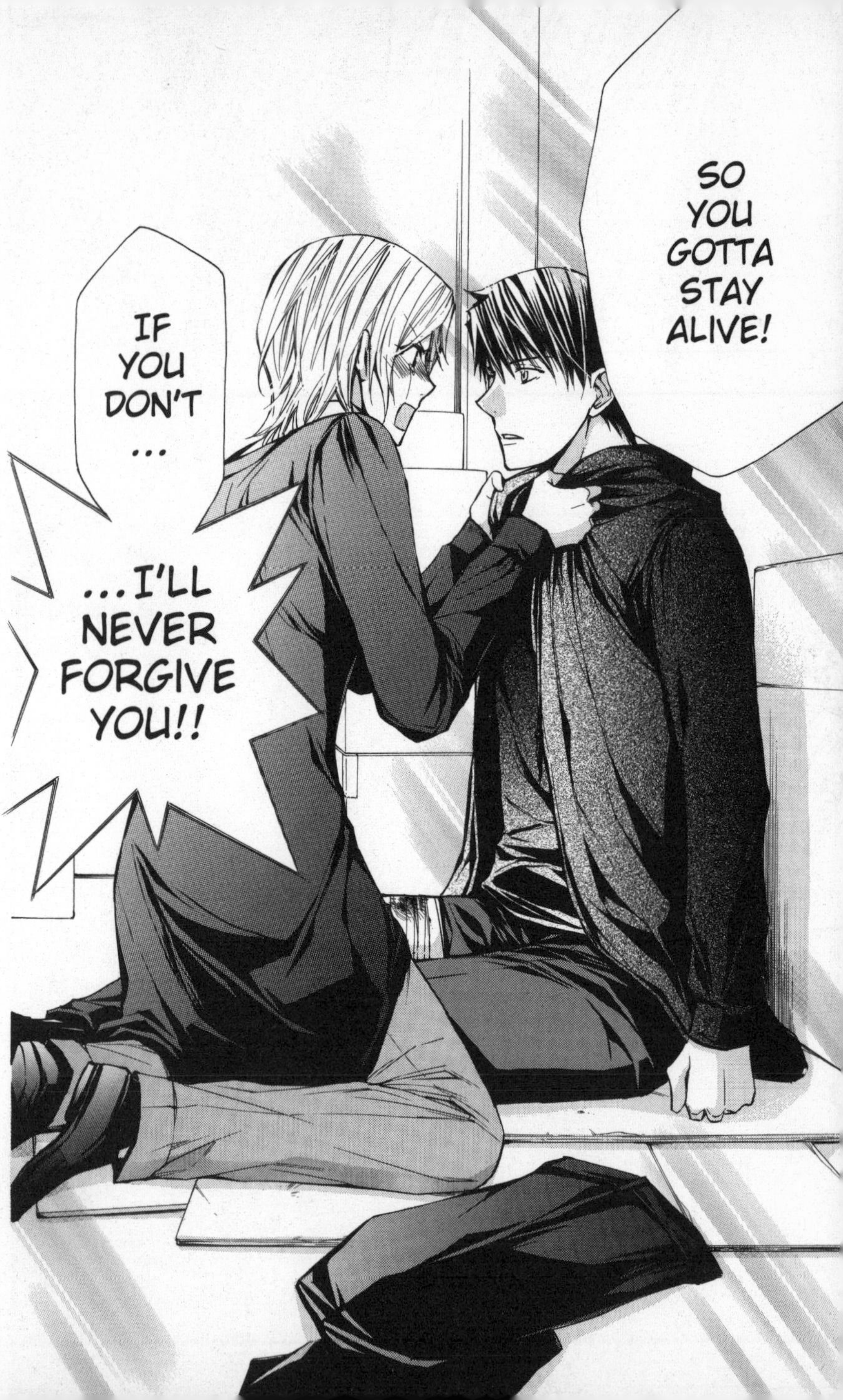
SO YOU GOTTA STAY ALIVE!
IF YOU DON'T ...
...I'LL NEVER FORGIVE YOU!!

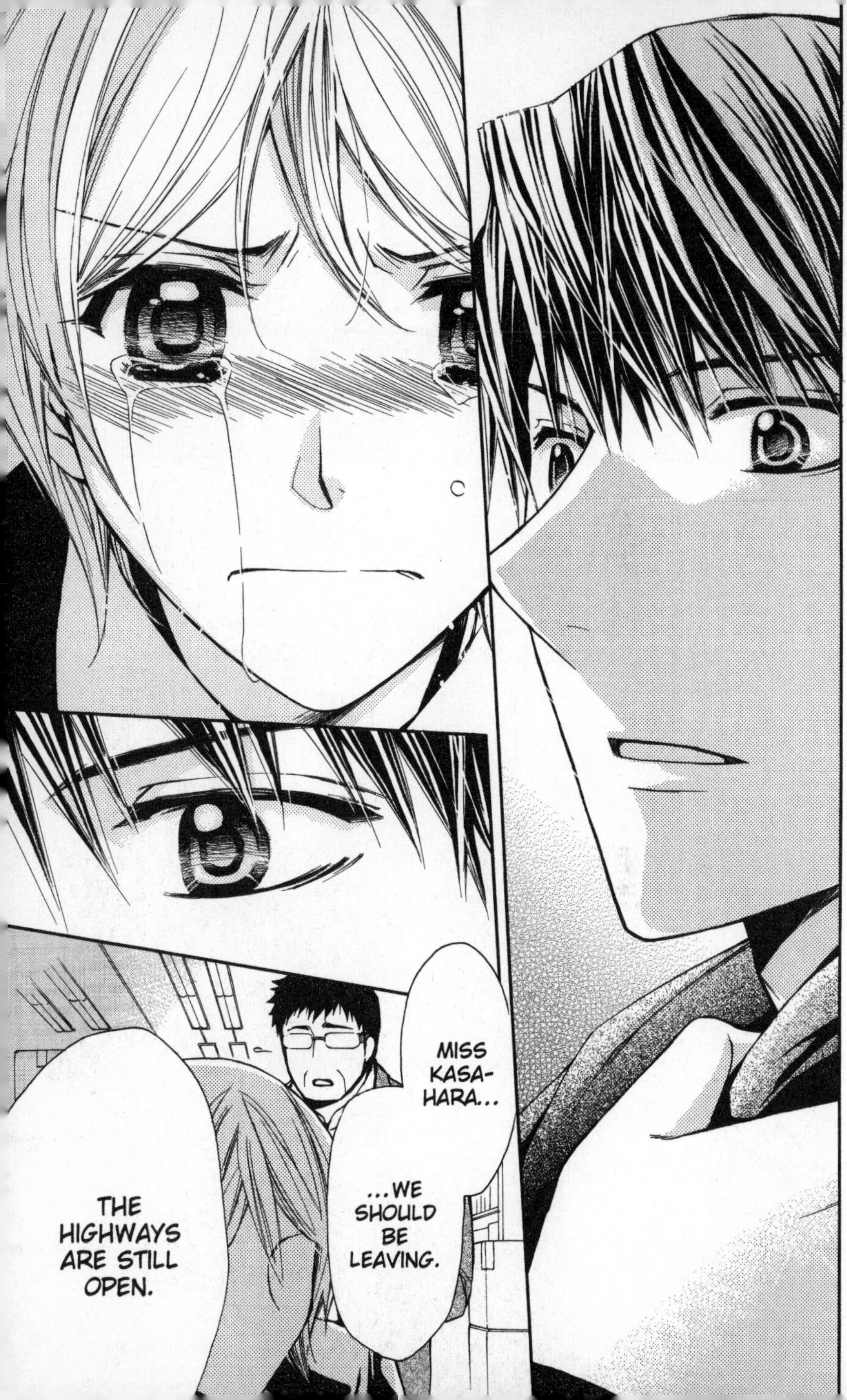
MISS KASA-HARA...
...WE SHOULD BE LEAVING.
THE HIGHWAYS ARE STILL OPEN.

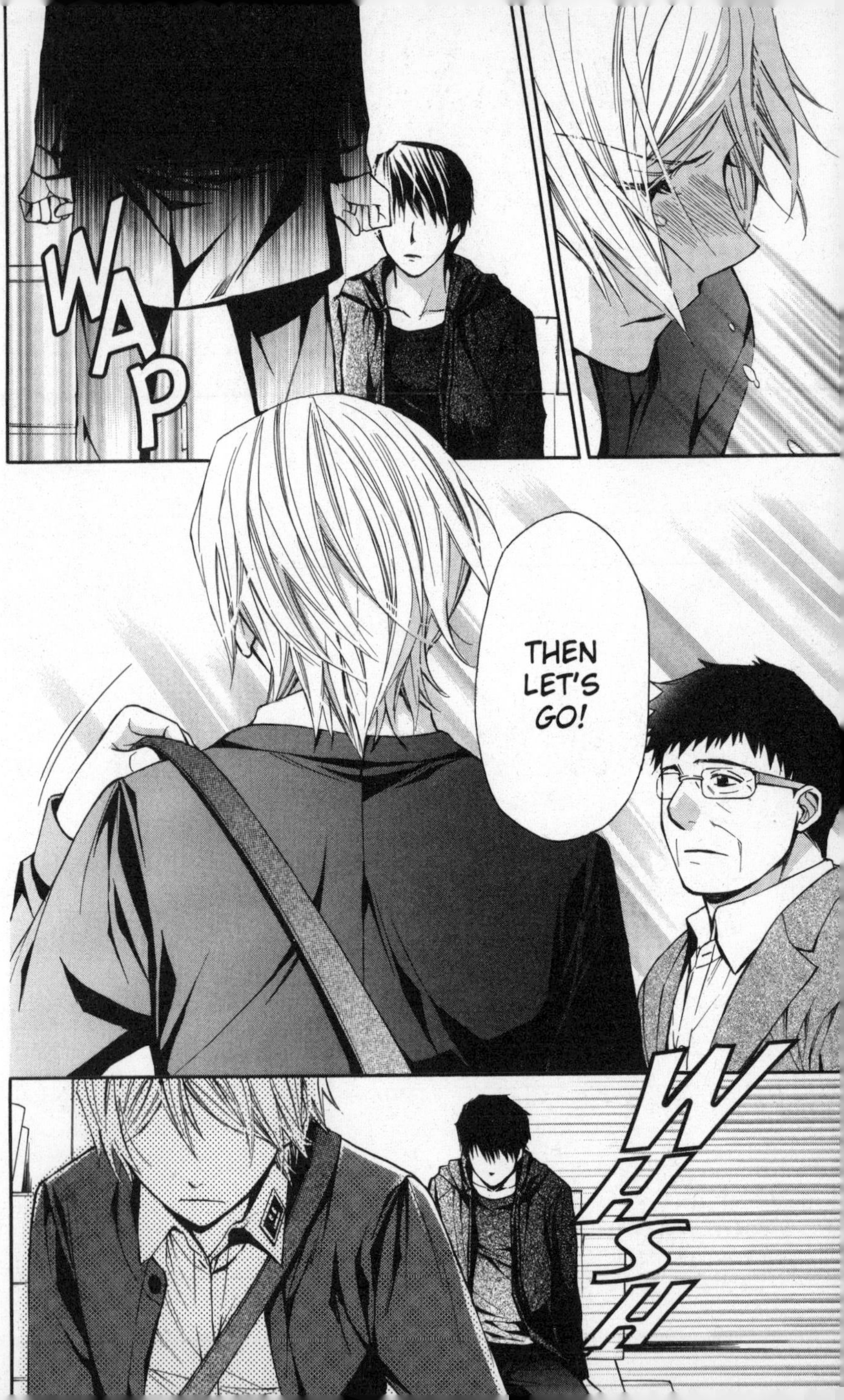
WAP
THEN LET'S GO!
WHSH

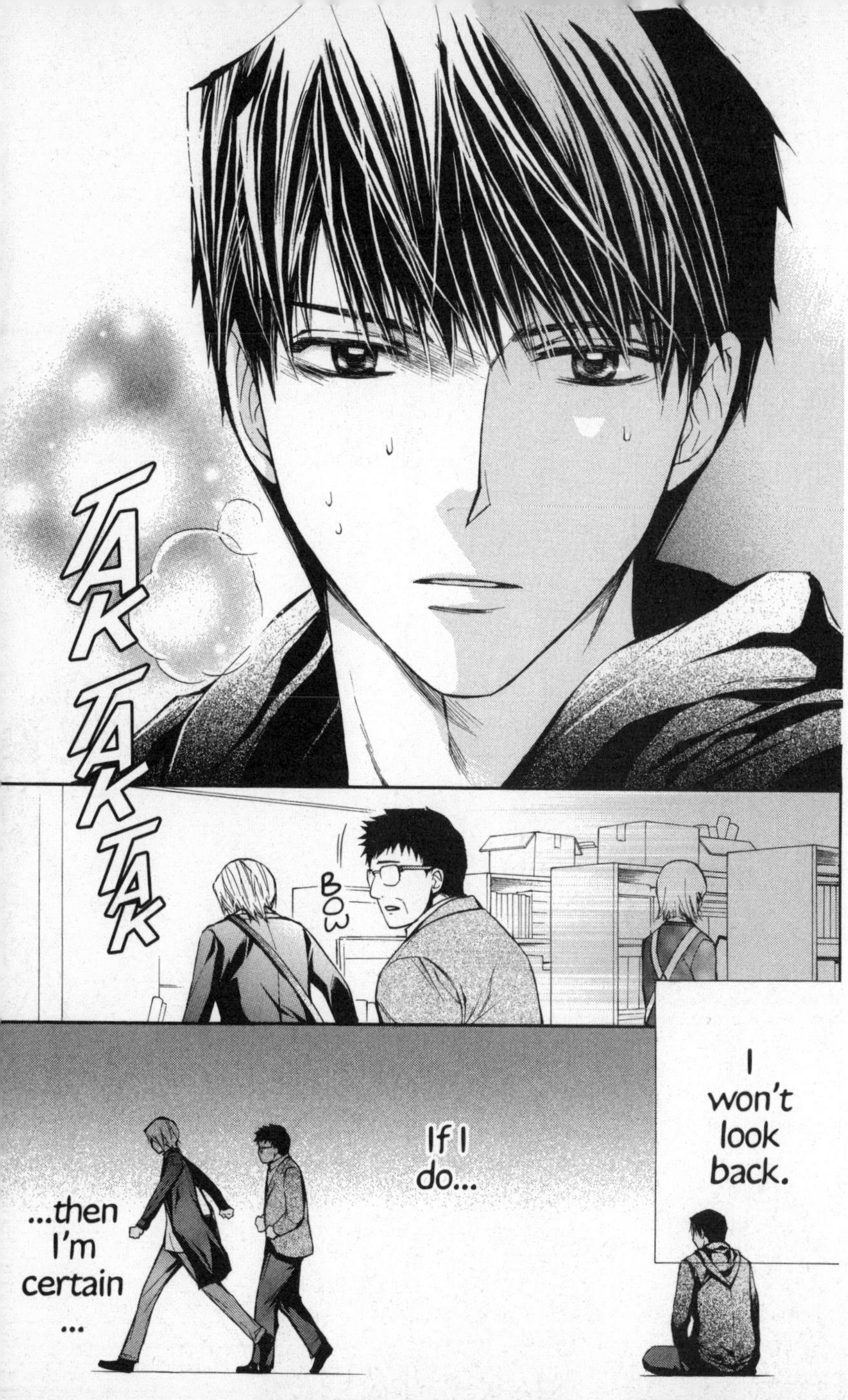
TAK TAK TAK
BOW
I won't look back.
If I do...
...then I'm certain ...

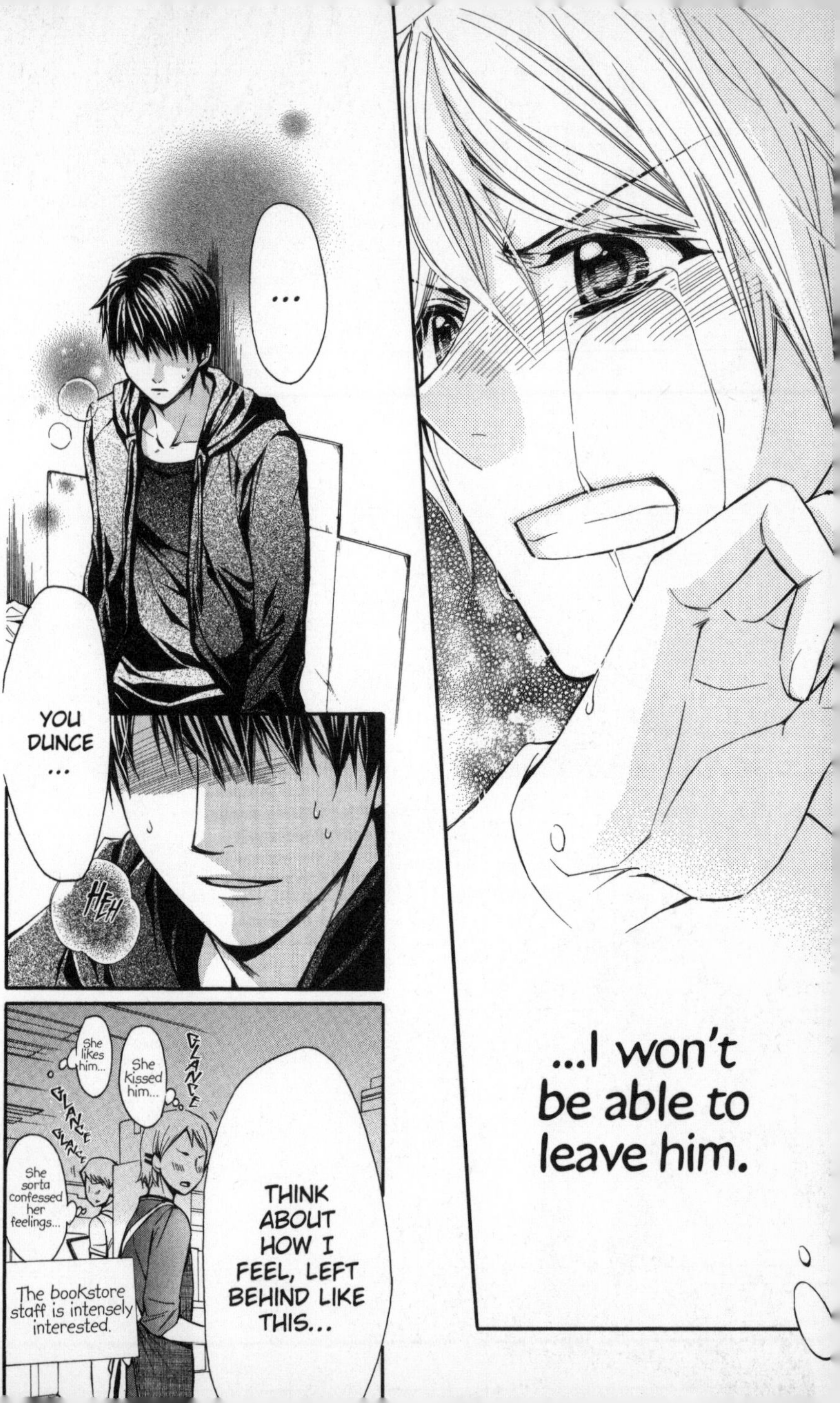
...I won't be able to leave him.
...
YOU DUNCE ...
HEH
THINK ABOUT HOW I FEEL, LEFT BEHIND LIKE THIS...
GLANCE
She kissed him...
She likes him...
She sorta confessed her feelings...
The bookstore staff is intensely interested.

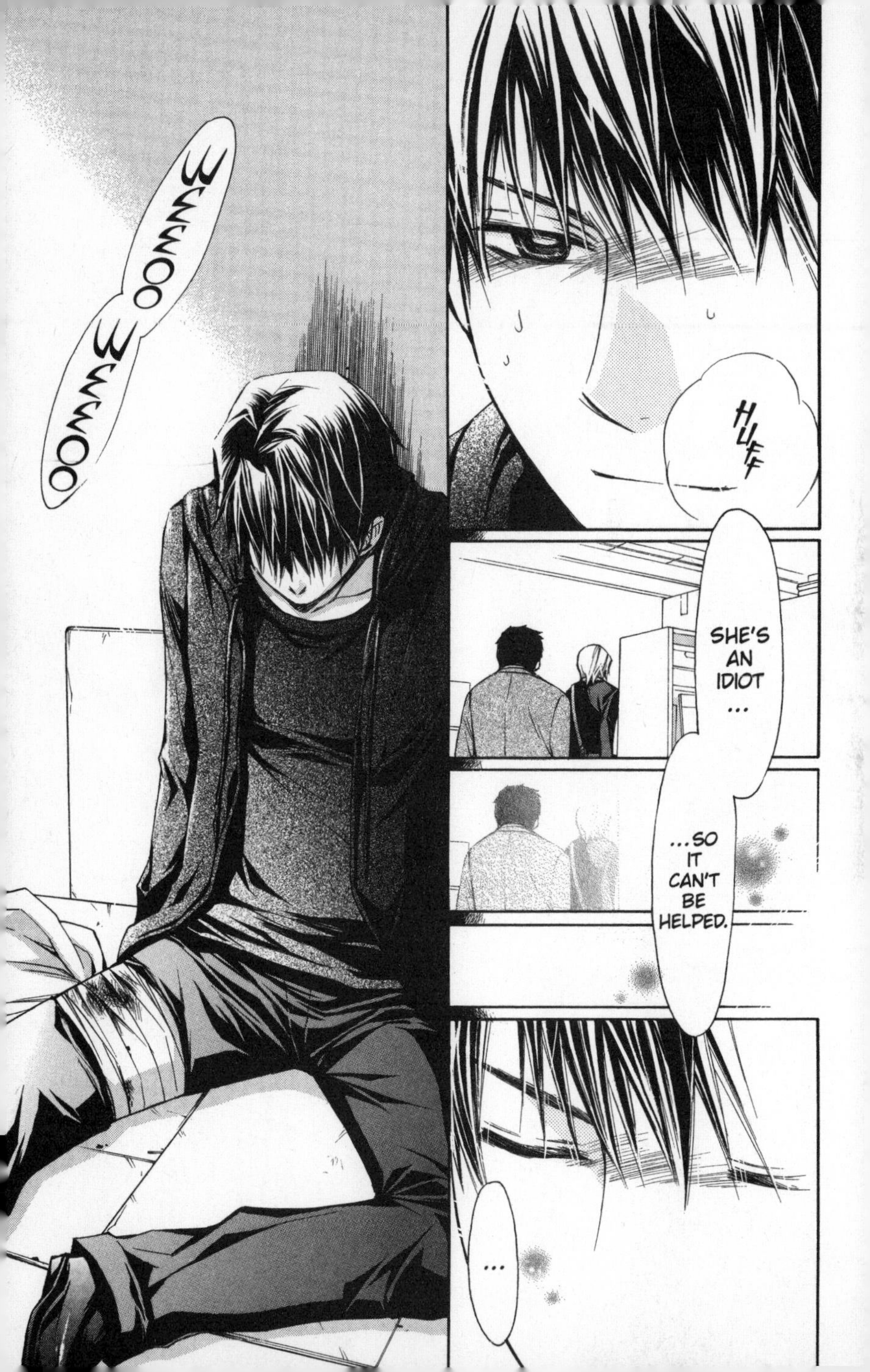
HUFF
SHE'S AN IDIOT...
...SO IT CAN'T BE HELPED.
...
WEEWOO WEEWOO

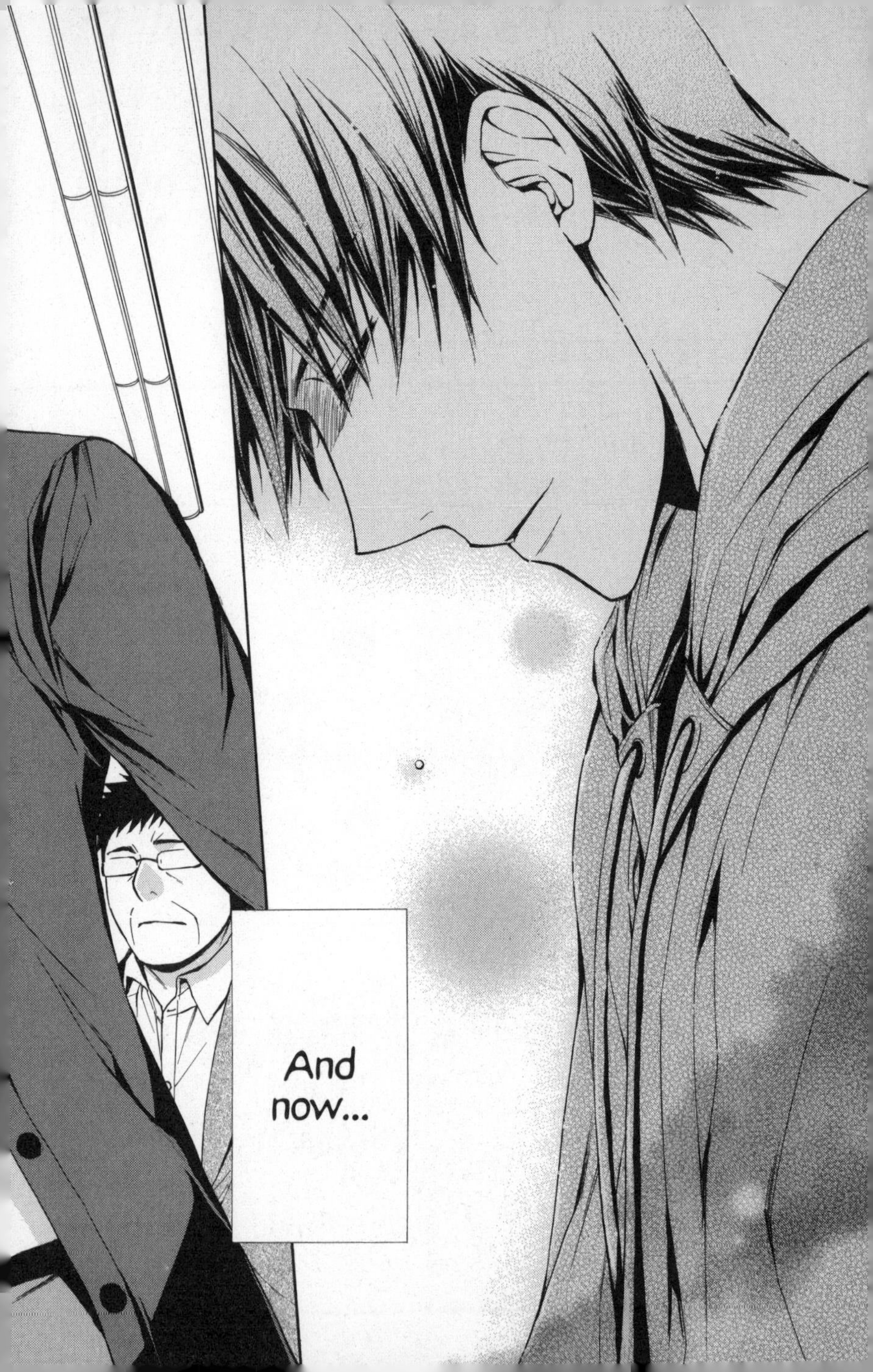
And now...

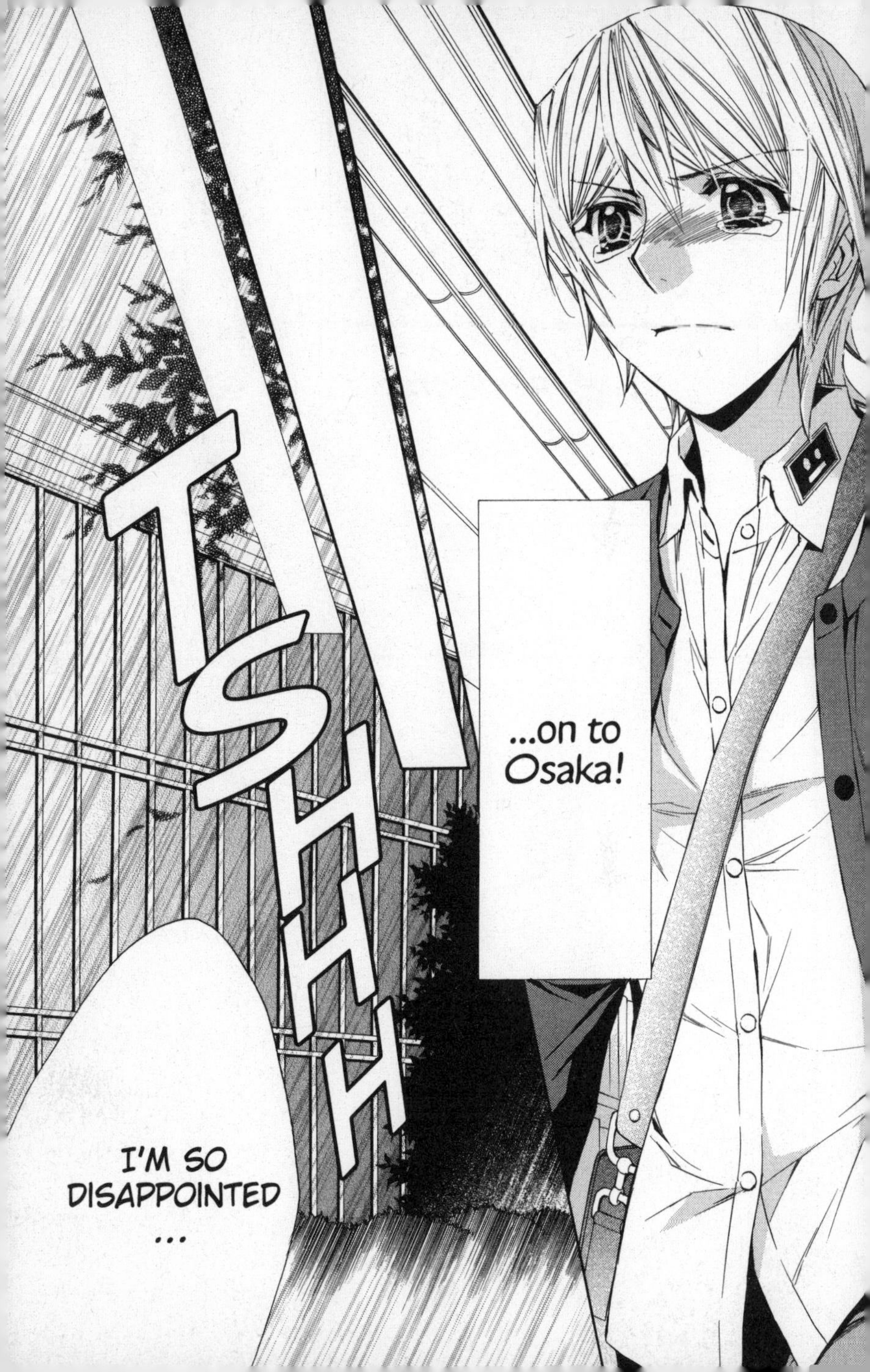
...on to Osaka!
TSHHH
I'M SO DISAPPOINTED ...

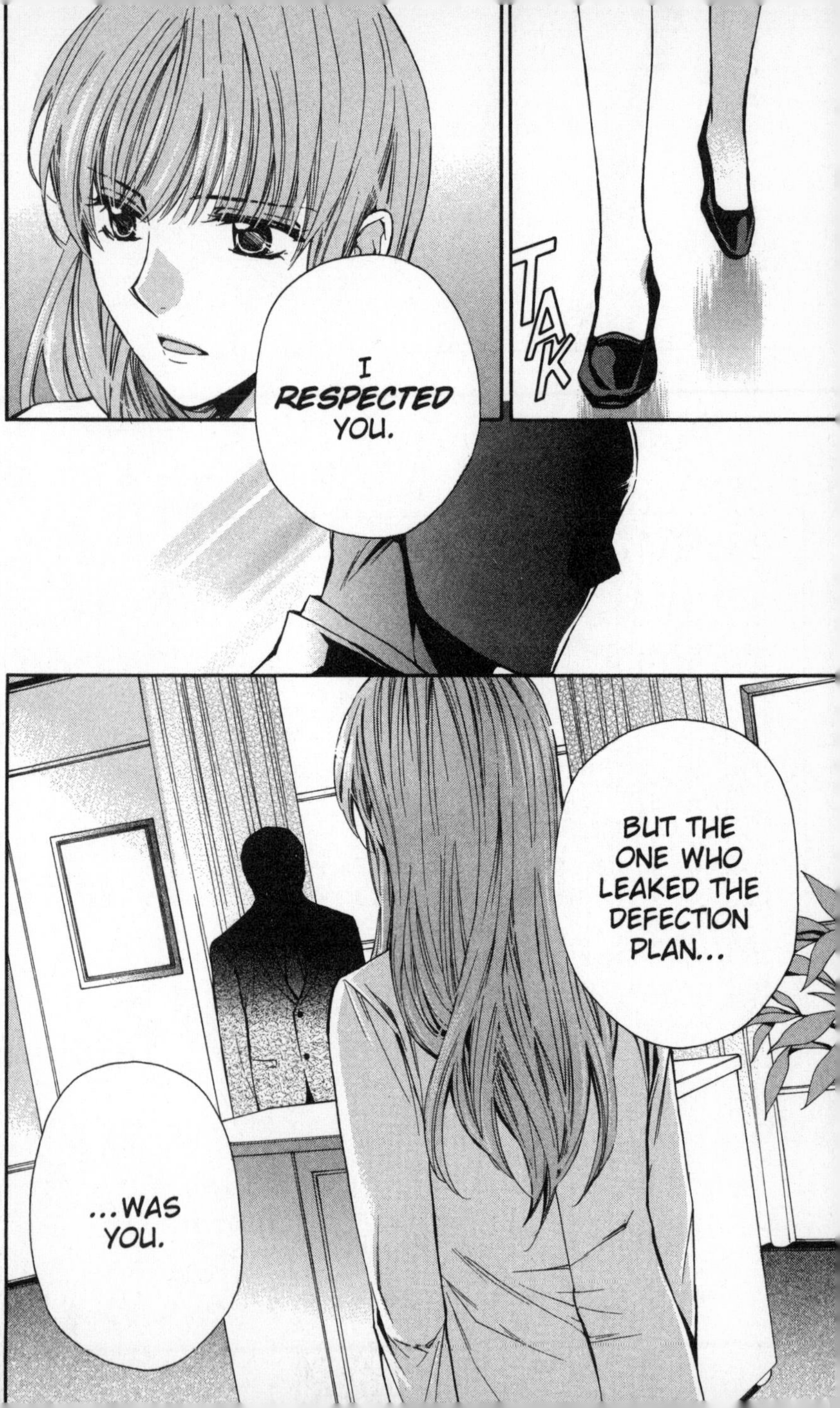
TAK
I RESPECTED YOU.
BUT THE ONE WHO LEAKED THE DEFECTION PLAN...
...WAS YOU.

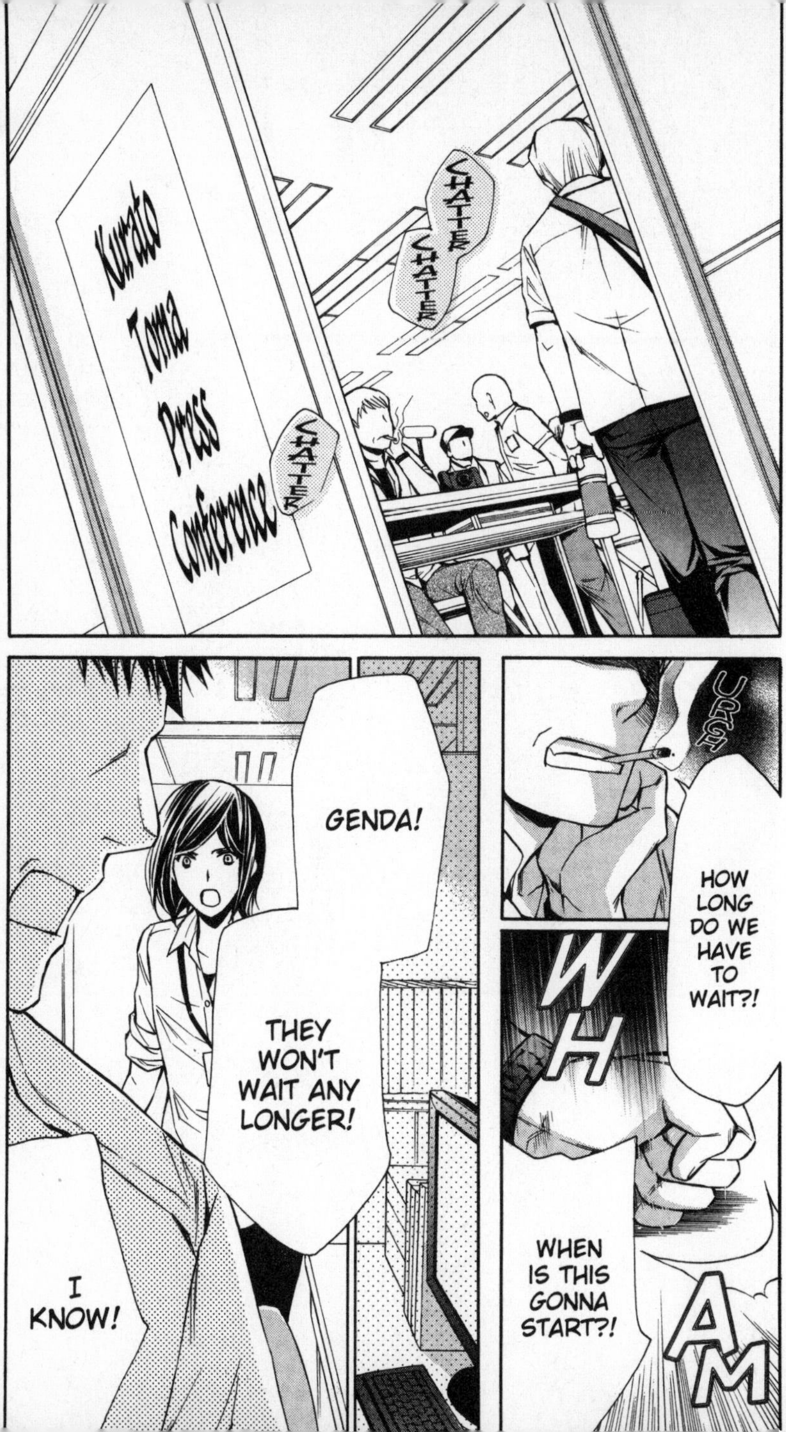
CHATTER
CHATTER
Kurato Toma Press Conference
CHATTER
URGH
HOW LONG DO WE HAVE TO WAIT?!
WHAM
WHEN IS THIS GONNA START?!
GENDA!
THEY WON'T WAIT ANY LONGER!
I KNOW!

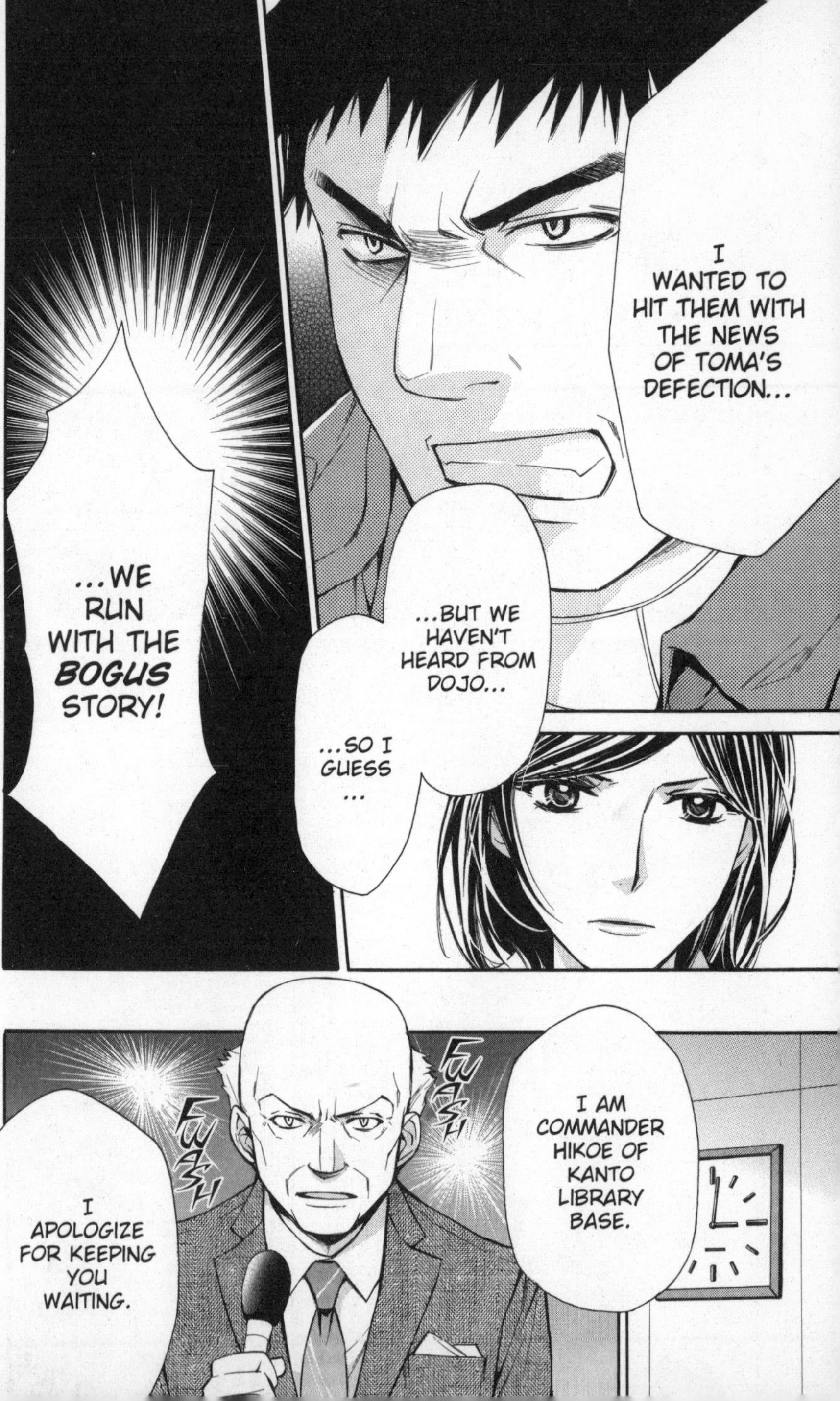
I WANTED TO HIT THEM WITH THE NEWS OF TOMA'S DEFECTION...
...BUT WE HAVEN'T HEARD FROM DOJO...
...SO I GUESS ...
...WE RUN WITH THE *BOGUS* STORY!
I AM COMMANDER HIKOE OF KANTO LIBRARY BASE.
FWASH
FWASH
I APOLOGIZE FOR KEEPING YOU WAITING.

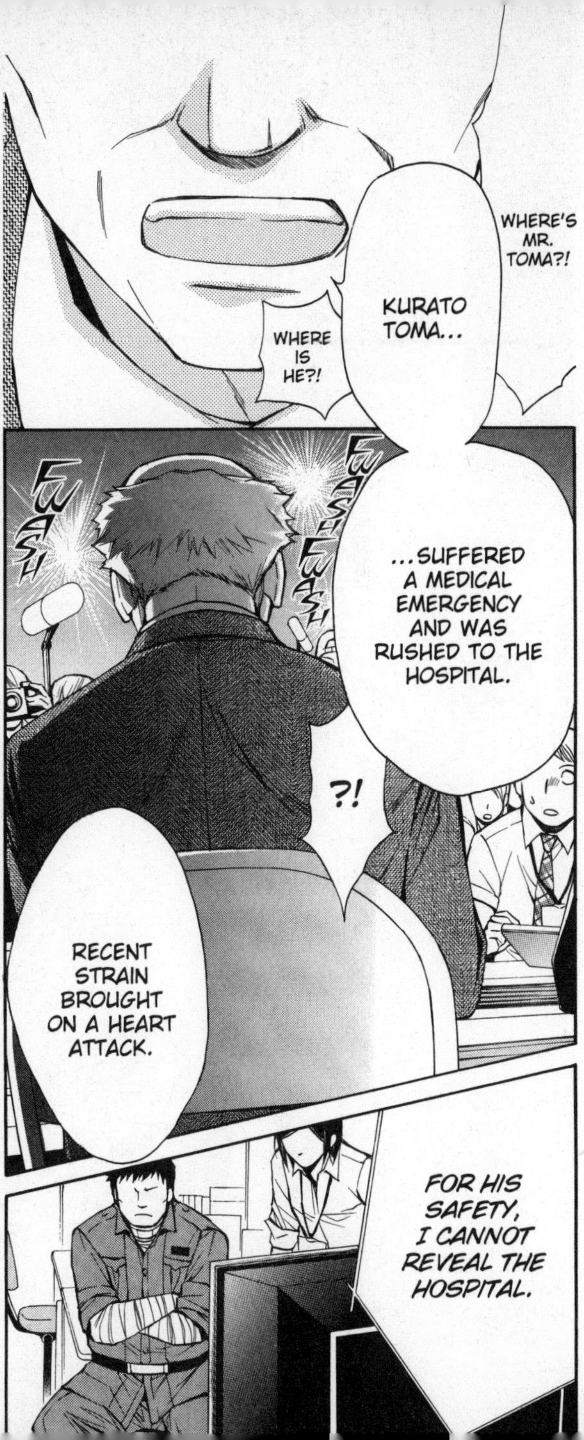
WHERE'S MR. TOMA?!
KURATO TOMA...
WHERE IS HE?!
FWASH
FWASH
FWASH
...SUFFERED A MEDICAL EMERGENCY AND WAS RUSHED TO THE HOSPITAL.
?!
RECENT STRAIN BROUGHT ON A HEART ATTACK.
FOR HIS SAFETY, I CANNOT REVEAL THE HOSPITAL.

5

*

This isn't very important, but the illustration on the back cover is summer-themed. (It was on the cover of *LaLa DX*.) If you ask me, it's of somewhat questionable moral taste, but that's all right.

After it was printed, I noticed there's no spoon for the parfait they're eating... so how are they gonna eat it? Huh? Just stick their faces in it?

*

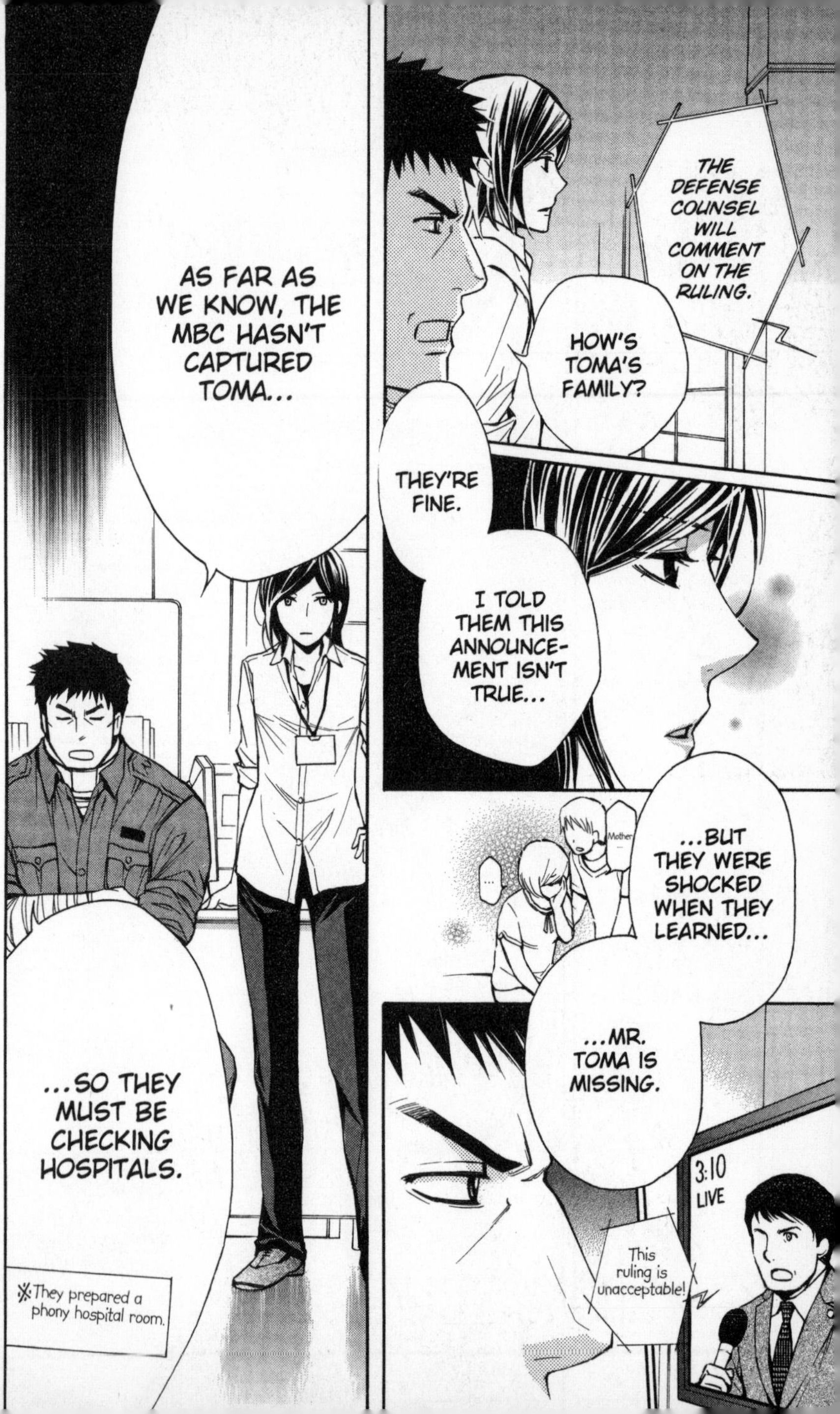
THE DEFENSE COUNSEL WILL COMMENT ON THE RULING.
HOW'S TOMA'S FAMILY?
THEY'RE FINE.
I TOLD THEM THIS ANNOUNCEMENT ISN'T TRUE...
...BUT THEY WERE SHOCKED WHEN THEY LEARNED...
Mother...
...
...MR. TOMA IS MISSING.
3:10
LIVE
This ruling is unacceptable!
AS FAR AS WE KNOW, THE MBC HASN'T CAPTURED TOMA...
...SO THEY MUST BE CHECKING HOSPITALS.
※They prepared a phony hospital room.

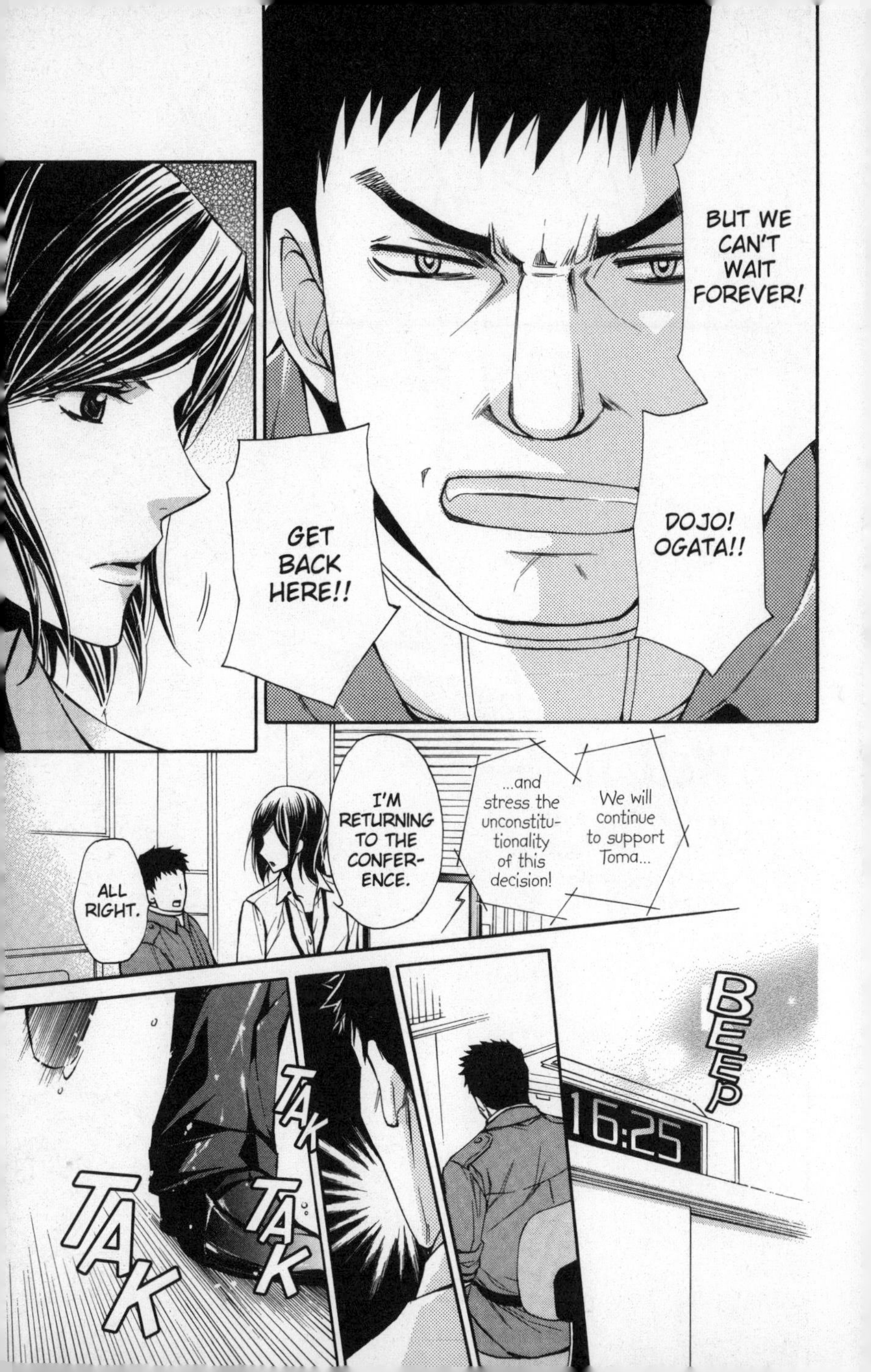
BUT WE CAN'T WAIT FOREVER!
DOJO! OGATA!!
GET BACK HERE!!
We will continue to support Toma...
...and stress the unconstitutionality of this decision!
I'M RETURNING TO THE CONFERENCE.
ALL RIGHT.
BEEP
16:25
TAK
TAK
TAK
TAK

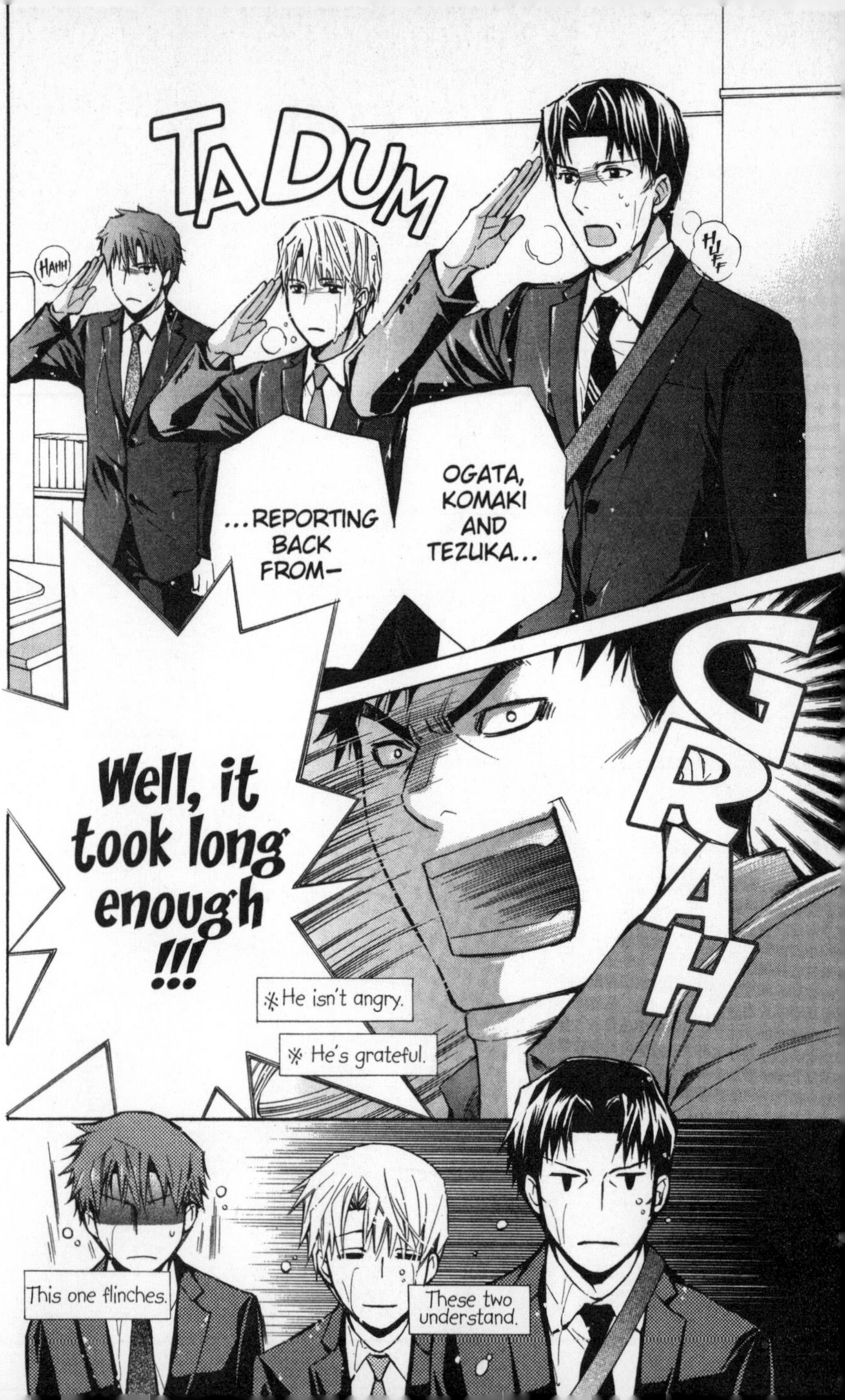
TA DUM
HUFF
HAHH
OGATA, KOMAKI AND TEZUKA...
...REPORTING BACK FROM—
GRAH
Well, it took long enough!!!
※ He isn't angry.
※ He's grateful.
These two understand.
This one flinches.

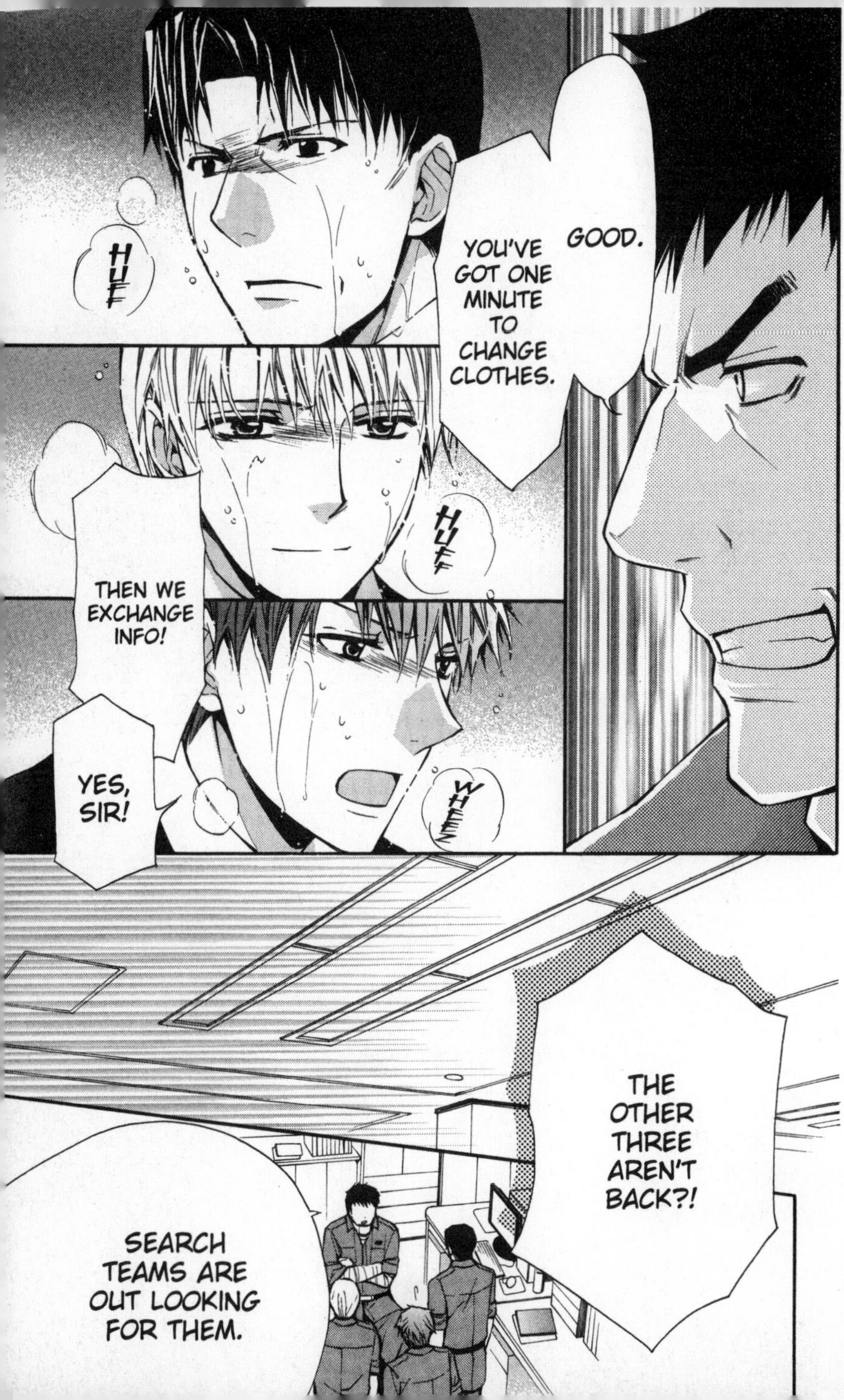
GOOD. YOU'VE GOT ONE MINUTE TO CHANGE CLOTHES.
HUFF
HUFF
THEN WE EXCHANGE INFO!
WHEEZ
YES, SIR!
THE OTHER THREE AREN'T BACK?!
SEARCH TEAMS ARE OUT LOOKING FOR THEM.

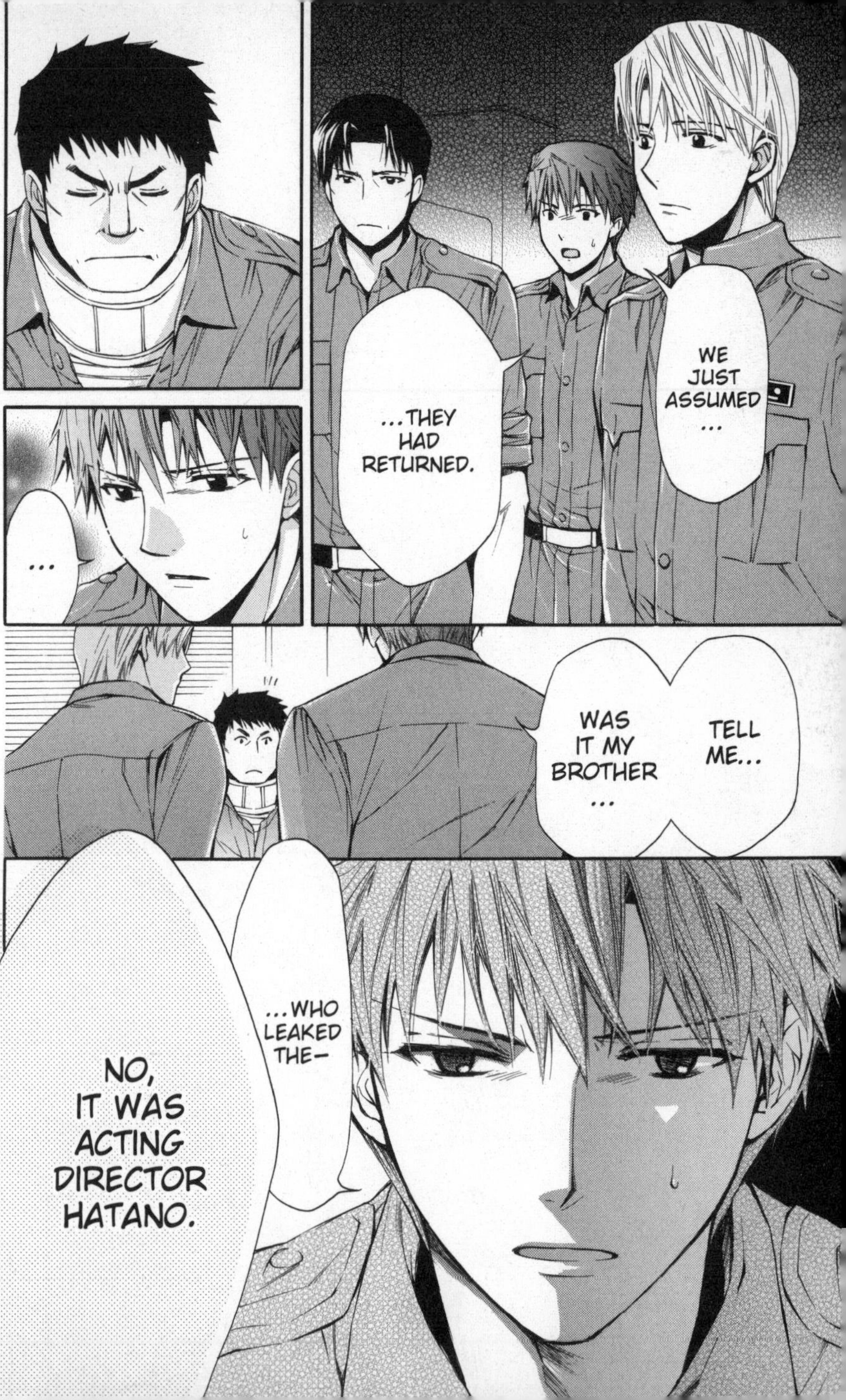
WE JUST ASSUMED...
...THEY HAD RETURNED.
...
TELL ME...
WAS IT MY BROTHER...
...WHO LEAKED THE–
NO, IT WAS ACTING DIRECTOR HATANO.

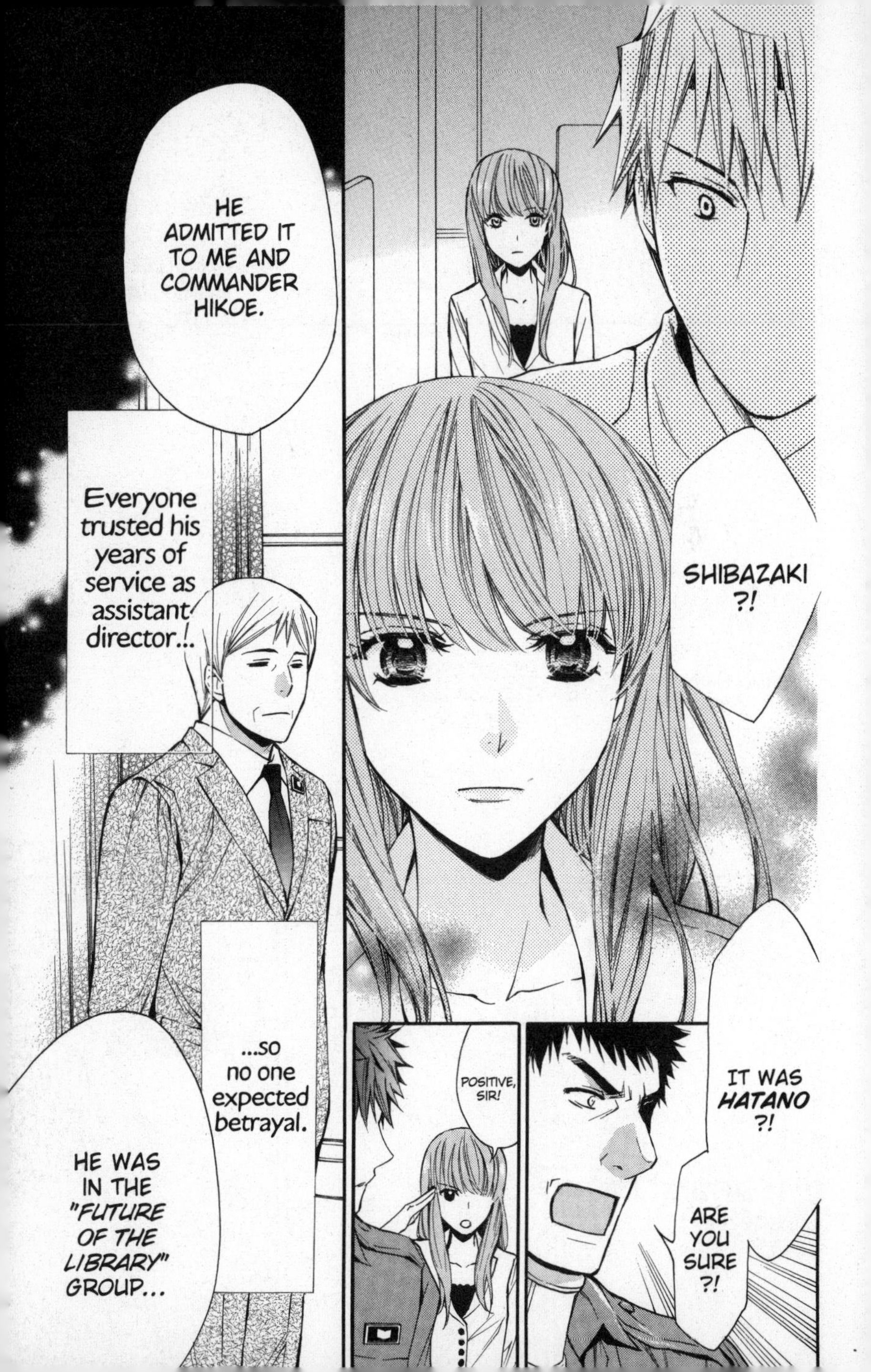
SHIBAZAKI ?!
IT WAS HATANO ?!
ARE YOU SURE ?!
POSITIVE, SIR!
HE ADMITTED IT TO ME AND COMMANDER HIKOE.
Everyone trusted his years of service as assistant director...
...so no one expected betrayal.
HE WAS IN THE "FUTURE OF THE LIBRARY" GROUP...

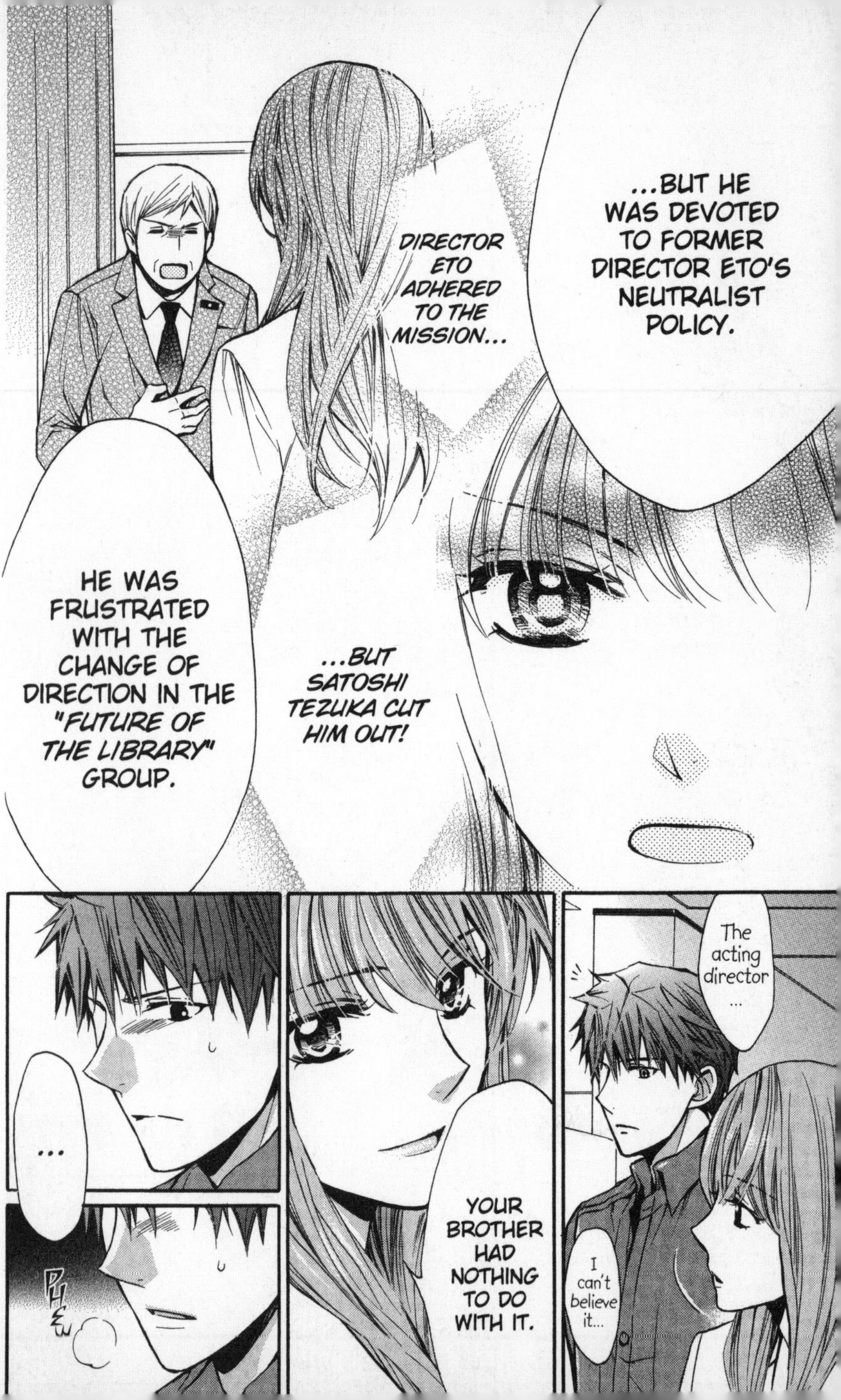
...BUT HE WAS DEVOTED TO FORMER DIRECTOR ETO'S NEUTRALIST POLICY.
DIRECTOR ETO ADHERED TO THE MISSION...
...BUT SATOSHI TEZUKA CUT HIM OUT!
HE WAS FRUSTRATED WITH THE CHANGE OF DIRECTION IN THE "FUTURE OF THE LIBRARY" GROUP.
The acting director ...
I can't believe it...
YOUR BROTHER HAD NOTHING TO DO WITH IT.
...
PHEW

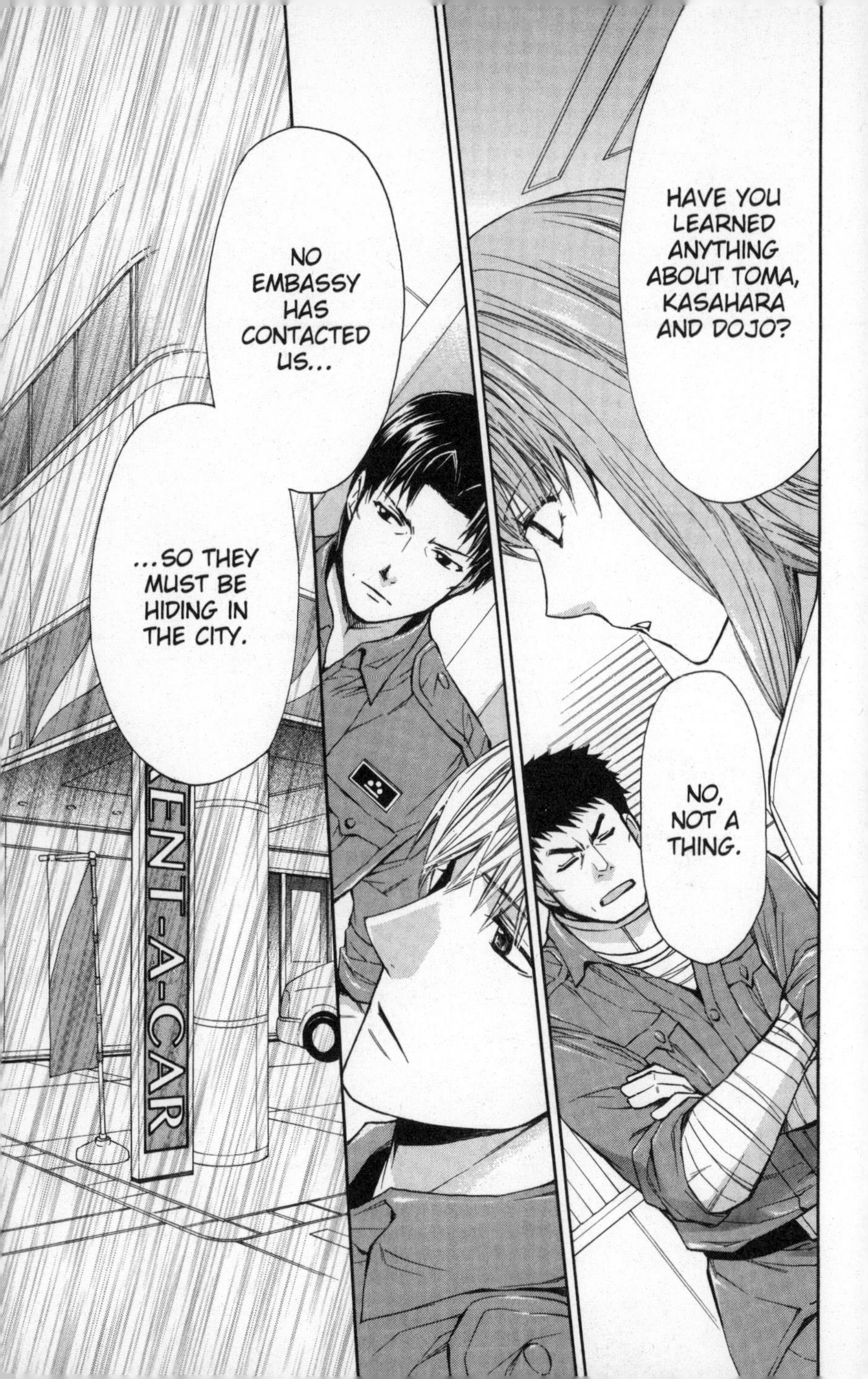
HAVE YOU LEARNED ANYTHING ABOUT TOMA, KASAHARA AND DOJO?
NO, NOT A THING.
NO EMBASSY HAS CONTACTED US...
...SO THEY MUST BE HIDING IN THE CITY.

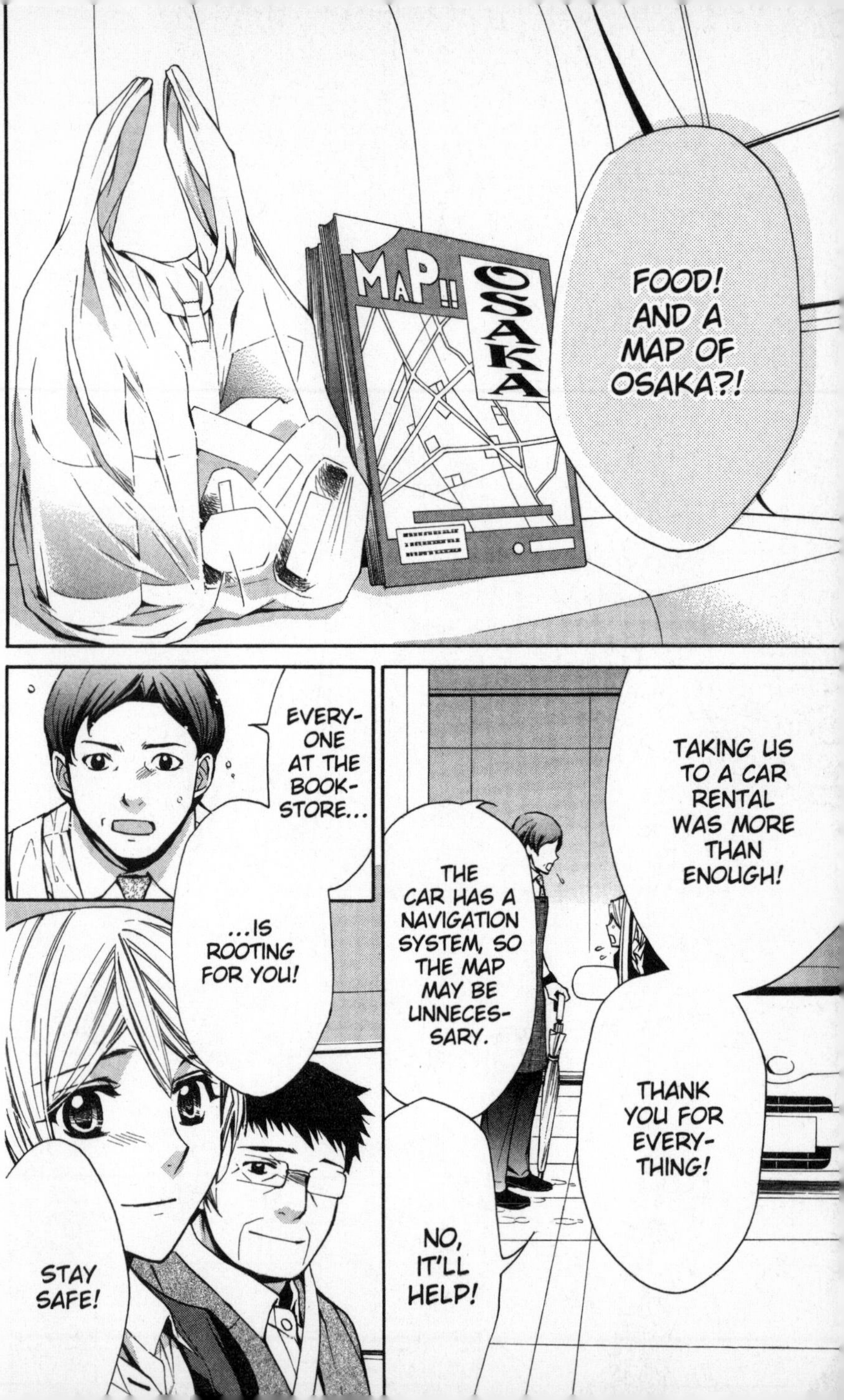
MAP!!
OSAKA
FOOD! AND A MAP OF OSAKA?!
TAKING US TO A CAR RENTAL WAS MORE THAN ENOUGH!
THE CAR HAS A NAVIGATION SYSTEM, SO THE MAP MAY BE UNNECES-SARY.
THANK YOU FOR EVERY-THING!
NO, IT'LL HELP!
EVERY-ONE AT THE BOOK-STORE...
...IS ROOTING FOR YOU!
STAY SAFE!

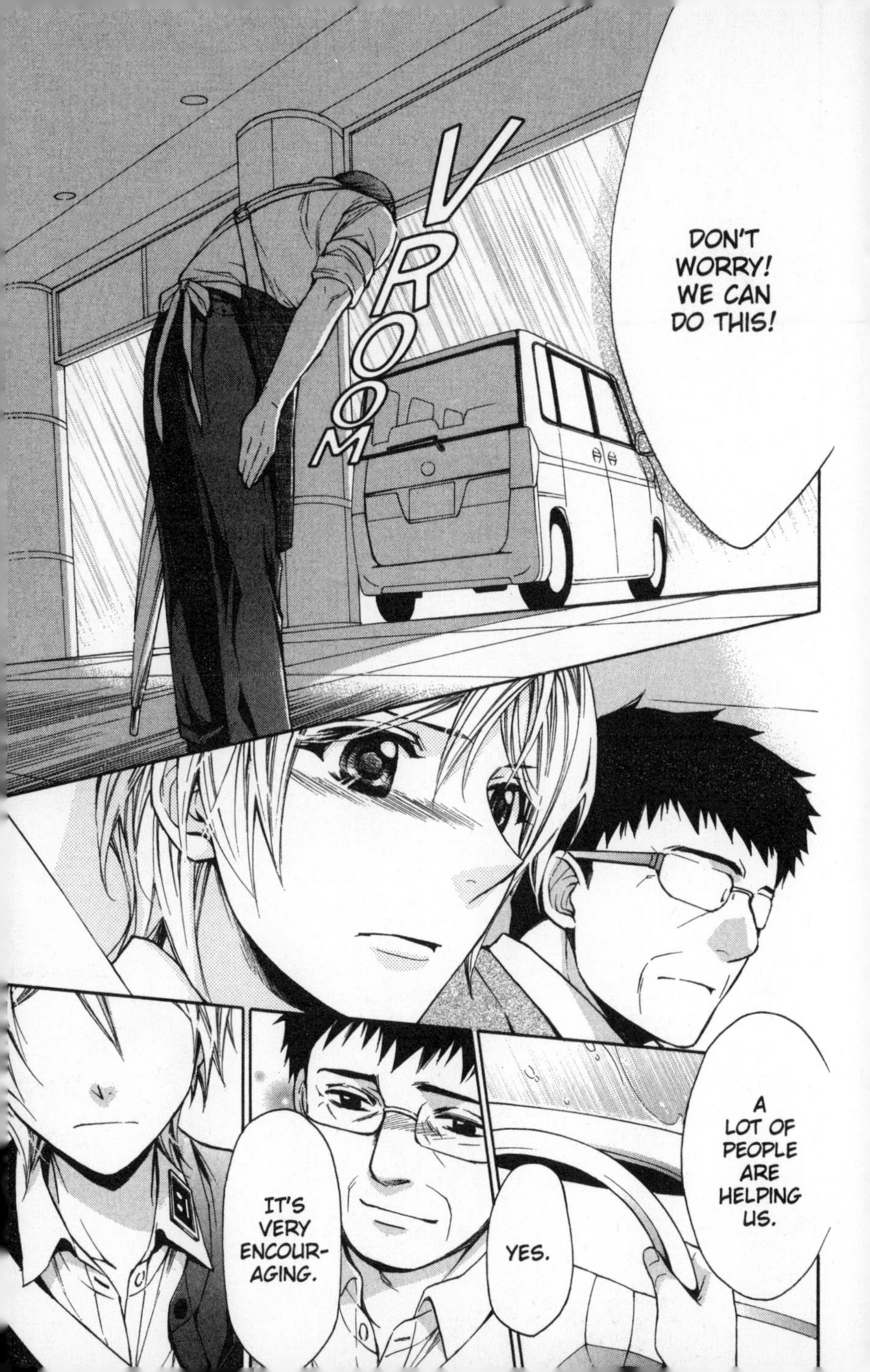
DON'T WORRY! WE CAN DO THIS!
VROOM
A LOT OF PEOPLE ARE HELPING US.
YES.
IT'S VERY ENCOURAGING.

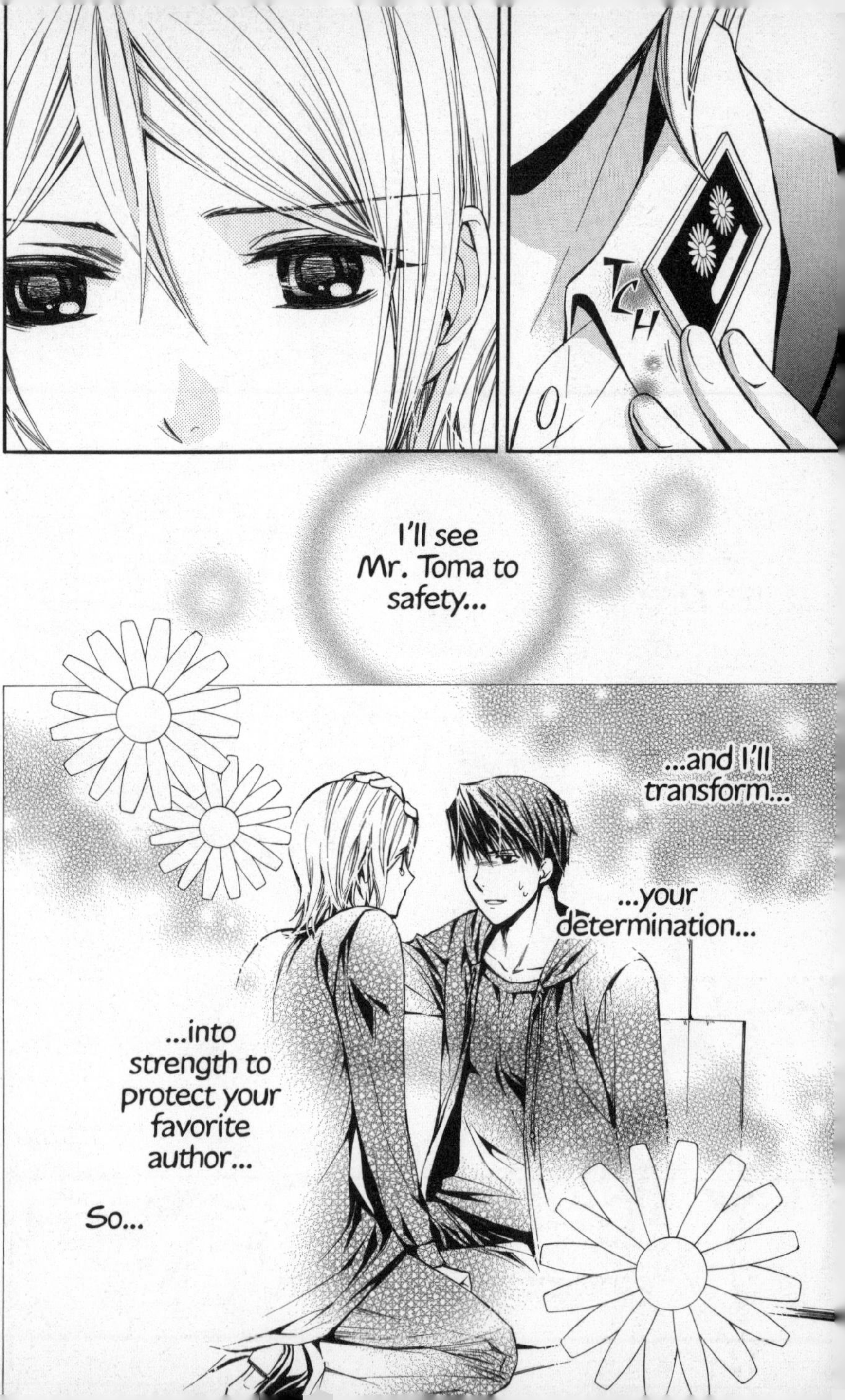
TCH
I'll see Mr. Toma to safety...
...and I'll transform...
...your determination...
...into strength to protect your favorite author...
So...

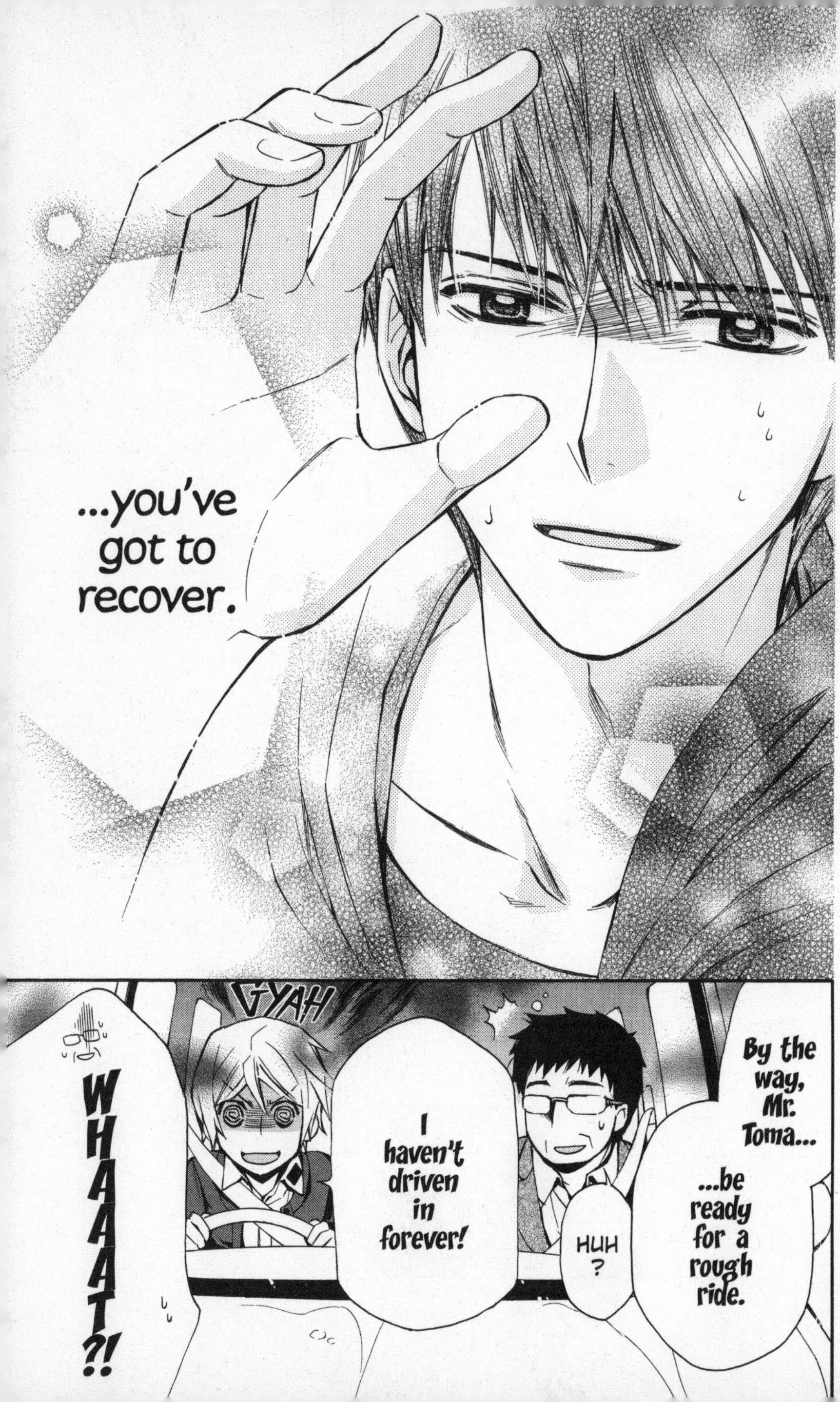
...you've got to recover.
By the way, Mr. Toma...
...be ready for a rough ride.
HUH?
I haven't driven in forever!
GYAH
WHAAAAT?!

Lingering Trembles

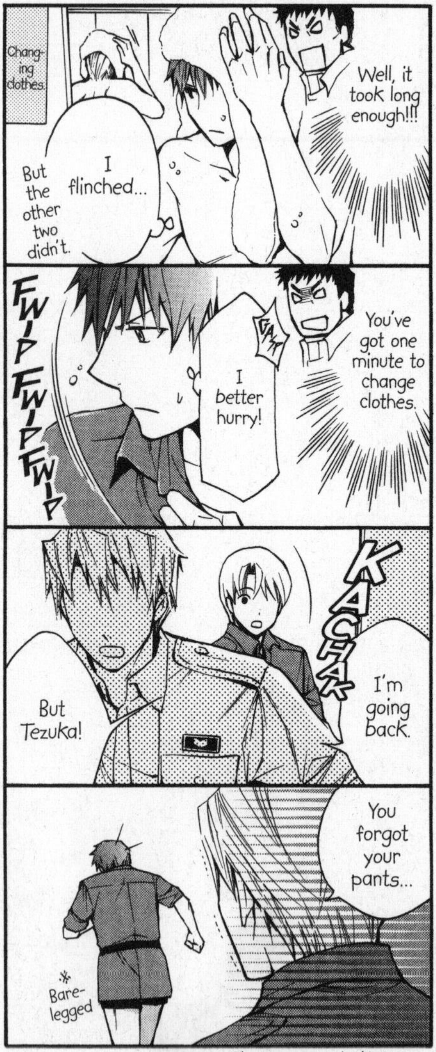
Well, it took long enough!!!
I flinched...
But the other two didn't.
Chang-ing clothes.
You've got one minute to change clothes.
I better hurry!
FWIP FWIP FWIP
KACHAK
I'm going back.
But Tezuka!
You forgot your pants...
※ Bare-legged

Three seconds before bursting out laughing.

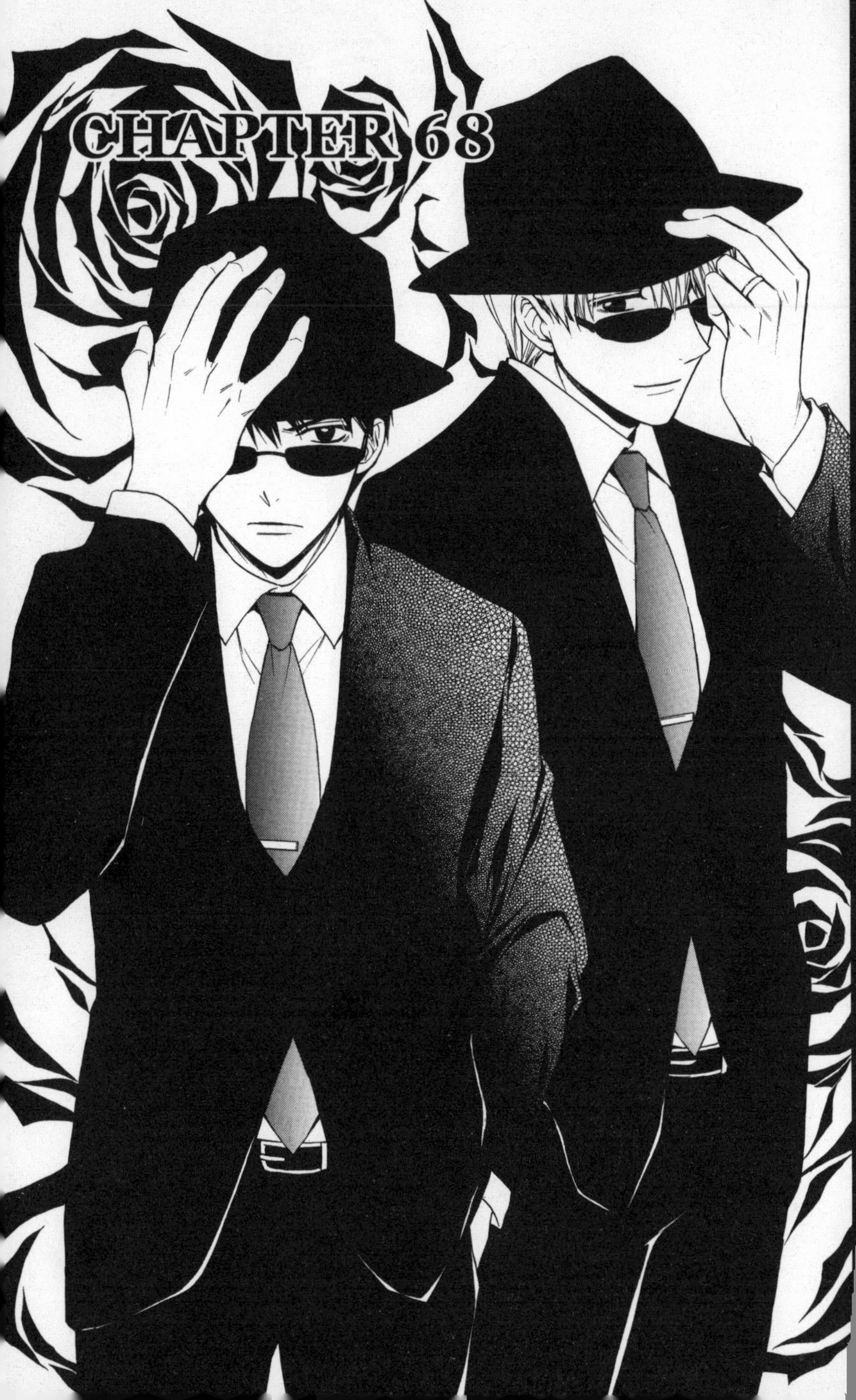
CHAPTER 68

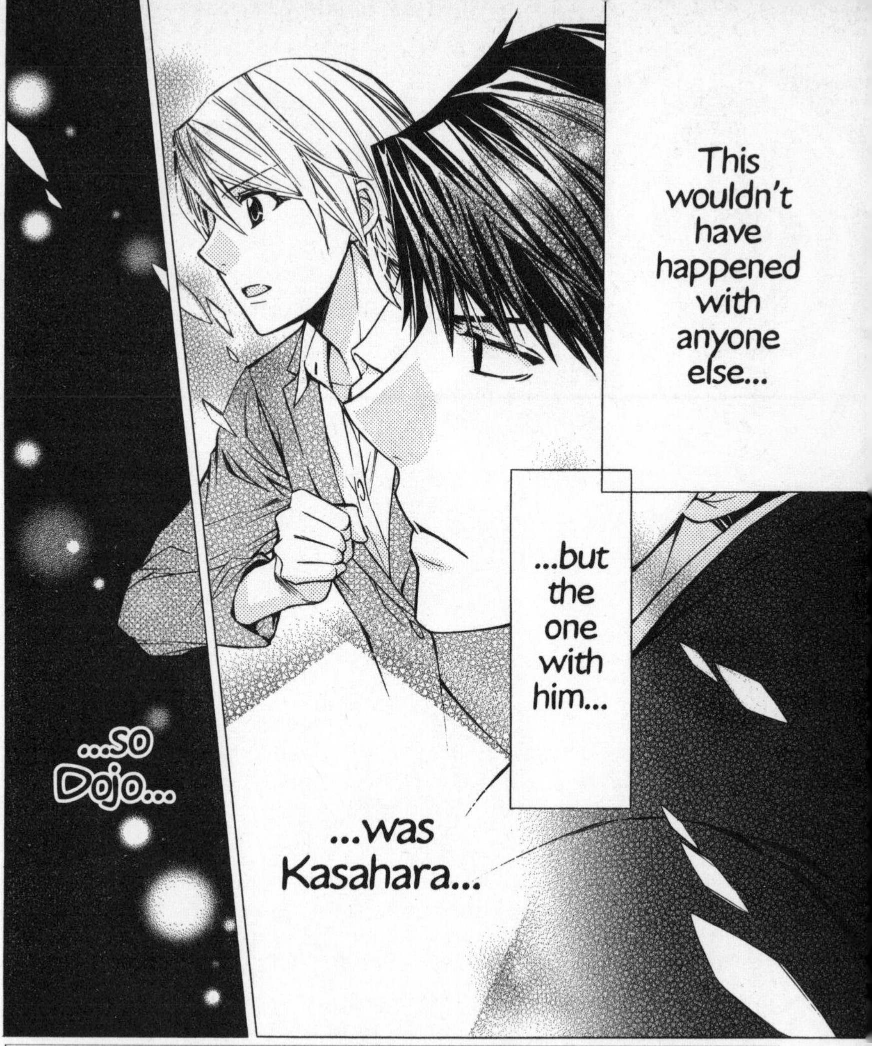
This wouldn't have happened with anyone else...
...but the one with him...
...was Kasahara...
...so Dojo...

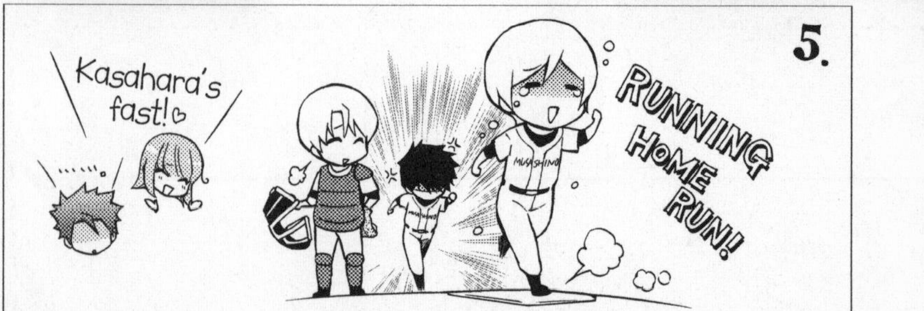
5.
RUNNING HOME RUN!
Kasahara's fast!

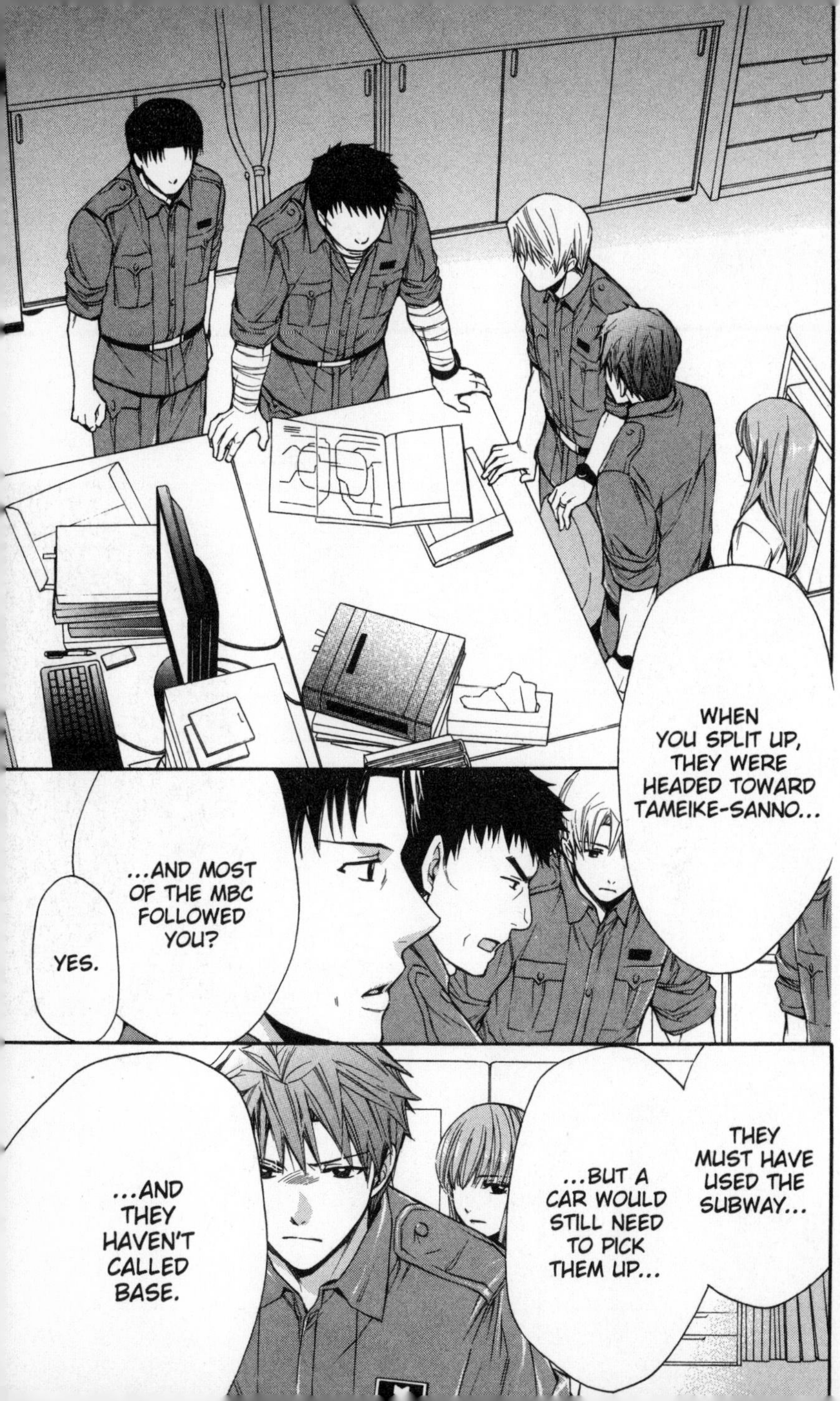
WHEN YOU SPLIT UP, THEY WERE HEADED TOWARD TAMEIKE-SANNO...
...AND MOST OF THE MBC FOLLOWED YOU?
YES.
THEY MUST HAVE USED THE SUBWAY...
...BUT A CAR WOULD STILL NEED TO PICK THEM UP...
...AND THEY HAVEN'T CALLED BASE.

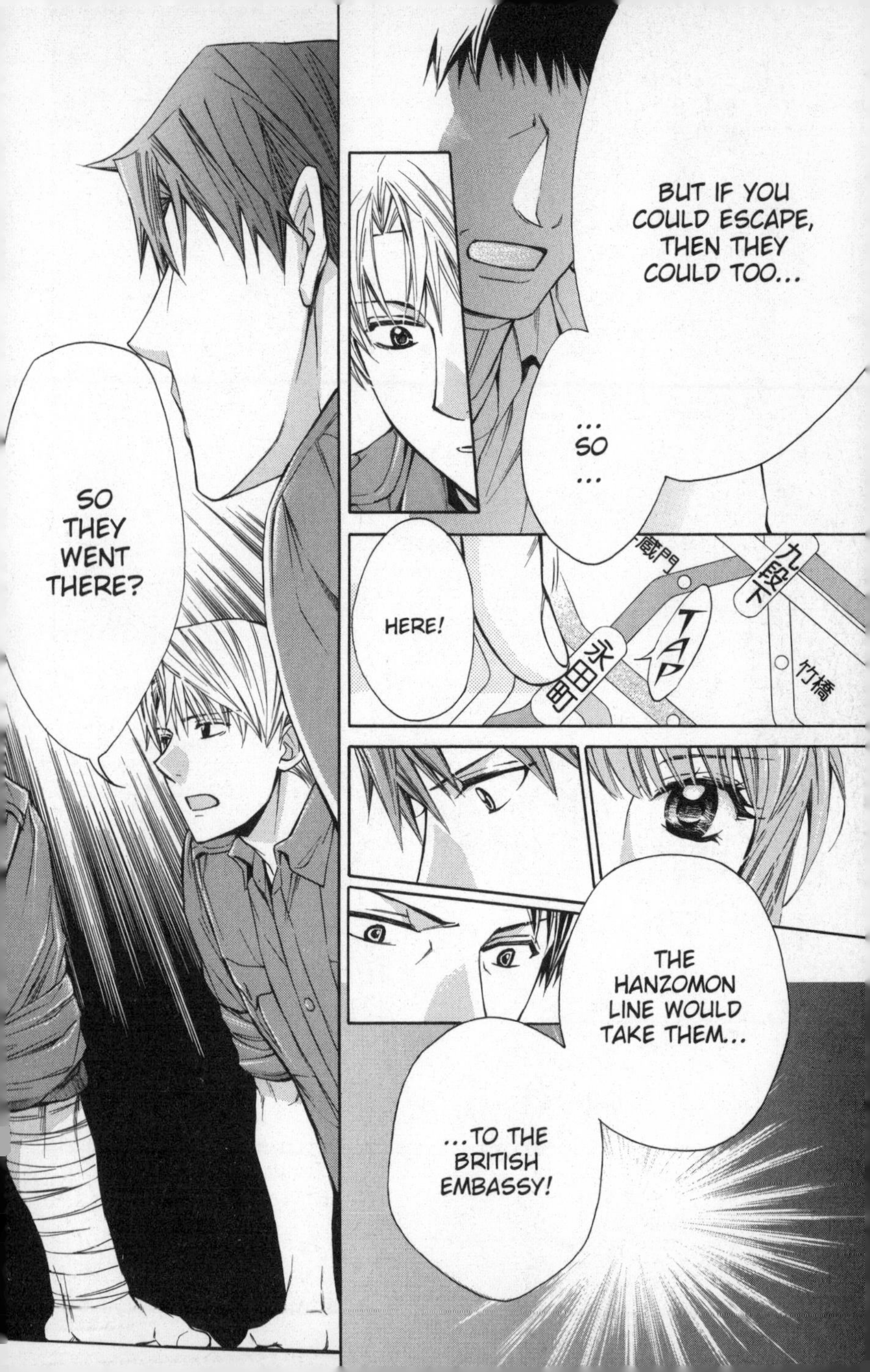
BUT IF YOU COULD ESCAPE, THEN THEY COULD TOO...
...SO...
HERE!
TAP
蔵門
九段下
永田町
竹橋
THE HANZOMON LINE WOULD TAKE THEM...
...TO THE BRITISH EMBASSY!
SO THEY WENT THERE?

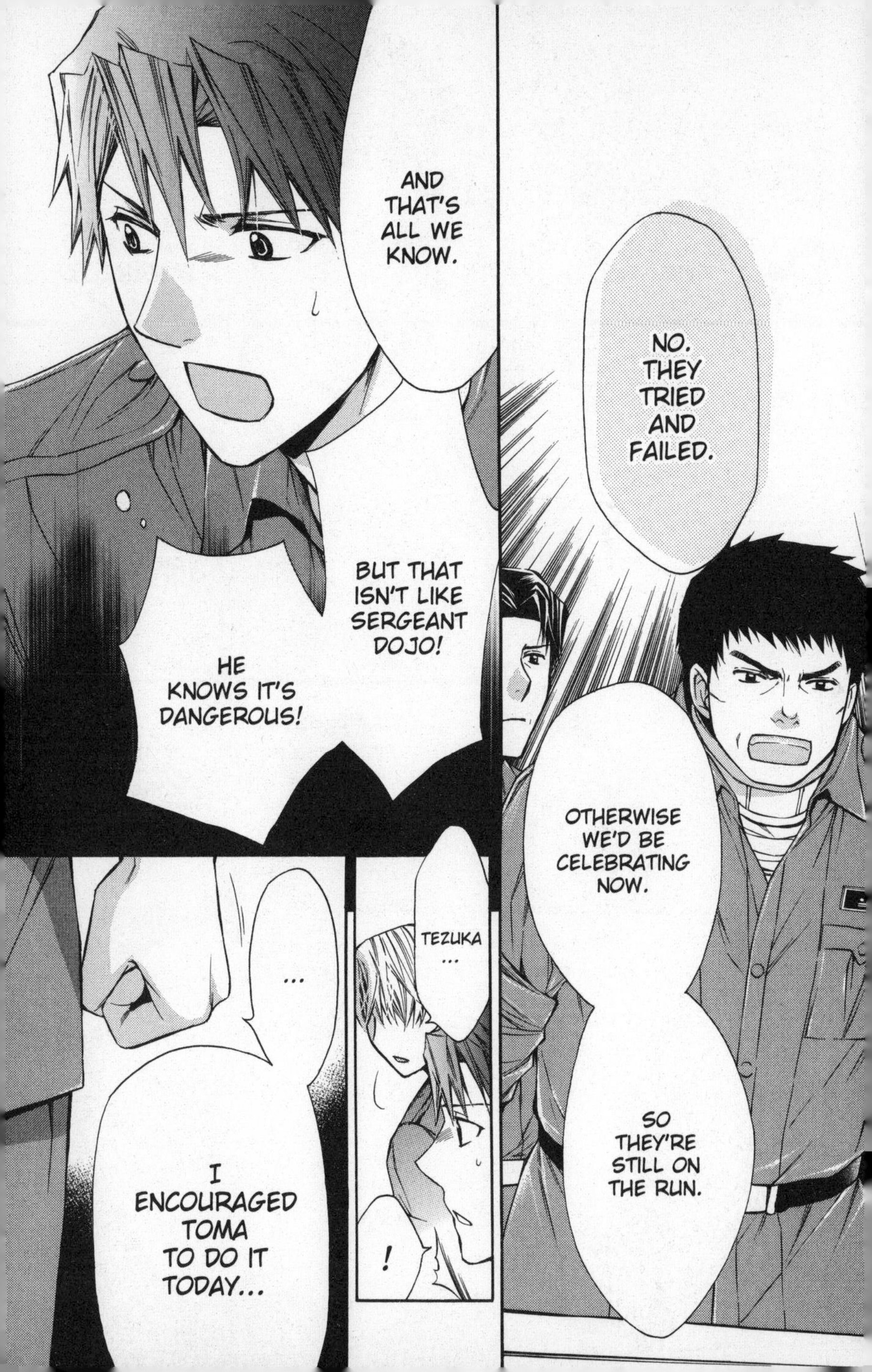
NO. THEY TRIED AND FAILED.
OTHERWISE WE'D BE CELEBRATING NOW.
SO THEY'RE STILL ON THE RUN.
AND THAT'S ALL WE KNOW.
BUT THAT ISN'T LIKE SERGEANT DOJO!
HE KNOWS IT'S DANGEROUS!
TEZUKA...
!
...
I ENCOURAGED TOMA TO DO IT TODAY...

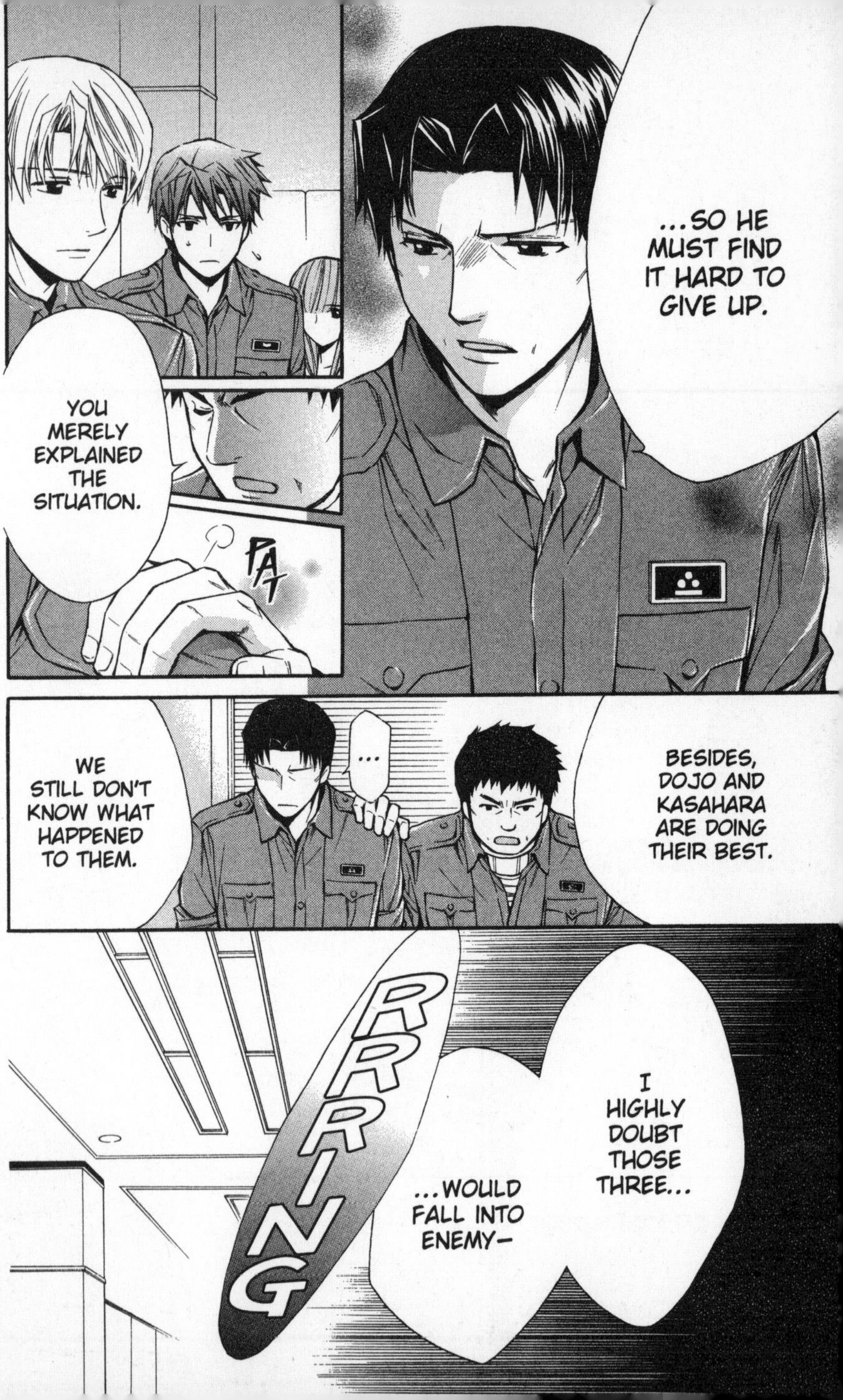

...SO HE MUST FIND IT HARD TO GIVE UP.
YOU MERELY EXPLAINED THE SITUATION.
PAT
BESIDES, DOJO AND KASAHARA ARE DOING THEIR BEST.
...
WE STILL DON'T KNOW WHAT HAPPENED TO THEM.
I HIGHLY DOUBT THOSE THREE...
...WOULD FALL INTO ENEMY–
RRRING

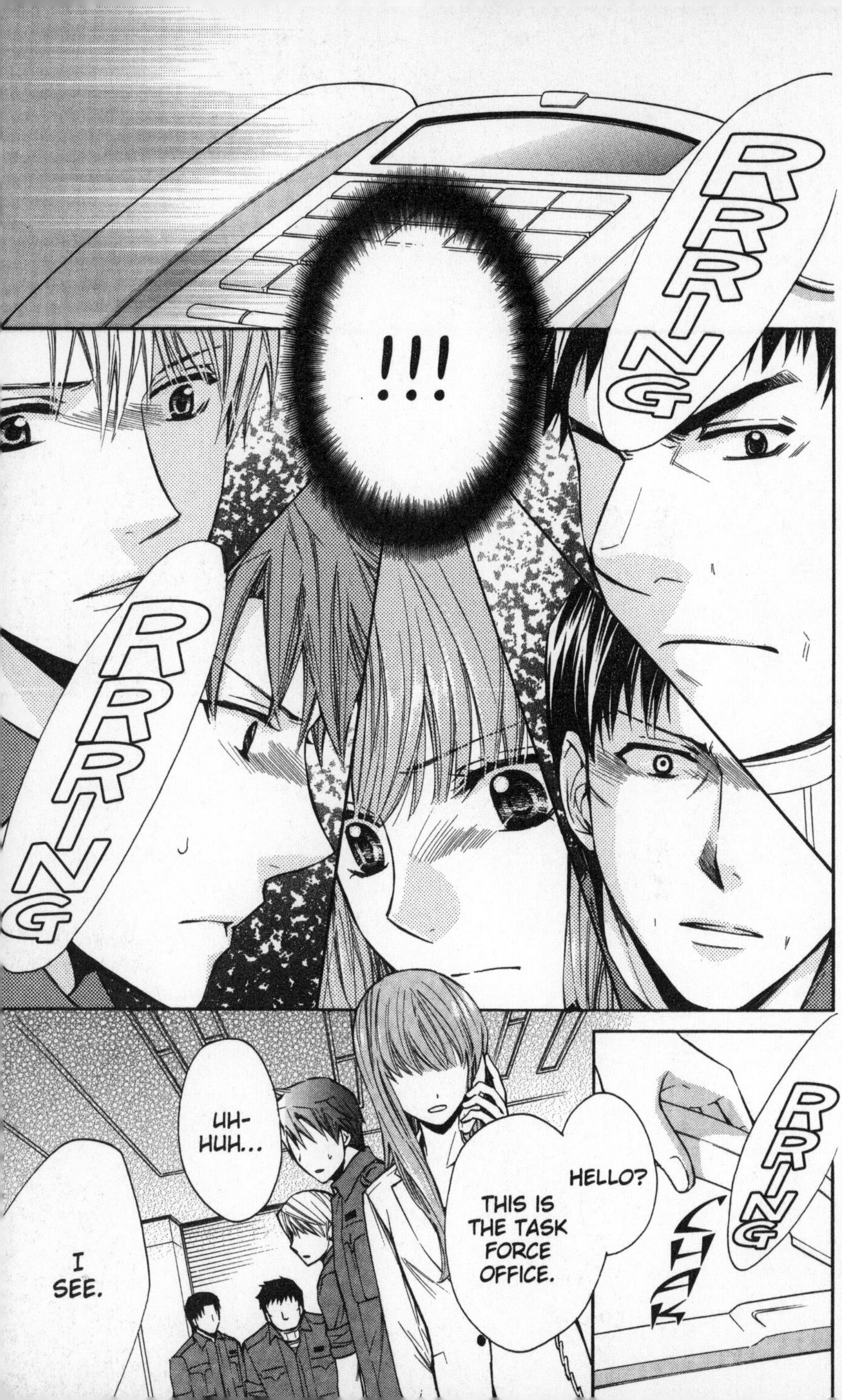
RRRING
!!!
RRRING
RRRING
CHAK
HELLO?
THIS IS THE TASK FORCE OFFICE.
UH-HUH...
I SEE.

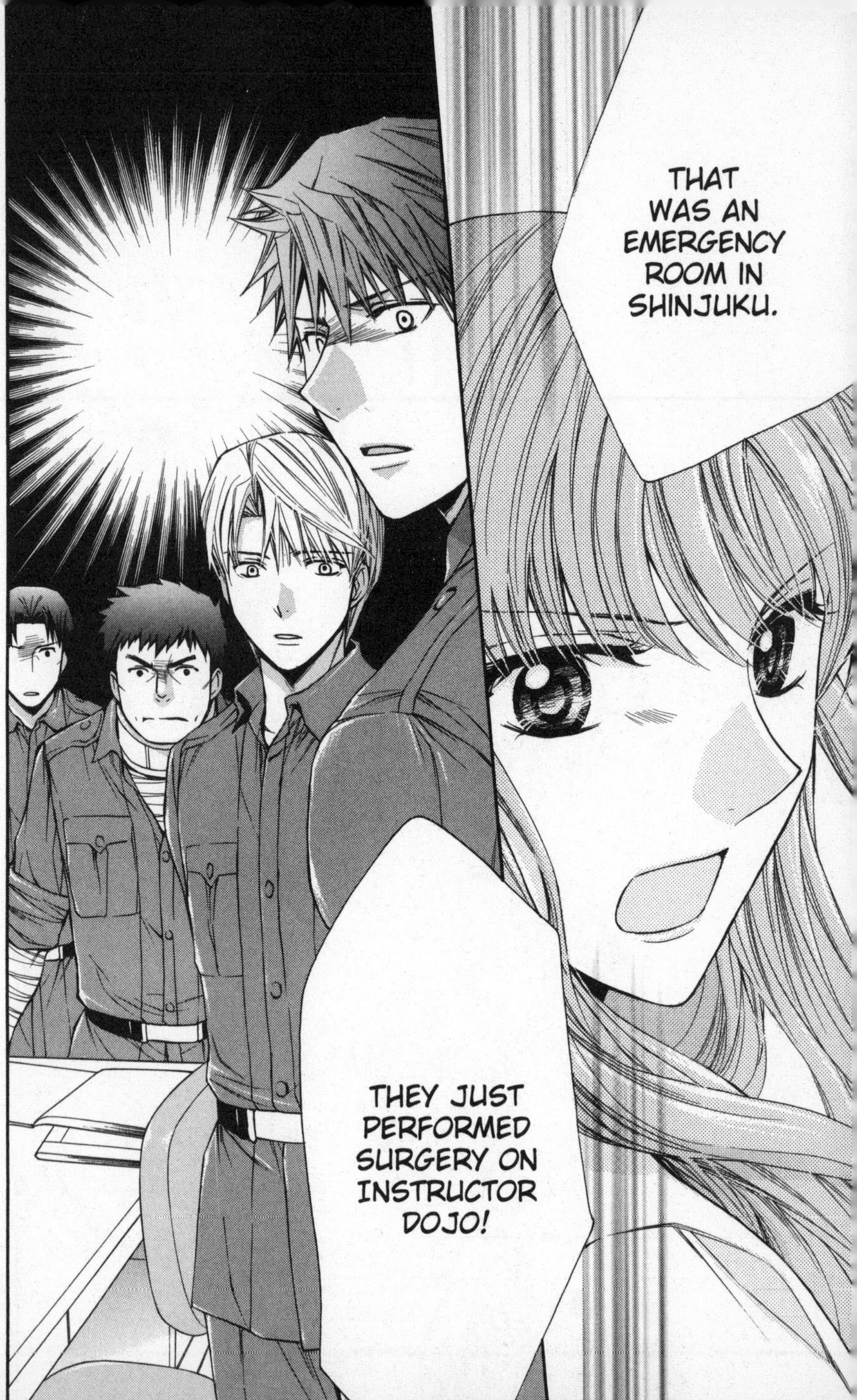
THAT WAS AN EMERGENCY ROOM IN SHINJUKU.
THEY JUST PERFORMED SURGERY ON INSTRUCTOR DOJO!

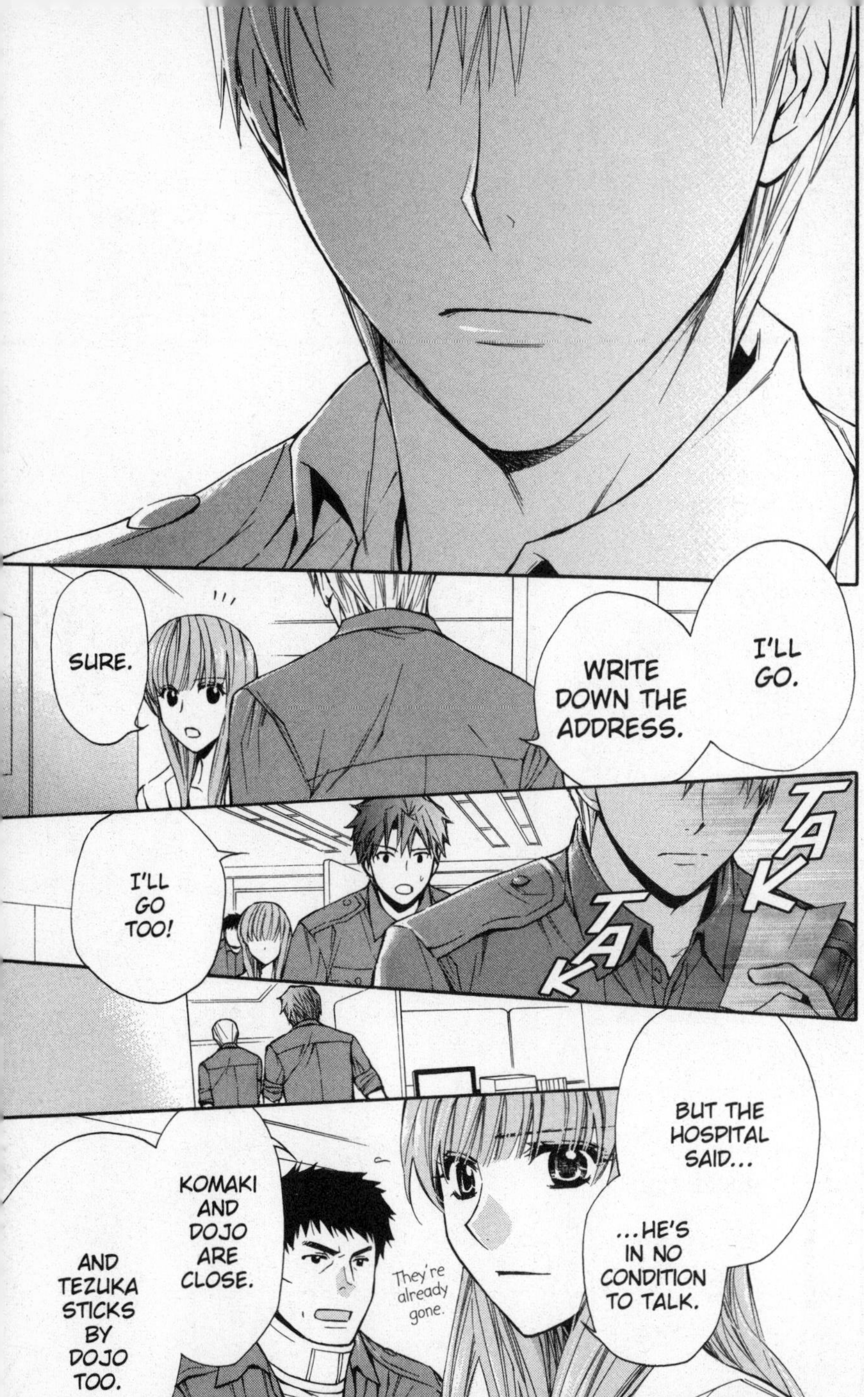
I'LL GO.
WRITE DOWN THE ADDRESS.
SURE.
TAK
TAK
I'LL GO TOO!
BUT THE HOSPITAL SAID...
...HE'S IN NO CONDITION TO TALK.
They're already gone.
KOMAKI AND DOJO ARE CLOSE.
AND TEZUKA STICKS BY DOJO TOO.

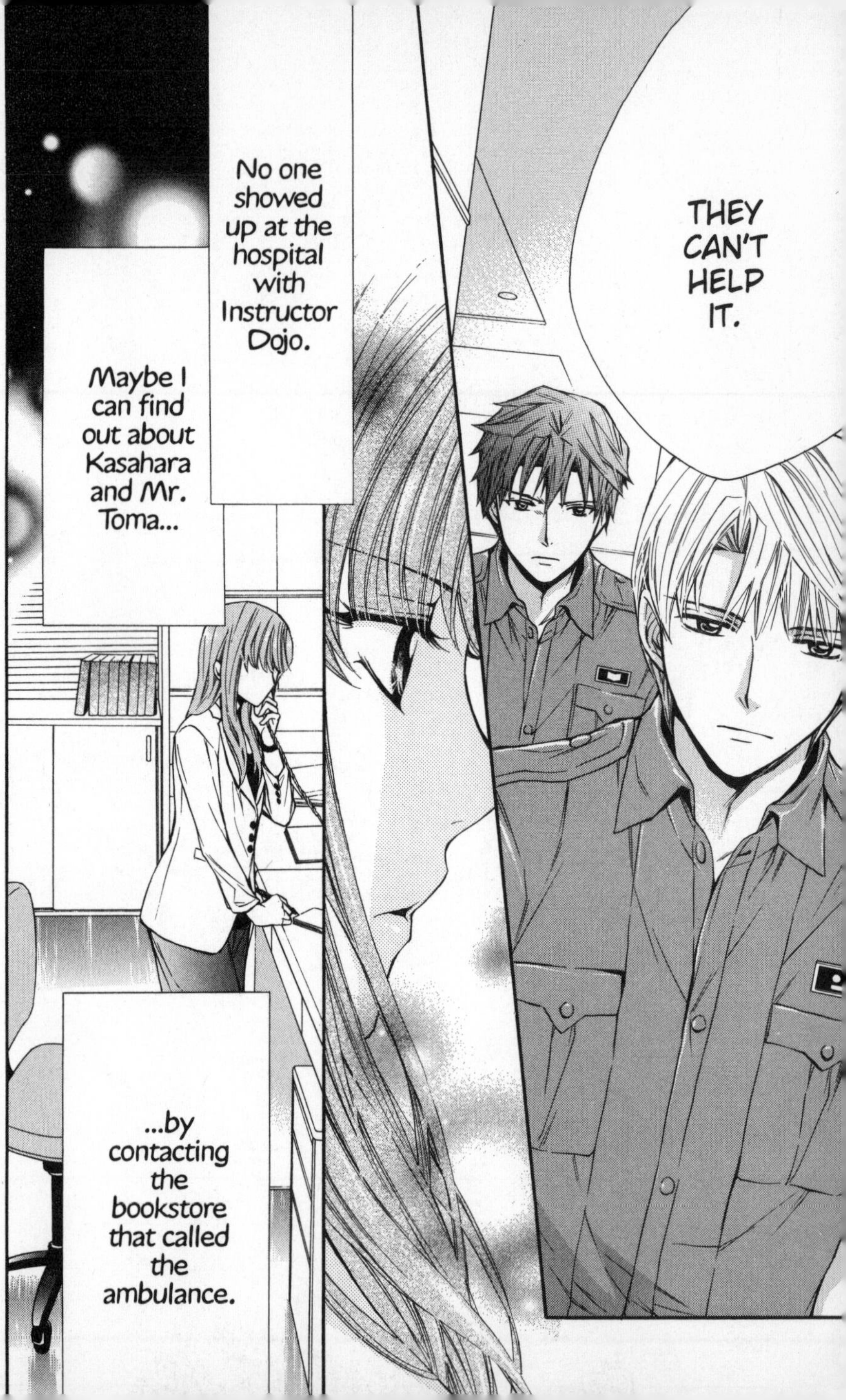
THEY CAN'T HELP IT.
No one showed up at the hospital with Instructor Dojo.
Maybe I can find out about Kasahara and Mr. Toma...
...by contacting the bookstore that called the ambulance.

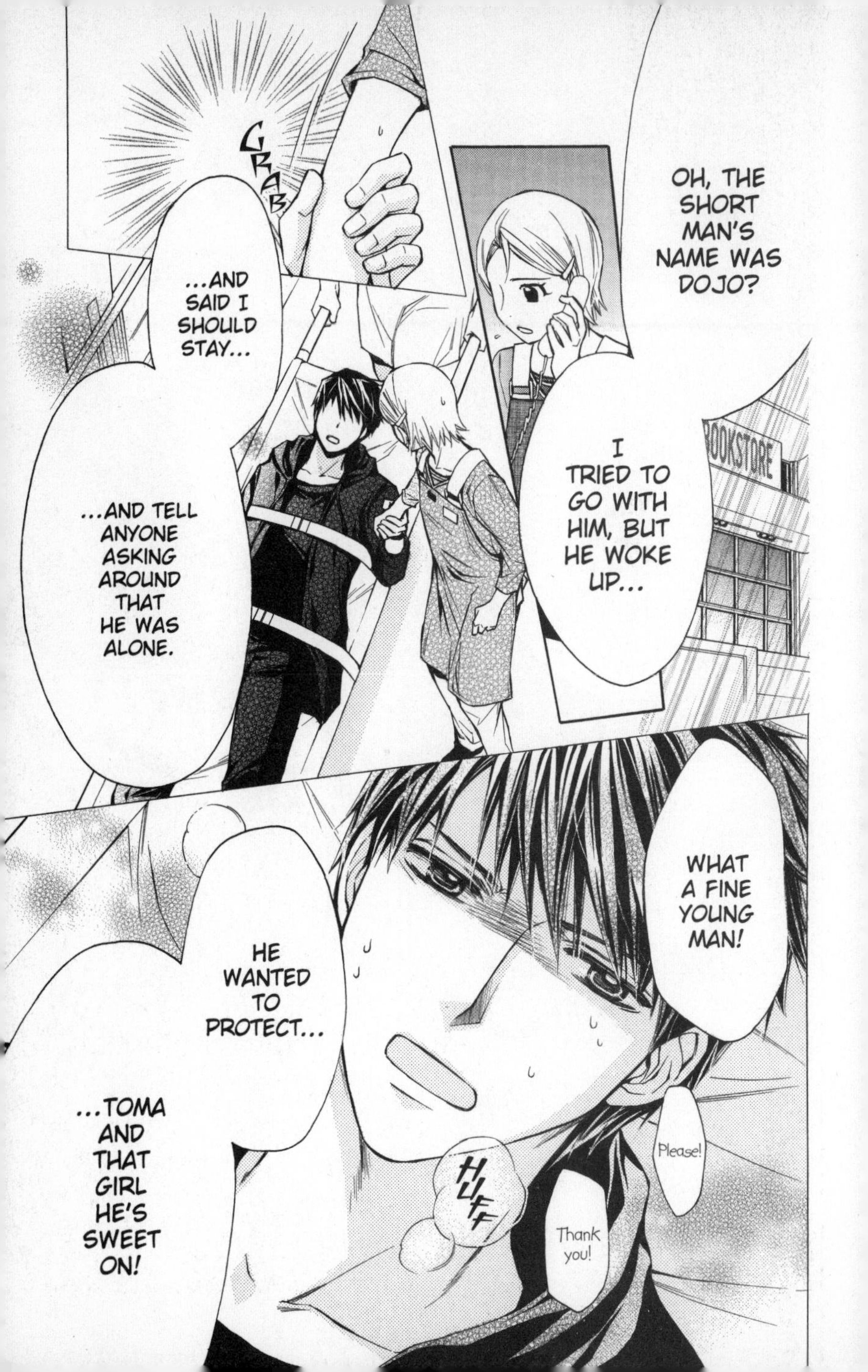
OH, THE SHORT MAN'S NAME WAS DOJO?
I TRIED TO GO WITH HIM, BUT HE WOKE UP...
BOOKSTORE
GRAB
...AND SAID I SHOULD STAY...
...AND TELL ANYONE ASKING AROUND THAT HE WAS ALONE.
WHAT A FINE YOUNG MAN!
Please!
Thank you!
HUFF
HE WANTED TO PROTECT...
...TOMA AND THAT GIRL HE'S SWEET ON!

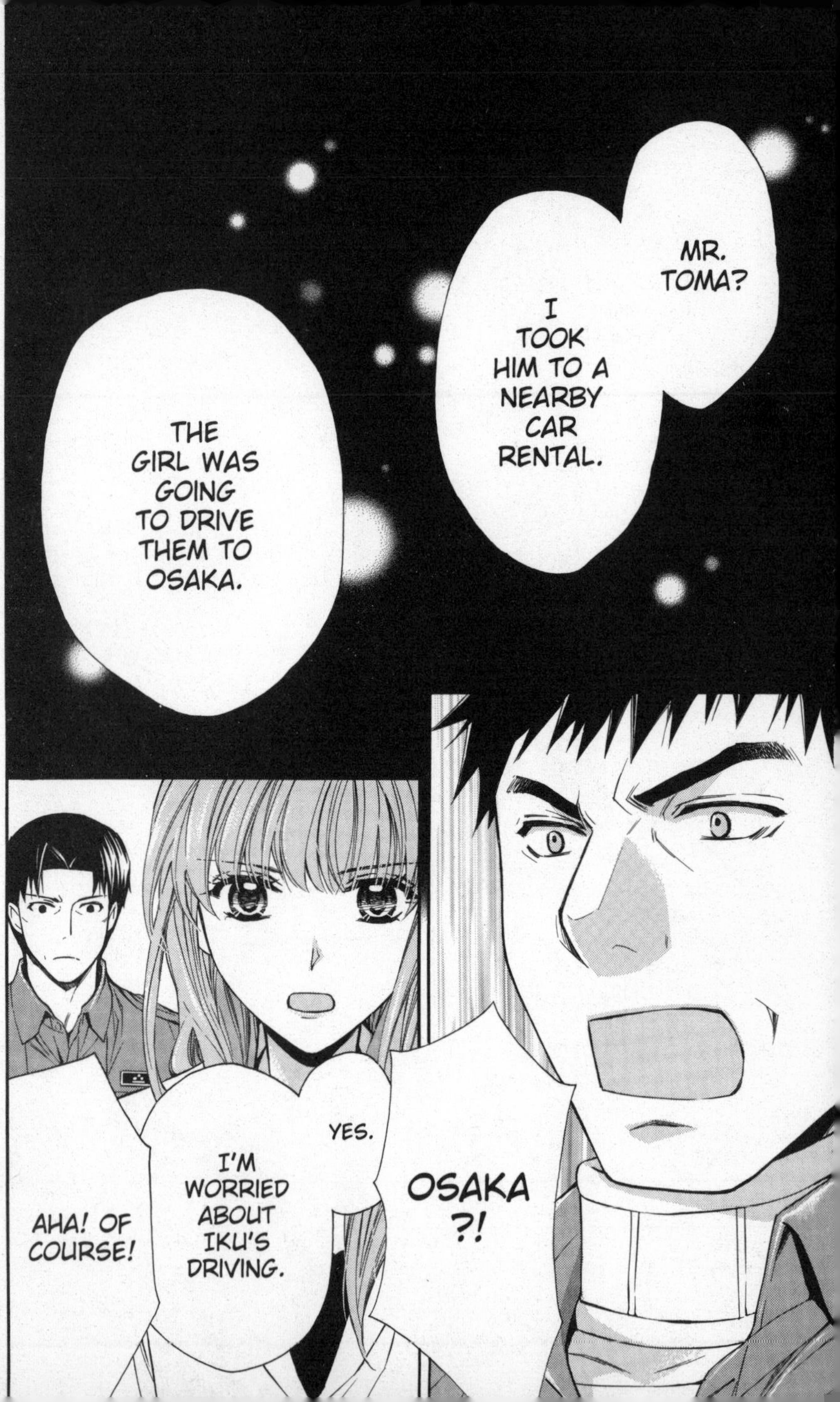
MR. TOMA?
I TOOK HIM TO A NEARBY CAR RENTAL.
THE GIRL WAS GOING TO DRIVE THEM TO OSAKA.
OSAKA?!
YES.
I'M WORRIED ABOUT IKU'S DRIVING.
AHA! OF COURSE!

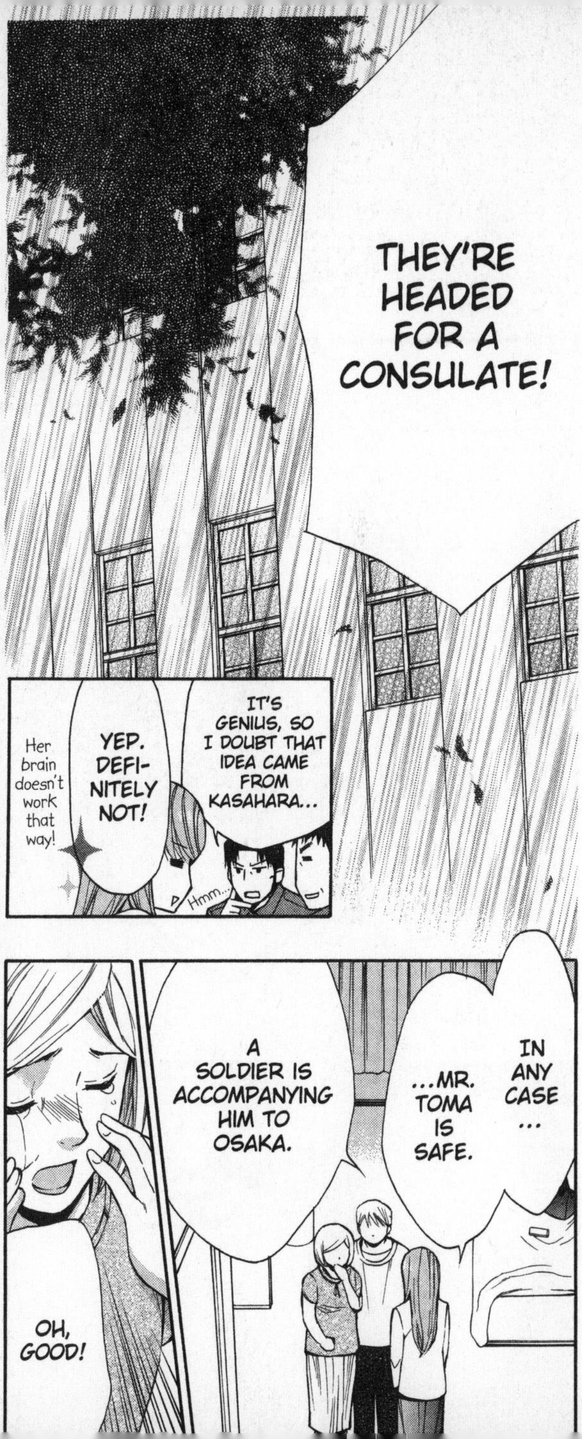
THEY'RE HEADED FOR A CONSULATE!
IT'S GENIUS, SO I DOUBT THAT IDEA CAME FROM KASAHARA...
YEP. DEFI-NITELY NOT!
Her brain doesn't work that way!
Hmm...
IN ANY CASE...
...MR. TOMA IS SAFE.
A SOLDIER IS ACCOMPANYING HIM TO OSAKA.
OH, GOOD!

6

*

In Volume 13, I rattled on about the video game *Monster Hunter*, and by the time this volume comes out, the next installment will be available. I can't wait! And surprisingly (?), it comes out the day after my birthday!

What an awesome birthday present! (But I have to buy it myself!)

I plan to play the heck out of that thing! I'm so super stoked! I hope they start a *MonHun* TV program and have all kinds of collaborations and events!

*

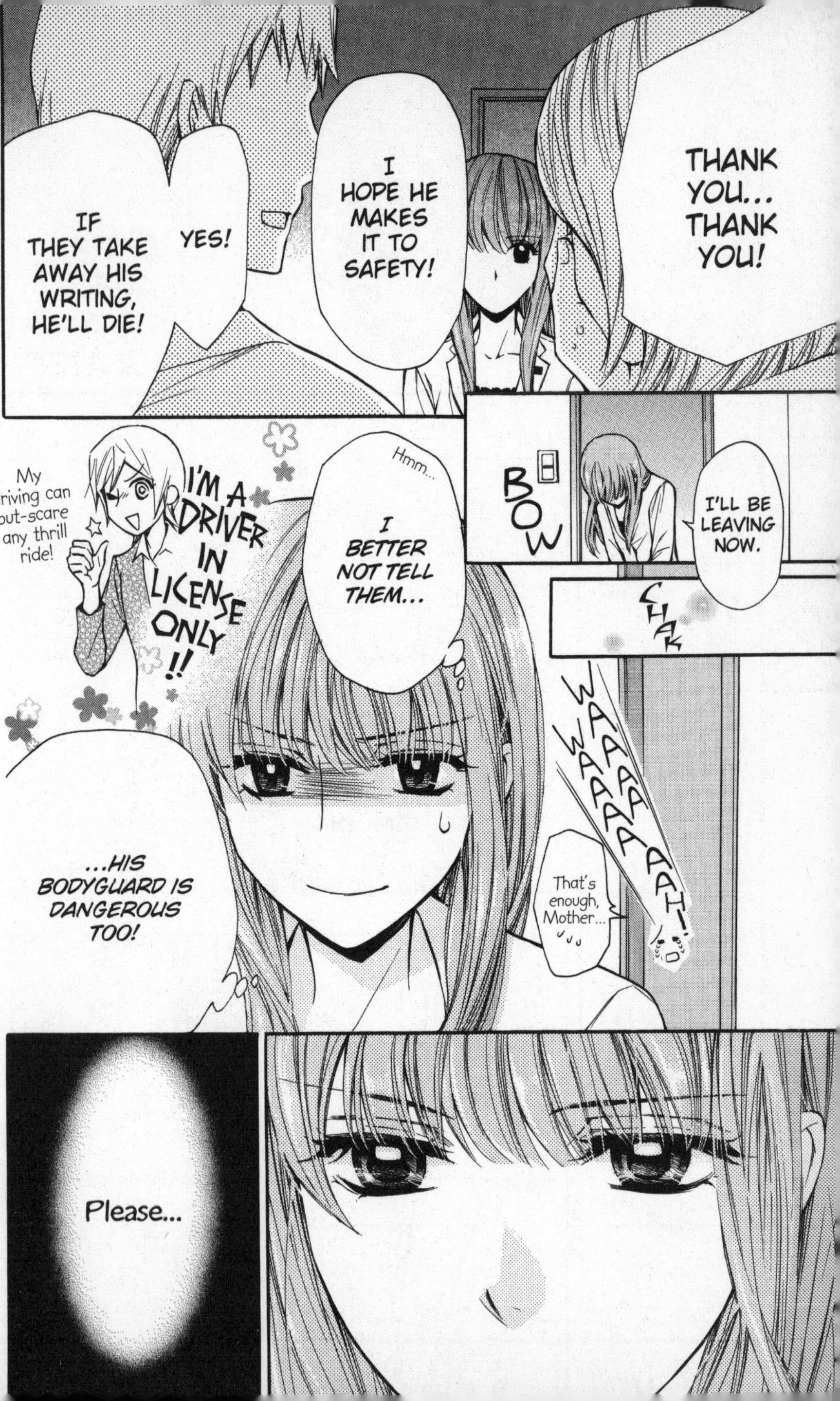
THANK YOU... THANK YOU!
I HOPE HE MAKES IT TO SAFETY!
YES!
IF THEY TAKE AWAY HIS WRITING, HE'LL DIE!
BOW
I'LL BE LEAVING NOW.
CHAK
WAAAAA WAAAAAAAAH!
That's enough, Mother...
Hmm...
I BETTER NOT TELL THEM...
I'M A DRIVER IN LICENSE ONLY!!
My driving can out-scare any thrill ride!
...HIS BODYGUARD IS DANGEROUS TOO!
Please...

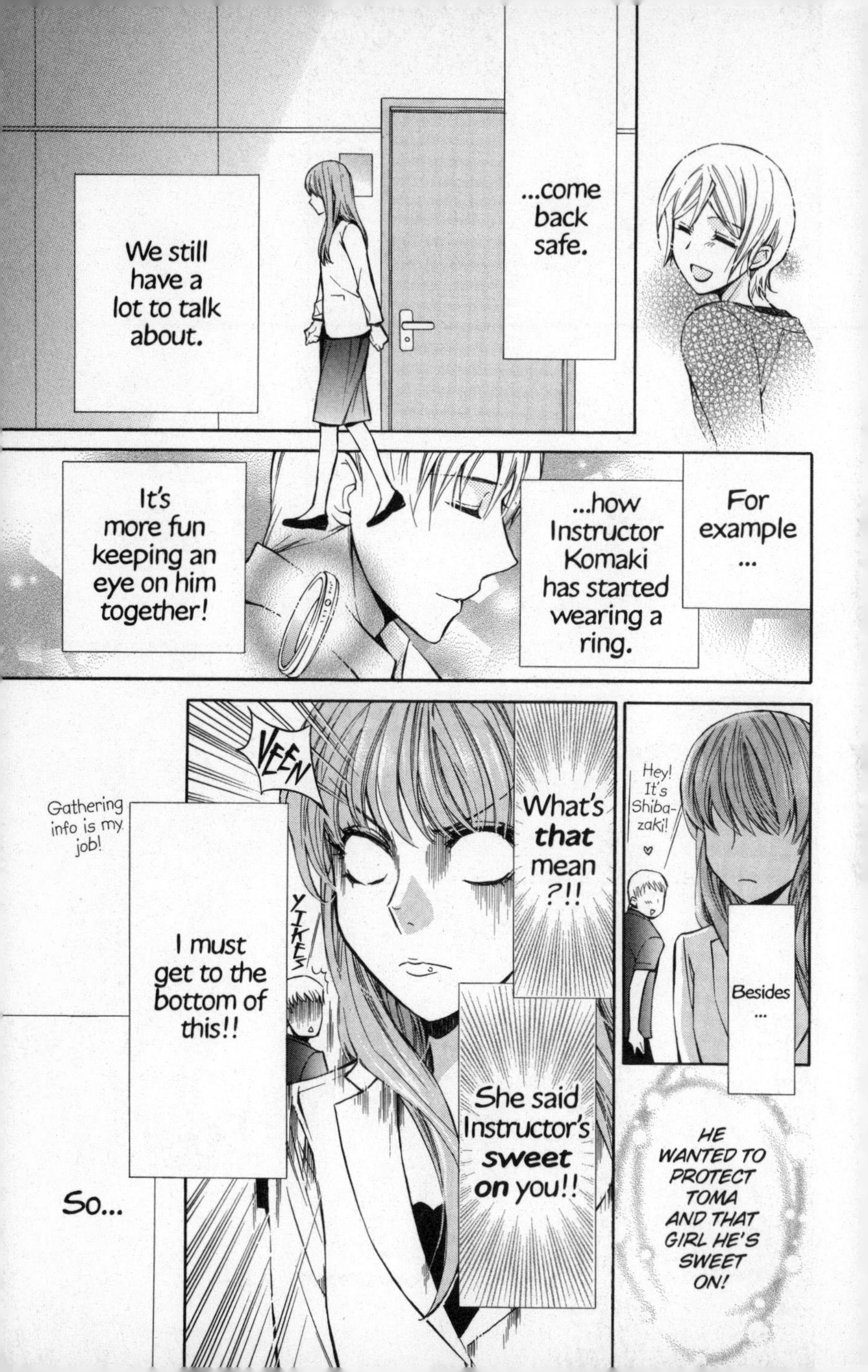
...come back safe.
We still have a lot to talk about.
For example...
...how Instructor Komaki has started wearing a ring.
It's more fun keeping an eye on him together!
Hey! It's Shiba-zaki! ♥
Besides...
HE WANTED TO PROTECT TOMA AND THAT GIRL HE'S SWEET ON!
VEEN
What's **that** mean?!!
She said Instructor's **sweet on** you!!
YIKES
I must get to the bottom of this!!
Gathering info is my job!
So...

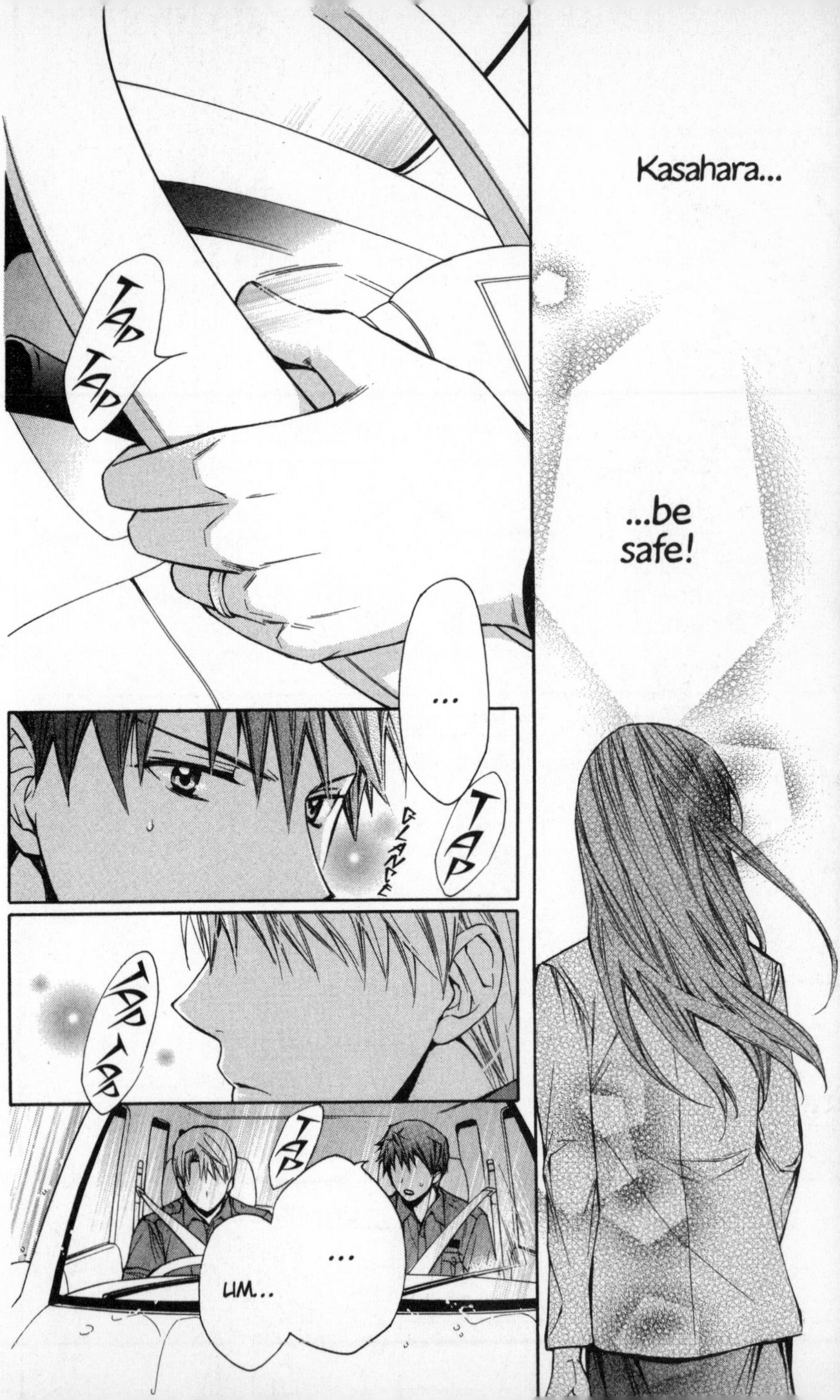
Kasahara...
...be safe!
TAP TAP
...
TAP
GLANCE
TAP TAP
TAP
...
UM...

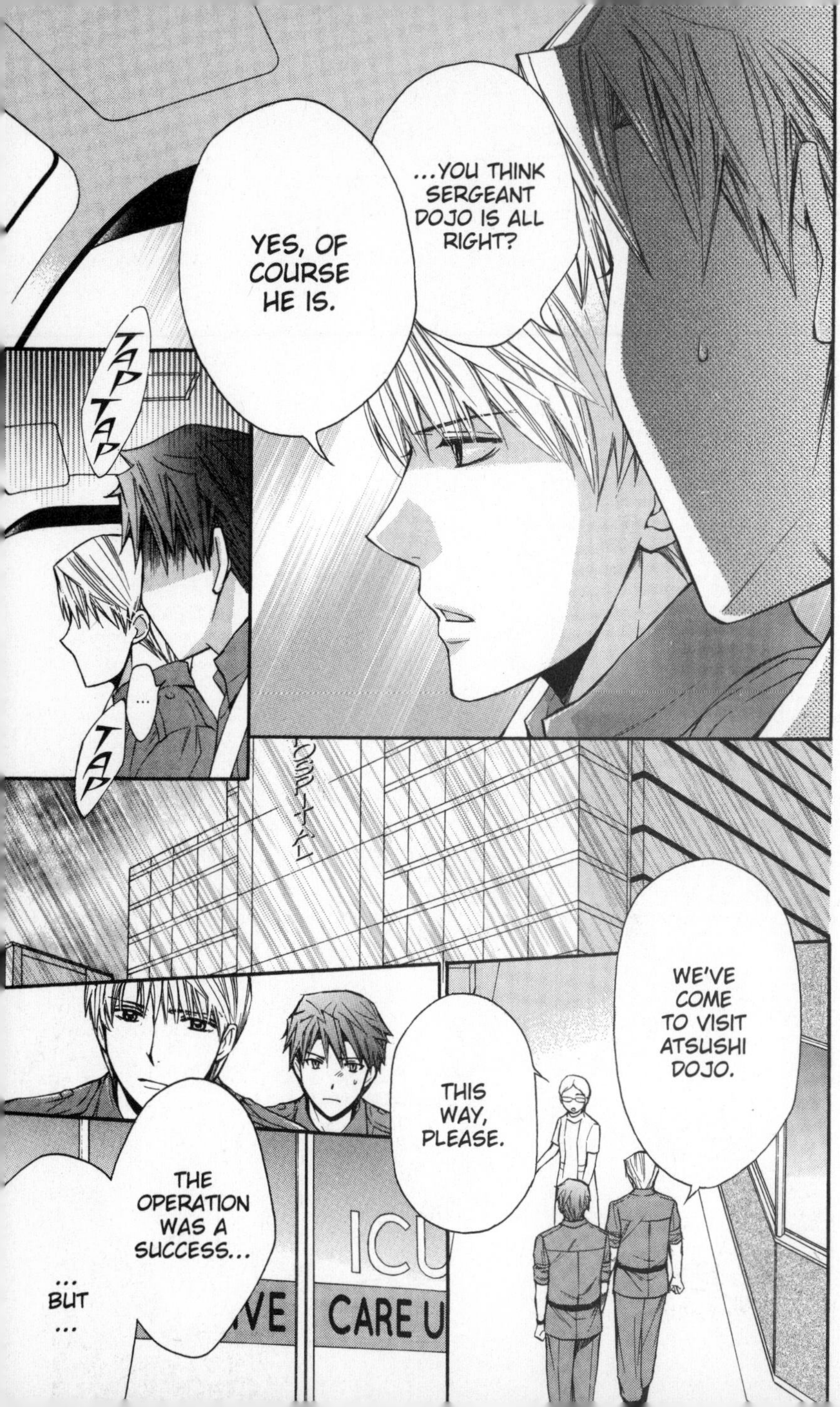
...YOU THINK SERGEANT DOJO IS ALL RIGHT?
YES, OF COURSE HE IS.
TAP TAP
...
TAP
WE'VE COME TO VISIT ATSUSHI DOJO.
THIS WAY, PLEASE.
ICU
THE OPERATION WAS A SUCCESS...
...BUT...

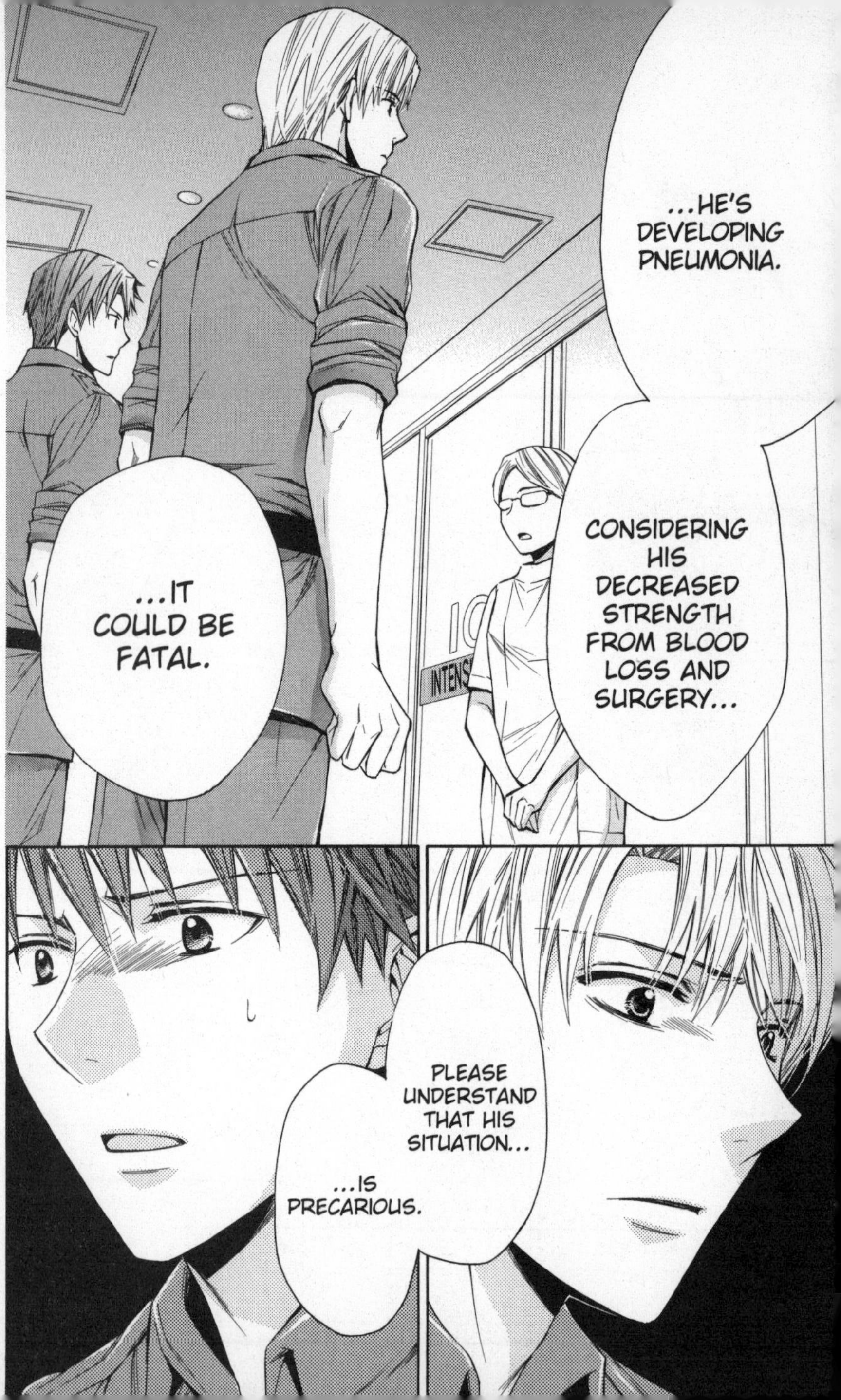
...HE'S DEVELOPING PNEUMONIA.
CONSIDERING HIS DECREASED STRENGTH FROM BLOOD LOSS AND SURGERY...
...IT COULD BE FATAL.
PLEASE UNDERSTAND THAT HIS SITUATION...
...IS PRECARIOUS.

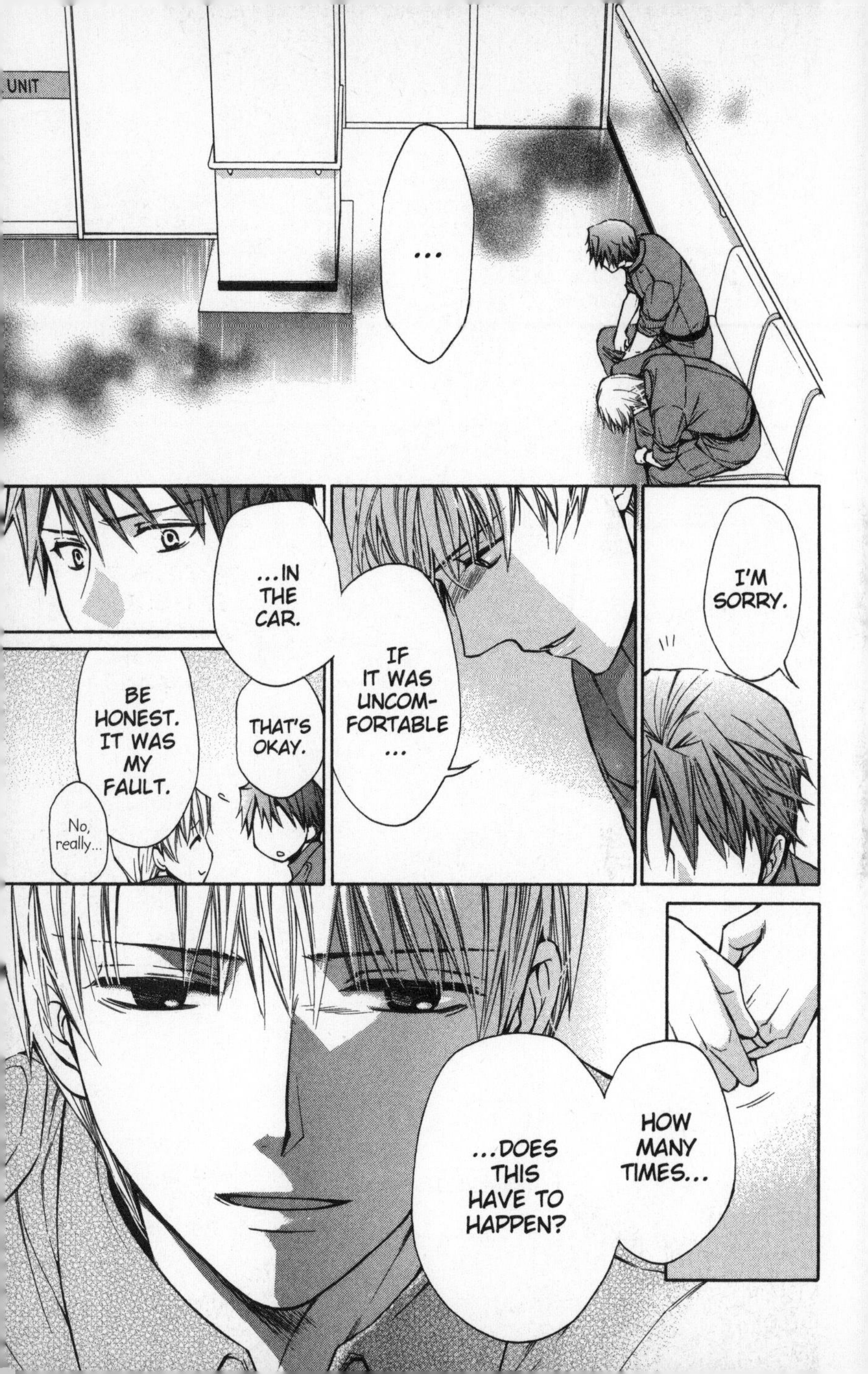
UNIT
...
I'M SORRY.
IF IT WAS UNCOMFORTABLE...
...IN THE CAR.
THAT'S OKAY.
BE HONEST. IT WAS MY FAULT.
No, really...
HOW MANY TIMES...
...DOES THIS HAVE TO HAPPEN?

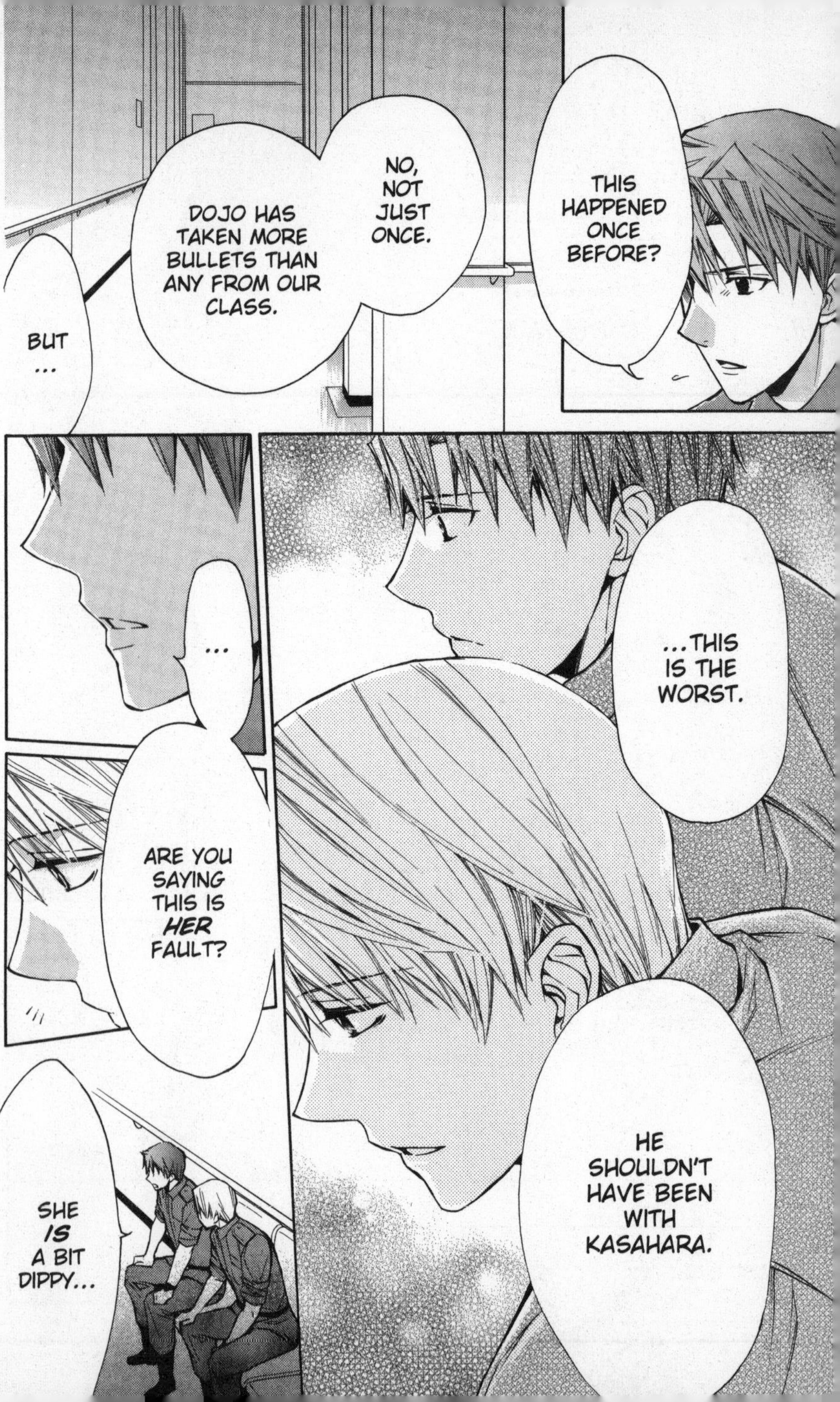
THIS HAPPENED ONCE BEFORE?
NO, NOT JUST ONCE.
DOJO HAS TAKEN MORE BULLETS THAN ANY FROM OUR CLASS.
BUT ...
...THIS IS THE WORST.
HE SHOULDN'T HAVE BEEN WITH KASAHARA.
...
ARE YOU SAYING THIS IS *HER* FAULT?
SHE *IS* A BIT DIPPY...

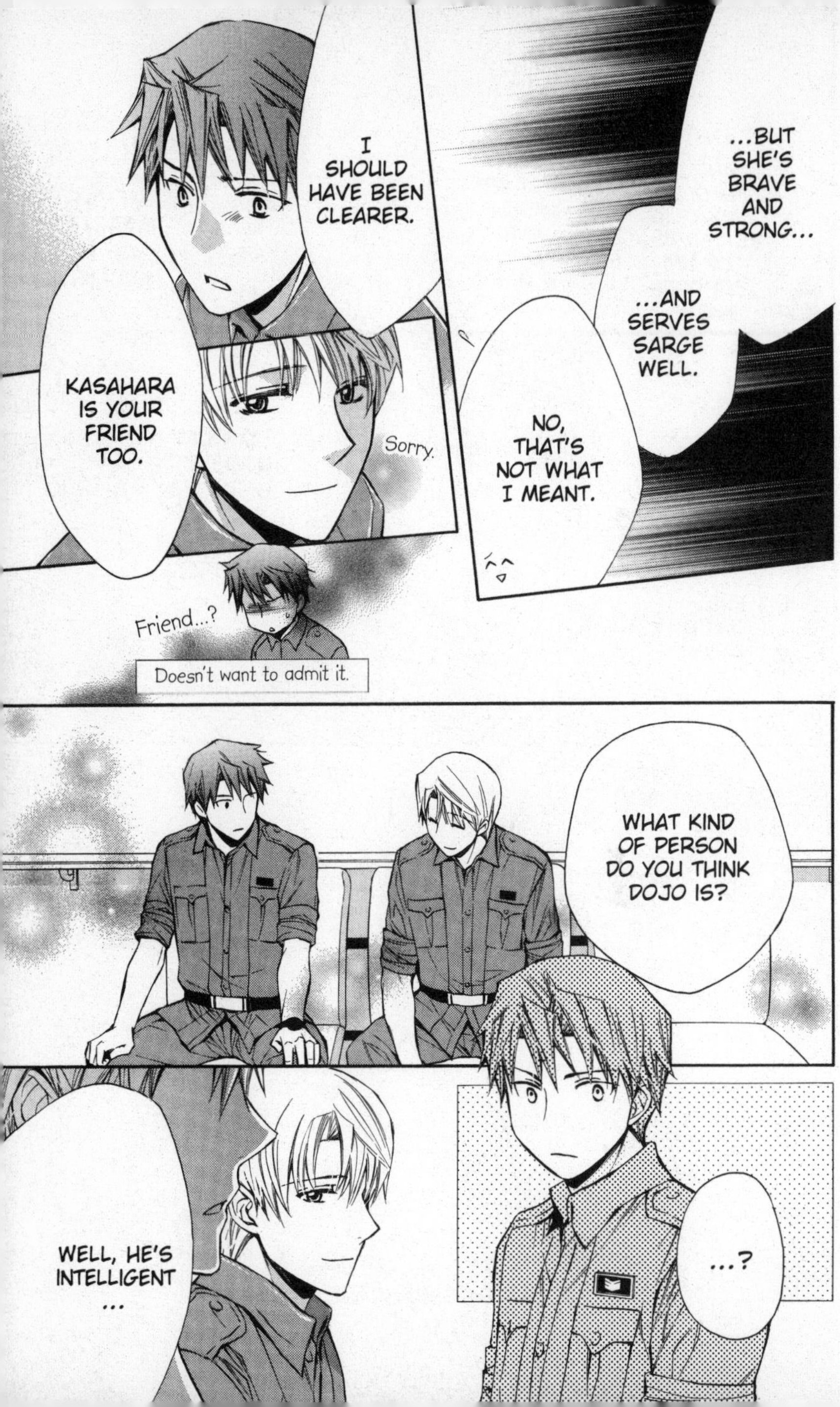
...BUT SHE'S BRAVE AND STRONG...
...AND SERVES SARGE WELL.
NO, THAT'S NOT WHAT I MEANT.
I SHOULD HAVE BEEN CLEARER.
KASAHARA IS YOUR FRIEND TOO.
Sorry.
Friend...?
Doesn't want to admit it.
WHAT KIND OF PERSON DO YOU THINK DOJO IS?
...?
WELL, HE'S INTELLIGENT ...

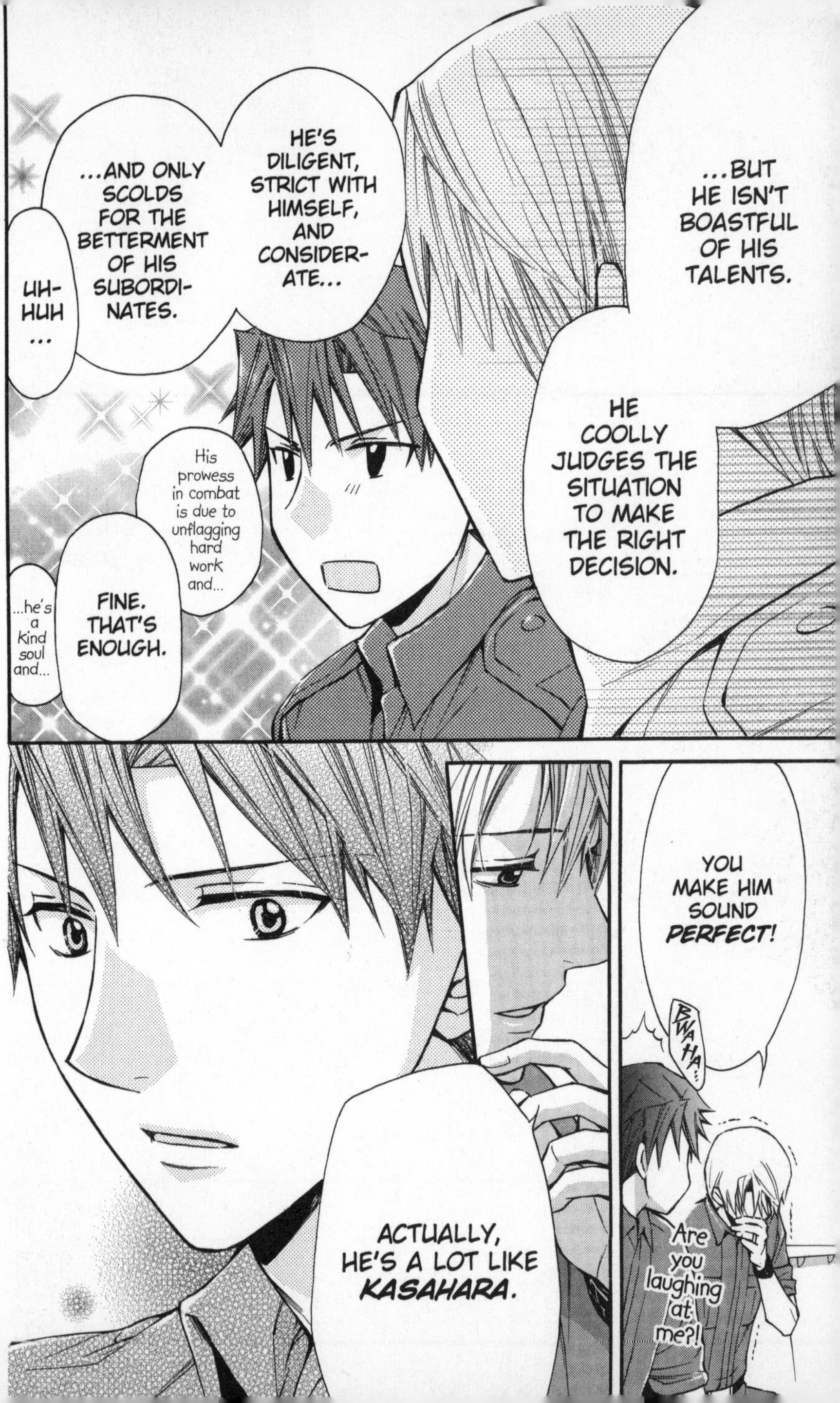
...BUT HE ISN'T BOASTFUL OF HIS TALENTS.
HE COOLLY JUDGES THE SITUATION TO MAKE THE RIGHT DECISION.
HE'S DILIGENT, STRICT WITH HIMSELF, AND CONSIDER-ATE...
...AND ONLY SCOLDS FOR THE BETTERMENT OF HIS SUBORDI-NATES.
UH-HUH...
His prowess in combat is due to unflagging hard work and...
...he's a kind soul and...
FINE. THAT'S ENOUGH.
YOU MAKE HIM SOUND *PERFECT*!
BWAHAHA
Are you laughing at me?!
ACTUALLY, HE'S A LOT LIKE *KASAHARA*.

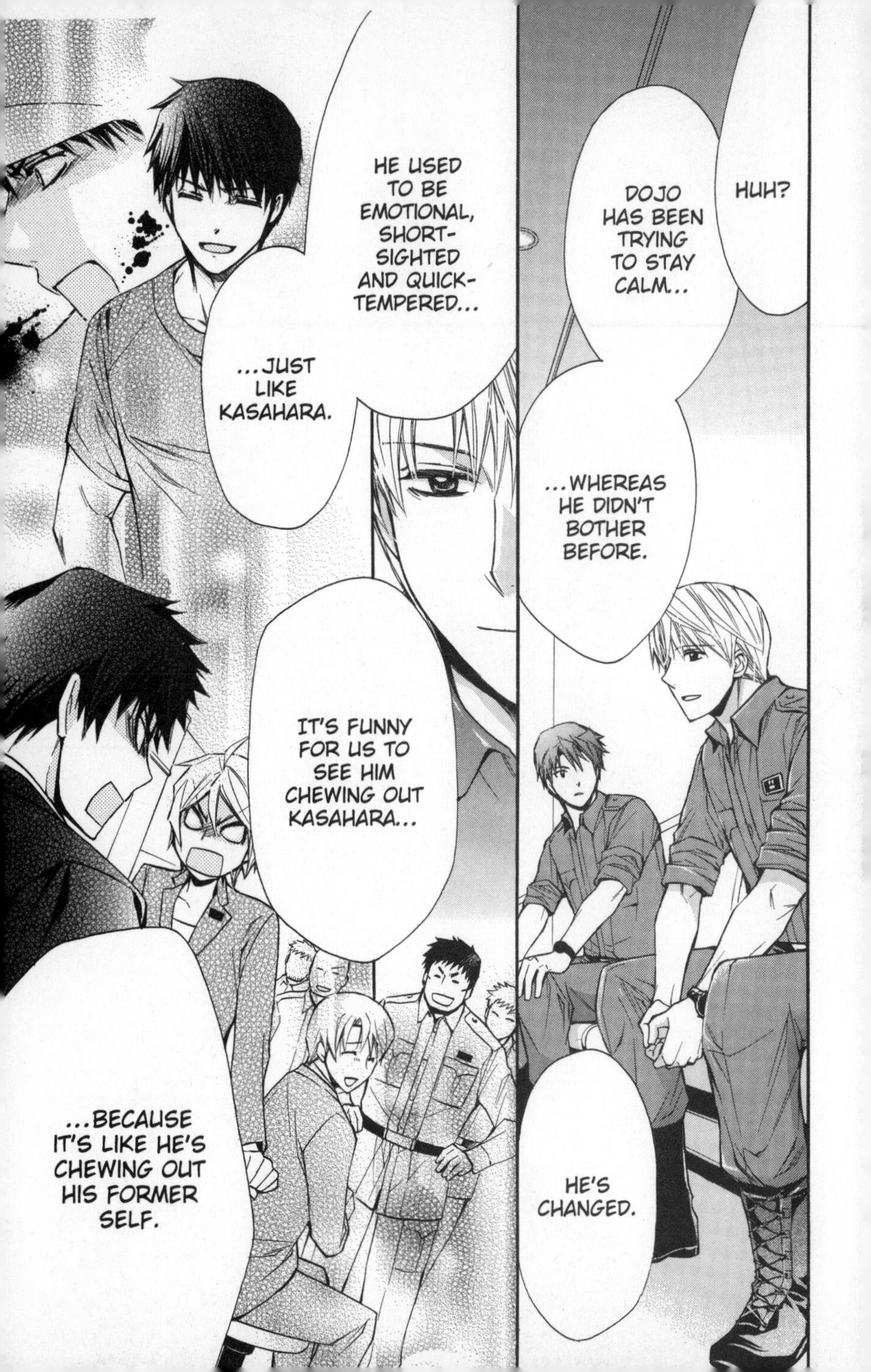
HUH?
DOJO HAS BEEN TRYING TO STAY CALM...
...WHEREAS HE DIDN'T BOTHER BEFORE.
HE'S CHANGED.
HE USED TO BE EMOTIONAL, SHORT-SIGHTED AND QUICK-TEMPERED...
...JUST LIKE KASAHARA.
IT'S FUNNY FOR US TO SEE HIM CHEWING OUT KASAHARA...
...BECAUSE IT'S LIKE HE'S CHEWING OUT HIS FORMER SELF.

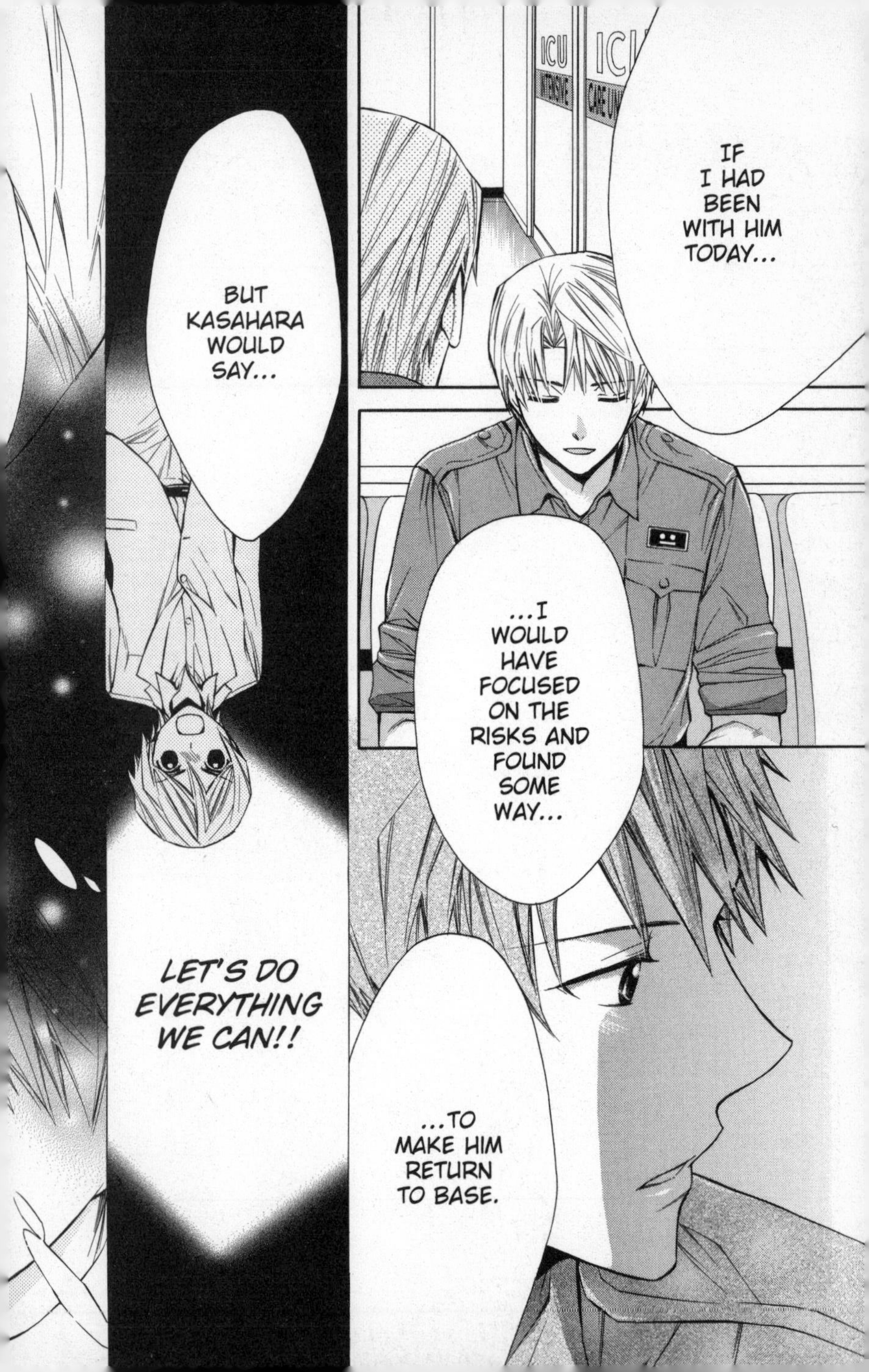
ICU
ICU
IF I HAD BEEN WITH HIM TODAY...
...I WOULD HAVE FOCUSED ON THE RISKS AND FOUND SOME WAY...
...TO MAKE HIM RETURN TO BASE.
BUT KASAHARA WOULD SAY...
LET'S DO EVERYTHING WE CAN!!

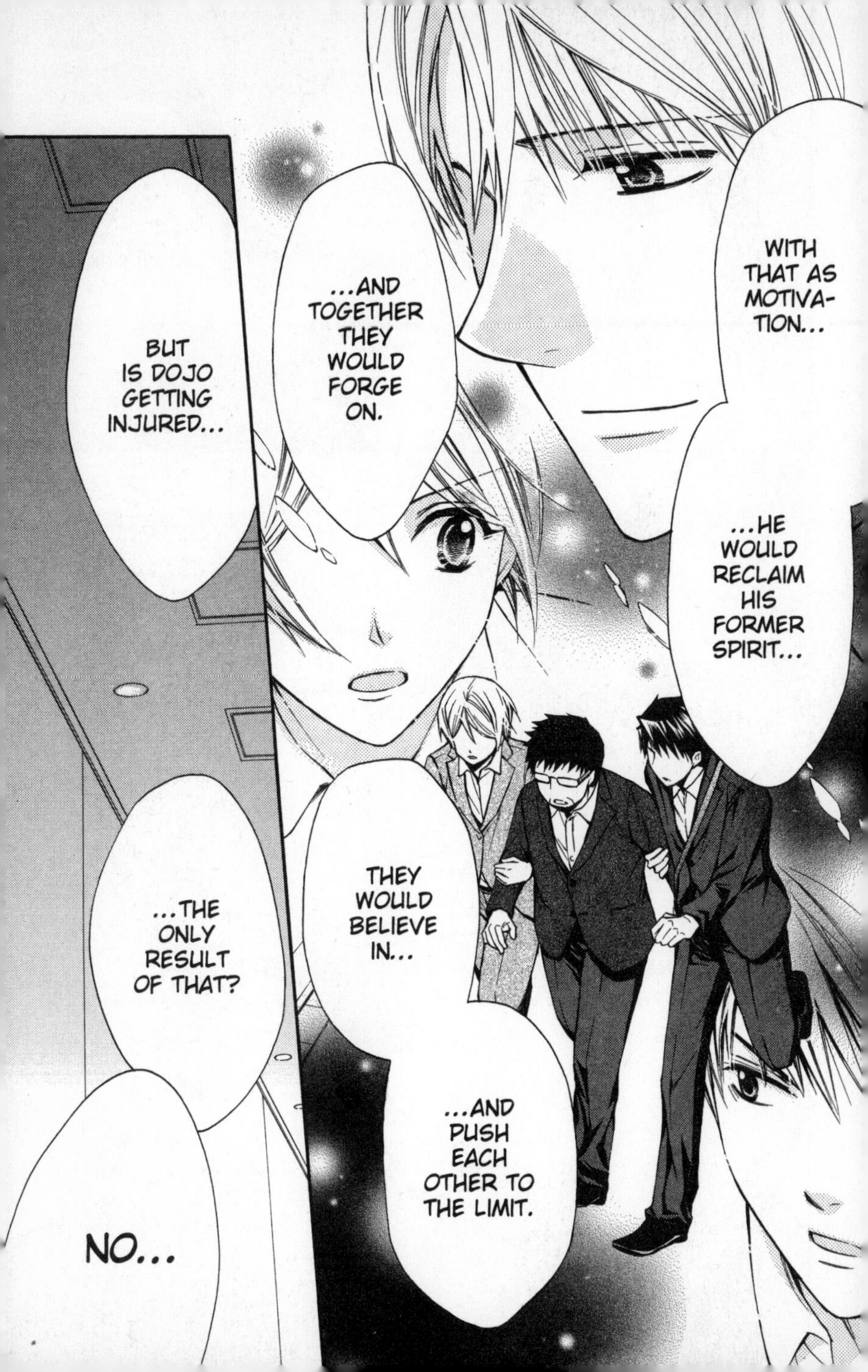
WITH THAT AS MOTIVA-TION...
...HE WOULD RECLAIM HIS FORMER SPIRIT...
...AND TOGETHER THEY WOULD FORGE ON.
THEY WOULD BELIEVE IN...
...AND PUSH EACH OTHER TO THE LIMIT.
BUT IS DOJO GETTING INJURED...
...THE ONLY RESULT OF THAT?
NO...

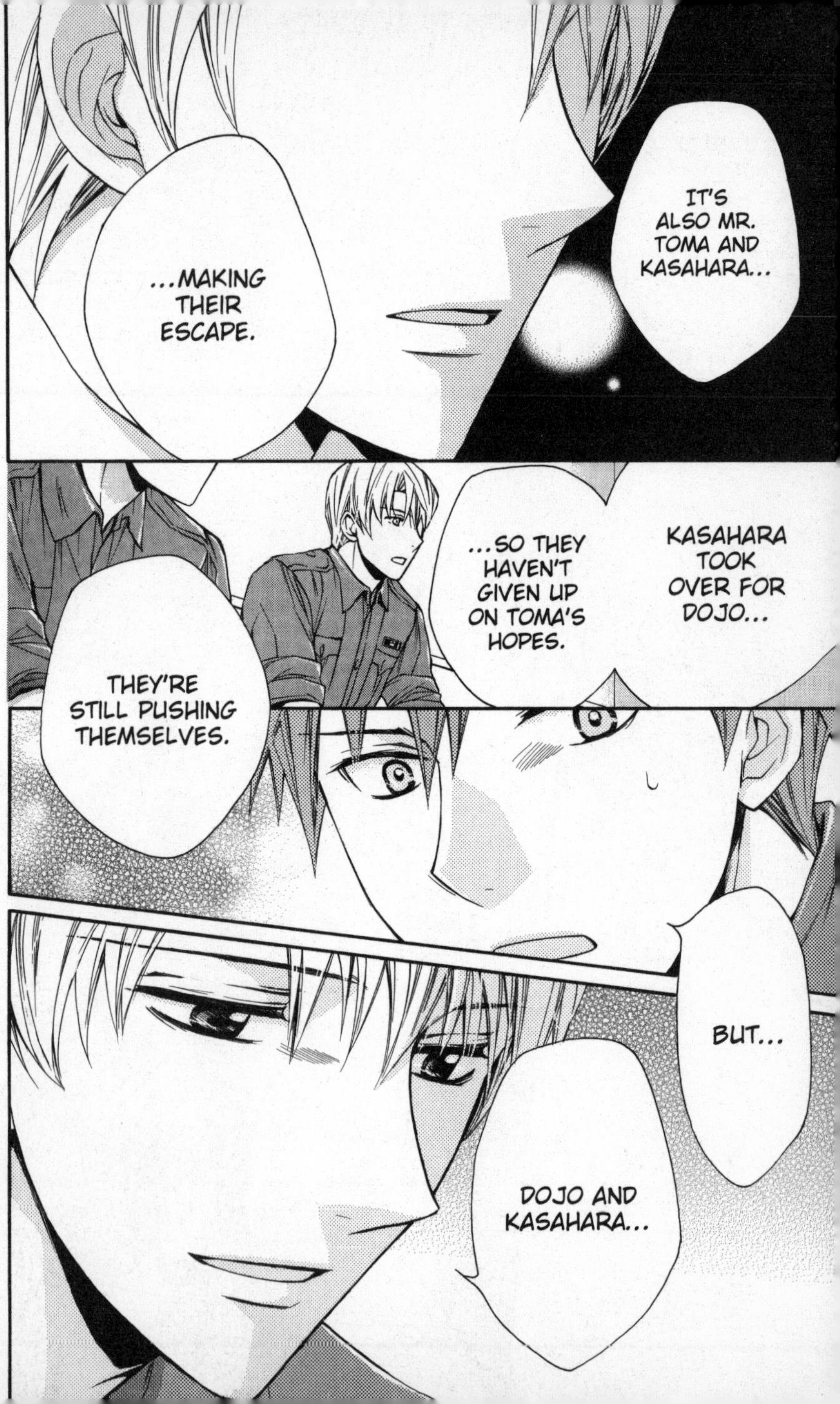
IT'S ALSO MR. TOMA AND KASAHARA...
...MAKING THEIR ESCAPE.
KASAHARA TOOK OVER FOR DOJO...
...SO THEY HAVEN'T GIVEN UP ON TOMA'S HOPES.
THEY'RE STILL PUSHING THEMSELVES.
BUT...
DOJO AND KASAHARA...

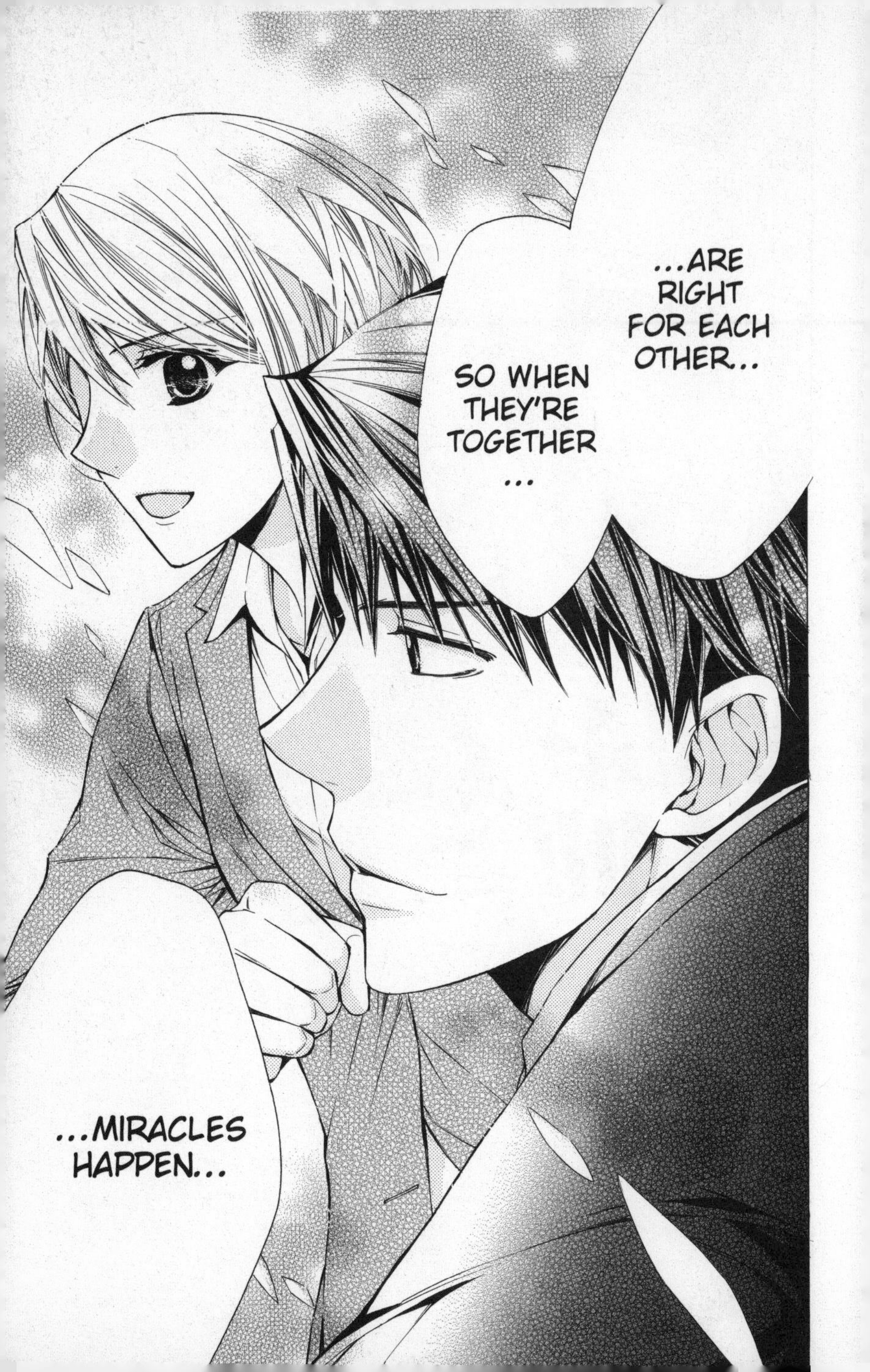
...ARE RIGHT FOR EACH OTHER...
SO WHEN THEY'RE TOGETHER ...
...MIRACLES HAPPEN...

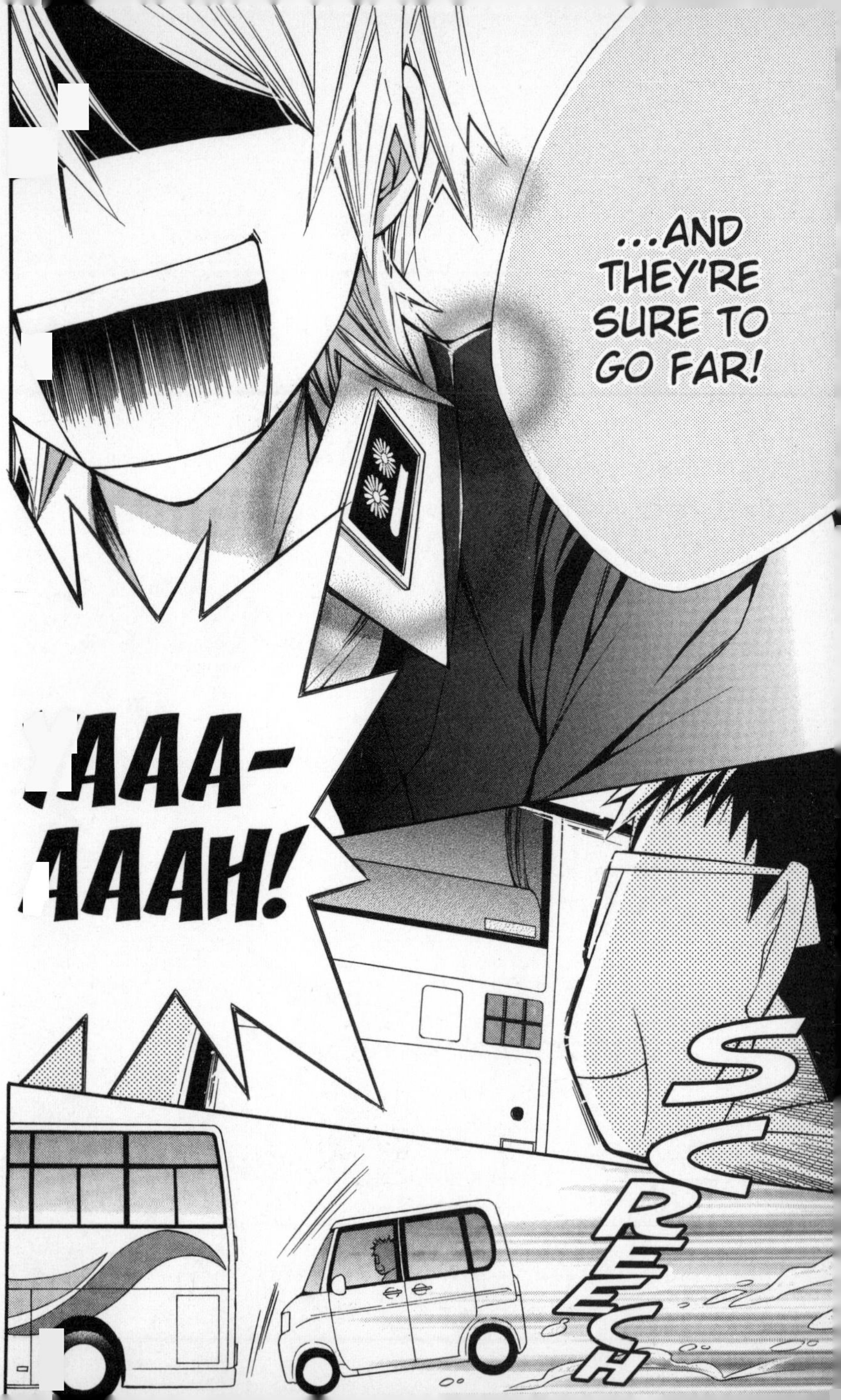
...AND THEY'RE SURE TO GO FAR!
AAA-AAAH!
SCREECH

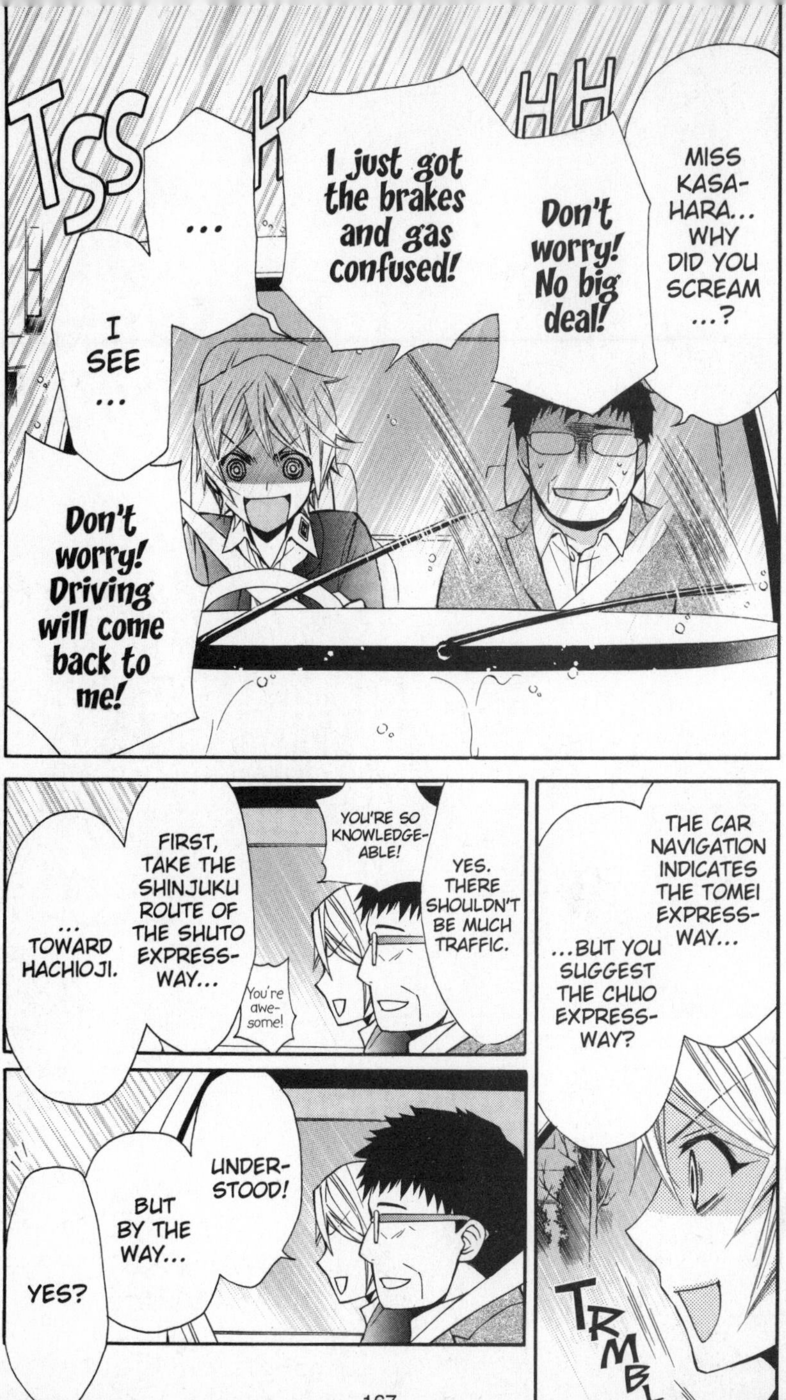
TSSHHH
MISS KASAHARA... WHY DID YOU SCREAM...?
Don't worry! No big deal!
I just got the brakes and gas confused!
...
I SEE...
Don't worry! Driving will come back to me!
THE CAR NAVIGATION INDICATES THE TOMEI EXPRESSWAY...
...BUT YOU SUGGEST THE CHUO EXPRESSWAY?
TRMBL
YES. THERE SHOULDN'T BE MUCH TRAFFIC.
YOU'RE SO KNOWLEDGEABLE!
You're awesome!
FIRST, TAKE THE SHINJUKU ROUTE OF THE SHUTO EXPRESSWAY...
...TOWARD HACHIOJI.
UNDERSTOOD!
BUT BY THE WAY...
YES?

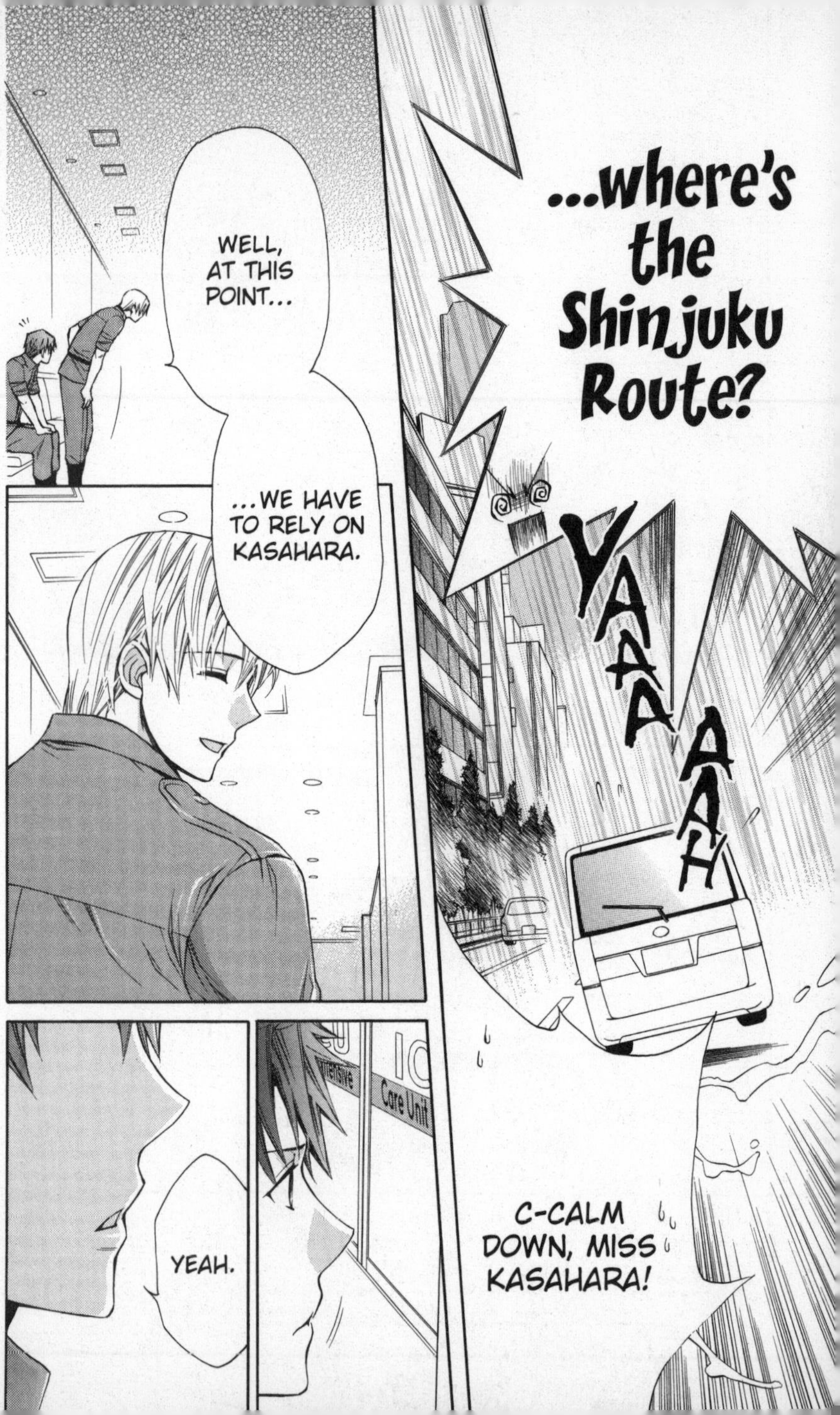
...where's the Shinjuku Route?
YAAAAAAH
C-CALM DOWN, MISS KASAHARA!
WELL, AT THIS POINT...
...WE HAVE TO RELY ON KASAHARA.
Care Unit
YEAH.

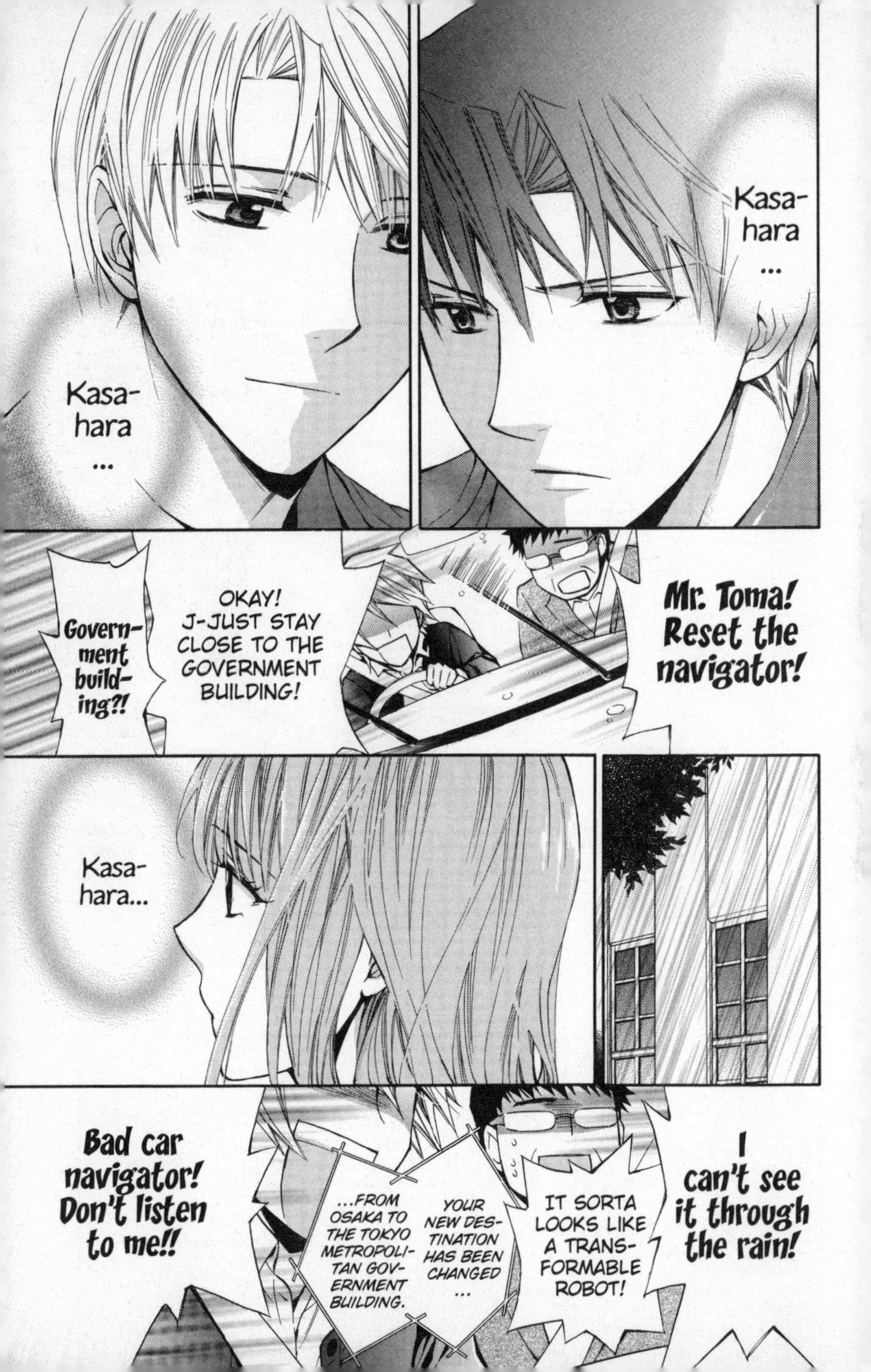
Kasahara ...
Kasahara ...
Mr. Toma! Reset the navigator!
OKAY! J-JUST STAY CLOSE TO THE GOVERNMENT BUILDING!
Government building?!
Kasahara...
I can't see it through the rain!
IT SORTA LOOKS LIKE A TRANSFORMABLE ROBOT!
YOUR NEW DESTINATION HAS BEEN CHANGED ...
...FROM OSAKA TO THE TOKYO METROPOLITAN GOVERNMENT BUILDING.
Bad car navigator! Don't listen to me!!

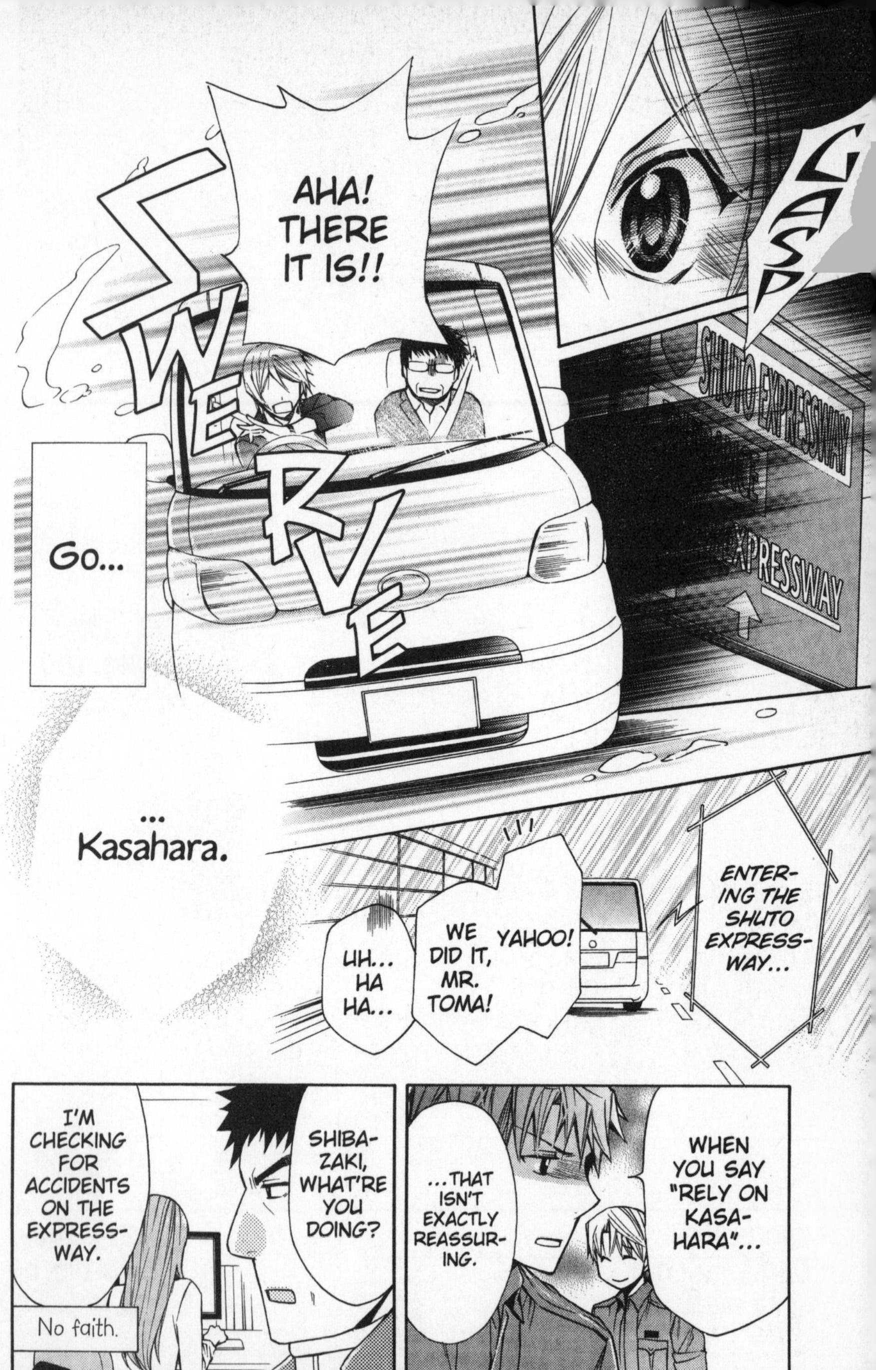
GASP
AHA! THERE IT IS!!
SWERVE
SHUTO EXPRESSWAY
EXPRESSWAY
Go...
... Kasahara.
ENTERING THE SHUTO EXPRESSWAY...
YAHOO!
WE DID IT, MR. TOMA!
UH... HA HA...
WHEN YOU SAY "RELY ON KASAHARA"...
...THAT ISN'T EXACTLY REASSURING.
SHIBAZAKI, WHAT'RE YOU DOING?
I'M CHECKING FOR ACCIDENTS ON THE EXPRESSWAY.
No faith.

LIBRARY WARS LOVE & WAR VOLUME 14 / THE END

BONUS MANGA

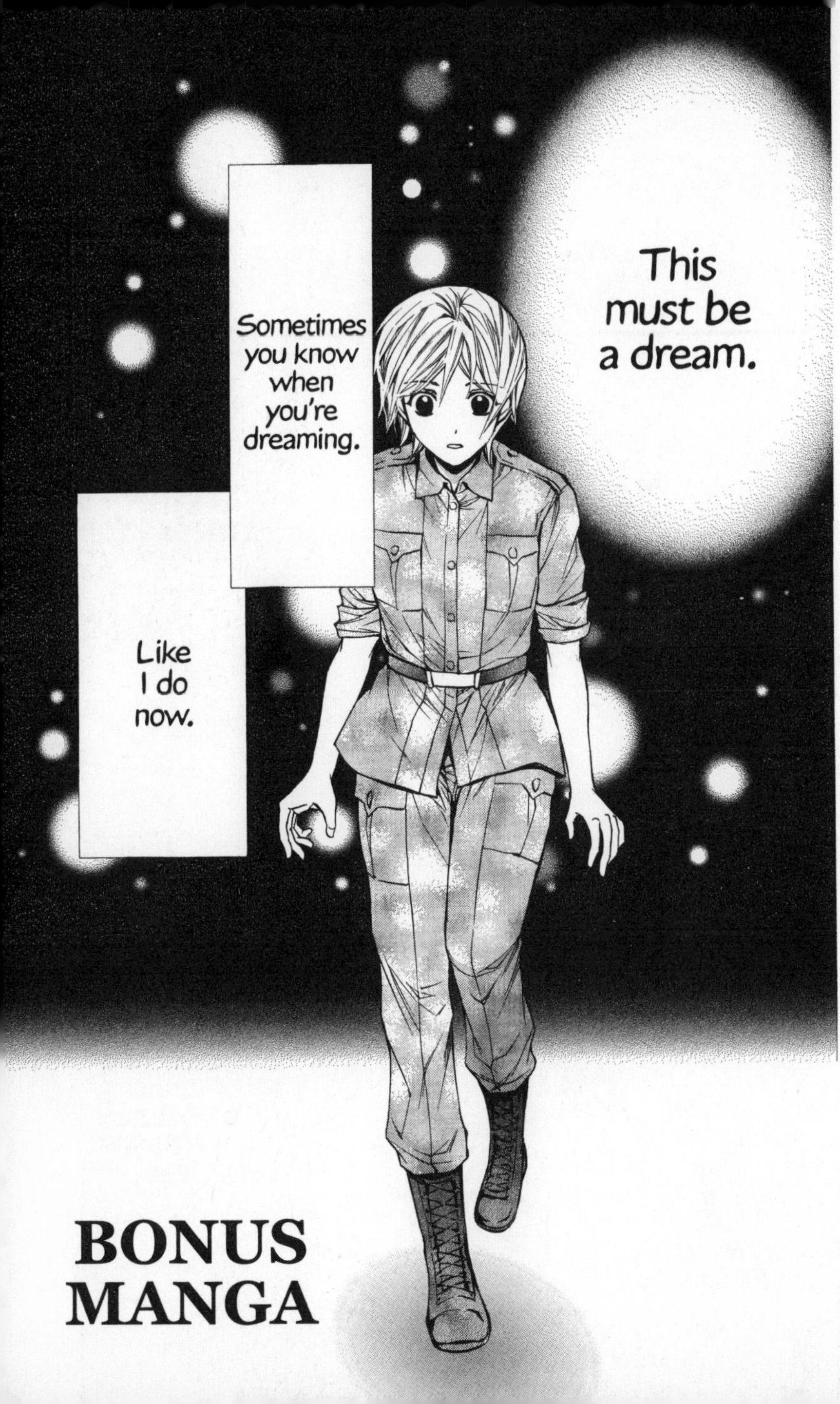
This must be a dream.
Sometimes you know when you're dreaming.
Like I do now.

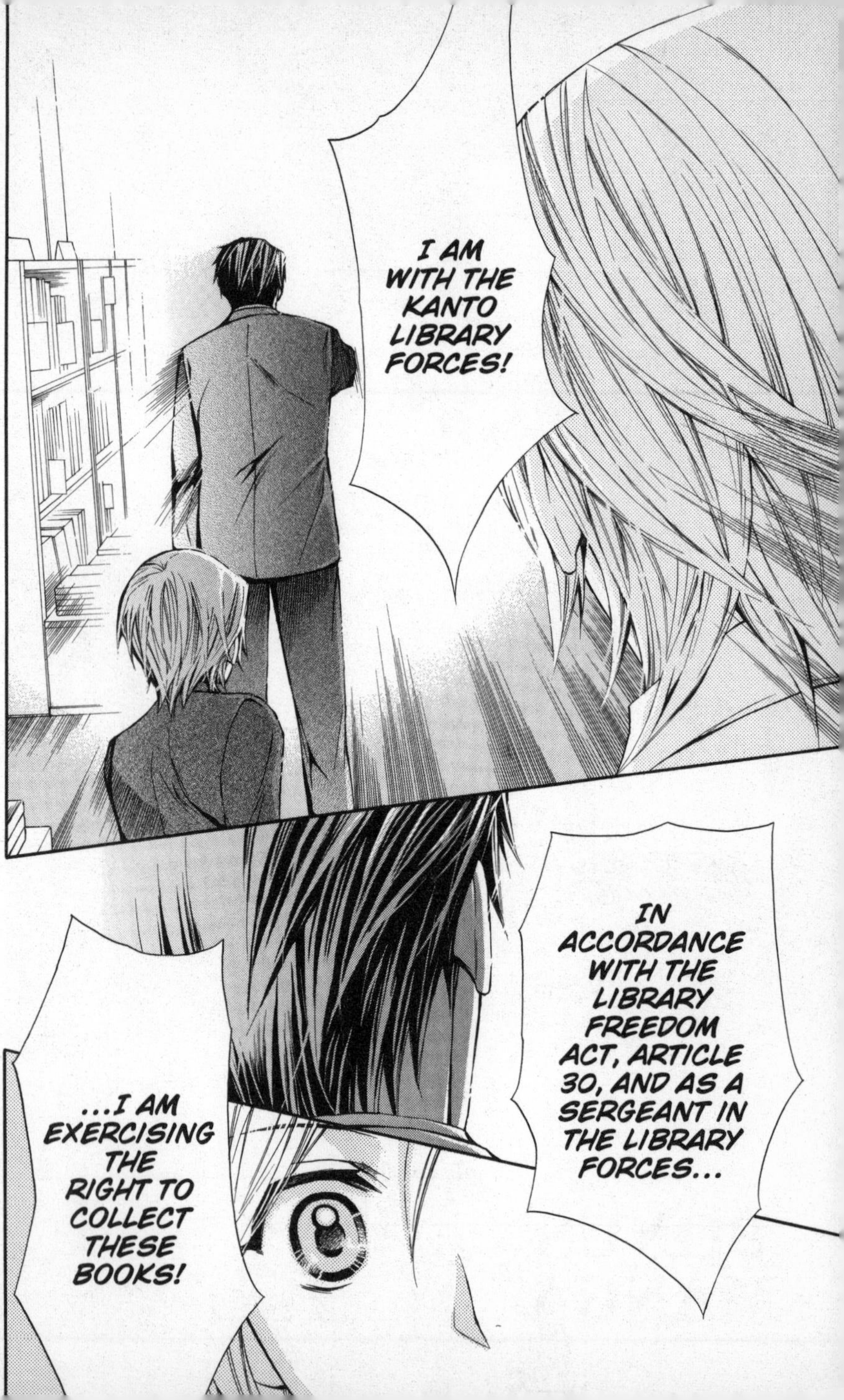
I AM WITH THE KANTO LIBRARY FORCES!
IN ACCORDANCE WITH THE LIBRARY FREEDOM ACT, ARTICLE 30, AND AS A SERGEANT IN THE LIBRARY FORCES...
...I AM EXERCISING THE RIGHT TO COLLECT THESE BOOKS!

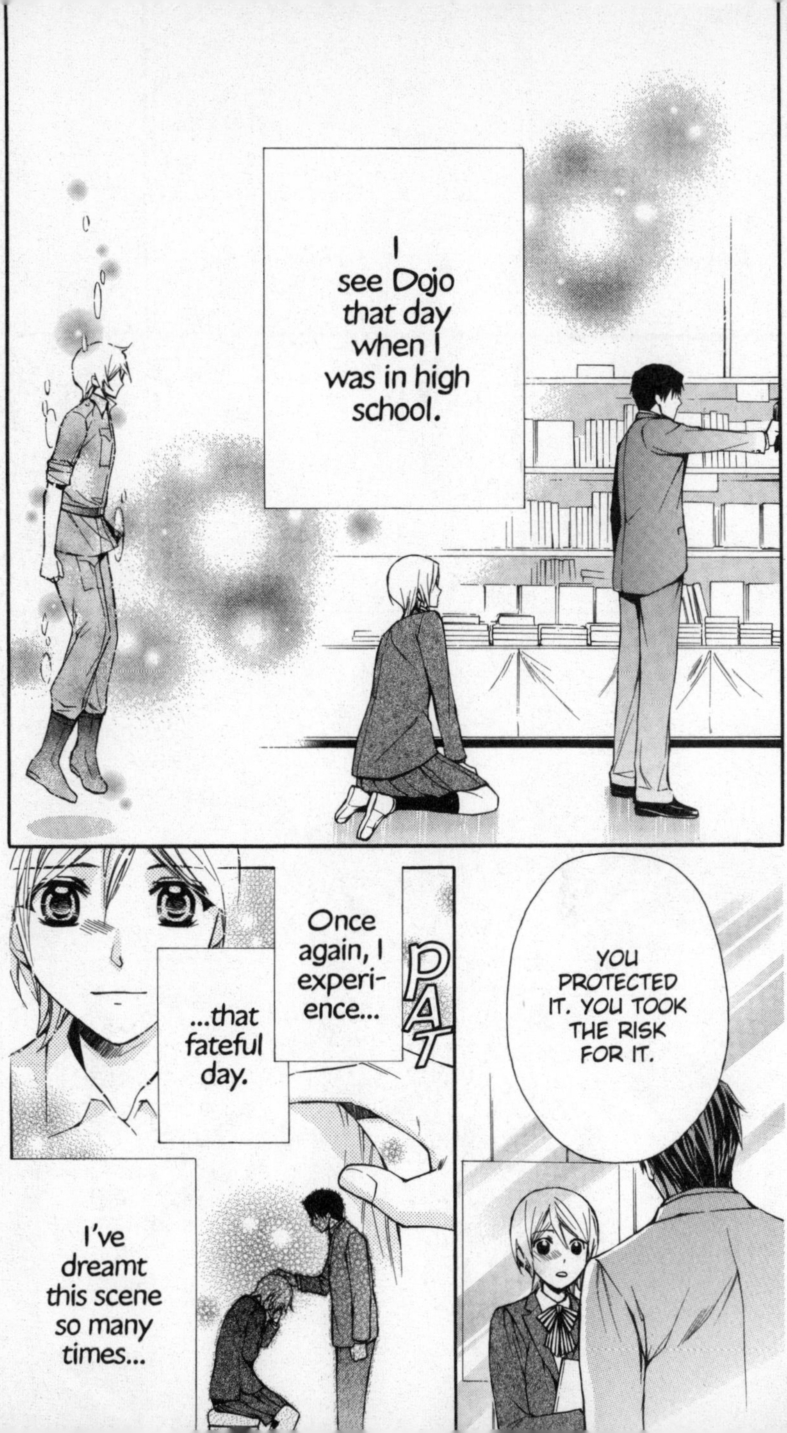
I see Dojo that day when I was in high school.
YOU PROTECTED IT. YOU TOOK THE RISK FOR IT.
Once again, I experience...
PAT
...that fateful day.
I've dreamt this scene so many times...

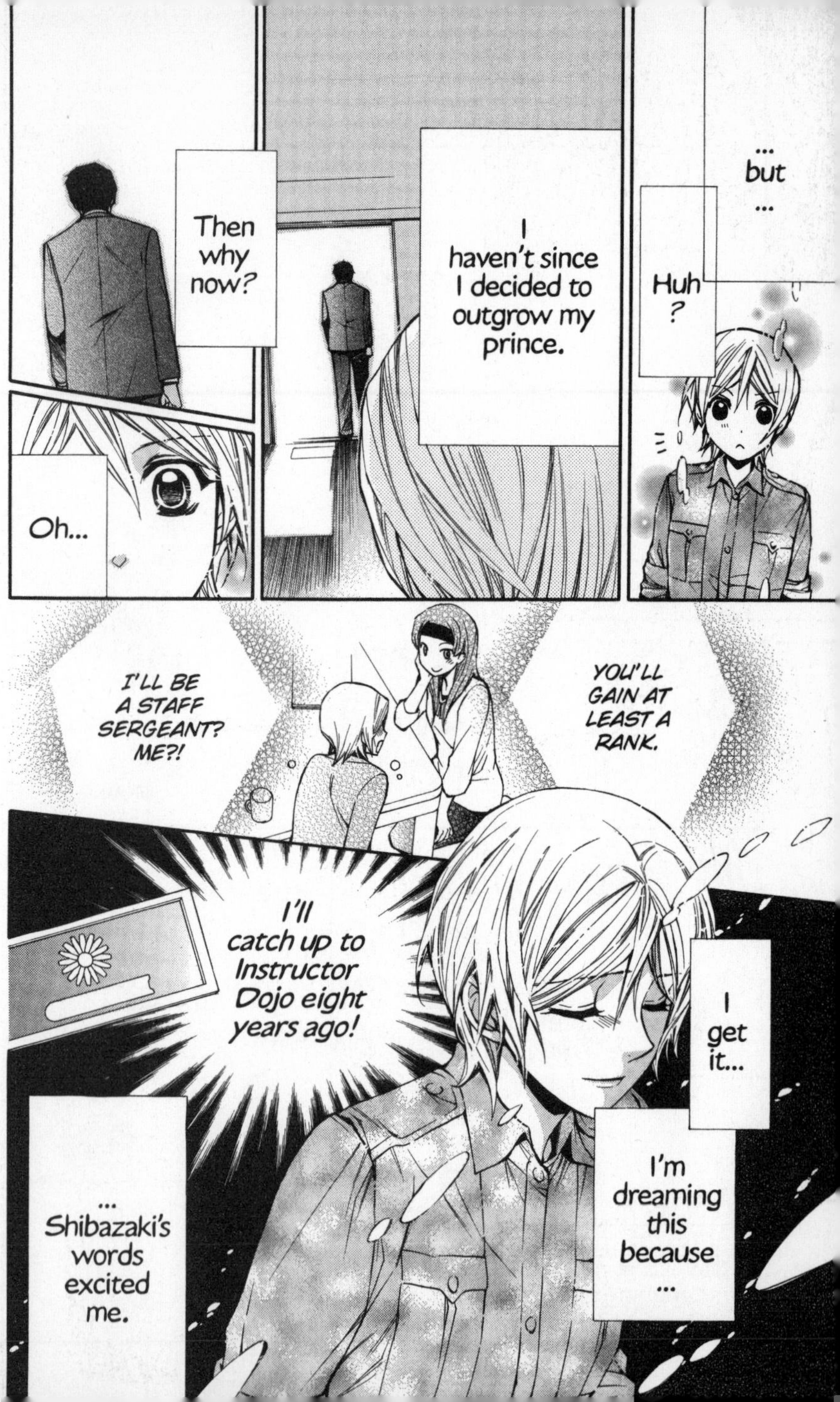
... but ...
Huh?
I haven't since I decided to outgrow my prince.
Then why now?
Oh...
YOU'LL GAIN AT LEAST A RANK.
I'LL BE A STAFF SERGEANT? ME?!
I get it...
I'm dreaming this because ...
I'll catch up to Instructor Dojo eight years ago!
... Shibazaki's words excited me.

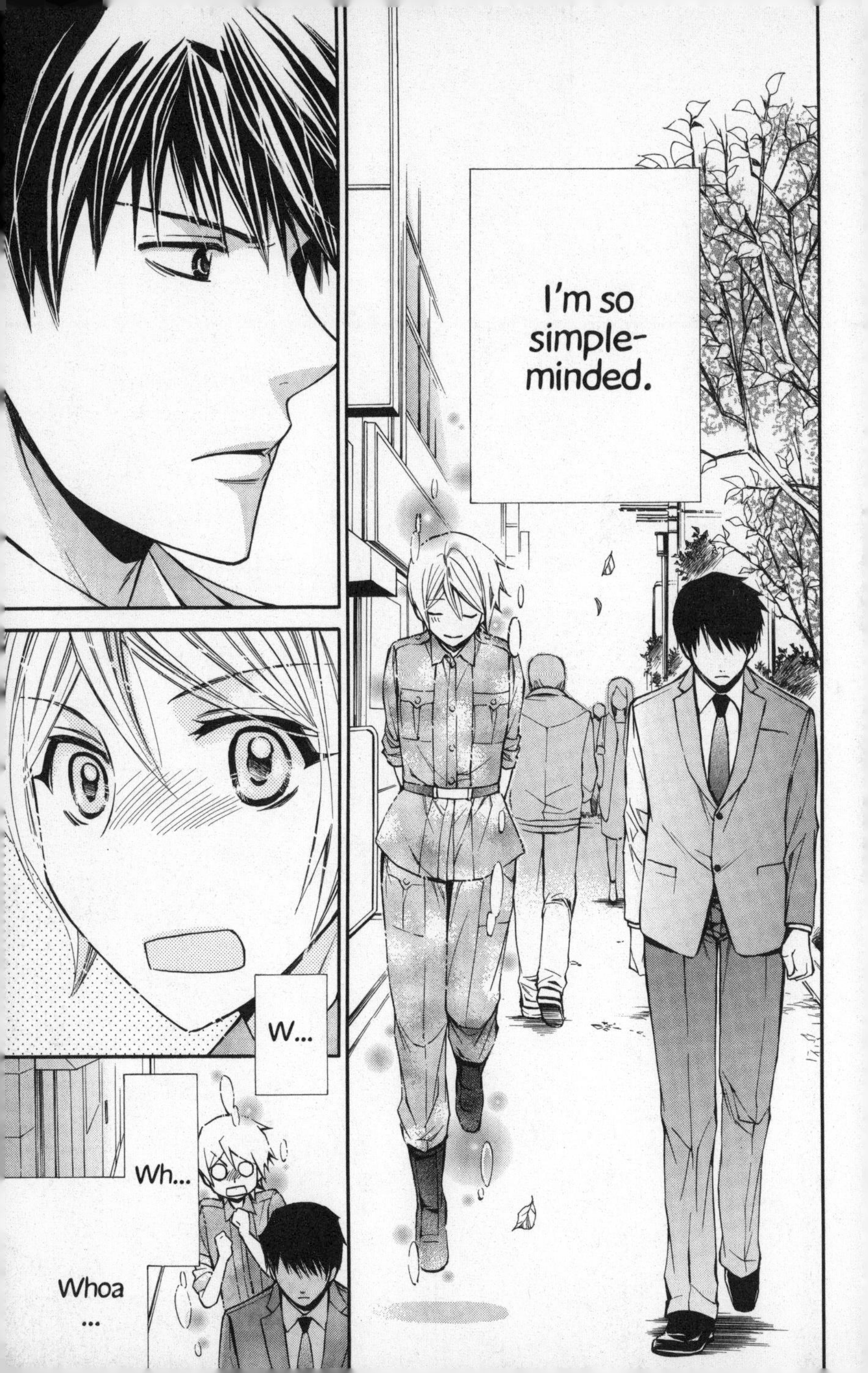
I'm so simple-minded.
W...
Wh...
Whoa ...

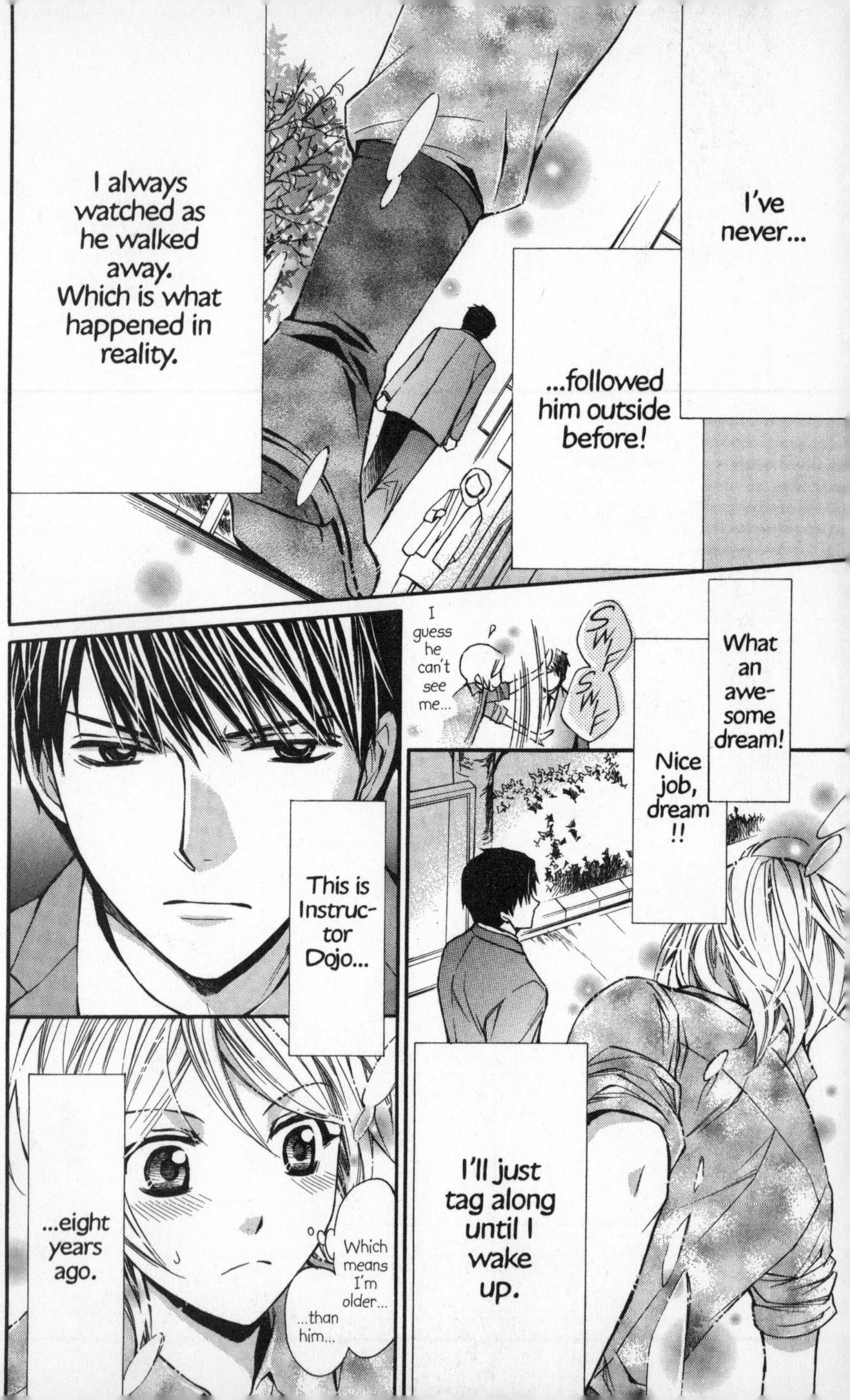
I've never...
...followed him outside before!
I always watched as he walked away. Which is what happened in reality.
SWF
SWF
I guess he can't see me...
What an awesome dream!
Nice job, dream!!
I'll just tag along until I wake up.
This is Instructor Dojo...
...eight years ago.
Which means I'm older...
...than him...

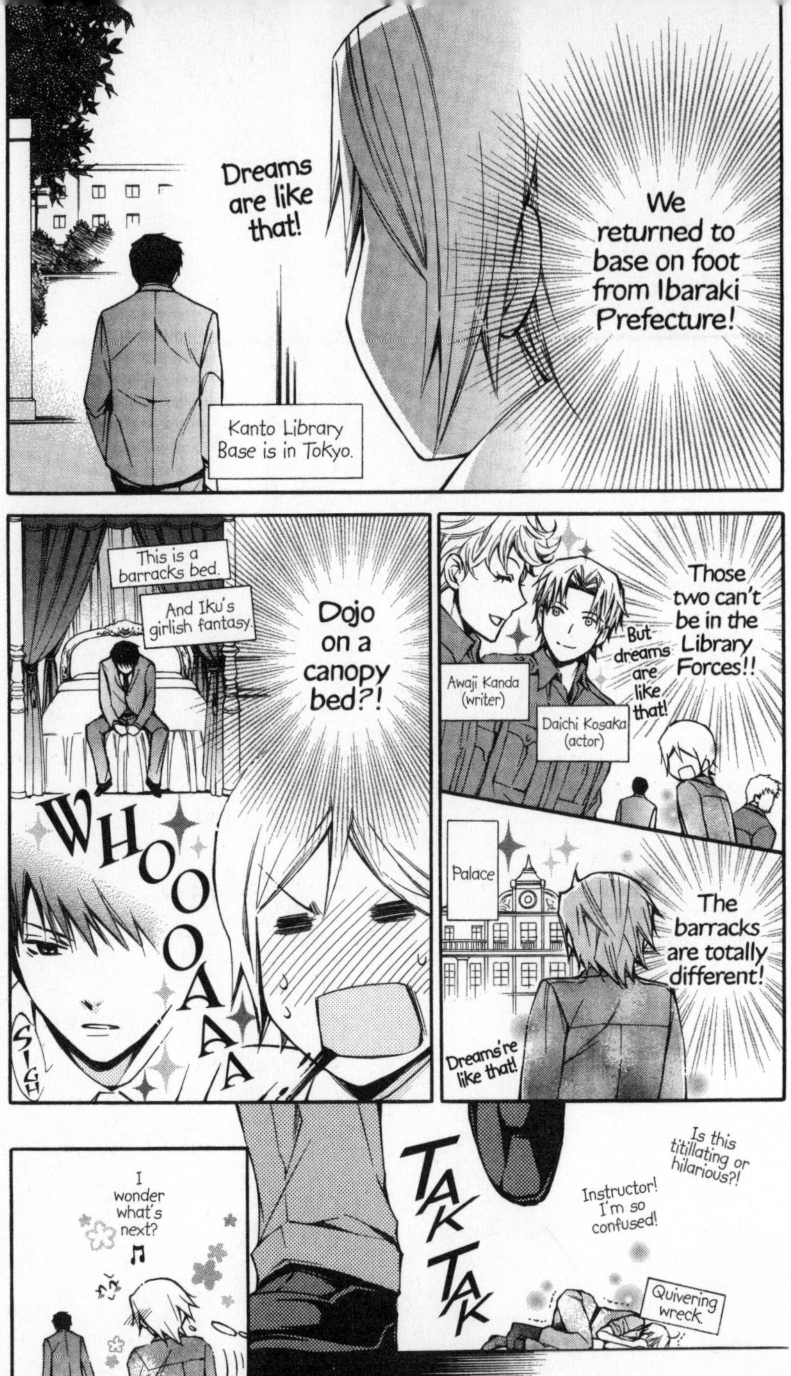
We returned to base on foot from Ibaraki Prefecture!
Dreams are like that!
Kanto Library Base is in Tokyo.
Those two can't be in the Library Forces!!
But dreams are like that!
Daichi Kosaka (actor)
Awaji Kanda (writer)
The barracks are totally different!
Palace
Dreams're like that!
Dojo on a canopy bed?!
This is a barracks bed.
And Iku's girlish fantasy.
WHOOOAAAA
SIGH
Is this titillating or hilarious?!
Instructor! I'm so confused!
Quivering wreck.
TAK TAK
I wonder what's next? ♪

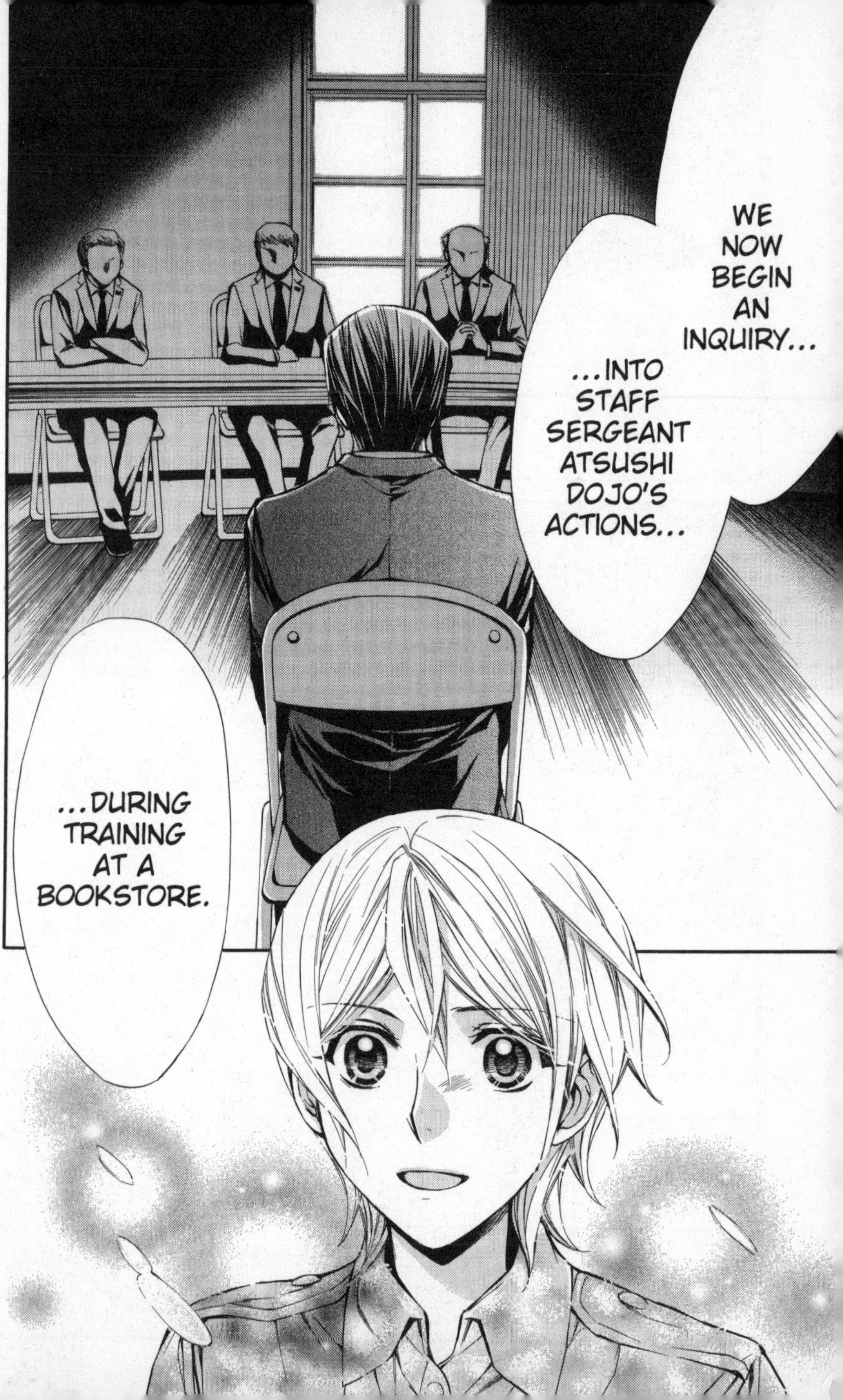
WE NOW BEGIN AN INQUIRY...
...INTO STAFF SERGEANT ATSUSHI DOJO'S ACTIONS...
...DURING TRAINING AT A BOOKSTORE.

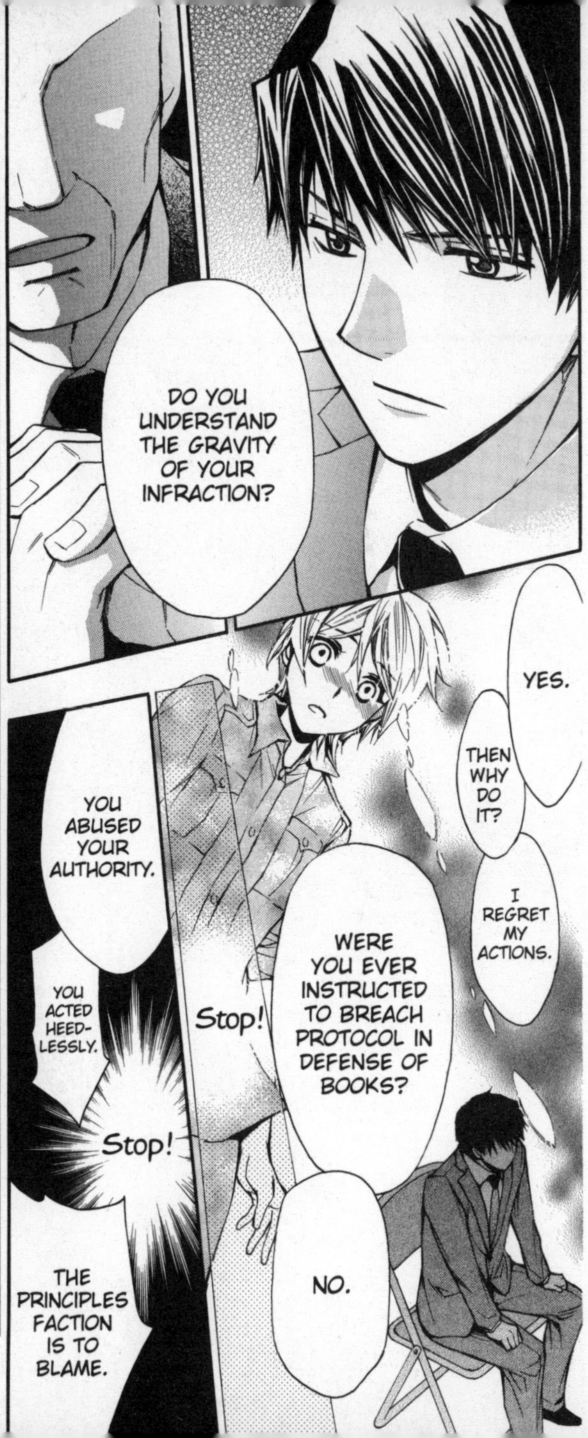
DO YOU UNDERSTAND THE GRAVITY OF YOUR INFRACTION?
YES.
THEN WHY DO IT?
I REGRET MY ACTIONS.
YOU ABUSED YOUR AUTHORITY.
WERE YOU EVER INSTRUCTED TO BREACH PROTOCOL IN DEFENSE OF BOOKS?
Stop!
YOU ACTED HEED-LESSLY.
Stop!
NO.
THE PRINCIPLES FACTION IS TO BLAME.

7

*

This is the final sidebar! Thanks for reading all this way! This time I was nervous and deeply moved at the same time because I got to write the show-stopper scene from the novel *Library Wars: Revolution*. I'll write all my feelings when *Revolution* finishes. I'll write a bunch next time! I'd love it if you stick around for Volume 15! Keep supporting me! Bye!

Special thanks are at the end of the book.

Kiiro Yumi

弓きいろ

*

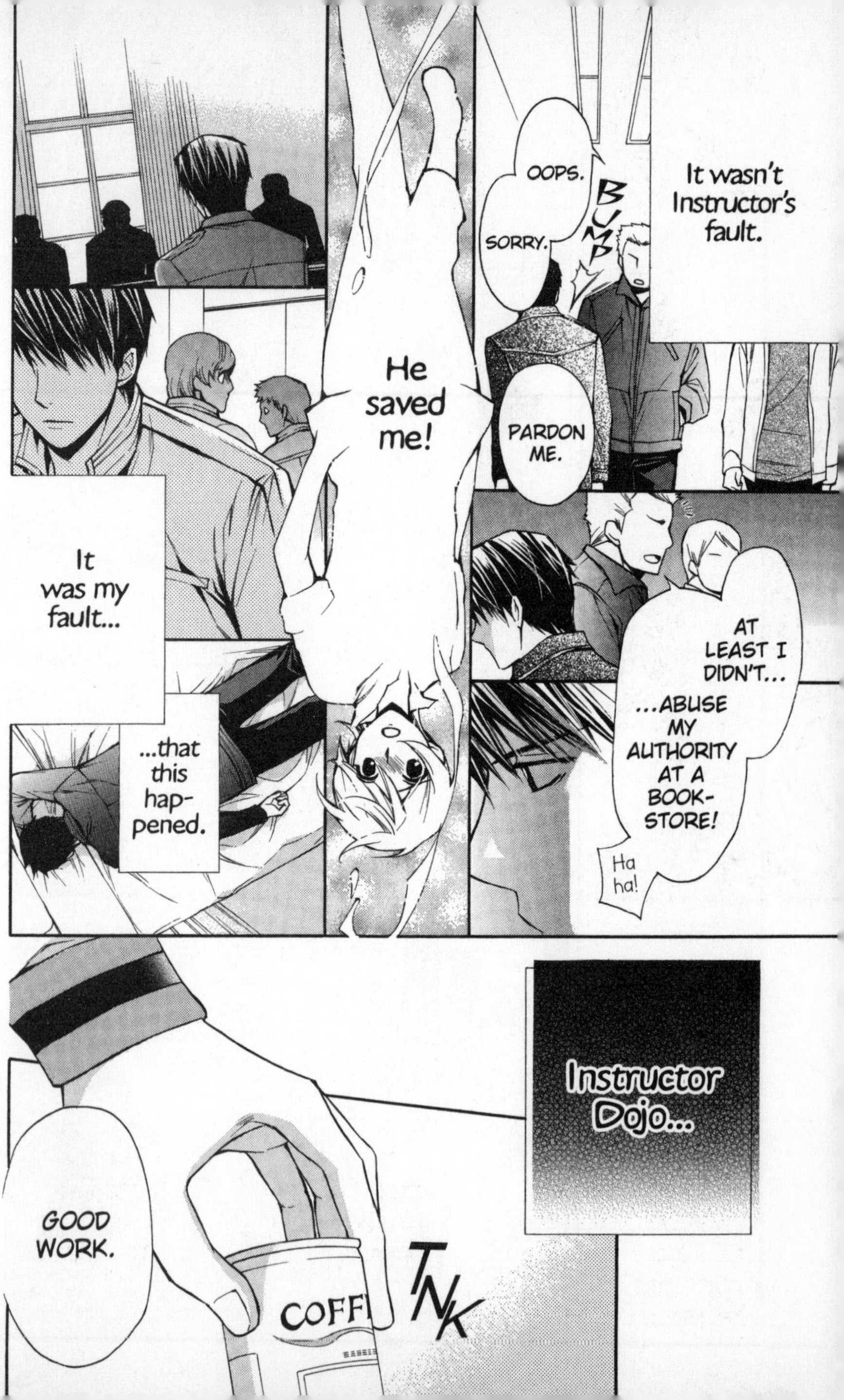
It wasn't Instructor's fault.
OOPS.
SORRY.
BUMP
PARDON ME.
AT LEAST I DIDN'T...
...ABUSE MY AUTHORITY AT A BOOKSTORE!
Ha ha!
He saved me!
It was my fault...
...that this happened.
Instructor Dojo...
GOOD WORK.
TNK
COFF

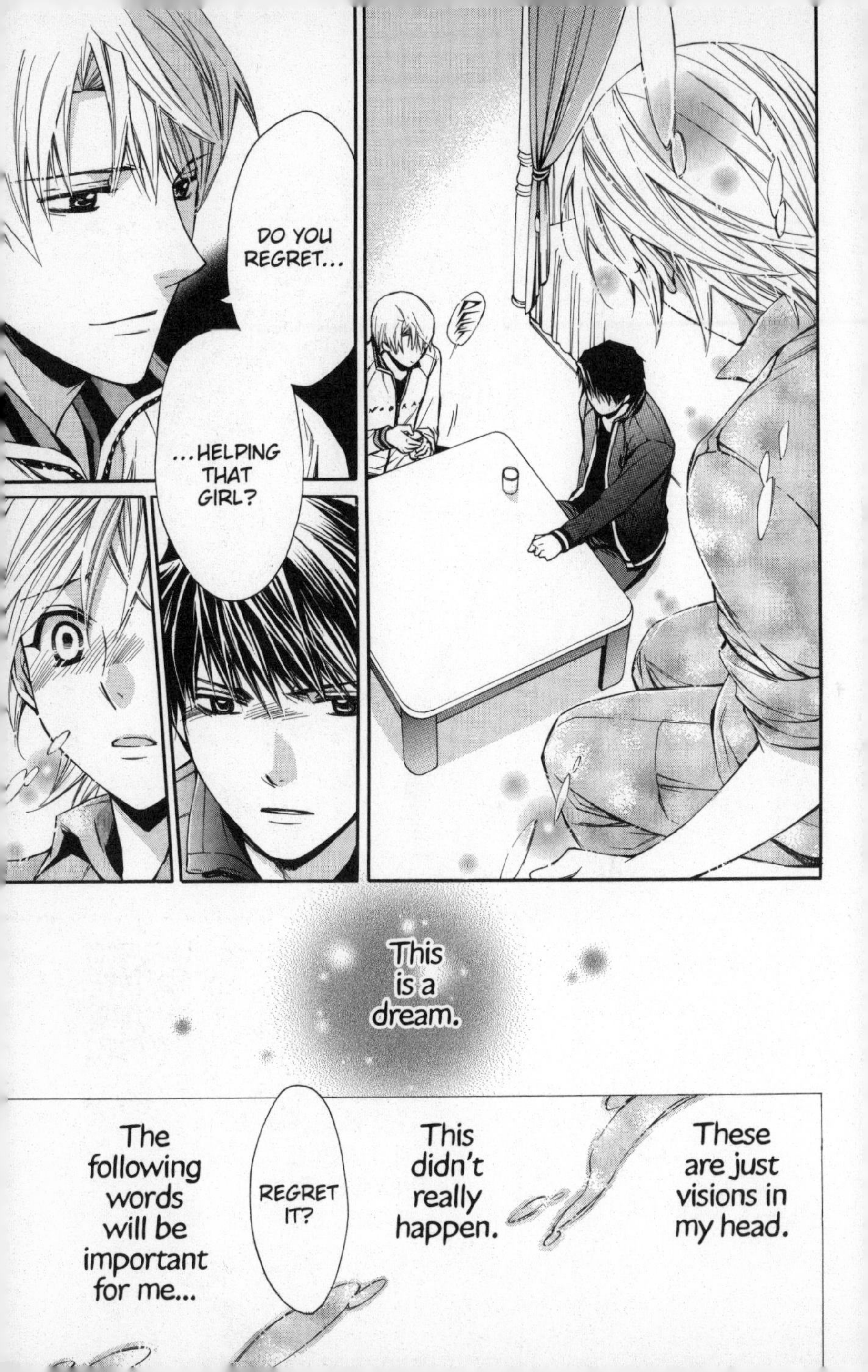
DO YOU REGRET...
...HELPING THAT GIRL?
This is a dream.
These are just visions in my head.
This didn't really happen.
REGRET IT?
The following words will be important for me...

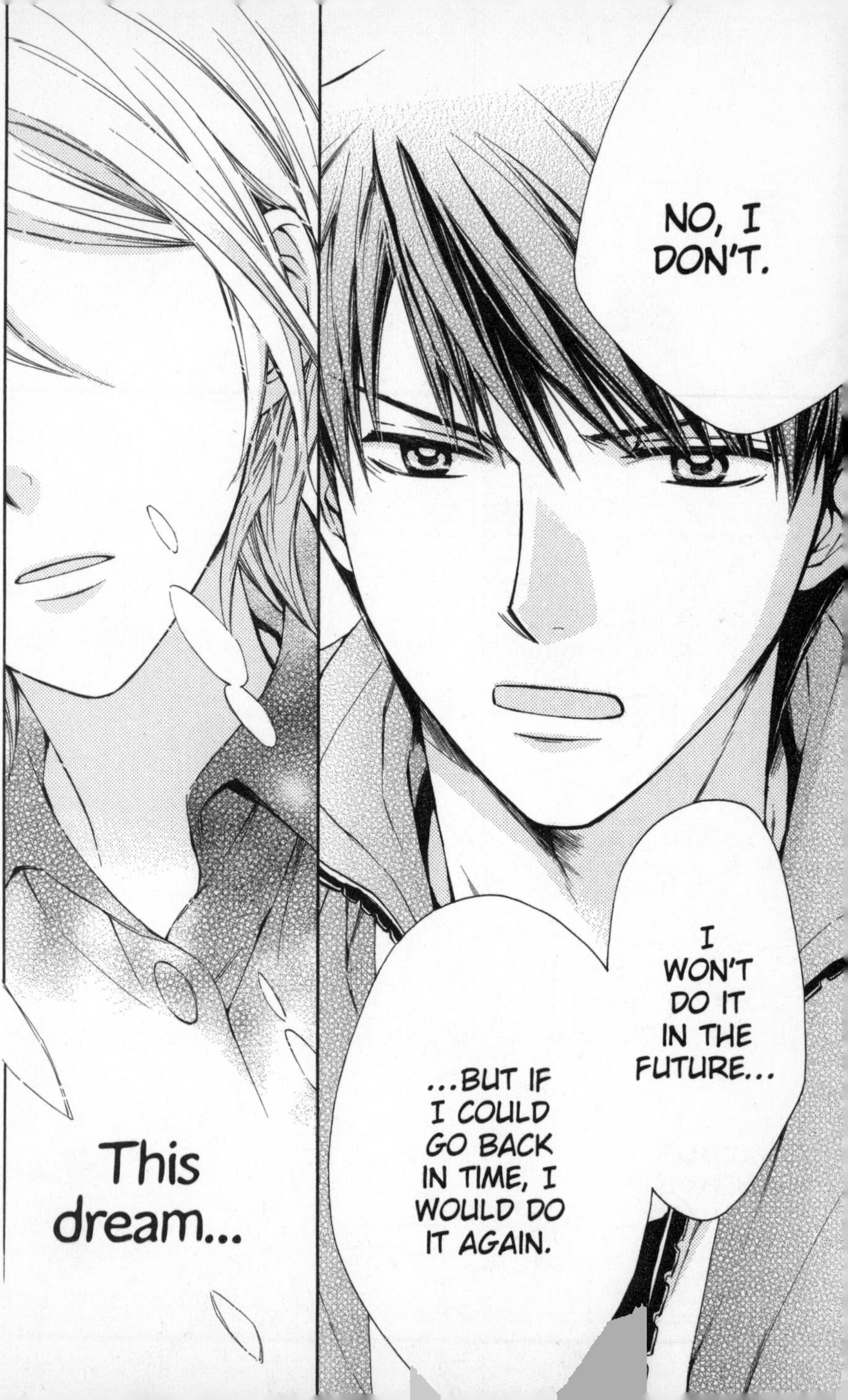
NO, I DON'T.
I WON'T DO IT IN THE FUTURE...
...BUT IF I COULD GO BACK IN TIME, I WOULD DO IT AGAIN.
This dream...

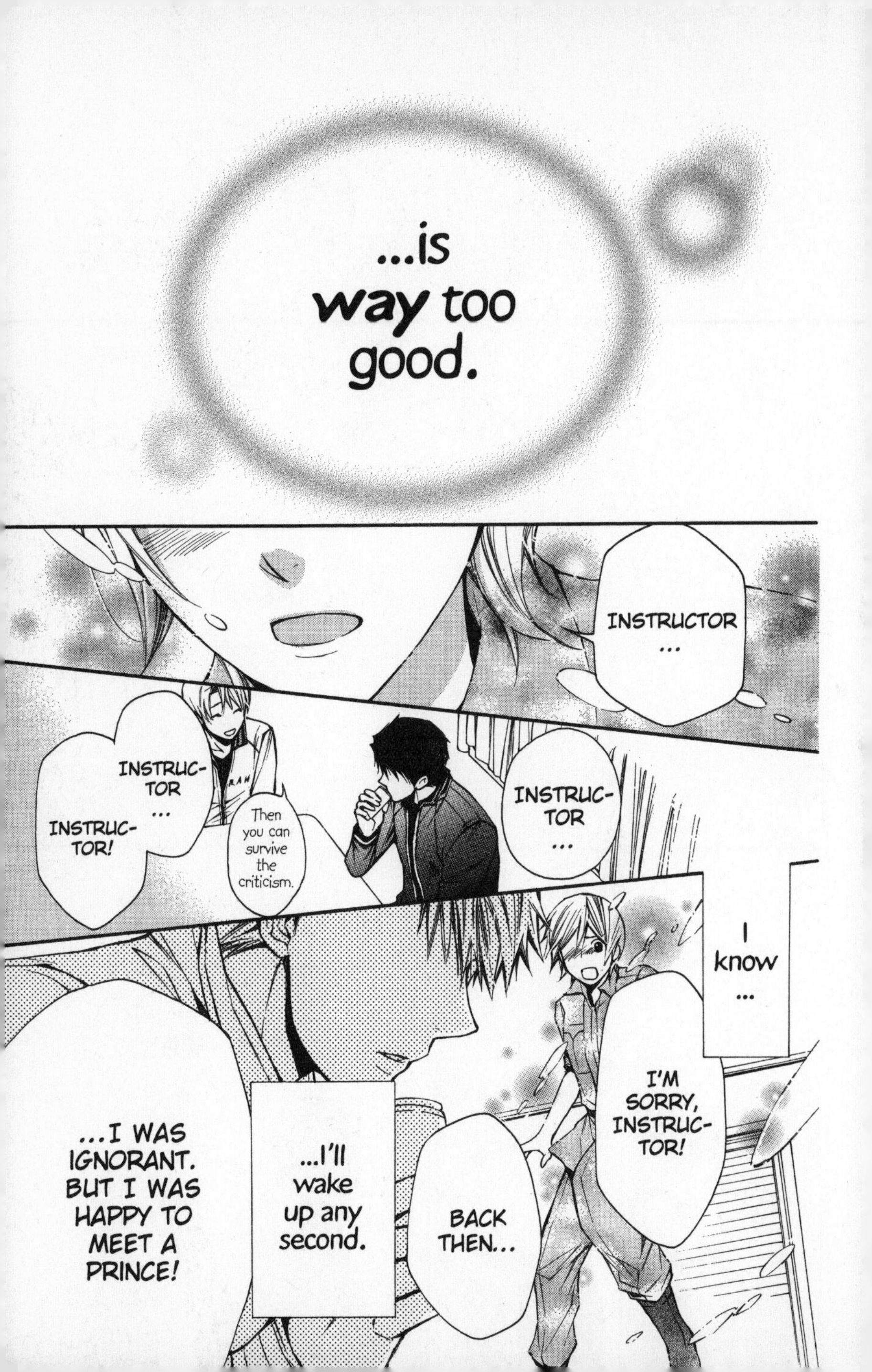
...is way too good.
INSTRUCTOR...
INSTRUCTOR...
Then you can survive the criticism.
INSTRUCTOR... INSTRUCTOR!
I know...
I'M SORRY, INSTRUCTOR!
BACK THEN...
...I'll wake up any second.
...I WAS IGNORANT. BUT I WAS HAPPY TO MEET A PRINCE!

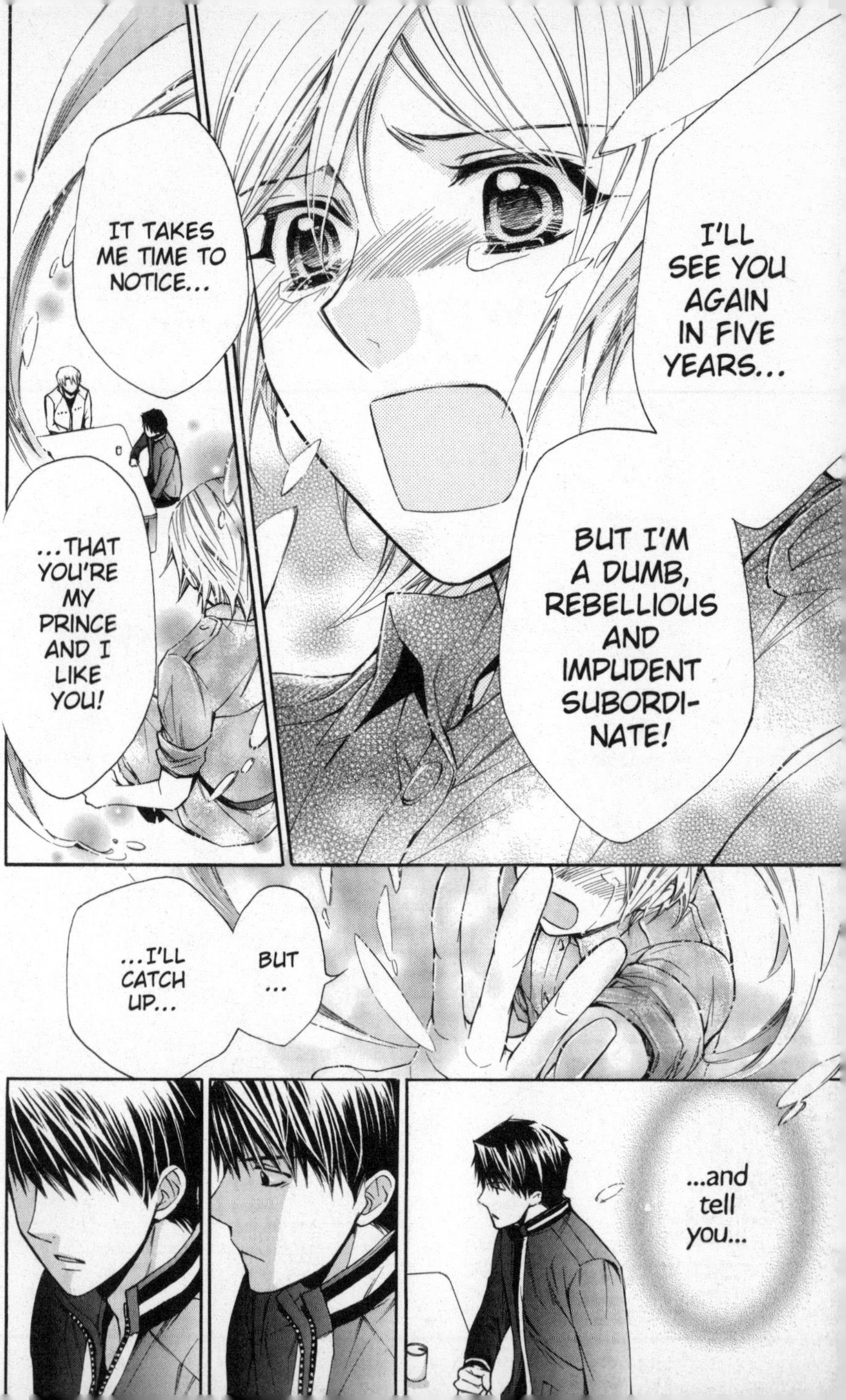
I'LL SEE YOU AGAIN IN FIVE YEARS...
BUT I'M A DUMB, REBELLIOUS AND IMPUDENT SUBORDI-NATE!
IT TAKES ME TIME TO NOTICE...
...THAT YOU'RE MY PRINCE AND I LIKE YOU!
BUT...
...I'LL CATCH UP...
...and tell you...

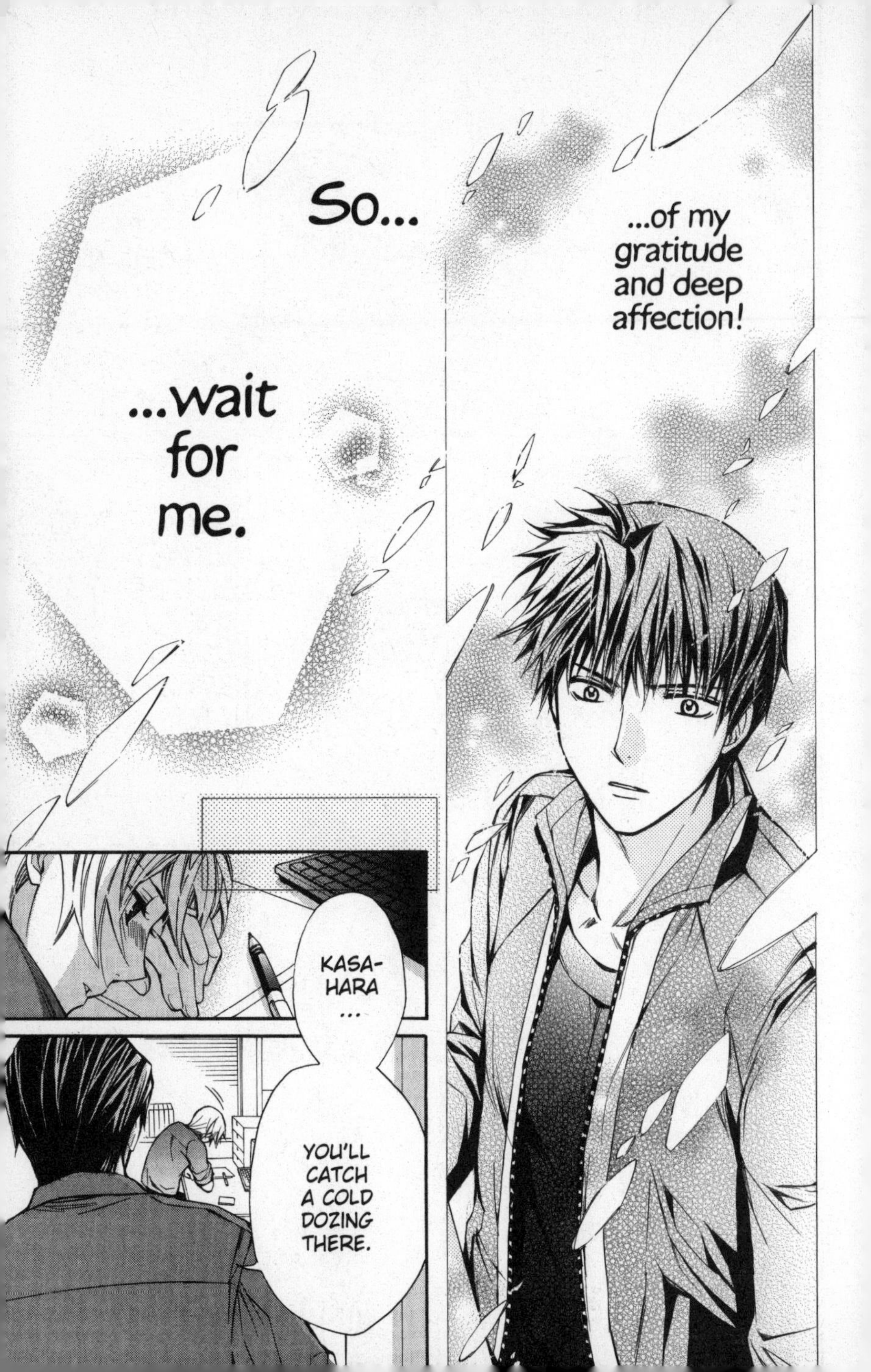
...of my gratitude and deep affection!
So...
...wait for me.
KASA-HARA ...
YOU'LL CATCH A COLD DOZING THERE.

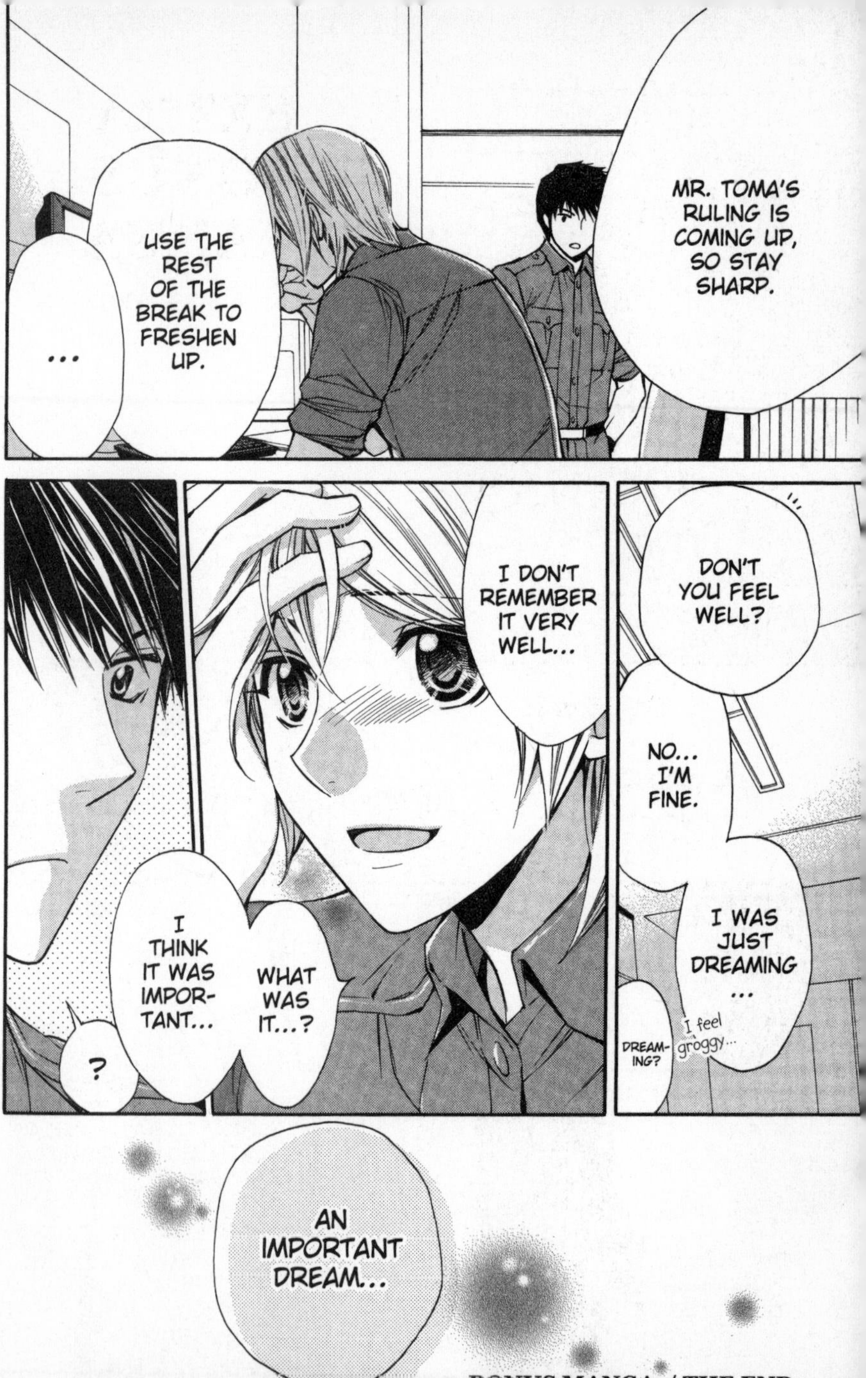
MR. TOMA'S RULING IS COMING UP, SO STAY SHARP.
USE THE REST OF THE BREAK TO FRESHEN UP.
...
DON'T YOU FEEL WELL?
NO... I'M FINE.
I WAS JUST DREAMING...
I feel groggy...
DREAMING?
I DON'T REMEMBER IT VERY WELL...
WHAT WAS IT...?
I THINK IT WAS IMPORTANT...
?
AN IMPORTANT DREAM...

BONUS MANGA / THE END

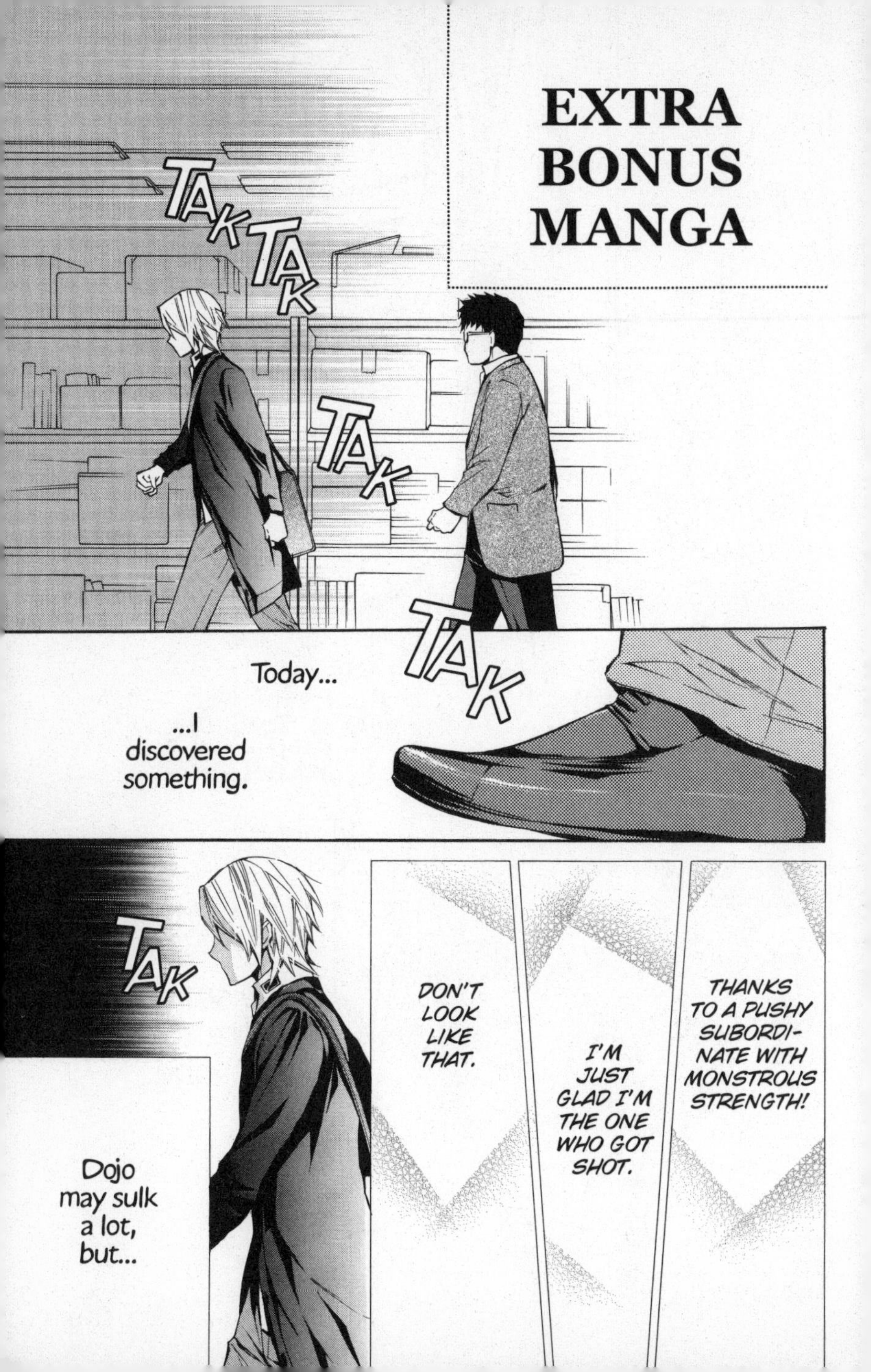
EXTRA BONUS MANGA
TAKTAKTAK
TAK
TAK
TAK
Today...
...I discovered something.
THANKS TO A PUSHY SUBORDINATE WITH MONSTROUS STRENGTH!
I'M JUST GLAD I'M THE ONE WHO GOT SHOT.
DON'T LOOK LIKE THAT.
TAK
Dojo may sulk a lot, but...

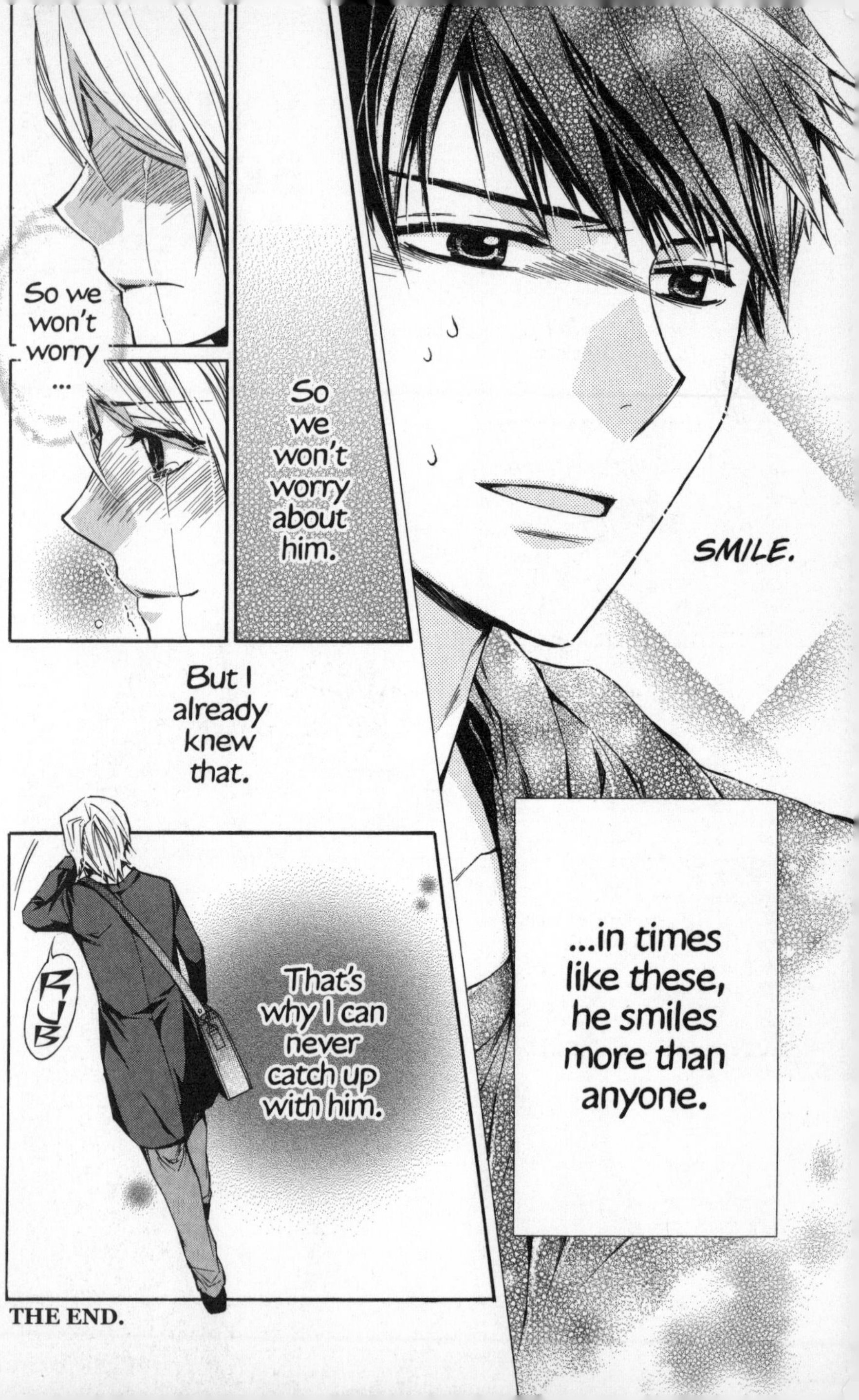

So we won't worry about him.
So we won't worry ...
But I already knew that.
...in times like these, he smiles more than anyone.
SMILE.
RUB
That's why I can never catch up with him.

THE END.

Special Thanks!!

Ms. Arikawa
Ms. Arikawa's editor
(ASCII Media)

★

Mamada,
Murakami, Aoki

★

My family

★

My editor, everyone
in *LaLa* editorial

★

Everyone who makes
this series possible.

★★ Thanks so, so much!

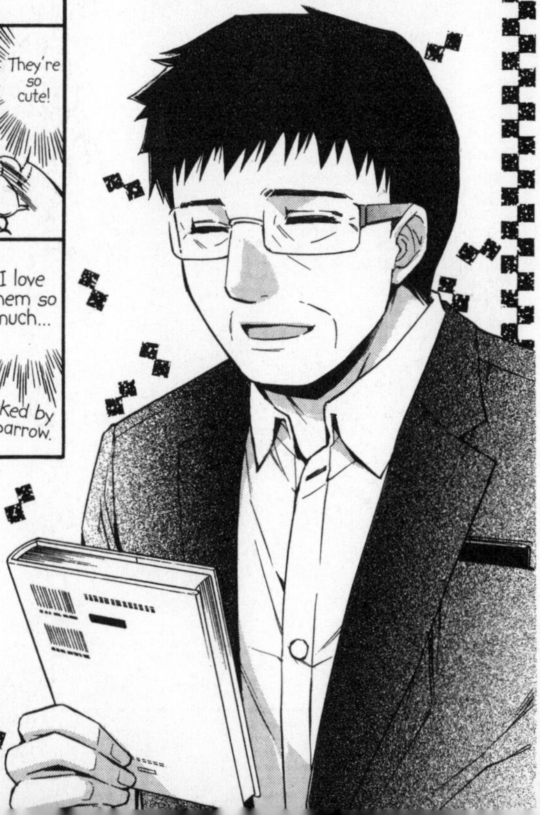

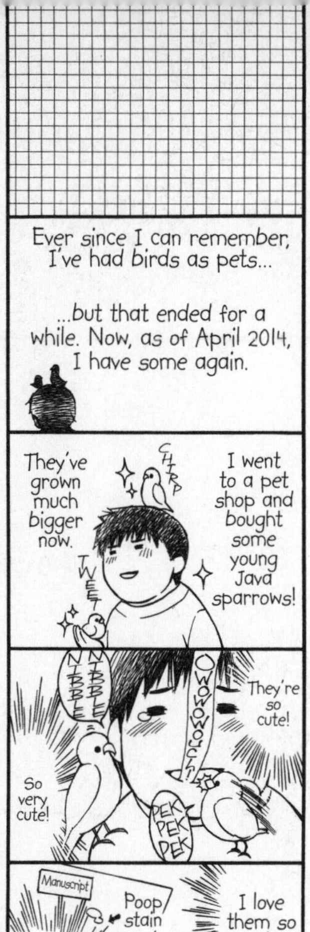

Ever since I can remember, I've had birds as pets...
...but that ended for a while. Now, as of April 2014, I have some again.
I went to a pet shop and bought some young Java sparrows!
CHIRP
TWEET
They've grown much bigger now.
They're so cute!
OWOWOWOUCH!
NIBBLE NIBBLE
PEK PEK PEK
So very cute!
I love them so much...
Manuscript
Poop stain
Manuscript
Pecked by a sparrow.
...that I don't even mind this!

Hope to see
you again
next volume!

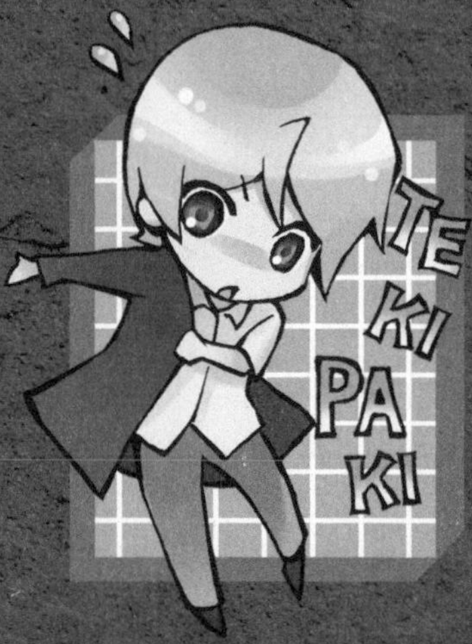
TE
KI
PA
KI

Kiiro Yumi won the 42nd *LaLa* Manga Grand Prix Fresh Debut award for her manga *Billy Bocchan no Yuutsu* (Little Billy's Depression). Her series *Toshokan Senso Love&War (Library Wars: Love & War)* ran in *LaLa* magazine in Japan, and its sequel is currently running in *LaLa*.

Hiro Arikawa won the 10th Dengeki Novel Prize for her work *Shio no Machi: Wish on My Precious* in 2003 and debuted with the same novel in 2004. Of her many works, Arikawa is best known for the *Library Wars* series and her *Jieitai Sanbusaku* trilogy, which consists of *Sora no Naka* (In the Sky), *Umi no Soko* (The Bottom of the Sea) and *Shio no Machi* (City of Salt).